DATE DUE

The War of the Unstamped

THE MOVEMENT TO REPEAL
THE BRITISH NEWSPAPER TAX, 1830–1836

The War of the Unstamped

THE MOVEMENT TO REPEAL
THE BRITISH NEWSPAPER TAX, 1830–1836

BY JOEL H. WIENER

City College of New York

Cornell University Press ✦ ITHACA and LONDON

First published 1969

Standard Book Number 8014-0522-x

Library of Congress Catalog Card Number 70-81598

PRINTED IN THE UNITED STATES OF AMERICA
BY THE VAIL-BALLOU PRESS, INC.

To My Mother

Acknowledgments

The initial research upon which this study is based, carried on over a two-year period in Great Britain, was made possible by the award of a Cornell-Glasgow Fellowship and by a University of Glasgow Research Fellowship. To both Cornell University and to the University of Glasgow I am very grateful. In addition, subsequent trips to Great Britain have been assisted by generous grants from Skidmore College and City College of New York.

Numerous librarians aided my research in countless ways. The staffs of the British Museum, the Public Record Office, the Manchester Central Reference Library, the Goldsmiths' Library of the University of London, the Mitchell Library in Glasgow, and the Cornell University Library are deserving of particular commendation. I also wish to thank the following persons and institutions for permitting me to make use of manuscripts in their possession: Mr. D. Flanagan, the Librarian of the Co-operative Union, Manchester (Owen Papers); the Trustees of the National Library of Ireland (Monteagle Papers); the Trustees of the British Museum (Place Papers); University College, London (Brougham Papers); the Huntington Library, San Marino, California (Richard Carlile Papers); the Trustees of the Birmingham Public Library (Lovett Papers); Earl Spencer (Althorp Papers); and the Controller of H.M. Stationery Office for permission to quote from Crown-copyright records in the Public Record Office (Home Office, Treasury Department Papers).

Of those—friends, teachers, and colleagues—who have assisted in the preparation of this book I can only make inadequate acknowledgment. Large thanks are owed to Professor Frederick G. Marcham of Cornell University for his continuing interest in the subject and for his many helpful suggestions. Professor David B. Davis of Cornell University commented perceptively on an earlier draft of the manuscript. James Tumelty and Geoffrey Finlayson of the University of Glasgow shared with me on many occasions their detailed knowledge of this period of English history and stimulated my own interest in the subject. My typists, Gladys Hartman and Shirley Lerman, worked diligently to complete the project. Finally, more praise than I am able to express is owed to my wife, Suzanne, for her encouragement and valuable editorial assistance.

JOEL H. WIENER

New York, New York
January 1969

Contents

Contents

Introduction

In June 1855 the final remaining penny of the British newspaper duty was removed, and in the following September the *Daily Telegraph* appeared at the price of 1*d*. The era of democratic journalism had formally arrived, and the daily newspaper became the cultural staple of all social classes. For the British working man in particular, the newspaper became what reformers of the 1830's predicted it would be, "the readiest, the commonest, the chief vehicle of knowledge." [1]

The story behind this development is a dramatic one, encompassing decades of struggle, persecution, resistance, and ultimate success. Historians have long recognized the significant effect of the financial restrictions on the press, known collectively as the "taxes on knowledge," in retarding the growth of a popular press in Great Britain. Their removal in 1861 has been correctly regarded as a landmark in the history of journalism, comparable, in its effects, to the termination of press censorship in 1695 and to the modification of the libel laws in 1843. But the series of steps by which these financial restraints were removed has never been studied adequately.

---

[1] Association of Working Men to Procure a Cheap and Honest Press, *Address* (London: The Association, 1836). A copy is in Place Papers, Add. MSS. 27,819, ff. 28–31.

Introduction

Although taxes on newspapers, advertisements, and paper were imposed as early as 1712, no sustained effort was made to remove them until the second quarter of the nineteenth century, when their redress became a standard radical grievance. The final, successful agitation for their repeal gathered momentum after 1849 as a by-product of the failure of the Chartist movement. It was led by John Bright, Richard Cobden, Joseph Hume, and other leading reformers, and its outlines have been traced by C. D. Collet, a participant in the campaign.[2]

The pre-1849 phase of the movement to repeal the "taxes on knowledge," however, concentrated in the critical years 1830–1836 and culminating in the reduction of the newspaper duty from 4*d*. to 1*d*., has not even been cursorily examined. This lack is so despite the fact that the movement shaped, and was in turn affected by, many of the important events of the 1830's. Neither Collet, whose description of the agitation is the most comprehensive in print, nor M. G. Moore, in an unpublished thesis entitled "The History of the Agitation against the Stamp Duty on Newspapers, 1830–1855," has ventured much beyond superficial references to this earlier movement.[3] Other historians have paid it even less attention. Standard histories of journalism such as Knight Hunt's *The Fourth Estate*, Fox Bourne's *English Newspapers*, and Alexander Andrews' *The History of British Journalism* provide short, inadequate summaries.[4] Francis Williams' *Dangerous Estate: The Anatomy of Newspapers* is perceptive in

[2] Collet D. Collet, *History of the Taxes on Knowledge: Their Origin and Repeal* (2 vols.; London: T. Fisher Unwin, 1899).

[3] Unpub. M.A. thesis, University of London, 1935. Moore fails to make adequate use either of primary source materials or of the numerous unstamped periodicals that survive.

[4] Frederick Knight Hunt, *The Fourth Estate: Contributions towards a History of Newspapers, and of the Liberty of the Press* (2 vols.; London: David Bogue, 1850); H. R. Fox Bourne, *English Newspapers: Chapters in the History of Journalism* (2 vols.; London: Chatto and Windus, 1887); Alexander Andrews, *The History of British Journalism from the Foundation of the Newspaper Press in England, to the Repeal of the Stamp Act in 1855, with Sketches of Press Celebrities* (2 vols.; London: Richard Bentley, 1859).

dealing with the later agitation against the "taxes on knowledge" but negligible on its earlier phase.[5] Likewise, neither Asa Briggs in *The Age of Improvement, 1783–1867,* an otherwise illuminating analysis of nineteenth-century Britain, nor Raymond Williams in his stimulating discussion of the popular press in *The Long Revolution* makes reference to this pre-Chartist agitation.[6] The present book seeks to rectify this imbalance by probing in depth the earlier movement to repeal the taxes on knowledge and evaluating its impact on the course of British development.

The decade of the 1830's in Great Britain has been aptly described, in a vein of understatement, as an "era of hope, pain, suffering, and fear." [7] It has, in fact, some claim to be regarded as the most critical one of the century. In addition to the campaign for the removal of press restrictions, it comprehended a semirevolutionary movement for parliamentary reform, an unprecedented outburst of trade union activity, continual factory and poor law agitation, and a host of constructive, reforming statutes. Less tangibly, the 1830's marked the culmination of the psychological process that E. P. Thompson has so brilliantly described—the development of a class consciousness among the British laborers.[8] On a cultural plane, this incipient class consciousness engendered questions involving mass literacy and the educational demands of a majority newly elevated to positions of political power. Politi-

[5] Francis Williams, *Dangerous Estate: The Anatomy of Newspapers* (London: Longmans, Green, 1957).

[6] Asa Briggs, *The Age of Improvement, 1783–1867* (London: Longmans, Green, 1959); Raymond Williams, *The Long Revolution* (New York: Columbia University Press, 1961). There is also a short summary in Brian Simon, *Studies in the History of Education, 1780–1870* (London: Laurence and Wishart, 1960), pp. 223–235.

[7] G. Kitson Clark, *The Making of Victorian England* (London: Methuen, 1962), p. 31.

[8] E. P. Thompson, *The Making of the English Working Class* (London: Victor Gollancz, 1963). Thompson views this collective self-consciousness as "the great spiritual gain of the Industrial Revolution, against which the disruption of an older and in many ways more humanly-comprehensible way of life must be set" (*ibid.,* p. 830).

cally and economically, it foreshadowed the emergence of the Chartist movement at the end of the decade.

The "traditional" analysis of the origins of Chartism, enunciated by G. D. H. Cole and other historians, presupposes a threefold setback for the working classes during the 1830's—that is, the limited nature of the Reform Act of 1832, the crushing impact of the Poor Law Amendment Act of 1834, and the unwillingness of successive Whig and Tory governments to rectify appalling factory conditions and to adopt a ten-hour working day. Additional sources of discontent, according to this analysis, were the failures of trade unionism between 1829 and 1834 and the onset of industrial depression in 1837. Chartism is interpreted as a product of the frustrations and tensions set into motion by this series of disappointments.[9] This interpretation is rendered partially inadequate by its failure to consider the significance of the movement to repeal the taxes on knowledge. The defects of the act of 1836, by which the duty on newspapers was reduced substantially, must likewise be assigned adequate weight in an assessment of working-class grievances. It is hoped that this study will provoke at least a qualified reinterpretation of Chartism.

The movement for the repeal of the taxes on knowledge during 1830–1836 was led primarily by working-class reformers. It was contended for in the byways of London and garreted alleyways of the urban complexes that were mushrooming throughout England and Scotland. It involved an overt attempt to violate the press laws, by means of the publication and dissemination of hundreds of illegal tracts and ephemeral newspapers. Gov-

---

[9] G. D. H. Cole, *Chartist Portraits* (London: Macmillan, 1941), pp. 1–19; A. Temple Patterson, *Radical Leicester: A History of Leicester, 1780–1850* (Leicester: University College, Leicester, 1954), pp. 275–301; Mark Hovell, *The Chartist Movement* (2d ed.; Manchester: Manchester University Press, 1959) pp. 78–98; Asa Briggs, "Chartism Reconsidered," *Historical Studies*, II (1959), 42–59. A somewhat different analysis is offered by F. C. Mather, who concludes that there was as much hostility against the aristocracy as between middle and working classes (*Chartism* [London: Historical Association, 1965], pp. 19–23).

ernmental authority was directly challenged in the pages of William Carpenter's *Political Letters and Pamphlets,* Henry Hetherington's *Poor Man's Guardian,* James Watson's *Working Man's Friend,* and their numerous progeny. The authorities responded by arresting and imprisoning hundreds of working-class vendors, taking punitive action against the publishers of illegal journals, and confiscating and destroying many of the illicit periodicals. This "war of the unstamped," as it came to be known, lasted for six years, and it constitutes the pivot of this book.

Concurrently with this working-class agitation, middle-class reformers waged a complementary struggle against the taxes on knowledge.[10] It was less spectacular though its hills and troughs are easier to discern, owing to better organizational techniques and to the more systematic exploitation of existing media. With a few exceptions, this phase of the conflict was restricted to legal and parliamentary channels. It was of importance both in its own right and as a touchstone affecting the relationship between different groups of reformers. The middle-class agitation is explored in the first part of this study while the "war of the unstamped" is treated in the second half.

This book leans heavily upon the assumption that broad social and economic groupings can, by the 1830's, be meaningfully identified as "middle-class" or "working-class." To a considerable extent, this assumption rests upon the research of such historians as E. P. Thompson and Asa Briggs. In an influential recent study, Thompson convincingly suggests that by the 1830's there were *"two* Radical publics: the middle-class, which looked forward to the Anti-Corn Law League, and the working class, whose journalists (Hetherington, Watson, Cleave, Lovett, Benbow,

---

[10] In the eyes of hostile contemporaries and of most later historians, the two campaigns were indissolubly blended. See Richard D. Altick, *The English Common Reader: A Social History of the Mass Reading Public, 1800–1900* (Chicago: University of Chicago Press, 1963), pp. 339–341; R. K. Webb, *The British Working Class Reader, 1790–1848: Literacy and Social Tension* (London: George Allen and Unwin, 1955), pp. 60–62.

O'Brien) were already maturing the Chartist movement."[11] Briggs postulates similarly a widening chasm in urban-industrial centers such as Leeds between "middle-class parliamentary reformers and working-class factory reformers," or as he expresses it elsewhere, between "popular radicals" and "mercantile and manufacturing groups."[12] Even historians such as Elie Halévy and S. Maccoby, who do not probe as deeply into the process of social change, dichotomize in their treatment of radical politics during the 1830's. For Halévy there are important distinctions between "philosophical Radicals" and "Ultra-Radicals," with the latter bitterly attacking the "industrial and commercial institutions" of the day.[13]

In fact, despite terminological differences and despite R. J. White's valid depiction of radicalism as "a truly nominalist concept, scarcely susceptible at all of universal categories or classification," most historians agree that two basic forms of radicalism existed in Britain during the 1830's.[14] Although they do not correspond to precise economic categories and although a variety of levels are comprehended within each, these two manifestations of radicalism are classifiable as "working-class" and "middle-class" (in the absence of agreement on better terms) since they closely

[11] Thompson, *Making of the English Working Class*, p. 727.

[12] Asa Briggs, "The Background of the Parliamentary Reform Movement in Three English Cities (1830–2)," *Cambridge Historical Journal*, X (1952), 312, 294; "The Language of 'Class' in Early Nineteenth-Century England," *Essays in Labour History*, ed. Asa Briggs and John Saville (London: Macmillan, 1960), pp. 43–73. The increasing articulation of a working-class self-consciousness is also stressed in David C. Morris, "The History of the Labour Movement in England, 1825–1852: The Problem of Leadership and the Articulation of Demands" (unpub. Ph.D. thesis, University of London, 1952).

[13] Elie Halévy, *The Triumph of Reform, 1830–1841*, trans. from the French by E. I. Watkin (London: Ernest Benn, 1950), p. 196; S. Maccoby, *English Radicalism, 1832–1852* (London: George Allen and Unwin, 1935), p. 25. There is a discussion of the tension between middle-class dissenting radicals and working-class reformers in L. S. Marshall, "The First Parliamentary Election in Manchester," *American Historical Review*, XLVII (1942), 519–522.

[14] R. J. White, *Radicalism and Its Results, 1760–1837* (London: Historical Association, 1965), p. 3.

touched upon social status, industrial change, and attitudes toward governmental power. They involved fundamentally differing reflex-responses to concrete issues. The precise nature of these responses was shaped by a fusion of social, economic, and political perspectives rather than by economic origins alone. Thus Francis Place and William Lovett, two persons of prime significance in this study, both emerged from the artisan class. Yet ideologically Lovett approached the question of the taxes on knowledge from a working-class or "ultra-radical" perspective, whereas Place's vision was conditioned substantially by the values of middle-class reformers.

The organization of this book is focused upon the dual nature of the campaign against the taxes on knowledge. Thus with the exception of the introductory and concluding chapters, an attempt is made to situate events within either a middle- or working-class context. Chapters 2, 3, and 4 trace the repeal activities of parliamentary reformers while Chapters 5 through 9 focus upon the war of the unstamped. A considerable segment of the second half of the book is devoted to an analysis of those periodicals that were published in violation of the law. Chapters 6 and 7 discuss the techniques employed by these periodicals to circumvent the law and deal with related questions of circulation, distribution, and prosecution. In Chapter 8 the ideas of the unstamped press are analyzed, and an attempt is made to weigh the extent to which these periodicals colored the thought of the period and sharpened its incipient "class" outlook. The number of illegal journals published between 1830 and 1836 exceeded 550; a complete descriptive listing of these journals, together with location of surviving copies, is available in another book by the author.[15]

A final introductory point concerns the exclusion of Ireland and Wales from this study. This exclusion did not occur entirely by choice, since the Irish press laws were similar to those in force in England and Scotland, while the Welsh press laws were iden-

[15] Joel H. Wiener, *A Descriptive Finding List of Unstamped British Periodicals, 1830–1836* (London: Bibliographical Society, 1969).

tical. And in both countries a minor campaign against the taxes on knowledge developed during the 1830's in response to events in England and Scotland. But the existence of adequate prior studies, particularly for Wales, as well as the inaccessibility of primary source material for these two countries, made it advisable to limit geographically the range of this book.[16]

[16] R. D. Rees, "Glamorgan Newspapers under the Stamp Acts," *Morgannwg: Transactions of the Glamorgan Local History Society*, III (1959), 61–94; R. D. Rees, "South Wales and Monmouthshire Newspapers under the Stamp Acts," *Welsh History Review*, I (1962), 301–324; Brian Inglis, *The Freedom of the Press in Ireland, 1784–1841* (London: Faber and Faber, 1954).

The War of the Unstamped

THE MOVEMENT TO REPEAL
THE BRITISH NEWSPAPER TAX, 1830–1836

CHAPTER I

Taxes on Knowledge

On 12 November 1830, the London *Examiner* carried, for the first time, the following signature on its masthead: "Paper and Print 3½d. Taxes on Knowledge 3½d." In January of the following year a Manchester working-class newspaper, *The Voice of the People*, commenced publication with an identical trademark on its front page. A new phrase had entered into the political consciousness of England, and for the next forty years radical orators were to invoke repeatedly the blessings of a free press by urging repeal of the "taxes on knowledge." Edwin Chadwick, who probably originated the phrase, had contributed not the least of his services to the reforming ideology of nineteenth-century Britain.[1]

What precisely were the "taxes on knowledge"? For the overwhelming majority of reformers—middle- and working-class alike—they were synonymous with the stamp duty on newspapers. Thus the agitation of the 1830's to eliminate the taxes on knowledge was concentrated predominantly upon efforts to repeal the newspaper impost. It virtually came to an end in 1836

[1] S. E. Finer attributes the phrase to Chadwick (*The Life and Times of Sir Edwin Chadwick* [London: Methuen, 1952], p. 35). George Jacob Holyoake credits Leigh Hunt with originating it (*Sixty Years of an Agitator's Life* [London: T. Fisher Unwin, 1893], I, 293).

[1]

when the latter was reduced to 1*d*. But the fact that this identification existed should not obscure the importance of other financial obstacles to the dissemination of printed matter. For the phrase "taxes on knowledge" was essentially a shibboleth behind which many journalistic grievances found expression.

The most important taxes on knowledge, in addition to the newspaper duty, were the levy on advertisements, the excise duty on paper, and smaller assessments on almanacs and pamphlets. However, some reformers classified the import duties on paper and on foreign books, which were not repealed until 1861, as taxes on knowledge.[2] Others perceived the main journalistic obstacle to be the Act of 54 Geo. III, c. 156, by which one free copy of every book or pamphlet had to be provided gratis to the eleven copyright libraries in the United Kingdom.[3] The verbal resources at the command of reformers and of those representing particular interest groups were in fact limitless. John Crawfurd, a participant in the conflicts of the 1830's, suggested on one occasion that the tax on stagecoaches, by increasing the cost of transporting newspapers, should be considered a tax on knowledge. Edwin Chadwick applied the same epithet to certain abuses which retarded the efficiency of the post.[4]

THE TAX ON NEWSPAPERS

The newspaper tax was first imposed in 1712 as part of a comprehensive measure which also encompassed taxes on advertise-

[2] For opposition to the duty on foreign books under the heading of a "tax on knowledge," see W. J. Fox, *On the Parliamentary Pledges to Be Required of Candidates at the Ensuing Elections: An Address to the Electors of Great Britain* (London: Charles Fox, 1832), p. 10; "The Revolution," *Tait's Edinburgh Magazine*, I (1832), 22. For information on the import duty on paper, see D. C. Coleman, *The British Paper Industry, 1495–1860: A Study in Industrial Growth* (Oxford: Clarendon Press, 1958), pp. 317–325.

[3] One of the best arguments against this tax is by "C. R. D." of Oxford in the *Parliamentary Review, and Family Magazine*, II (1834), 717–718.

[4] Crawfurd's speech at a Paisley by-election meeting as reported in the *Glasgow Argus*, 13 March 1834; Edwin Chadwick, *On the Taxes on Knowledge: From the Westminster Review, No. XXIX, for July 1, 1831* (London: Robert Heward, 1831).

ments and pamphlets. Although the statute was designed principally to place a curb on newspapers, revenue considerations being
secondary, the initial stamp duty of $\frac{1}{2}d$. was not prohibitive; [5] but
during the remainder of the century, the incidence of the tax was
increased gradually until in 1797 it was raised to $3\frac{1}{2}d$. and in
1815 to $4d$.[6]

This "slave-mark," in the words of a leading working-class agitator,[7] restricted the circulation of most newspapers to upper-
income groups. Few persons could afford to pay a minimum daily
price of $6d$. or $7d$. for a newspaper. In the midst of such con-
comitants to industrial change as rising literacy and accelerating
cultural expectations, a restrictive policy of this nature was short-
sighted. Moreover, mechanical advances in printing, in particular
the invention of the steam press and its initial use by the *Times* in
1814, made this impost economically indefensible.[8]

During 1815–1819, political and economic tensions increased
in Britain, as the problems engendered by the ending of the
Napoleonic Wars were fused with those produced by the Industrial Revolution. In an atmosphere of increasing violence, radical
journalists, circumventing the ambiguous phraseology of the act
of 1815, began to publish a spate of cheap periodicals with titles
such as the *Cap of Liberty* and the *Black Dwarf*. In 1816, William Cobbett commenced his *Weekly Political Register* in an

[5] For a summary of the act of 1712, as well as the hostile journalistic reaction
to it, see Lucy M. Salmon, *The Newspaper and Authority* (New York: Oxford
University Press, 1923), pp. 181–186; Frederick S. Siebert, *Freedom of the
Press in England, 1476–1776: The Rise and Decline of Government Control*
(Urbana, Ill.: University of Illinois Press, 1965), pp. 305–318.

6 For the many changes in the newspaper duty during the eighteenth and
nineteenth centuries, see Donald Read, *Press and People, 1790–1850: Opinion in
Three English Cities* (London: Edward Arnold, 1961), p. 66; Arthur Aspinall,
Politics and the Press, c. 1780–1850 (London: Home and Van Thal, 1949), pp.
16–24; John Crawfurd, *Taxes on Knowledge: A Financial and Historical View
of the Taxes Which Impede the Education of the People* (London: Charles Ely,
1836), pp. 5–12.

[7] Richard Carlile, in a speech at the Rotunda, *Prompter*, 20 Aug. 1831.

[8] Bourne, *English Newspapers*, I, 358. There is a general account of the
mechanical improvements in Charles Knight, *The Old Printer and the Modern
Press* (London: John Murray, 1854), pp. 249–259.

open, unfolded edition at the price of 2*d*. He sold it as a "pamphlet," thus paying only a nominal duty to the government, and it soon acquired a circulation of more than 40,000.[9] Thomas Wooler, William Hone, Richard Carlile, and other working-class journalists joined in this struggle with the Tory government.

In December 1819, in the aftermath of the "Peterloo" incident, Viscount Castlereagh, the leader of the House of Commons, and Viscount Sidmouth, the Home Secretary, decided to suppress the journalistic outlets through which extreme dissentient views were being expressed. In the conviction that "internal tranquility" could be restored only by the suppression of "mischievous and detestable libels," they took an active role in securing Parliamentary approval of the Six Acts, two of which sought directly to destroy the incipient radical press.[10] Under the provisions of one of these statutes an extensive "security system" was established to guard against seditious or blasphemous libel. Every publisher was compelled to deposit a bond with the government as surety against any future conviction. The bond was £300 if the publisher resided in London, £200 if he resided in the provinces.[11]

But another of the Six Acts was even more stringent. It applied the 4*d*. newspaper duty to all periodicals that appeared more frequently than every twenty-six days, that sold for less than 6*d*., and that contained "any Public News, Intelligence or Occur-

[9] G. D. H. Cole, *The Life of William Cobbett* (3d ed.; London: Home and Van Thal, 1947), p. 207.

[10] Letter from Sidmouth to the Mayor of Exeter (1819), Home Office (hereafter cited as H.O.) 41/5/43, reprinted in G. D. H. Cole and A. W. Filson, *British Working Class Movements: Select Documents, 1789–1875* (London: Macmillan, 1965), pp. 297–298. In a Commons debate on the Six Acts, Castlereagh proclaimed his intention to punish the "lower portion" of the press in order to eliminate "licentiousness" (*Hansard's Parliamentary Debates* [hereafter cited as *Hansard*], H. of C., 22 Dec. 1819, XLI, 1470–1479).

[11] Richard Carlile's unrelenting opposition to this "security system" is described ably in William H. Wickwar, *The Struggle for the Freedom of the Press, 1819–1832* (London: George Allen and Unwin, 1928).

rences, or any Remarks or Observations thereon, or upon any Matter in Church or State." The preamble to this Act clearly announced its intent, which was to drive out of circulation "pamphlets and printed papers containing Observations upon public Events and Occurrences, tending to excite Hatred and Contempt of the Government and Constitution of these realms as by law established, and also vilifying our holy religion." [12] The penalty for publishing or selling an unstamped newspaper was fixed at the prohibitive sum of £20 per violation.

The provisions regarding frequency of publication were particularly significant. A cheap newspaper that published only monthly stood little chance of survival since it could neither serve as a regular organ of communication nor, in the words of Albany Fonblanque, as "the poor man's book of knowledge." [13] Thus when moderate Manchester trade unionists sought in 1830 to convert an unstamped weekly, the *United Trades' Co-operative Journal*, into a legal monthly periodical, John Doherty and other reformers resisted on the ground that "the utility of the work would be thereby destroyed." [14] William Carpenter, a radical journalist, undoubtedly lost most of his influence with the poorer classes when he directed his efforts toward producing *Carpenter's Monthly Political Magazine* after being prosecuted in 1831 for publishing an unstamped weekly periodical. [15]

The discretionary powers of the authorities accentuated the obstacles posed by the act of 1819. Only the Attorney-General or a Stamp Office official could initiate effectively a prosecution under the provisions of the statute. This meant that the decision as to which publishers or publications faced legal punishment was made frequently for political reasons. Innocuous or progovern-

[12] 60 Geo. III, c. 9.
[13] Albany Fonblanque, *England under Seven Administrations* (London: Richard Bentley, 1837), III, 55.
[14] *United Trades' Co-operative Journal*, 24 April 1830.
[15] Carpenter's unstamped *Political Letters and Pamphlets* circulated an estimated 900 weekly in Birmingham alone. This was reduced to about 50 for the *Political Letter*, a short-lived legal successor (*Ballot*, 4 Dec. 1831).

ment weeklies were often encouraged to publish, irrespective of the amount of "news" that they printed, whereas critical journals faced the prospect of suppression. The issue of legal discretion remained an explosive one until the final repeal of the newspaper duty in 1855.[16]

Despite its severity the act of 1819 proved instantaneously "successful." During the succeeding years most radical journalists either fled into exile or "legalized" their periodicals. Legalization was achieved by increasing the price of the paper to 6*d*. or more or by issuing it in a stamped edition. Although the latter meant a selling price of 7*d*. or higher, it was frequently the preferred alternative since it carried with it the privilege of free postal transmission. This ensured an expeditious delivery to customers who resided in rural areas. It became the practice for some publishers to pay the stamp duty on the country editions of their periodicals, which might otherwise cost 8*d*. or more to send. At the same time, they would circulate the London editions unstamped and run the risk of prosecution.[17]

William Cobbett, against whom the act of 1819 was principally directed, adopted this stratagem. From 1820 on he began to issue *Cobbett's Weekly Political Register* in both stamped and unstamped editions. Its price varied during the succeeding decade but never again fell below 6*d*. in either edition. More effective transmission of the stamped *Register* was assured though Cobbett's readership precipitately and permanently declined as a result of the substantial increase in price. His importance as a molder of public opinion declined likewise.[18]

[16] Middle- and working-class reformers agreed that critical publications were suppressed whereas others, such as the *Penny Magazine*, were encouraged. See, for example, the National Political Union's petition against the dispensing power of the Stamp Commissioners, a copy of which is in Place Papers, Add. MSS 27,796, f. 56.

[17] Great Britain, House of Commons, *Select Committee on Newspaper Stamps* (1851), pp. 124–128, qq. 776–804. The *Athenaeum* adopted this practice consistently in the 1840's. (John C. Francis, *John Francis, Publisher of the Athenaeum: A Literary Chronicle of Half a Century* [London: Richard Bentley and Son, 1888], I, 37).

[18] Cole, *Cobbett*, pp. 239–241.

During the 1820's a surface calm predominated in the field of journalism, a situation that mirrored the quiescent political atmosphere. Many grievances were mitigated temporarily as economic conditions revived and as the Tory party came under the moderating influences of William Huskisson, George Canning, and Robert Peel. The working classes, for their part, remained politically apathetic until a fresh external stimulus, the French Revolution of 1830, aroused many of them to renewed journalistic activity. Few unstamped periodicals were published during the 1820's, and several of those that did appear were suppressed quickly, such as the *Harlequin,* a minor dramatic miscellany with no political pretensions.[19] Inasmuch as no major challenge was launched against the Tory governments of Liverpool, Canning, and Wellington, they were enabled to retain their moderate image though few in positions of power were other than hostile to the prospects of a cheap press. In the years after 1830 numberless radicals were unjustly to heap scorn upon the Whigs for failing to emulate the example set by their Tory predecessors.[20]

Due to the discretionary nature of the enforcement power, the effects of the 4*d.* stamp duty were felt most sharply by radical journalists; but most newspaper proprietors suffered from the impost as a result of the higher selling price that the tax compelled. For example, a recent study has demonstrated that "the consumption of newspapers per head of population was actually stationary between 1815 and 1835." [21] This statement is striking in the context of the near-revolutionary transformations that were occurring in other areas, and by comparison to journalistic developments taking place in the United States.

[19] Diary, Place Papers, Add. MSS 35,146, f. 107; Francis Place, *A Letter to a Minister of State, Respecting Taxes on Knowledge* (2d ed.; London: Privately distributed, 1831), p. 10.

[20] One working-class radical denounced the Whigs as "sham-reformers . . . hypocrites and traitors, the malignant executioners of barbarous laws, which, when out of office, they pretended to denounce" (*Le Bonnet Rouge,* 23 Feb. 1833).

[21] Arthur Aspinall, "Statistical Accounts of the London Newspapers, 1800–1836," *English Historical Review,* LXV (1950), 222–223; *Politics and the Press,* p. 23.

Comparisons with the United States were instructive and opponents of the impost never ceased to offer them. It was estimated, for example, that on the basis of an estimated readership of one thousand persons per newspaper, the United States (with a considerably smaller population than Great Britain) had an annual newspaper circulation of sixty-four million, compared to one of twenty-eight million in the latter country.[22] It was also shown that whereas about 320 newspapers were published annually in Great Britain prior to 1833, approximately 850 per year were produced in the United States.[23] Using these and other statistics, Charles Knight maintained in 1836, on the eve of the reduction of the newspaper duty, that about $1\frac{1}{2}$ stamped papers were published annually per head of population in Great Britain compared to 6 newspapers per head in the United States.[24]

The effect of the newspaper tax was especially pronounced because of the need to secure stamped paper in advance from one of the several Stamp Offices established for that purpose. If a newspaper was published in the provinces, the obstacles were even greater. The transportation costs incurred in connection with the stamping might undercut its economic viability, as seems to have been the case with John Doherty's abortive Manchester weekly, *The Voice of the People*. Doherty blamed the periodical's failure on the need to purchase paper initially in Manchester, then ship it to London for stamping, and, finally, return it to Manchester, all at the expense of the proprietor.[25]

Even when such a circuitous process could be avoided, the stamping of a newspaper necessitated a considerable outlay of

[22] *Scotsman*, 27 Sept. 1828.

[23] R. Montgomery Martin, *Taxation of the British Empire* (London: Effingham Wilson, 1833), p. 11.

[24] *Morning Chronicle*, 25 July 1832.

[25] John Doherty, *A Letter to the Members of the National Association for the Protection of Labour* (Manchester: Alexander Wilkinson, 1832), p. 14. Stamped paper was occasionally patched and sold, even if torn (Stanley Morison, *The English Newspaper: Some Account of the Physical Development of Journals Printed in London between 1622 and the Present Day* [Cambridge: Cambridge University Press, 1932], p. 207 n.).

[8]

capital, perhaps several hundred pounds per day for a daily newspaper.[26] Since a refund was not obtainable, the owner of stamped paper that became spoilt or that could not be sold was not compensated for his substantial initial investment. If the stamped paper was purchased in bulk and at least £10 was paid in cash, and if the proprietor agreed not to charge more than 7*d.* for the periodical, then a discount of 20 per cent on the 4*d.* stamp duty was granted. But this failed to ease the burden of the duty, which according to the calculation of one contemporary amounted to 137 per cent—an effective tax of 3⅕*d.* on an income of 5⅝*d.*[27]

So long as the 4*d.* stamp duty remained in existence, only a publisher of independent wealth, possessed of a speculative temperament, could consider the possibility of publishing a legal newspaper. Thus the stamp duty created an effective monopoly which sharpened animosity between supporters and opponents of the statute. It imparted to the struggle over the newspaper tax the emotional dimension of a conflict waged for economic survival.

THE TAX ON ADVERTISEMENTS

The advertisement duty was levied initially in 1712 as a complement to the tax on newspapers. Like the latter, it had been increased repeatedly during the eighteenth century. In 1789 it was raised to 3*s.* per advertisement and after 1815 it stood at the prohibitive level of 3*s.* 6*d.* per advertisement.[28] Opposition to the impost was widespread, and a reduction of the duty to 1*s.* 6*d.* in 1833 reduced substantially but did not eliminate resistance to it. As in the case of the newspaper duty, much of this opposition

[26] *Morning Chronicle,* 25 July 1832.

[27] R. K. D., *Letter to Lord Viscount Althorp, on the Proposed Reduction in the Newspaper Stamp and Advertisement Duties* (London: Hurst, Chance, 1831), pp. 4–5.

[28] Read, *Press and People,* p. 66; Alfred P. Wadsworth, "Newspaper Circulations, 1800–1914," *Paper Read for Manchester Statistical Society, 9 March 1955* (Manchester: Norwood, Lockbury, 1955), p. 3.

took the form of overt violation of the law. The advertisement duty was finally abolished in 1853.

By the nineteenth century the economic potential of advertising had become increasingly clear. Advancing material progress and rising commercial expectations accelerated this recognition. Businesses such as the book trade sensed the advantages to be gained from advertising in newspapers and periodicals. Mechanics' institutes, literary associations, trades unions, and other organizations perceived likewise the need to give regular publicity to their activities.[29] As a complement to this rising demand, advertisements were becoming a major source of revenue for newspaper proprietors whose other means of income, notably the profit derivable from the sale of newspapers, was curtailed by the stamp duty.

Not surprisingly, the levy on advertisements was labeled repeatedly as a "tax on knowledge" by its opponents on the ground that it retarded the dissemination of newspapers, books, and pamphlets, as well as the general interchange of ideas. Political economists, such as J. R. McCulloch, James and John Stuart Mill, and Francis Place, who were seeking to convert the working classes to their doctrines, gave repeated expression to this view. They maintained that, as a result of the advertisement duty and the consequent difficulties of adequately publicizing new works, only about one pamphlet in fifty, or 2 per cent, repaid the expense of publication.[30] Other reformers, some drawn from the working classes, opposed the tax as part of a general resistance to governmental restrictions. Many radical journalists simply ignored the impost and opened the advertising columns of their

[29] For a petition from the Manchester New Mechanics' Institution, see *Journals of the House of Commons*, 10 May 1833, LXXXVIII, 37. For a petition from the "Library of the People," Boston, Lincs., see *Journals of the House of Lords*, 2 July 1833, LXV, 467.

[30] Crawfurd, *Taxes on Knowledge*, p. 20. McCulloch claimed that less than 2 percent of the pamphlets issued showed a profit as a result of the paper and advertisement duties ("Taxes on Literature," *Edinburgh Review*, LIII [1831], 430–432).

illicit journals to all who paid a nominal fee, usually about 25 per cent of the price charged by stamped newspapers.[31]

Economic factors were, in most instances, of greater importance than pedagogical ones in arousing opposition to the advertisement tax. Resistance to the duty can, therefore, be most effectively placed within the context of the free-trade movement. In the view of free traders, the tax was "a millstone on commerce and industry," and, even worse, one which seriously penalized inventiveness and flexibility.[32] It assertedly created "monopolies" since the limited advertising undertaken by private business tended to gravitate toward one influential newspaper in each city. In support of this contention, it was calculated that the *Times,* the most important newspaper in the country, published 60 per cent of all London advertisements in 1834.[33] Furthermore, free traders repeatedly accused the government and the Stamp Office of employing discretionary powers to reinforce these monopolies. Inasmuch as payment of the duty could legally be demanded within ten days, pressure was often exerted subtly on radical journals.[34]

The effects of the advertisement duty were undoubtedly

[31] *Le Bonnet Rouge* charged 1s. for up to six lines and 3d. per additional line, *Voice of the West Riding* 1s. for up to five lines and 2d. per additional line, and *Hetherington's Twopenny Dispatch* 1s. 6d. for six lines and 2d. for every succeeding line. The *Thief,* an illegal periodical which collected the advertisement duty, charged 7s. for up to ten lines and 4d. for each succeeding line.

[32] Martin, *Taxation of the British Empire,* pp. 114–115; *The Spectator's Key to Political Knowledge,* No. III: *Taxation* (1833)—appended to 1833 volume of the *Spectator.*

[33] *Scotsman,* 16 March 1836. This seems accurate and it is, therefore, difficult to accept seriously Richard Carlile's assertion that the reduction of the duty in 1833 was meant as a "bribe" to the *Times* (*Prompter,* 28 April 1833; *Cosmopolite,* 27 April 1833).

[34] Arthur Aspinall, "Statistical Accounts of the London Newspapers in the Eighteenth Century," *English Historical Review,* LXIII (1948), 205. The government could penalize opposition newspapers by placing official advertisements, constituting an important percentage of the total number, with cooperative journalists (Aspinall, "The Irish 'Proclamation' Fund, 1800–1846," *English Historical Review,* LVI [1941], 265–280).

severe. Statistical comparisons with the United States were employed once again to advantage. The *Scotsman,* a leading reform journal, printed a series of influential articles during 1828 in which it maintained that the twelve New York daily newspapers published about 50 per cent more advertisements annually than all 344 newspapers in the United Kingdom. It further contended that the number of press advertisements that appeared weekly in Liverpool was only about 2.5 per cent of those printed in New York, a city of approximately equal commercial importance.[35] The reduction of the duty in 1833 produced effects that tended to substantiate these and similar assertions. Within a year there was a large increase in the number of newspaper advertisements, possibly to the extent of 35 per cent.[36]

Despite its impact, the reduction of the duty to 1*s.* 6*d.* was at best a palliative. Until its total repeal in 1853 the advertisement duty continued to be a major obstacle to the unfettered development of the press. But after 1833 an increasing number of reformers began to concentrate their efforts upon removal of the newspaper duty.

THE EXCISE DUTY ON PAPER

The excise duty on paper was levied initially in 1712 and totally repealed in 1861. During its existence, it proved to be one of the more burdensome taxes on knowledge. Class One paper, used extensively in printing, was assessed at a rate of 3*d.* per pound between 1803 and 1836, after which it was levied at a rate of 1½*d.* per pound.[37] This assessment did not prove as onerous

[35] *Scotsman,* 1 Oct. 1828. The first argument was slightly misleading. Inasmuch as the newspaper duty greatly reduced the number of *daily* newspapers in the United Kingdom, the actual number of copies of newspapers issued in both countries was markedly closer than the figures cited would indicate.

[36] For an estimate that the immediate increase in London was 35 per cent and in the provinces 27 per cent, see Aspinall, "Statistical Accounts, 1830–1836," pp. 223, 226. A contemporary estimates it at 14 per cent (Crawfurd, *Taxes on Knowledge,* p. 49 n.).

[37] For a detailed analysis of the excise duty, see Coleman, *British Paper Industry,* p. 318; J. R. McCulloch, *Observations, Illustrative of the Practical*

to newspaper proprietors, who used comparatively small quantities of paper, as it did to book publishers. Inasmuch as additional stamp duty had to be paid if a newspaper exceeded one sheet or four folio pages, an effective statutory limit existed. Thus, the paper duty added only about one farthing to the price of a newspaper.

Publishers of books and pamphlets, on the other hand, suffered considerably, and those who specialized in cheap literature, such as Charles Knight and William and Robert Chambers, were at a particular disadvantage. They were attempting constantly to reduce their expenses in order to be able to sell their volumes at the lowest possible price. But on an eighty-page pamphlet (that is, five sheets), five hundred copies of which were printed, the excise duty amounted to £6. This meant that the tax on the cost of producing the volume fluctuated on the average between 20 and 30 per cent and that it influenced significantly the price at which a new work could be sold.[38]

The effect of this tax on tracts and other cheap publications was striking. The Society for the Diffusion of Useful Knowledge, headed by Knight, had to limit the size of its fortnightly *Library of Useful Knowledge* to thirty-two pages in order to be able to sell individual copies at 6*d*.[39] Although denying Lord Brougham's assertion in the spring of 1835 that retention of the excise duty on paper would compel the S.D.U.K. to give up one or more of its publications, Knight admitted that "it might prevent

---

Operation and Real Effect of the Duties on Paper, Showing the Expediency of Their Reduction or Repeal (London: Longman, Rees, Orme, Brown, Green, and Longman, 1836), pp. 3–11.

[38] McCulloch "Taxes on Literature," pp. 428–433. According to Charles Knight the duty on an octavo volume of 36 sheets, 1,000 copies of which were printed, amounted to 1*s*. per volume (*The Newspaper Stamp and the Duty on Paper, Viewed in Relation to Their Effects upon the Diffusion of Knowledge* [London: Charles Knight, 1836], p. 48).

[39] Henry Brougham, 1830, to Thomas Creevey, cited in *The Creevey Papers: A Selection from the Correspondence and Diaries of the Late Thomas Creevey, M.P.*, ed. Sir Herbert Maxwell (London: John Murray, 1903), II, 207.

new valuable works being undertaken." [40] Knight's denial seems to have been borne out by events in the case of the S.D.U.K., but the *Miscellany of Useful and Entertaining Tracts*, a publication issued by the Chambers brothers, was effectively forced out of existence as a result of the excise duty. [41] Other inexpensive miscellanies undoubtedly befell a similar fate during these years.

Despite opposition to the paper tax, the vogue of cheap literature gathered momentum during the first half of the nineteenth century, and revenue accruing to the government as a result of the duty was substantially greater than that yielded by any of the other taxes on knowledge. According to the *Spectator*, the net sum realized by the tax on Class One paper for the year ending January 1832 was £677,103, compared to £451,657 for the newspaper duty. [42] In 1834, a year in which many new journalistic ventures were commenced, the yield to the Exchequer was £823,- 000. [43] One of the best-known cheap publications, *Chambers' Edinburgh Journal*, paid an average of £2,000 per year in excise duty, while the S.D.U.K. paid approximately £7,000 per year for the paper used in its popular *Penny Magazine*. [44] According to Charles Knight, the same group expended a total of £32,000 on paper duty over an eleven-year period in order to publish a less successful weekly, the *Penny Cyclopaedia*. [45]

The excise duty on paper possessed one feature that distinguished it sharply from the newspaper and advertisement duties.

[40] Charles Knight, letter to Henry Brougham, [May 1835?], Brougham Papers, No. 18,193.

[41] William Chambers, *Story of a Long and Busy Life* (Edinburgh: W. and R. Chambers, 1882), pp. 93–94.

[42] *The Spectator's Key to Political Knowledge*, No. III: *Taxation* (1833)— appended to 1833 volume of the *Spectator*.

[43] *Scotsman*, 8 Aug. 1835.

[44] *Chambers' Edinburgh Journal*, 31 Jan. 1835; Henry Brougham, "On the Diffusion of Knowledge," National Association for the Promotion of Social Science, *Transactions*, II (1858), 38.

[45] Knight, *Old Printer*, p. 301. It was demonstrated that the public paid the equivalent of 8*s.* 7*d.* per ream of paper duty although only about 4*s.* 8½*d.* accrued to the revenue ("Taxes on Knowledge—Duty on Paper—Direct and Indirect Taxation," *Tait's Edinburgh Magazine*, II [1833], 610–613).

Since it was levied during the distributive stage and not after the product was in the control of the retailer, its payment could not easily be evaded. No publisher could avoid paying the tax unless he chose to publish his tracts on calico or a similar substance. Such an uneconomic alternative was resorted to on several occasions, notably by Richard Carlile, but was never widely adopted.

Thus opponents of the paper duty, irrespective of their political persuasion, had to limit the form of their protest to the printed page, though technical frauds might occasionally be perpetrated in order to diminish the burden of the tax.[46] This circumstance had the effect of weakening a "class" division between radicals on this issue. Middle-class reformers, who were active in the publication of books and pamphlets, agitated more vigorously against the tax than did working-class journalists who were involved in the printing of newspapers. But at no time did this difference provoke a serious conflict over aims or tactics, since the question whether to violate the law or not was largely an academic one.[47] When the Melbourne government reduced the paper duty by 50 per cent in 1836, many opponents of the tax were mollified.

DUTIES ON PAMPHLETS AND ALMANACS

The pamphlet duty was comparatively noncontroversial and, from its inception in 1712, was never intended to be more than a "registration duty."[48] The levy of 3*s*. was assessed on the entire edition of a pamphlet and not, as was the case with newspapers and advertisements, on each individual number. Working-class journalists attempted, therefore, to publish their illegal newspa-

---

[46] Fraud was facilitated by loose definition of the several classifications of paper, each of which was subject to different rates of taxation (Coleman, *British Paper Industry*, pp. 322–323; McCulloch, *Observations*, pp. 10–15).

[47] William Carpenter, the working-class journalist who initiated the publication of unstamped newspapers, complained as vigorously as Knight and Chambers about the effects of the paper tax (*Carpenter's Monthly Political Magazine*, I [Oct. 1831], 68).

[48] Aspinall, "Statistical Accounts in the Eighteenth Century," p. 202.

pers as "pamphlets," in order to avoid payment of the newspaper duty. William Carpenter's *Political Letters and Pamphlets,* Henry Hetherington's *Penny Papers for the People,* and Henry Hunt's *Address to the Radical Reformers of England, Ireland, and Scotland,* as well as other periodicals, were legally registered as "pamphlets" at the Stamp Office. This stratagem was deliberately intended to deceive the authorities and, in a technical sense, deserved prosecution. However, ambiguity in legal phraseology was capable of working in both directions. In 1834, Francis Place abandoned his intention to publish a series of pamphlets on trade unions, since he feared a Stamp Office prosecution of the tracts as an illegal newspaper.[49]

Despite its relative leniency, reformers condemned the pamphlet duty in terminology that was frequently as harsh as that reserved for the other taxes on knowledge. It was regarded as an obstacle in the path of the dissemination of "cheap knowledge" and was widely evaded by working-class radicals, particularly in the provinces, where the enforcement of any statute was more difficult.[50] The miniscule sum yielded by the duty was scarcely sufficient to repay the costs of collection and was recognized by the Grey government to be inadequate compensation for the intensity of the antagonism it aroused. As a result, the tax was totally repealed in 1833.

From the beginning of the eighteenth century, almanacs could justly claim to have fulfilled the role later predicated by the *Examiner* for newspapers as "the poor man's history of laws, customs, institutions, and opinions."[51] Their quality varied consid-

[49] Francis Place, letter to Ebenezer Elliott, 9 July 1835, Place Papers, Add. MSS 35,149, f. 307a; John A. Roebuck, *On the Means of Conveying Information to the People* (London: John Longley, 1835), p. 4. This pamphlet forms part of a series often bound together as John A. Roebuck, ed., *Pamphlets for the People* (London: John Longley, 1835–1836). This series will be referred to hereafter as *R. Pamphlets.*

[50] Aspinall, "Statistical Accounts in the Eighteenth Century," p. 204 n.; "Statistical Accounts, 1800–1836," p. 223.

[51] *Examiner,* 10 Feb. 1833.

[16]

erably, ranging from the illegal, semiliterate *Paddy's Watches* of the eighteenth century, to the high-quality almanacs issued under the superintendence of the Stationers' Company.[52] By the provisions of an act of 1815, which modified several earlier statutes, a duty of 1s. 3d. was payable on each individual almanac that was printed in England or Scotland. As a result of the duty, an illegal almanac trade flourished even before working-class publishers began to issue unstamped newspapers. After 1830 resistance to the almanac duty largely merged into the general agitation against the taxes on knowledge.

During 1830–1834 a "war" against the tax on almanacs was waged in London, Scotland, and the provinces. Its history closely paralleled and overlapped that of the newspaper repeal campaign. Many of the same radical journalists, including James Watson, Richard Carlile, and Richard E. Lee, were involved, and similar techniques of subterfuge were employed.[53] Sizable numbers of illegal almanacs, the majority selling at about 2d., were distributed in all sections of the country. According to James Guest, a participant in the campaign, the price of an illegal almanac was usually not marked, and so hawkers

sold for what they could get, at prices varying from 2d. to 6d., sometimes a good supper and leave to sleep in the barn or outhouse, often when they could get the blind side of the old dame or the young one with their Pamphlets, Books of Dreams, fortune telling, Nixon's prophecies, books of fate, ballads, etc.[54]

Illegal almanacs were printed on calico in order to evade payment of the duty which, it was argued, applied only to printed paper. Carlile issued the *Untaxed Cotton Almanack* during two

[52] Abel Heywood, Jr., *English Almanacks during the First Third of the Century* (Manchester: Privately pub., 1904), p. 25.

[53] See, for example, *Poor Man's Guardian*, 12 Oct. 1833; *Man*, 13 and 27 Oct. 1833.

[54] James Guest, "A Free Press, and How It Became Free," in W. Hutton, *The History of Birmingham* (6th ed.; Birmingham: James Guest, 1861) p. 496.

successive years, as well as another cotton almanac known as the *Atlas*. Benjamin D. Cousins, another radical journalist, published on cotton an almanac entitled *A Political Pocket Handkerchief, a Duster for the Whigs*, for which he was prosecuted in December 1831.[55]

Watson ingeniously fathered several editions of the *Working Man's Almanack*, which was allegedly printed and published by "John Doyle" at Liberty Street, New York. This almanac was theoretically "imported," though, in fact, it was entirely conceived and executed at a small printing shop in Finsbury.[56] The authorities were deceived, and no prosecutions were initiated. Even the *Times*, ignorant of its true paternity, unwittingly praised it, thus providing an evening of delight for many working-class radicals.[57]

The struggle for repeal of the almanac duty achieved success in 1834 when the Whig government totally repealed the duty. This decision was probably speeded up as the result of an influential report submitted to the government by Charles Knight, in which he detailed innumerable violations of the act during the preceding four years and contended that the sale of legal almanacs would increase tenfold if the duty were repealed.[58]

Predictably, the effect of repeal was striking. At least two hundred new almanacs were published almost immediately in London and the provinces, and several of them, according to the

---

[55] *Cosmopolite*, 8 June 1833; *Poor Man's Guardian*, 17 Dec. 1831; Heywood, *English Almanacks*, p. 21.

[56] *Working Man's Friend*, 22 Dec. 1832. *Franklin Moore's Almanack* was professedly printed in the United States but actually printed in London by Cousins (Heywood, *English Almanacks*, p. 21). Other almanacs were smuggled illegally into England from the Isle of Man where no stamp duty was in effect.

[57] Heywood, *English Almanacks*, pp. 22–25.

[58] Charles Knight, Report on Unstamped Almanacs, 14 Nov. 1833, reprinted in Monica C. Grobel, "The Society for the Diffusion of Useful Knowledge, 1826–1846" (unpublished M.A. thesis, University of London, 1933), IV, App. VI, 1–6; Charles Knight, *Passages of a Working Life during Half a Century* . . . (London: Bradbury and Evans, 1864–1865), II, 64–65.

Commissioners of Excise Report, achieved a circulation of more than 250,000.[59] With this specific object achieved, still another of the taxes on knowledge was removed from the arena of discontent. Thus after 1834, with the almanac and pamphlet duties removed and with the advertisement duty substantially reduced, much of the energy of reformers was directed toward the most substantive and important goal—repeal of the newspaper duty.

[59] Crawfurd, *Taxes on Knowledge*, p. 56; *Scotsman*, 30 July 1834; Heywood, *English Almanacks*, p. 28.

CHAPTER 2

The Middle-Class Background

A divisiveness along class lines permeated the reform movements of the 1830's. This polarity of sentiment and economic interest increased in intensity throughout the decade. An accelerating sense of working-class grievance emerged as a consequence of the parliamentary reform agitation of 1830–1832. The Reform Act of 1832, by its creation of a uniform £10 borough franchise, effectually transferred political power from the landed to the rising commercial classes. Simultaneously, it eliminated the traces of a democratic suffrage that existed in the "potwalloper" and "scot and lot" boroughs, thus depriving the urban laborers of any direct participation in the electoral process.

The struggles for factory and poor law reform sharpened this pattern of working-class frustration. Benthamites, led by Edwin Chadwick and Southwood Smith, and Tory reformers, such as Richard Oastler, Lord Ashley, and Michael Sadler, secured a factory act in 1833 that laid the groundwork for massive intervention by the central government but that seemed pitifully inadequate to those denouncing the evils of "infant slavery."[1] In the

[1] One unstamped journal condemned the statute as "a cheat, a gross, a scandalous fraud upon the people of England, and a cruel mockery and cheat on British infancy" (*Poor Man's Advocate, and Scourge of Tyranny*, 11 Oct. 1834).

following year an even more serious wedge between middle- and working-class reformers was opened by the enactment of the Poor Law Amendment Act. This Act terminated the Speenhamland system of outdoor relief. Subsequent directives issued by the Poor Law Commissioners provided that in many areas public assistance was to be restricted to inhabitants of workhouses. To the Benthamites this statute and the changes emanating from it seemed a model of efficiency; the poorer classes, for their part, regarded it as a manifestation of class inhumanity. An abortive and violent three-year struggle to prevent implementation of the Act followed.

The movement to repeal the taxes on knowledge forms an important episode in this developing pattern. Chronologically, the agitation for removal of the restrictions on the press spanned the better part of the decade. More importantly, repeal of the taxes on knowledge was one of the few concrete reforms of the 1830's that was favored unqualifiedly by both middle- and working-class reformers. It was a grievance behind which persons representing every hue of the radical political spectrum could be expected to unite. Hence, its resolution might have been expected to generate attitudes of mutual trust and respect between reformers of varying backgrounds. Had this situation occurred, a movement of seemingly endemic class bitterness, such as Chartism, might conceivably not have been spawned. The inability of working- and middle-class radicals to achieve unity on the demand for press reform was, therefore, significant. It is not the exclusive key to the history of the 1830's and 1840's since many other areas must be explored fully before a convincing explanation of the breakdown in political and social unity can be offered. But the increasing polarity of reformers on the issue of repealing the taxes on knowledge was an important development in the chain of events that linked the Reform Act of 1832 to the Chartist movement. An attempt is made in this chapter to explore the ideological roots of this failure from the middle-class perspective.

The middle-class demand for removal of the taxes on knowl-

[21]

edge represented an amalgam of the several currents of thought that dominated moderate reform thinking in the early 1830's. A commitment to Benthamite utilitarianism and to the doctrines of political economy, educational reformism, the movement for free trade, demands for improvement of the postal system, and a host of concrete economic grievances composed the core of this amalgam. The theme of journalistic freedom enunciated by James Mill and others to the effect that "no limit whatsoever ought to be imposed upon the liberty of the press" was a further, though lesser, element in this middle-class ideology.[2]

Much of the antagonism between middle and working classes on the newspaper issue lay in the former's antipathy to the illegal periodicals that inundated England after 1830. These journals largely expressed working-class attitudes and often employed violent imagery to articulate their point of view. Though the particular ideas enunciated by each of them differed, the following comment extracted from the *Man*, a leading unstamped journal, is only slightly stronger than hundreds of other such statements: "Any doctrine that may be promulgated, which falls short of an utter and total annihilation of Priestcraft, Kingcraft, Lordcraft, Profit, Monopoly, and Competition, is an absolute mockery of reason and common sense." [3] The constant reiteration of such sentiments tended to overshadow the more restrained analyses provided by other unstamped journals. Not surprisingly, many propertied reformers, irrespective of their motivation in seeking repeal of the stamp duty, were alienated.

As a result, these reformers condemned with near-unanimity the "foul and pernicious doctrines" being disseminated by the illegal penny press.[4] They castigated the unstamped journals for their presumed association with "the seditious, the factious,

<hr />

[2] James Mill, "Liberty of the Press," *Supplement to the 4th, 5th, and 6th Editions of the Encyclopaedia Britannica*, V (1824), 258–272; Alexander Bain, *James Mill: A Biography* (London: Longmans, Green, 1882), pp. 237–240.

[3] George Petrie ("Agrarius") in the *Man*, 22 Sept. 1833.

[4] Henry Brougham, "Working and Prospects of the Reform," *Edinburgh Review*, LVI (1832), 260.

the incendiary, and the destructive forces in the country." [5] James Mill, author of an eloquent and widely-circulated essay on the freedom of the press, gave expression to this viewpoint in a letter to John Black, the editor of the *Morning Chronicle*. After berating the latter for his failure to *"suppress* all knowledge" of certain working-class meetings at Birmingham, Mill denounced

the illicit cheap publications, in which the doctrine of the right of the labouring people . . . to all that is produced, is very generally preached. The alarming nature of this evil you will understand when I inform you that these publications are superseding the Sunday newspapers. . . . I am sure it is not good policy to give the power of teaching the people exclusively to persons violating the law, and of such desperate circumstances and character that neither the legal nor the moral sanction has sufficient hold upon them.[6]

The essence of the middle-class position was that both extremes, the monopoly of the "demagogue" and the monopoly of the stamped press, were equally undesirable, and that "respectable," propertied, moderate persons had the best qualifications to disseminate cheap journals.[7] Few concerted efforts were made to evaluate objectively the diversified themes expounded in the numerous unstamped periodicals. Instead, an indiscriminate assault was launched against most journals that published without a government stamp. Such condemnations were usually accompanied by demands for repeal of the newspaper duty, but such a dual approach only intensified working-class resentment. Thus

[5] Brougham, in a well-publicized speech on raising the foundation stone of the Mechanics' Institute in Liverpool, in Henry Brougham, *Works* (Edinburgh: Adam and Charles Black, 1872–1873), X, 79. W. B. Adams ("Junius Redivivus") condemned "the fantastic trash now selling in the streets of London" (*Examiner*, 24 June 1832). In Francis Place's opinion the unstamped publications were "sad trash" (Place Papers, Add. MSS 27,819, f. 26a).

[6] James Mill, letter to Henry Brougham, 3 Sept. 1832, quoted in Bain, *Mill*, pp. 364–67.

[7] Fox, *On Parliamentary Pledges*, p. 11; *Monthly Repository*, VI (1832), 269, VI (1832), 440. Men of "virtue and talent" could, if given an opportunity, drive out the "wicked" and "contemptible" smugglers (*Spectator*, 6 Sept. 1833).

Lord Brougham, despite his eloquent testimony on behalf of an untaxed press before the Select Committee on Libel Law in 1834, alienated working-class radicals. He coupled his support for repeal of the newspaper duty with the questionable assertion that

any one of [the unstamped journals] contains more atrocious matter in any one number, than all the respectable daily papers of London contain in a year . . . [including] personal slander as well as political . . . blasphemy in very great abundance, obscenity in considerable store, every species of ribaldry, personal, political, and irreligious.[8]

Francis Place and other reformers likewise forfeited influence with the same groups when they undertook a widespread agitation for an untaxed press primarily on the ground that it offered the best antidote to "the poison already in existence." [9]

Much of the middle-class antipathy to the illegal journalism of the 1830's was a product of genuine ideological revulsion. The bulk of opinion enunciated in the unstamped journals was predictably unsettling to persons of property, even to those who were strongly sympathetic to reform. The reiterated attacks upon the competitive economic system shocked many middle-class reformers, as did the uncompromising demands for political and social equality. But another factor of at least equal importance in shaping middle-class antipathy to illicit journalism was a genuine reluctance on the part of many reformers to sanction any overt violation of the law.[10]

[8] Henry Brougham, *Taxes on Knowledge: Stamps on Newspapers: Extracts from the Evidence . . . before the Select Committee of the House of Commons, on Libel Law, in June 1834* . . . (London: J. R. and C. Childs, 1834), p. 3. Brougham's testimony was not published officially until 1843. (Great Britain, House of Commons, *Appendix to the Report of the Campbell Committee*, 1843 [512], CCLIX).

[9] *Monthly Repository*, VII (1834), 106.

[10] Joseph Hamburger maintains that middle-class reformers faced a similar dilemma with respect to the Chartist movement, but he describes their rejection of illegality as "no more than a minor source of their alienation from Chartism" (*Intellectuals in Politics: John Stuart Mill and the Philosophic Radicals* [New Haven, Conn.: Yale University Press, 1965], pp. 253–254).

Working-class radicals, from the commencement of the movement to repeal the newspaper tax in 1830, demonstrated few scruples regarding the publication of illegal periodicals. Several, including William Carpenter, a London printer who produced the first significant illegal newspaper of the decade, the *Political Letters and Pamphlets,* argued against such a policy on theoretical grounds. Despite imprisonment for publishing the *Letters* and in spite of a continuing association with the unstamped press, Carpenter stressed the advantages of a legal petitioning campaign. He maintained that "knowledge and moral power and not violence or brute force, [are] the only means [the working classes] could successfully employ in the pursuit of political and social happiness." [11] James Watson, an even more active participant in the war of the unstamped, expressed similar scruples. "If, after having tried every effort which moral combination could effect," he warned, "[the working classes] still failed to accomplish their liberty, then . . . physical effort . . . might be necessary." [12] Carlile, the publisher of several unstamped journals, enunciated similar views on many occasions. But as legal methods of demonstrating antipathy to the newspaper tax began to seem increasingly futile, the doubts of Carpenter, Watson, Carlile, and others who hesitated to use illegal means to oppose the newspaper duty were gradually overborne.

Middle-class reformers, on the other hand, were almost uni-

[11] *Spectator,* 17 March 1832. In January 1832, Carpenter was refused an opportunity to speak at a meeting of the National Union of the Working Classes because he had assertedly attacked the vendors of illegal newspapers (*Poor Man's Guardian,* 28 Jan. 1832).

[12] Celebration of the third anniversary of the French Revolution, as reported in the *Working Man's Friend,* 4 May 1833. But Watson had reportedly left the Third Co-operative Congress during the previous year after several speakers agreed to support repeal only to the extent of a petitioning campaign (*Proceedings of the Third Co-operative Congress; Held in London . . . on the 23rd of April 1832, and by Adjournment on each of the Six Following Days, Sundays Excepted,* ed. William Carpenter [London: William Strange, 1832), pp. 69–73). William Cobbett, who published no unstamped newspapers during the 1830's, favored strict adherence to the law (letter to Joshua Hobson, 24

formly reluctant to endorse a policy of flagrant illegality. To a considerable extent they were prepared to identify their fortunes with the several Whig governments that were in office during the 1830's. The ministries of Lords Grey and Melbourne were regarded as generally sympathetic with their aims, and the prospect of enacting desired reforms through conventional parliamentary channels remained a viable one to them. During the period 1833–1835 it even seemed fleetingly possible that those radical M.P.'s who championed their views might secure a dominant position within the Whig party.[13]

This division on the question of whether or not to evade openly the stamp duty and to publish illegal newspapers severely embittered relations between the two groups of reformers. Edward L. Bulwer, a leading spokesman for middle-class reformers on the newspaper issue, postulated an intrinsic connection between "seditious" journalism and disregard for the law. He contended that "the very circumstance of wrestling against the law sharpens animosity into passion and substitutes for wise weapons —which are never passionate—the heated notions which are never safe." [14] This dubious analysis was accepted by most propertied reformers. Matthew Davenport Hill of Birmingham articulated this theme in a House of Commons debate held in 1834. After categorizing illegal journalists as "men of desperate fortunes, reckless of a gaol, and urged by their own pressing wants to adopt the style best calculated to stimulate the curiosity of the buyer," he predicted self-confidently that "their sincere opinions are almost certain to be on the side of violent changes. . . . Even if the unstamped newspapers were harmless in their doctrines (which they are not), the very fact of their being printed

---

Aug. 1833, Tolson Memorial Museum, Huddersfield, cited in J. T. Ward, *The Factory Movement, 1830–1855* [London: Macmillan, 1962], p. 111).

[13] A definitive analysis of the parliamentary maneuverings during these years has not yet appeared. See Halévy, *Triumph of Reform,* pp. 60–241; Norman Gash, *Reaction and Reconstruction in English Politics, 1832–1852* (Oxford: Clarendon Press, 1965).

[14] *New Monthly Magazine,* XXXV (1832), 400.

and sold in violation of the law, would produce a mischievous effect on the minds of the buyers." [15]

The *Examiner*, an influential weekly that vigorously championed repeal of the newspaper tax, also expressed this viewpoint when it cautioned against contempt for the law in these terms: "In connexion with the more prudent opinions are the scruples which will not permit of an illicit enterprise." [16] Even Thomas Wakley, after 1835 the M.P. most in sympathy with working-class demands, disappointed many of his Finsbury constituents by his pronounced opposition to illegal journalism. Although admitting that "resistance may lead to the sought-for relief," Wakley urged that "members of a civilized society will ever find it more prudent to attempt to *alter* the law, then obstinately to violate the law." [17] The *Constitutional*, a radical morning newspaper, did not commence publication until 15 September 1836 (the day on which reduction of the newspaper duty to 1*d.* took effect), despite the fact that Place, Hume, and other reformers had conceived it as early as January 1833. Its projected financial underpinning was not secure enough to warrant publication while the 4*d.* stamp remained; the scruples of its sponsors, on the other hand, would not sanction an overt violation of the law. [18]

Thus two considerations of a general nature shaped the attitudes of propertied reformers on the issue of the newspaper duty: fear of the "seditious" doctrines being disseminated by the unstamped press and a repudiation of the illegal tactics employed by working-class opponents of the newspaper act. Both factors helped to widen intraradical divisions, particularly during the

[15] Matthew Davenport Hill, *Speech . . . on Mr. Bulwer's Motion for a Repeal of the Stamp Duty on Newspapers, in the House of Commons, on Thursday, May 22, 1834: Extracted from the Mirror of Parliament* (London: *Mirror of Parliament*, 1834), pp. 7–8.

[16] *Examiner*, 15 Sept. 1833.

[17] *Ballot*, 26 June 1831; newsclipping of a Finsbury meeting of Feb. 1836, in Place Newspaper Collection, Set 70, ff. 313–315.

[18] See the printed circular issued by the "Society for the Diffusion of Political and Moral Knowledge," in Jan. 1833. A copy is in Place Papers, Add. MSS 35,154, ff. 167–168.

period 1830–1834. After 1834 many middle-class reformers tempered their earlier opposition to the unstamped press. Several, including William E. Hickson who had previously been a critic of the illegal press, now perceived a qualitative improvement in many of the illicit periodicals. In the spring of 1836, Hickson wrote a widely-circulated tract entitled *Taxes on Knowledge: Reduction or Abolition of the Newspaper Stamp-Duty?*, in which he lauded their remarkable improvement and suggested that "the quantity of general information they collect and diffuse (for the most part of an unexceptionable nature) is . . . truly astonishing." [19]

Other reformers gave a conditional endorsement to the widespread defiance of the law. William B. Adams, who popularized Benthamite ideas under the pseudonym "Junius Redivivus," virtually repudiated his mentor's doctrines when he wrote in 1835:

Laws made expressly to prevent the dissemination of opinion . . . are utterly untenable by any reasoning process, and the friends of freedom and improvement are justified in warring upon them as they would war on pirates. No quarter should be given to an enemy who denies his adversary the freedom of speech, and cuts out his tongue for talking.[20]

D. W. Harvey, the M.P. for Southwark, argued that "when laws are morally dead, acts of parliament, are of no more value than a blank sheet of parchment." [21] The *Manchester Advertiser*, a stamped weekly, rejected advice to "cram the goals" but likewise extended qualified approval to violation of the law:

We will have the law altered, and it may come to pass that we shall have to agree one and all upon repealing it without waiting for the sanction of parliament. Such things have happened before, and the law will not dare to gainsay it. Anybody who chooses to violate it, as it

[19] William E. Hickson, *Taxes on Knowledge: Reduction or Abolition of the Newspaper Stamp-Duty?* (London: C. Ely, 1836), p. 10.

[20] William B. Adams, "The Roebuck Pamphlets," *Monthly Repository*, IX (1835), 546.

[21] *Cleave's Weekly Police Gazette*, 23 Jan. 1836.

stands, is at liberty to incur its penalties. But there the utmost limit of his right ceases. He has no right to tempt and persuade others to their ruin.[22]

In a more pronounced expression of approbation, several reformers emulated the tactics of the illegal journalists by publishing during 1835–1836 a nationally circulated unstamped weekly known as the *Pamphlets for the People*. This was supported by a number of M.P.'s, foremost among whom was John A. Roebuck, and it amassed a substantial circulation. Thus in the final stages of the campaign for repeal of the newspaper duty, an accommodation between middle- and working-class reformers became once again a distinct possibility.

BENTHAMITE RADICALISM

Benthamite utilitarianism when linked to the ideas of the political economists was a leading intellectual impulse behind the attempt of middle-class reformers to repeal the taxes on knowledge. Within this movement a broad stratum of reformers and reforming journals adhered to the "utilitarian" doctrines enunciated by Jeremy Bentham and superimposed upon them a belief in the laissez-faire political economy of Adam Smith, Thomas Malthus, and David Ricardo. These reformers also expressed an almost messianic desire to disseminate "useful" knowledge amongst the masses, and to "uplift" them.[23] A firm Enlightenment faith in progress and in the efficacy of reason reinforced their commitment insofar as it related to the issue of an untaxed press.

Major proponents of this approach to the newspaper question were Francis Place, the Westminster "wire-puller" and lobbyist, the parliamentary reformers Joseph Hume, John A. Roebuck,

[22] *Manchester Advertiser*, 6 Feb. 1836.

[23] For a succinct analysis of the doctrines of these reformers see Webb, *British Working Class Reader*, pp. 97–102; Jessie K. Buckley, *Joseph Parkes of Birmingham and the Part Which He played in Radical Reform Movements from 1825 to 1845* (London: Methuen, 1926), p. 188.

[29]

and Henry Warburton, and W. J. Fox, the Unitarian minister, publicist, and political organizer. Fox's thinking typifies that of many of his colleagues and he can serve to exemplify their approach to the question of repeal.[24] As editor of the *True Sun*, a radical evening newspaper, and the *Monthly Repository*, a Unitarian journal, he popularized the utilitarian faith in a free press. Many of his articles were reprinted in illicit working-class journals, thus enabling him to maintain some influence with the poorer classes.

Fox regarded mankind as undergoing an inevitable progression toward a higher social order. Knowledge was the crucial mechanism in this advancement; its unobstructed dissemination could alone stimulate a general demand for improvement.[25] A free press was an essential component of this view of society, especially during the 1830's, a decade that Fox perceived as one of transition and conflict.

The "middle-class" element in Fox's thinking emerges most strikingly in the emphasis which he gave to the pedagogical role of journalism. Information was to be diffused to the "natural teachers of the poor," the artisans and skilled mechanics, and the latter were in turn to serve as a conduit in reaching the semiliterate base of society.[26] A limitless vista of progress was envisaged,

[24] Never an original thinker, Fox has been described aptly by his biographer as "a Preacher, not a Prophet" (Richard Garnett, *The Life of W. J. Fox, Public Teacher and Social Reformer: 1786–1864* [London: J. Lane, 1910], p. 114).

[25] W. J. Fox, *The Duties of Christians towards Deists: A Sermon Preached . . . on Occasion of the Recent Prosecution of Mr. Carlile for the Republication of Paine's "Age of Reason"* (London: George Smallfield, 1819); "On the State and Prospects of the Country at the Close of the Year 1831," *Monthly Repository*, VI (1832), 2; "The True Spirit of Reform," *Monthly Repository*, IX (1835), 1–8.

[26] W. J. Fox, "Taxes on Knowledge," *Monthly Repository*, VI (1832), 268. Brougham argued that if artisans were given correct opinions, "it will spread downwards till it reached the very lowest description of the community" (address to the Manchester Mechanics' Institute (1835) in Henry Brougham, *Speeches . . . upon Questions Relating to Public Rights, Duties, and Interests; with Historical Introductions, and a Critical Dissertation upon the Eloquence of the Ancients* (Edinburgh: Adam and Charles Black, 1838), III, 175.

albeit of an ill-defined nature. To conservative opponents, Fox offered the meagre consolation that "he who can read Paine can read the Bible." [27] But he anticipated that the working classes, through the medium of a free press, would assimilate and give effect to his own preferred doctrines of political economy.

Fox and others active in the movement for an untaxed press eloquently articulated their belief in the idea of progress. This theme was the mainstay of the middle-class demand for unstamped newspapers since it implied an unqualified faith in the power of the printed word, a faith that was summarized in the common description of the press as a "mighty engine" or "grand vehicle" of progress.[28] It was assumed that truth had the ineluctable ability to surmount "every intellectual obstacle, every impediment but mere brute force," and that "where there is no motive to attach a man to error, it is natural for him to embrace the truth." [29] According to John Stuart Mill:

Up to this time error has had the field to itself. Truth will now, for the first time, have its *natural chances of superiority*. In the immensely increased number of readers which will be the effect of the cheapness of newspapers and political tracts, any *writers of talent* may hope, whatever be their sentiments, to find the quantity of support necessary for a moderate degree of success.[30]

The masses needed, therefore, only the "capability of reasoning," to ensure "nearly a perfect government." [31]

[27] Fox, *Duties of Christians*, p. 41.

[28] Speech at Glasgow by a reformer named Brash, as reported in the *Glasgow Argus*, 10 oct. 1833; Chadwick, *On the Taxes on Knowledge*, p. 6. The newspaper was described as an "instrument of civilization" (*Examiner*, 10 Feb. 1833); newspapers are "the great pulpits of the time" (testimony of Henry Cole, *S.C. on Newspaper Stamps* [1851], p. 407, q. 2738).

[29] [Samuel Bailey], *Essays on the Formation and Publication of Opinions, and on Other Subjects* (London: R. Hunter, 1821), pp. 138-139; Mill, "Liberty of the Press," p. 267.

[30] "The Chancellor's Declaration against the Taxes on Political Information," *Monthly Repository*, VIII (1834), 594.

[31] William B. Adams ("Junius Redivivus"), *The Rights of Morality; An Essay on the Present State of Society, Moral, Political, and Physical, in England: Addressed to the Productive Classes of the Community* (London: Effingham Wilson, 1832), p. 75.

When applied specifically to journalistic activity, this belief in progress fortified the middle-class reformer's confidence that his periodicals could easily outdistance those produced by more radical competitors. How, it was argued, could a working-class reader prefer "immoral publications" to a better class of journal, one that prudently counselled "the right course of conduct?" [32] Or, expressed more poignantly, how could "a meal of healthful, useful, and agreeable mental instruction" be refused gratuitously? [33]

Evidence to refute this optimistic assumption seemed to be available during the 1830's when many illegal working-class publications amassed considerable circulations. Moderate publicists were quick to denigrate this phenomenon. They retorted somewhat disingenuously that these journals "only maintain a feeble existence by means of their illegality, and that the moment they shall lose their notoriety as victims to government persecutions . . . they shall die a natural death." [34] There was a modicum of validity to this assertion as the several unsuccessful prosecutions of Carlile during the 1820's, each resulting in greater notoriety and mounting circulation, had amply demonstrated.[35] Nonetheless, events of the succeeding years were to invalidate this simplistic assertion further. Despite being placed at a disadvantage by the reduction of the stamp duty to 1*d.* in 1836, ultra-radical newspapers such as the *Northern Star* and the *London Dispatch* were to outdistance in popularity many of their more restrained competitors during the late 1830's and 1840's.[36]

[32] Testimony of Samuel Bucknall, a publisher, *S.C. on Newspaper Stamps* (1851), pp. 196–200, qq. 1214–1229; "On the Necessity for Popular Instruction," *Examiner*, 6 Nov. 1831. For an unusual dissenting view by a leading political economist, see McCulloch, *Observations*, p. 29.

[33] *Chambers' Edinburgh Journal*, 4 Feb. 1832, cited in Chambers, *Story of a Long and Busy Life*, p. 31.

[34] *Monthly Repository*, VIII (1834), 107.

[35] Theophila C. Campbell, *The Battle of the Press as Told in the Story of the Life of Richard Carlile* (London: A. and H. B. Bonner, 1899), chaps. 5–13.

[36] C. D. Collet contended rather naïvely that the *Northern Star* prospered only because "a good paper, a moderate paper" was not available (testimony, *S.C. on Newspaper Stamps* (1851), p. 152, q. 927.

The other key strands of this point of view—a pronounced emphasis upon "political economy" and a sense of mission in eliminating the final vestiges of ignorance—were closely intertwined, and reformers used the terms "political economy" and "knowledge" interchangeably.[37] The transformations that they envisaged as a result of the dissemination of cheap newspapers were to be achieved largely through propagandization on behalf of the principles of political economy. This hope was often stated overtly, as when Place affirmed that cheap periodicals should teach workers the "doctrine of wages and profits," or when Brougham urged the need to expound "the true principles and mutual relations of population and wages."[38] According to Place, in the absence of restrictions on the press, "the important doctrine of profit and wages would ere long be as well as generally understood, than for which nothing is of more importance to the working people, and few things much more essential to the happiness of the country."[39] Edwin Chadwick envisaged as a consequence of a free press, an outpouring of tracts "expository of the circumstances influencing wages, and on other subjects involving the principle of political and domestic economy, and of morals and legislation, which contribute to the welfare of the whole community."[40]

[37] "Taxes on Newspapers," *Monthly Repository*, IX (1835), 348; Rowland Detrosier, *Lecture on the Utility of Political Unions for the Diffusion of Sound Moral and Political Information amongst the People* . . . (London: John Brooks, 1832), pp. 11–12; *Bennet's Glasgow Magazine*, I (1833), 425.

[38] Francis Place, letter to Sir Francis Burdett, 6 Dec. 1833, Place Papers, Add. MSS 35,149, f. 241a; Brougham, "Practical Observations on the Education of the People," in *Works*, VIII, 422–424. Political economy was "a lever which will move the world" (Samuel Bailey, *Essays on the Pursuit of Truth, on the Progress of Knowledge, and on the Fundamental Principle of All Evidence and Expectation* [London: R. Hunter, 1829], p. 125). *Manchester Advertiser*, 9 May 1835, urged that "the great object is to make every adult, man and woman, as good a reasoner upon . . . political economy, as those who now compound and perplex into a maze of mischievous folly the clear and lucid writings of Dr. Adam Smith."

[39] *Newspaper Stamps: Deputation . . . to Procure the Total Repeal of the Stamp Duty on Newspapers* . . . (London: C. Ely, 1836), p. 11.

[40] "The Real Incendiaries and Promoters of Crime," *Examiner*, 20 Feb. 1831.

It was regarded as essential that the Ricardian doctrine of the wages-fund be disseminated through the instrumentality of a cheap press. If this economic law were inculcated successfully, then "ignorance" would disappear from the sphere of industrial relations. Rick-burning, machine-breaking, the formation of trade unions, and all analogous manifestations of antisocial behavior would be obliterated.[41] This contention was employed with particular effectiveness during the agricultural disturbances of 1830–1832 when the propertied classes foresaw the likelihood of a general conflagration. The fact that rural laborers were overwhelmingly illiterate, and that scarcely any of the illegal journals were circulated among them, did not prevent reformers from proclaiming that "mobs, rioting, and all the other deplorable manifestations of popular folly and extravagance" would disappear if they were permitted to circulate untaxed tracts.[42] As a concomitant to the above, it was alleged that the universal acceptance of the doctrines of "political economy" would decrease permanently the incidence of crime, since the latter was a direct manifestation of ignorance.[43] Roebuck's view, in a tract written for the National Political Union, that educated people would automatically be industrious, peaceable, and incapable of feeling themselves oppressed, was widely accepted.[44]

[41] *Spectator*, 1 Aug. 1835; W. J. Fox, *Finsbury Lectures: Reports of Lectures Delivered at the Chapel in South Place, Finsbury* (London: Charles Fox, 1835), pp. 8–10.

[42] *Greenock Intelligencer*, cited in *Glasgow Argus*, 27 March 1834; *Monthly Repository*, VIII (1834), 105, maintained that "the more newspapers the fewer rioters." Still other middle-class reformers argued that if they were permitted to circulate their doctrines "mobs would not be known" (*The Moral and Political Evils of the Taxes on Knowledge* . . . [London: Effingham Wilson, 1830], p. 8). "Cheap newspapers . . . were the only means of stimulating the people to desire knowledge" (Joseph Hume, in a speech quoted in *Newspaper Stamps: Deputation*, p. 5).

[43] "Increase of Knowledge—Decrease of Crime," *Bennet's Glasgow Magazine*, I (1833), 592.

[44] John A. Roebuck, *Report of the Council to the First Annual General Meeting of the Members, Held at Saville House, on Thursday, February 2nd, 1832* (London: Effingham Wilson, 1832), p. 5.

It was likewise believed that intemperance, an accelerating social evil and a presumed product of ignorance and misery, would be eliminated if the fiscal regulations on the press were removed. Most reformers adhered unhesitatingly to Place's dictum that if a worker was properly educated, "he will become decent in his conduct and language, sober, discreet, taking reasonable pride in his own person and in that of those who are dependent on him." [45] This presumed link between intemperance and the restrictions on the press was at least partly valid since some workmen seem to have attended public houses solely in order to read a newspaper. The evidence of one such laborer as conveyed to the Select Committee on Newspaper Stamps is instructive in this regard:

I tell you, Sir, I never go to the public-house for beer, I go for the news; I have no other way of getting it; I cannot afford to pay five-pence, but unfortunately I go on drinking till I have spent a shilling, and I might as well have bought the paper in the first instance; still that is my reason, my only reason for going to the public house; I hear people read the paper, and say what is going on in London, and it is the only place where I get the news. [46]

Not surprisingly, the Select Committee on Drunkenness, which was established in 1834 under the chairmanship of John Stuart Buckingham, strongly condemned the taxes on knowledge. [47]

A final aspect of the arguments of Benthamites and political economists for removal of the newspaper tax proved especially irritating to working-class activists. This aspect involved the condescending manner in which the virtues of diffusing knowledge were advocated. Repeated references to the necessity for "lifting

---

[45] Francis Place, *Improvement of the Working People: Drunkenness—Education.* (London: Charles Fox, 1834), pp. 9, 17; Adams, *Rights of Morality*, p. 47.

[46] *S.C. on Newspaper Stamps* (1851), p. 352, q. 2364; *ibid.*, p. 356, q. 2380.

[47] Great Britain, House of Commons, *Select Committee on the Inquiry into Drunkenness* (1834), p. ix. See also the evidence of Edwin Chadwick before this committee, *ibid.*, p. 38, q. 325.

the labouring people out of the degrading ignorance in which they have been sunk" and for "the highly-gifted to raise their fellows, however low they may be sunk," were not likely to lead to political harmony.[48] Neither was the following formula for the establishment of adult education programs:

There is no *desire* for learning; the ground is in a fallow state; and therefore it is not enough to purchase manure, and secure the implements of cultivation; they must be applied, the ground must be broken up, the manure must be spread, and then we may hope that the results will be good.[49]

Nonetheless, the theme of "elevating" the uneducated masses was a crucial cog in the middle-class dynamic. If newspapers had not been viewed almost evangelically as "vehicles of public instruction," much of the moral fervor behind the movement for repeal of the newspaper duty would have been dissipated.[50] These reformers agitated strongly and influentially on behalf of an untaxed press because they felt an urgent need to reinvigorate the "practical morality" of the lower orders.[51] But the one-sided perspective of their commitments bred an emotional counter-reaction from working-class journalists which severely weakened the possibility of a radical alliance.[52]

[48] "Popular Instruction," *Examiner*, 27 Nov. 1831; Fox, *Finsbury Lectures*, pp. 31, 34–35. J. F. C. Harrison perceptively describes middle-class newspapers as "designed primarily to strengthen the social fabric rather than provide cultural or emotional enrichment for the individual" (*Learning and Living, 1790–1960: A Study in the History of the English Adult Education Movement* [London: Routledge and Kegan Paul, 1961], pp. 40–43).

[49] [Joseph Livesey], "The Preston Institution for the Diffusion of Knowledge," *Moral Reformer*, III (1833), 296–297, quoted in Harrison, *Learning and Living*, p. 5.

[50] Brian Simon's argument that the "industrial middle-class" sought to educate the masses solely to propagate capitalistic ideas ignores this important idealistic strain (Simon, *Studies in the History of Education*, pp. 125–129).

[51] Henry Brougham, "Newspaper Tax," *Edinburgh Review*, LXI (1835), 183.

[52] See the letter from Thomas Morrison in *Cobbett's Weekly Political Register*, 23 May 1835, in which the "pedantry and presumption" of Roebuck and Chadwick are condemned.

THE EDUCATIONAL REFORMERS

Educational reformism represented a distinct strain of thought within the middle-class repeal movement though its outlook frequently resembled that of the Benthamites and political economists. Several of the latter, including Roebuck, Fox, and William E. Hickson, are classifiable as educational reformers. Their concern was primarily with pedagogy but when they did focus upon the content of education, their attitudes blended with those described in the preceding section.

Hickson, the future proprietor of the *Westminster Review*, George Birkbeck, the founder of Mechanics' Institutes, and Matthew Hill, a radical M.P. who achieved subsequent legal prominence as Recorder of Birmingham and whose father, Thomas Hill, established the famous Hazelwood School, were educational reformers who worked for repeal of the taxes on knowledge. Each placed primary stress upon the *process* of reading and learning. They hoped to stimulate the development of newspapers because they viewed them as essential prerequisites to the spread of literacy. The working classes, they maintained, had a unique need for literacy since their rapid political advancement had left them intellectually and morally unequipped to perform a responsible social role. Only the unhampered dissemination of "MORAL AND POLITICAL KNOWLEDGE" could fortify them effectively for the arduous task that lay ahead.[53]

In the opinion of the educational reformers, newspapers were a fundamental "implement" of learning, inasmuch as "the generality of persons are too much occupied in life to receive instruction through any other source." [54] According to Birkbeck, newspapers "were of great use in spreading the habit of reading, which was

---

[53] Detrosier, *Lecture on the Utility of Political Unions*, pp. 3, 6–7; Roebuck, *Report of the Council*, pp. 5–8; speech of Dr. James Browne, *Scotsman*, 19 March 1836.

[54] Testimony of Hickson, *S.C. on Newspaper Stamps* (1851), p. 472, q. 3212; testimony of Collet. *ibid.*, p. 160, q. 981.

[37]

the first great step in human improvement." [55] They were effective instruments of learning because of their simplicity, readability, and relevance to ordinary activities.

Thus if the skill of reading was to be effectively disseminated, all barriers to journalistic expression had to be removed. It was argued that semiliterate laborers would forget how to read if they lacked unrestricted access to daily newspapers, particularly to those of local interest. The latter, it was generally agreed, were more likely than national newspapers to create a habit of reading among small farmers and agricultural laborers. [56] And unless a high rate of literacy could be maintained, the prospect of developing a temperate, stable society would be materially reduced. As Hickson stated in testimony before the Select Committee of 1851: "Readers are not rioters; readers are not rick-burners." [57]

Many educational reformers asserted that literacy developed self-reliance in intellectual matters. Matthew Hill gave emphasis to this conviction in his efforts to secure repeal of the newspaper tax. He affirmed that the content of a newspaper was fundamentally irrelevant. It was the process of expression itself that was of supreme importance, since "every man who has had a really good education, has done infinitely more for himself than his best teachers have done for him." [58] Such an analysis placed Hill in almost direct theoretical opposition to many political economists for it implied that "habits of thought" had to emerge from within the individual. [59] Hickson likewise eloquently pleaded: "Let us give up the attempt to force our own opinions, or habits

[55] *Newspaper Stamps: Deputation*, p. 3; Hunt, *Fourth Estate*, II, 82.

[56] William E. Hickson, *Mister Spring Rice and His Penny Stamp: From the London and Westminster Review* (London: 1836), p. 3; Hickson testimony, *S.C. on Newspaper Stamps* (1851), p. 476, q. 3240.

[57] Testimony of Hickson, *S.C. on Newspaper Stamps* (1851), p. 479, q. 3254.

[58] Hill, *Answer to a Letter from the Secretary of a Society for Political Instruction, Formed by Working Men, Asking for Advice on the Conduct of Such Institutions* (1836), quoted in Rosamond and Florence Davenport-Hill, *The Recorder of Birmingham: A Memoir of Matthew Davenport Hill; with Selections from His Correspondence* (London: Macmillan, 1878), pp. 135–139.

[59] *Ibid.*, p. 372.

of thinking, upon minds unprepared to receive them. . . .
Grown-up men and women are not to be disciplined into knowledge as children may be taught in schools." [60] Thus working-
class journalism might be encouraged, despite its potential "extremism," if it contributed to the process of educational development. Edwin Chadwick, more easily classifiable as a Benthamite
than an educational reformer, gave eloquent expression to this
viewpoint:

No matter how poor, how inadequate, low, coarse and distasteful to
cultivated minds might be the nature of the publications first sent forth;
if they are read, they can scarcely fail to be of service in contributing
to the formation of a habit of reading, which will facilitate the diffusion
of publications of a more *useful and elevated character*.[61]

The views expounded by educational reformers were often
more palatable to the poorer classes than those offered by the
Benthamites and political economists. They tended, at their best,
to impart to the middle-class movement for repeal of the stamp
duty a sense of tolerance which could have had a harmonizing
effect. Unfortunately, the assumptions of the educational reformers were less influential in shaping the ideological structure
of the newspaper agitation than those of the political economists.
Furthermore, another variety of educational reformism possessed
at least an equal degree of influence. This type was represented
by those reformers who sought to disseminate "useful" learning
by means of publications like the *Penny Magazine*, a journal produced by the Society for the Diffusion of Useful Knowledge.

The sponsors of the S.D.U.K. included Lord Brougham, Lord
John Russell, Thomas Spring Rice, and other prominent Whig
and radical politicians. Their principal objective was to circulate
doctrines of a broadly "utilitarian" character, without at the same
time pandering to the presumed irresponsibility of the masses.
The method selected was the indirect albeit effective one of
avoiding, with careful exceptions, references to controversial sub-

[60] Hickson, *Taxes on Knowledge*, pp. 12–13.
[61] Chadwick, "The Real Incendiaries and Promoters of Crime!" *Examiner*,
20 Feb. 1831.

jects, political or otherwise.[62] In the words of the Society itself, "any interference with theology or politics would have endangered the existence of a union which demanded the most cordial co-operation from all who wished well to the cause." [63]

In the *Penny Magazine* the needs of working-class readers were met by a mixture of engravings and essays on a variety of pedantic, unrelated subjects. Politically conscious laborers were offended by this supercilious approach since it appeared to ignore their demands for political expression. Thus despite a weekly circulation reliably estimated at 200,000, the *Penny Magazine* was an object of derision and contempt among working-class radicals.[64] Brougham, who exerted an influence over the contents of the magazine, described political knowledge as "the most valuable of all Knowledge" and, in accordance with this view, played an important role in the agitation for repeal of the stamp duty.[65] But his seemingly inconsistent association with the *Penny Magazine*, combined with a reputation for political instability, earned for him wide detestation in the pages of the illicit press.[66] Thus

[62] Defenders of the *Penny Magazine*, including Matthew Hill, argued unconvincingly that it was merely obeying a bad law (*Speech on Bulwer's Motion*, pp. 9–10).

[63] Society for the Diffusion of Useful Knowledge, *Address of the Committee* . . . (London: Charles Knight, 1846), pp. 4–5. Charles Knight, the publisher of the *Penny Magazine*, attacked those who "quarrel with us for leading the people into trains of agreeable thought, and require that we should be always preaching to them the doctrines of political economy" (letter to Henry Brougham, 29 Aug. 1832, Brougham Papers, No. 10,061).

[64] For an estimated circulation of 200,000, see Knight, *Old Printer*, pp. 280–281. For a working-class attack on the *Penny Magazine*, see *Poor Man's Guardian*, 4 Aug. 1832. Place wrote: "The unionist will read nothing which the Diffusion Society meddles with—they call the members of it *Whigs* —and Whig means with them a treacherous rascal, a bitter implacable enemy" (letter to Joseph Parkes, 21 April 1834, Place Papers, Add. MSS 35,149, f. 281).

[65] Speech at Liverpool in July 1835, as reported in *Manchester Advertiser*, 25 July 1835. He described political knowledge as "that which was most important to the people" (*Sun*, c. March 1836, newscutting in Place Newspaper Collection, Set 70, f. 437).

[66] The *Poor Man's Guardian* referred to him typically as a "mean-spirited, fawning, sycophantic, slavish ARISTOCRAT" (13 Oct. 1832).

it is probably the case that the over-all effect of the thinking of educational reformers upon the movement to repeal the newspaper tax was to exacerbate further the division between middle- and working-class reformers.

FREE TRADE

The movement for repeal of the taxes on knowledge formed a segment of the broader campaign for free trade. By the 1840's the latter dominated reforming activity to a considerable extent, thus imparting a more marked "free trade" quality to the post-Chartist press agitation than to the earlier one. Many free traders were, nonetheless, attracted to the cause of press reform during the 1830's. For some the advertisement duty appeared to be the largest obstacle to the unfettered commercial development of the press. Others viewed the existence of the newspaper stamp as of at least equal importance since any form of taxation was regarded as undesirable. Speirs, the radical M.P. for Paisley and a pronounced opponent of the taxes on knowledge, expressed this attitude in a speech to his constituents when he promised to "vote for the abolition of any tax, but . . . strenuously oppose the imposition of a new one." [67] Chadwick, in an influential article which appeared in the *Westminster Review* during 1831, placed repeal within the context of "bold reductions of fiscal imposts on articles of general consumption." [68]

Buttressing this opposition to the newspaper tax on general grounds was the specific belief that it represented a formidable obstacle to "free trade in politics." [69] By this view, news was a commodity analogous to any other, and the principle of free discussion was fully comprehensible only within a commercial context. As expressed by Samuel Bailey:

To check inquiry and attempt to regulate the progress and direction of opinions, by proscription and penalties, is to disturb the order of na-

[67] Speech at a political dinner, as reported in *Glasgow Argus*, 23 April 1835.
[68] Chadwick, *On the Taxes on Knowledge*, p. 30.
[69] *Moral and Political Evils*, p. 7.

ture, and is analogous, in its mischievous tendency, to the system of forcing the capital and industry of the community into channels, which they would never spontaneously seek, instead of suffering private interests to direct them to their most predictable employment.[70]

If the laws of supply and demand were permitted to operate upon news and greater competition was allowed, then the informal "monopoly" of the "Gentlemen of the Press," particularly that of the *Times,* would be terminated.[71] The intolerable "monopoly" of those who published illegal newspapers would likewise be ended, since the inferior product would be compelled to give way to its superior. "If you remove the stamps," Brougham asserted in testimony before the 1834 Libel Committee, "you apply the common principle of destroying the smuggler, by lowering the duties." [72] Similarly, he stated in a letter to Spring Rice, the Chancellor of the Exchequer, repeal "puts an end to the obscure, blasphemous and seditious press and it at once dethrones the *3 or 4 unknown persons* who now tyrannise over the town altogether." [73] In the view of Chadwick: "A journalist would be bound to good behaviour, under penalties of the loss of hundreds or thousands of his circulation for each act of misbehaviour." [74]

An automatic improvement in the tone and quality of journalism would then be assured, and individuals could invest their "enterprise and capital" in the publishing field without fear of

[70] Bailey, *Essays on the Formation and Publication of Opinions,* p. 100. It was argued that cheaper newspapers would make labor more flexible and transferrable (testimony of Rev. Thomas Spencer, *S.C. on Newspaper Stamps* [1851], p. 359, q. 2395).

[71] Place, "The Taxes on Knowledge" (*R. Pamphlet,* No. 8), pp. 10–11; Roebuck, "The Stamped Press and Its Morality" (*R. Pamphlet,* No. 3), pp. 2–3.

[72] Brougham, *Taxes on Knowledge,* p. 4; Hill, *Speech on Bulwer's Motion,* pp. 7–8.

[73] Henry Brougham, letter to Thomas Spring Rice, 8 May 1835, Monteagle Papers, folder, 13,378 (1).

[74] Chadwick, *On the Taxes on Knowledge,* pp. 21–23.

unethical competition from either rich or poor.[75] From the rather simplistic perspective of a contemporary writer, whenever there is variety the better product will dominate since "the bane and the antidote will commonly come together."[76]

Amongst the free traders most directly involved in the press agitation of the 1830's were Charles Poulett Thomson, Vice President of the Board of Trade in the Grey ministry, John Crawfurd, a surgeon employed by the East India Company, and T. Perronet Thompson, M.P. for Hull and former owner of the *Westminster Review*. Poulett Thomson abandoned interest in the question of taxes on knowledge after an abortive free trade motion on the subject in March 1830, but Perronet Thompson continued to play an active role on behalf of repeal.[77] He possessed some influence with the working classes, despite his unqualified commitment to the doctrines of laissez faire and political economy. Thompson was one of only two radical M.P.'s to vote against reduction of the newspaper duty in 1836 in the conviction that the only acceptable policy was total repeal of the impost.[78]

THE POSTAL REFORMERS

The movement for rationalization of the Post Office and for the rectification of postal abuses was linked closely to the middle-

[75] Crawfurd, *Taxes on Knowledge*, p. 34; leader in *Glasgow Argus*, 17 Nov. 1834; J. S. Buckingham, *Parliamentary Review, and Family Magazine*, III (1833), 449–452.

[76] R. K. D., *Letter to Viscount Althorp*, pp. 10, 15.

[77] *Hansard*, H. of C., 25 March 1830, XXIII, 857–919; "Taxes on Knowledge," *Examiner*, 17 June 1832. Place's important tract, *A Letter to a Minister of State*, was dedicated to Thomson, who was attacked repeatedly by reformers for abandoning the cause of repeal. See William Carpenter, *The People's Book; Comprising Their Chartered Rights and Practical Wrongs* (London: William Strange, 1831), p. 382.

[78] *Hansard*, H. of C., 25 July 1836, XXXV, 560–568. Thompson denounced the Whigs as "enemies" of the people for their retention of the penny stamp ("Lecture at the Opening of the Westminster Mechanics' Institute," reprinted in T. Perronet Thompson, *Exercises, Political and Others* [London: Effingham Wilson, 1842], IV, 369).

class repeal agitation. Persons active in both aspects of the reform movement included Rowland Hill, the initiator of the uniform penny postage that was adopted in 1839, and Robert Wallace, M.P. for Greenock. Wallace, who described the stamp duty as "the most degrading and injurious tax ever inflicted on a free people," successfully secured the abolition of several postal abuses.[79] Hill, a lesser-known personality during the early stages of the movement, participated in several important repeal meetings and took part in delegations to the government.

The aspect of the postal question that most directly related it to the newspaper agitation was the attempt by reformers to affix a uniform postal charge to newspapers and other printed materials transmitted through the mails. Under the provisions of the act of 1819, periodicals and newspapers that bore a 4*d.* government stamp were permitted free use of the postal service whereas other publications, including pamphlets, had to pay high, frequently uneven, duties. This anomalous situation, immeasurably assisting the powerful London dailies and weeklies which relied heavily on the post, aroused the wrath of reformers, including the Westminster group centered around Francis Place.

Place proposed in January 1831 that a small uniform postal duty be substituted for the 4*d.* newspaper stamp. His initial medium for testing this suggestion was an influential pamphlet he wrote entitled *A Letter to a Minister of State*.[80] In this tract Place supported a ½*d.* postal duty rated proportionately on the number of sheets transmitted through the mails. Folio-sized London newspapers such as the *Times* and the *Morning Chronicle*, which ordinarily contained two demy sheets per number, would, by the terms of this proposal, pay twice as much as their

[79] A letter from Wallace which appeared in the *Greenock Intelligencer* during January 1836; reprinted in the *Liberator* (Glasgow), 16 Jan. 1836.

[80] This tract was published in at least four editions. An edition published in March 1831 was financed by a society of "Gentlemen in the City," presumably the City of London Literary and Scientific Institution. Two further editions appeared in 1835. The second was distributed by the Society for the Diffusion of Political and Moral Knowledge at the price of 1*d.*

poorer competitors. Place calculated that the Whig *Morning Chronicle* would probably sell for 3½d. if the duty was repealed and a postal charge substituted; a radical competitor on the order of the projected *Constitutional* would, on the other hand, be enabled to sell for 2d.[81]

Most subsequent proposals for postal reform were similar to Place's original one, though occasionally differing in specifics. For example, the reduction of the advertisement duty in 1833 weakened the monopolistic control exercised by the most powerful London newspapers, and size differential, a factor closely related to the number of advertisements per issue, was no longer as important. Place then modified his earlier proposals so as to conform with those in effect in the United States. He advocated the imposition of a postal duty proportionate to the distance of transmission. By this scheme, an automatic ½d. would be levied on all newspapers and periodicals that were transported up to a distance of 120 miles. For distances beyond that, an additional ½d. would be charged, provided that the weight of the article did not exceed one ounce.[82] Chadwick endorsed Place's original proposal in a widely distributed tract; John Crawfurd, who provided much of the expertise for the repeal movement, also favored this suggestion but was willing to accept even a 3d. postage in preference to retaining part of the original stamp duty.[83] Both Fox and Hickson publicized variations of Place's postage proposals, the former in his *Monthly Repository*, the latter as a member of the City of London Literary and Scientific Institution and as the author of several tracts and articles on the subject of taxes on knowledge.[84]

[81] Place, *Letter to a Minister of State*, pp. 11–13; Place, letter to Sir Francis Burdett, 6 Dec. 1833, Place Papers, Add. MSS 35,149, f. 241a.

[82] Place Papers, Add. MSS 27,790, f. 216a; *Radical*, 20 March 1836.

[83] Chadwick, *On the Taxes on Knowledge*, pp. 26–28; Crawfurd, *Taxes on Knowledge*, p. 54.

[84] *Monthly Repository*, VI (1832), 270, 439. An article that Hickson wrote for the *London Review* of January 1836 was reprinted as a 2d. pamphlet entitled *Taxes on Knowledge: Reduction or Abolition of the Newspaper Stamp-Duty?* Proof of Hickson's authorship is in William E. Hickson, letter to Place, 19 Dec. 1835, Place Newspaper Collection, Set 70, f. 270.

The motivation behind the consistent espousal of postal reform was twofold. As suggested previously, reformers hoped by this stratagem to weaken the *Times* and the other London "Gentlemen of the Press." In this endeavor they were supported by the provincial press which would profit financially if a postage were imposed since about 85 per cent of the journals transmitted through the mail were published in London.[85] The only provincial newspapers which stood aloof from the increasingly pronounced demand for a postage were those (such as the *Scotsman*) that had a national circulation and were thus favored by the franking privilege.[86]

A more impelling reason for the injection of the postal issue into the repeal agitation was the desire of reformers to undercut ministerial opposition to repeal on financial grounds. Extravagant claims were made by reformers as to the increase in revenue which would accrue from the imposition of a postage. Place estimated absurdly that the number of printed papers to be transmitted through the post after repeal of the stamp duty would be increased eighteenfold. By this calculation, the revenue would be tripled at a minimum. According to Place: "Loss of revenue is impossible, gain of revenue is certain." [87]

This optimistic assertion was echoed by other reformers, in Parliament as well as outside, despite a recognition that the circulation of newspapers would have to increase between five- and tenfold merely for the revenue to break even.[88] Not surprisingly, neither Lord Althorp nor Spring Rice, his successor as Chancellor of the Exchequer, was visibly impressed.[89] The

[85] John Crawfurd, *The Newspaper Stamp, and the Newspaper Postage; Compared* (London: J. Reid, 1836), pp. 9–10.

[86] *Scotsman*, 22 Feb. 1833.

[87] Place, *Letter to a Minister of State*, p. 13.

[88] *The Spectator's Key to Political Knowledge*, No. III: *Taxation* (1833)— appended to 1833 volume of the *Spectator*.

[89] In June 1832 and in May 1834, Bulwer, in presenting motions for repeal of the newspaper duty, affirmed that the revenue would be doubled if a 1*d*.

government held fast to its determination to retain the newspaper stamp as a safer political and financial alternative than
adoption of a postage, and in 1836 it reduced the stamp duty to
1d. without taking any action on the postage.[90]

Opposition to the postal scheme, apart from that generated by
its financial uncertainties, came from vendors and distributors
who feared an increase in direct sales to subscribers and from
those who felt vaguely that the interests of the public would be
damaged by adoption of the proposal. Many critics believed that,
if postal reform was adopted, newspapers would somehow become "the party organ of local interests," and that the national
character of the periodical press, as "the safety valve of the
state," would disappear.[91] Althorp, the Whig Chancellor, and
others who opposed changes in the postal structure, employed
this argument effectively on several occasions. Thus demands for
a postal duty were conveniently ignored, and no proposal was
considered seriously until the adoption of Rowland Hill's proposals for a penny postage in 1839.

Despite the intensity of the agitation generated on behalf of a
postal duty, an exercise that received pronounced support from
the National Political Union, working-class reformers remained
genuinely uninterested in postal reform. Their demands for total
repeal of the stamp duty seemed likely to be compromised if any
of the postal proposals were adopted and this prospect was
anathema to them. Even the smallest shift of the argument from
the theoretical to the expediential plane signified a retreat from
total victory and was regarded by them as a breach of integrity. A
further factor was that working-class journalists increasingly ma-
tured a system of rapid transmission of their illegal newspapers

---

postage was adopted (*Hansard*, H. of C., 14 June 1832, XIII, 619–648; *ibid.*,
22 May 1834, XXIII, 1193–1223).

[90] A by-product of the postal agitation was the adoption of prestamped adhe-
sive paper for letters. This adoption was the outgrowth of a proposal made by
Charles Knight to facilitate the efficiency of a 1d. postal charge.

[91] Martin, *Taxation of the British Empire*, pp. 120–121.

by private coaches. This was recognized by Althorp who argued effectively in an 1833 budget debate that stagecoaches were able to transmit newspapers for less than 1*d.*, thus nullifying the potential advantage of a penny postage.[92]

SPECIAL INTEREST GROUPS

Groups with specific economic interests composed a final element of the middle-class repeal ideology. Pressure exerted by these groups was often so substantial that a recent historian has described the movement for repeal of the taxes on knowledge as a compound of "idealism and sharp commercial practice."[93]

Skilled workers connected with journalism formed one major pressure group. Although artisans, they invariably grounded their demands upon arguments drawn from the perspective of middle-class reformers. Their emphasis was predictably moderate. Members of the printing trades, for example, demanded repeal of the taxes on knowledge on the assumption that thousands of additional jobs would be created if all restrictions were removed.[94] Trade societies of compositors and journeymen bookbinders likewise demanded governmental action, but their sentiments were aroused sharply only when economic conditions were poor, as in 1830.[95] Like other skilled workers, they phrased their arguments in moderate terms and, in many instances, favored only a *reduction* of the newspaper and advertisement duties.[96] In proportion as economic conditions improved and as the unstamped press developed, many of the artisans who worked for established journals became increasingly "conservative." They attempted to protect their own positions, irrespective of where this

[92] *Hansard*, H. of C., 19 April 1833, XVII, 332.

[93] Williams, *Dangerous Estate*, pp. 75–76.

[94] This argument was supported by the political economist McCulloch (Fourteenth Report of the Commissioners of Excise Inquiry [1835], app. 2, pp. 43–50, cited in Coleman, *British Paper Industry*, pp. 321–322).

[95] See the petitions in *Journals of the House of Commons*, 2 July 1830, LXXXV, 606; *Political Letters and Pamphlets*, 21 Oct. 1830.

[96] *Journals of the House of Commons*, 25 March 1830, LXXV, 229.

led them ideologically. Thus in 1836 the letterpress printers of York publicly petitioned *against* repeal of the stamp duties.[97]

Other groups connected with publishing maintained a steady opposition to the taxes. Paper manufacturers, booksellers, libraries, and literary institutions denounced the financial imposts in the belief that their own operating costs were thereby increased substantially. Mechanics' Institutes also petitioned for repeal since the expansion of newsrooms, which held the key to their success or failure, was dependent upon the availability of cheap newspapers.[98] Many of the political unions that emerged in the aftermath of the parliamentary reform agitation likewise attacked the "knowledge" duties on the ground that they obstructed their development by making the attachment of reading rooms to their organizations more difficult. The National Political Union, for example, bewailed its inability to acquire sufficient newspapers and periodicals to retain the allegiance of its membership after the subsidence of the parliamentary reform crisis in 1832.[99]

Leading provincial newspapers, including the *Scotsman*, the *Manchester Guardian*, the *Leeds Mercury*, and the *Leeds Times*, vigorously opposed the taxes on knowledge. Their motivation varied, but one consistent theme was resentment of the informal monopoly exercised by the London dailies. Since every newspaper had to pay a 4*d.* stamp duty, the provincial journals were at a distinct disadvantage. The free postal privileges that accompanied the stamp were of relatively little value to most of them whereas they aided immeasurably the better-financed London dailies. The latter could maintain a national circulation more easily and, in the process, outstrip the provincial competitors.

[97] *Ibid.*, 15 June 1836, XC, 340.

[98] Testimony of Thomas Hogg, Secretary to the Union of Mechanics' Institutions in Lancashire and Cheshire, *S.C. on Newspaper Stamps* (1851), pp. 168–169, 173–175, qq. 1029–1036, 1062–1075; petition of Birmingham Mechanics' Institution, reprinted in *Midland Representative*, 14 April 1832; petition from the Worcester Literary and Scientific Institution, reprinted in *Spectator*, 17 March 1832.

[99] Minutes of the National Political Union, Place Newspaper Collection, Add. MSS 27, 796, ff. 36–37, 40.

In economic terms, the newspaper stamp was regarded as a "bonus" paid to London newspapers at the expense of their country competitors, one that, in the words of Lord Brougham, should be on "the publick charge." [100] There was not, in fact, a single daily provincial newspaper in existence during the entire period 1830–1836. Even where provincial journals existed, their circulation was extremely limited, primarily due to the newspaper duty. The *Manchester Guardian,* a weekly that ranked only behind the *Leeds Mercury* and the *Stamford Mercury* in provincial circulation, had a paid readership of approximately two thousand at the time of the Reform Act. But prior to 1836 a weekly circulation in the provinces of six or seven hundred was considered satisfactory.[101]

The ardor for repeal expressed by many provincial journals waned considerably as the illegal working-class press gained support. In 1828 the *Scotsman* had provided an impetus to the campaign against the taxes on knowledge by publishing several important statistical articles. By 1836, however, it was merely paying lip service to the principle of total repeal. Other provincial journals remained lukewarm to repeal despite a commitment to reform and despite the prospect of financial gain if the newspaper duty were removed.

The *Glasgow Argus,* a newspaper established in 1833 to champion corn law repeal and financial reform, was unenthusiastic about removal of the stamp duty through fear of the consequences of an unregulated penny press. Its conditional endorsement of total repeal in 1834 was extended only in the belief that "the Penny Magazines, the Journals of Messrs. Chambers and Hunt, to say nothing of the unstamped political press, are jostling newspapers out of remunerative competition." [102]

As a result of the newspaper tax, weekly London journals fre-

[100] Brougham, letter to Dr. Shepherd, 18 April 1836, Brougham Papers, letters, No. 162.
[101] Williams, *Dangerous Estate,* p. 106; Read, *Press and People,* p. 64.
[102] *Glasgow Argus,* 26 May 1834, 17 Nov. 1834.

quently found themselves in serious financial straits because they faced powerful competition from the London dailies. John Stuart Mill reported in 1833 that the *Examiner* "may stop any week. [Fonblanque] can retrench so as to cover the weekly loss if he had £1000 in hand. . . . And for which (without counting on any increase of sale) he can carry it on on the chance of a reduction of the stamp duties within that time." [103] During these years the policies of the *Examiner* were staunchly directed against the press restrictions, but by 1835–1836 it had largely recovered its financial stability, and its energies were then directed mainly toward procuring a reduction of the advertisement duty. The *Spectator*, a London radical weekly, pursued a similar course.[104]

Not all of the London and provincial weeklies favored repeal of the newspaper duty despite the possibility of financial gain. Many newspapers sensed the intangible factors of great dimension that were involved in the question of the taxes on knowledge, and shied away from a total commitment to repeal.[105] The majority of provincial and weekly London journals did, however, favor an untaxed press, and the effect of their efforts, together with those of other interested pressure groups, was to strengthen considerably the middle-class repeal movement.

[103] Quoted in Garnett, *Fox*, p. 152; *The Life and Labours of Albany Fonblanque*, ed. E. B. de Fonblanque (London: Richard Bentley and Son, 1874), pp. 35–36.

[104] *Spectator*, 12 Jan. 1833, 29 Aug. 1835.

[105] This point is made by Francis Williams in his perceptive study *Dangerous Estate*, pp. 108–109.

CHAPTER 3

The Parliamentary Campaign

The middle-class campaign for repeal of the taxes on knowledge was waged, to a considerable extent, at the parliamentary level. This fact reflected the belief of propertied reformers that the major channels of government remained open to them. A small phalanx of M.P.'s, such as Roebuck, Hume, D. W. Harvey, and George Grote, represented their interests in the Commons while sympathetic politicians of influence, including Edward Ellice, Grey's brother-in-law, and Lord Durham, served frequently as intermediaries on their behalf. Furthermore, the weaknesses of party ties during the 1830's enabled the parliamentary radicals to act as a buffer between the two parties—the Whigs and the Tories—and to try to pressure successive governments into making concessions.

By contrast, few working-class radicals considered seriously the possibility of securing repeal of the newspaper tax by parliamentary means. The Reform Act of 1832 had persuaded them that their interests, once "betrayed," were not likely to be further satisfied by the narrowly-elected Parliament. Hume and other M.P.'s who had supported the statute were condemned for "abandoning" the laboring classes. Some working-class activists would not even direct petitions to Parliament or to the monarch since they regarded such a form of expression as servile. Remonstrances, which *demanded* redress of grievances, were proffered instead and, not surprisingly, the bulk of the working-class agitation against the newspaper duty was conducted through the channels of illegal journalism. This dichotomy between the middle- and working-class approaches to repeal of the taxes on knowledge increased as the former pursued their parliamentary activities.

Francis Place and Joseph Hume were the leaders of the parliamentary movement for repeal of the taxes on knowledge. Place masterminded several of the reform agitations of the period from his Charing Cross residence and, after 1834, from his home in Brompton Square. Amidst his many reform activities, he took a special interest in repeal of the newspaper duty, describing it on more than one occasion as "by far the most important matter in the power of ministers." [1] Place's support for an untaxed press stemmed primarily from his advocacy of the doctrines of political economy which he sought to disseminate to the working classes via the medium of a cheap press.[2] Not surprisingly, Henry Hetherington, James Watson, and the other "Rotundaists" who were circulating "dangerous" doctrines in the illegal journals, were attacked repeatedly by him.[3]

Psychologically, Place was driven to manage events, and his correspondence is replete with caustic references to the apathy of the masses.[4] Even Hume, one of the most energetic and persis-

---

[1] Place, letter to Thomas Young, 8 Jan. 1834, Add. MSS 35,149, ff. 266a, 269.

[2] Place, letter to Burdett, 6 Dec. 1833, *ibid.*, ff. 241–241a. His advocacy of birth control as a means of solving the population problem prompted the Tory *Morning Herald* to dub him "Celibacy Place, the Malthusian breeches-maker" (27 Feb. 1836).

[3] Place, letter to Joseph Hume, 3 June 1831, Place Papers, Add. MSS 35,149, f. 75a; letter to James Mill, 26 Oct. 1831, *ibid.*, f. 120a.

[4] In January 1832 he assured a sceptical John Cam Hobhouse that "there was so little real feeling or spirit in the people" (Lord Broughton, *Recollections of a Long Life*, ed. Lady Dorchester [London: John Murray, 1909–1911], IV, 164).

tent men ever to hold a seat in the Commons, was frequently lectured for his tardiness in acting. Place was particularly intolerant of any delay in repealing the newspaper duty since so long as the masses remained "ignorant," arbitrary, despotic government would continue. Only when the poorer classes had been given the proper materials with which to think and consciously to eliminate abuses would the power of government "diminish." [5] "Lord Johnism," that is to say, any tendency to compromise with the detested Whigs, was anathema to him.[6]

Place propelled himself into the newspaper agitation with predictably unrestrained enthusiasm. On several occasions, he organized delegations to plead with members of the government, including the Prime Minister and the Chancellor of the Exchequer, for repeal of the stamp duty. His extensive library of source material on working-class history was placed at the disposal of radical M.P.'s, and both Hume and Edward L. Bulwer, among others, were provided with ample matter for their parliamentary speeches on the subject. Motions were framed and discussions held at his home, and the latter became the effective headquarters of the parliamentary repeal campaign. Place also conducted an extensive correspondence with reformers in many sections of the country on the subject of the taxes on knowledge, seeking thereby to stimulate a "genuine" national agitation, one that would impress upon the Whig ministers the need for change. He had a measured amount of success in generating a response among reformers, particularly during 1835–1836 when a London committee for repeal of the newspaper duty was organized under his direction.

Place's closest parliamentary ally in the taxes on knowledge campaign was Joseph Hume. Hume was an indefatigable member of the Commons for nearly forty years. During that time, he developed a reputation for perseverance, independence of mind, and tireless energy in championing unpopular causes. Although

[5] Place Papers, Add. MSS 27,809, f. 42.
[6] The reference, common among reformers, was to the moderate views of the Whig leader, Lord John Russell.

limited oratorical ability and lack of a commanding intelligence
prevented him from attaining a political position of the first rank,
John Stuart Mill and other reformers regarded him warmly as
one of the few politicians who was ready "to force discussions on
all the great issues." [7] During the 1830's many of Hume's
efforts were expended vigorously on behalf of an untaxed press
and, despite periodic disagreements with Place, the two men
worked closely together on most aspects of the repeal question.

Hume's thought was predictably Benthamite but unlike Place
he rarely theorized about his beliefs. Instead, he responded prag-
matically to concrete instances of injustice, often exhibiting decidedly "popular" tendencies. He deplored imposts on literature not
only as inefficient obstacles to economic and moral development
and to the dissemination of "useful knowledge" but also as
anachronisms which discriminated unjustly between rich and
poor.[8] When William Carpenter, the first journalist to challenge
the newspaper act of 1819 openly, was convicted for publishing
an unstamped newspaper in June 1831, Hume publicly sprang to
his defense in a letter that was widely circulated. He contended
that "the liberty of a free state" was endangered by Carpenter's
prosecution and by the subsequent prosecution of Henry Hetherington, and that such actions were "against the very essence of
the Constitution." [9] Instead of resorting to measures "unparalleled in the entire history of the country," Hume argued, the

[7] *Monthly Repository*, VIII (1834), 174. The *Spectator* described Hume as
"a model of a good and worthy member of a Reformed Parliament" (23 June
1832). For less uncritical contemporary estimates, see Sir Denis Le Marchant,
Memoir of John Charles Viscount Althorp Third Earl Spencer (London:
Richard Bentley and Son, 1876), pp. 235–236; John A. Roebuck, *History of the
Whig Ministry of 1830, to the Passing of the Reform Bill* (London: John W.
Parker and Son, 1852), I, 284. A conservative contemporary described Hume
accurately as "a teasing, biting flea . . . that would let no minister of any
department sit easy in his seat" (Samuel C. Hall, *Retrospect of a Long Life:
From 1815 to 1883* [London: Richard Bentley and Son, 1883], I, 218).

[8] See Hume's speech as a member of a delegation to Lord Melbourne during
February 1836 (*Newspaper Stamps: Deputation*, pp. 5–8).

[9] For copies of the letter, see *Cobbett's Weekly Political Register*, 4 June
1831; *Political Letter*, 4 June 1831; *Midland Representative*, 4 June 1831;
Ballot, 5 June 1831; *Hansard*, H. of C., 28 June 1831, IV, 415–421.

government should "show more sympathy with the wishes of the people, and not deprive them of the means of buying this cheap knowledge."[10]

On at least three occasions Hume moved for official returns of the numbers of publishers and vendors imprisoned, while repeatedly condemning such actions. And at least three times—in cases involving Peter Mackenzie, the Glasgow journalist, William Cobbett, who was tried for seditious libel in 1831, and Richard Carlile—Hume attempted to intercede with the authorities on behalf of imprisoned journalists. In another less-publicized instance he was apparently responsible for securing the release of an obscure vendor named Joseph Forster, who had served nine weeks of a three months' prison sentence.[11]

Hume's attempts to gain repeal of the newspaper duty commenced in May 1827, even before Place's sentiments had been sufficiently aroused. At that time, Hume offered a parliamentary motion calling for repeal of the provisions of the act of 1819 on the ground that its sole purpose had been that of "checking the circulation of opinion, and putting an end to the freedom of remark."[12] This motion was defeated by a vote of 120 to 10 amidst allegations that Hume was seeking deliberately to embarrass the short-lived reform ministry of George Canning and that he had reneged on a private pledge not to raise the issue if

[10] *Hansard*, H. of C., 13 Aug. 1833, XX, 583. After several bitter denunciations of the government by Hume, Althorp wrote testily of him, "He never was famous for taste or tact and never was quick enough to see what was the real position in which he was placed" (letter to Sir Herbert Taylor, 9 Feb. 1833, Althorp Papers).

[11] *Cobbett's Weekly Political Register*, 16 July 1831. In agreeing to support Carlile, Hume wrote: "I abominate prosecution for opinions sake (worthy only of the most barbarous and fanatical people)" (letter to Richard Carlile, 7 Aug. 1831, Carlile Papers). See also Joseph Forster, *The Rejected Address to the Editor of the Weekly Dispatch of Sunday, October 5, 1834, on Being Sentenced to Three Months' Imprisonment in That Horrible Bastile, the House of Correction, Cold Bath Fields, for Selling Unstamped Newspapers* (London: Howlett and Son [1835]).

[12] *Hansard*, H. of C., 31 May 1827, XVII, 1065.

requested by the Attorney-General.[13] He continued to demonstrate interest in newspaper reform, however, and during the years 1830–1832 he presented several petitions on the subject, spoke at repeal meetings, and acted as unofficial leader of those M.P.'s who were agitating on the subject in Parliament.[14] Between June 1832 and August 1835 the more conservative Edward L. Bulwer, a brilliant orator, presented three well-publicized motions for repeal of the newspaper duty but in spite of this Hume's implicit leadership of the parliamentary movement remained unchallenged.

Neither Hume nor Place could generate sufficient working-class enthusiasm for their efforts to repeal the taxes on knowledge. Place possessed extensive contacts with a segment of the London artisan class and with several working-class journalists including William Lovett, Richard Carlile, and John Cleave. The latter described Place with some affection as "a gentleman to whom the working classes must entertain feelings of gratitude and respect, for his well-known benevolence and many active labours in their behalf—labours which, if not always guided by sound principle, have been at least generally able, and always disinterested." [15] And as W. J. Fox perceptively noted, Place was "one who forms a valuable portion of the few links that yet hold together the different orders of this classified country in their unhappily progressive alienation." [16]

---

[13] Speech of Sir Robert Wilson, *Hansard*, H. of C., 31 May 1827, XVII, 1075–1077. In December 1826, Hume had suggested that the newspaper duty be reduced to 1½d. (*ibid.*, 13 Dec. 1826, XVI, 400–401). Aspinall asserts that Lord Howick, Grey's son, probably acted out of "factious motives" in voting for Hume's motion (*Politics and the Press*, p. 59).

[14] *Midland Representative*, 2 July 1831.

[15] *Cleave's Weekly Police Gazette, c.* 1836?, Place Newspaper Collection, Set 70, f. 425. Place privately characterized Cleave as "passionate and revengeful, and not at all scrupulous as to the use of any means of accomplishing his purpose the end of which was improving the condition of the working people" (*c.* 1835?, Place Papers, Add. MSS 27,791, ff. 67–68).

[16] *Monthly Repository*, VIII (1834), 625. Popay, the police spy, inaccurately informed the Home Office that Place "never had any influence or any com-

Place's uncompromising aversion to every impediment to journalistic expression enhanced his influence with some of the working classes. Under no circumstances, in his opinion, was any degree of governmental interference with printed matter to be tolerated. This implied not only that fiscal imposts on the press had to be removed, but that a public libel was not to be construed as a legal crime. Place defined libel solely as a civil wrong to be adjudicated by juries on financial grounds.[17] Despite these "extreme" views, however, and in spite of his pronounced determination to shape events, Place's influence with the politically articulate segment of the working classes remained minimal. His uncompromising antipathy to the burgeoning trade union and cooperative movements, together with his contemptuous references to the unstamped press, proved too substantial a handicap.[18]

Hume commanded even less support from working-class activists, some of whom referred to him contemptuously as "Mr. West-end-of-the-town." [19] During 1831 he worked closely with several working-class political unions in the establishment of penny reading rooms in the Tyneside area.[20] His enthusiastic endorsement of the Reform Act had weakened his standing, however, and his detractors justifiably suspected him of being too ready to surrender the principle of an unstamped press in order to secure a political compromise.

Despite his readiness in 1827 to challenge the Canning government on this subject, Hume was not prepared to endanger the Grey ministry on a "subsidiary" question such as repeal of the

munication individually with the Radical Party of the Union or the Rotunda" (S.S. report, 29 Nov. 1831, H.O. 64/11).

[17] Place, letter to Hume, 6 June 1834, Place Papers, Add. MSS 35,149, ff. 296–297.

[18] There are scores of references in Place's correspondence to buttress these points. See, for example, Place, letter to Thomas Young, 8 Jan. 1834, *ibid.*, ff. 266a, 269.

[19] *Poor Man's Guardian*, 23 July 1831.

[20] Hume, letter to the Northern Political Union, as reprinted in Northern Political Union, *Objects and Rules* (Newcastle-upon-Tyne: The Union, 1831), p. 12.

taxes on knowledge until the Reform Bill had become law.[21]
Even after 1832 he frequently defended the seeming inconsisten-
cies of Althorp, Russell, and other Whig ministers on the issue,
though confessing in May 1834, that "the [Grey] Ministry have
had a fair trial, and have woefully disappointed the just expectations of the people." [22] As late as the spring of 1835, immediately after the formation of Melbourne's second ministry which
survived until 1841, Hume was cautioning reformers to exercise
prudence and restraint. Although avowing that he had personally "put every iron in the fire to promote our object, the repeal
of the newspaper impost," he did not think it proper "by our petitions to urge any reaction, when I knew the members of the new
administration were with us." [23]

On the related subject of libel law Hume's opinions were more
restrained than those of Place, thus reducing further his influence
with working-class journalists. Unlike Place, he favored only a
partial repeal of the "security system" that had been established
in 1819. As a member of the Select Committee on Libel Law of
1834, he supported not only the retention of portions of this system but its application to pamphlets as well as to periodicals. His
main concern, irrespective of the legal phraseology employed,
was to assure that "none should libel with impunity." [24]

Neither Hume nor Place was sufficiently popular with working-
class reformers to provide leadership for a unified campaign to
repeal the newspaper tax. The emergence of Bulwer as titular
leader of the parliamentary agitation after 1832, however, most
strikingly undermined the possibility of an effective alliance. Bulwer's "radicalism" was a very transitory phase in his political and
literary career. After entering the Commons in 1831, he became

---

[21] Hume, letter to Thomas Wakley, read at a public meeting during July
1831, as reported in *Poor Man's Guardian*, 16 July 1831.

[22] Letter from Hume to Aytoun, the radical candidate at Edinburgh, reprinted
in *Glasgow Argus*, 29 May 1834.

[23] Hume, letter to Place, 10 May 1835, Place Papers, Add. MSS 35,150, ff.
47–47a.

[24] Memorandum from Hume, 6 June 1834, *ibid.*, Add. MSS 35,149, f. 295a.

identified closely with its radical phalanx. His marked oratorical abilities combined with a knowledge of "literary" subjects enabled him to attach his name to the agitation for repeal of the taxes on knowledge, and during the sessions of 1832, 1834, and 1835 he introduced unsuccessful motions for repeal of the newspaper duty.[25] Though the cause of an untaxed press was not advanced appreciably on these occasions, the set speeches that Bulwer delivered received nationwide publicity and enabled him to promote his literary ambitions.[26]

The markedly restrained quality of Bulwer's "radicalism" antagonized many reformers. He advocated repeal of the newspaper stamp, primarily because he regarded it as the most effective means of undercutting cheap, unlicensed literature. In his view the latter posed a threat to society since it generated "an aversion to sober industry, an unsettled and vague dissatisfaction; an indifference to moderate benefits, and a grasping and shadowy experiment, which, if it may not destroy constitutional authority, will deeply injure the cause of constitutional freedom." [27] "Honest men," he professed during the parliamentary debate on his first motion for repeal of the newspaper duty, must be legally permitted to rebut the "superficial and dangerous notions" being disseminated by the "pernicious" penny press. Only then could the worker become enlightened and a "community of intelligence" between governors and governed be formed.[28] He expressed similar sentiments in May 1834, when he presented his

[25] Bulwer withdrew another repeal motion that was planned for August 1833, and for this he was criticized by James S. Buckingham and other reformers (*Parliamentary Review, and Family Magazine*, III [1833], 450).

[26] Baron Lytton, *The Life, Letters, and Literary Remains of Edward Bulwer, Lord Lytton* (London: Kegan Paul, Trench, 1883), II, 326.

[27] Edward L. Bulwer, "The New Year," *New Monthly Magazine*, XXXIV (1832), 1–7.

[28] Edward L. Bulwer, *Taxes on Knowledge: Debate in the House of Commons on the 15th June, 1832, on Mr. Edward Lytton Bulwer's Motion . . . with a Comment in the Form of Notes [by Francis Place]; and the Article from the "Examiner" Newspaper, of Sunday, 17th June, 1832* (Southwark: W. Barnes, 1832), pp. 1–12.

second motion to the Commons on the subject of the taxes on knowledge. On this occasion he produced one memorable epigram ("It was said, that the schoolmaster was abroad; he saw his rod, but not his books") and a number of oratorical flourishes, including an exhortation to the Chancellor of the Exchequer to "open the prison-house of the mind." [29] The effectiveness of his appeal to reformers was vitiated, however, by his announced willingness to agree to a year's postponement of any substantive change in the law.

By 1835, Bulwer's conservative "radicalism" had become even more sharply etched. According to Place, he conspicuously failed to attend an important repeal meeting held at the Crown and Anchor Inn in July.[30] Amidst charges of "treachery" by several reformers, he then refused in August of that year to press to a division his third motion for repeal of the newspaper duty.[31] Hume, Warburton, and other opponents of the taxes on knowledge who were present at the debate, urged him to divide the House. With only a handful of ministerial supporters present and with "the utmost apathy and indifference" prevailing, it was agreed even by Bulwer, that the motion would have carried.[32] Instead, Bulwer was content to accept a vague "pledge" from Spring Rice, the Chancellor of the Exchequer, that the stamp duty would be reduced during the next session of Parliament.[33]

The reaction to these tactics was overwhelmingly unfavorable.

[29] *Hansard*, H. of C., 22 May 1834, XXIII, 1194–1205.

[30] Francis Place, "The Examiner and the Tax on Newspapers," *Radical*, 21 March 1836.

[31] Speech by Benjamin Warden, a working-class radical, as reported in *Glasgow Argus*, 11 Feb. 1836. Henry Chapman, a middle-class reformer, asserted that Bulwer had "sold out" on this issue ("Mr. Bulwer's Sham Motion for the Repeal of the Tax on Knowledge" [*R. Pamphlet*, No. 12], pp. 10–13).

[32] Edward L. Bulwer, letter, *Spectator*, 5 Sept. 1835. According to Buckingham, when Bulwer presented his motion apathy was manifested by all except "the small knot of personal and political friends by which [Bulwer] was surrounded" (*Parliamentary Review, and Family Magazine*, II [1834], 693).

[33] Bulwer maintained that his motion merely proposed the establishment of a committee and that the government could have easily defeated a concrete motion for repeal at any time in the future (*Spectator*, 5 Sept. 1835).

The *Spectator* accused Bulwer of being a publicity-seeker, while Brougham, then trying to ingratiate himself with reformers, described the incident as "one of the most mortifying, and . . . most inexplicable things which have happened in Parliament during the late session." [34] *Cleave's Weekly Police Gazette*, a working-class newspaper, accused Bulwer of acting "very culpably" and speculated that Hume would not have seconded the motion if he had known that his colleague was planning to withdraw it. [35] Recriminations continued even after reduction of the stamp to 1*d*. in 1836, and as late as 1851, Hickson, a participant in the movement, asserted confidently that the tax would have been totally repealed in 1835 "if we could have over-ruled the opinions of Sir Edward Bulwer Lytton . . . but we were not so far fortunate." [36] Thus Bulwer's questionable handling of the issue on those occasions when national attention was focussed upon him did much to destroy the possibility of unity with working-class reformers in support of a national campaign for removal of the newspaper tax.

The parliamentary history of the "taxes on knowledge" during the period 1830–1836 follows an unorthodox pattern. Few governmental supporters attacked openly the proposition that the duties should be repealed, while the Conservative opposition under the leadership of Peel took no official position. Though Peel believed that the newspaper duty should be retained in order to provide "permanent restraints on the licentiousness of the press," he and his supporters rarely intervened in debates on the subject. They undoubtedly hoped that a policy of silence would help to exacerbate tensions between Whigs and radicals. [37] Only a hand-

[34] *Ibid.*, 29 Aug. 1835; Henry Brougham, "Taxes on Knowledge," *Edinburgh Review*, LXII (1835), 129.

[35] *Sun, c.* Jan. 1836, cited in *Cleave's Weekly Police Gazette*, 6 Feb. 1836. Bulwer was described as a "moral poltroon" by the *Liberator*, a radical Glasgow newspaper (16 Jan. 1836).

[36] Testimony of William E. Hickson, *S.C. on Newspaper Stamps* (1851), p. 466, q. 3187.

[37] *Hansard*, H. of C., 31 May 1827, XVII, 1072.

ful of independent M.P.'s, representing agricultural districts, rejected directly the notion that the imposts should be repealed. But despite this seeming lack of opposition, the "knowledge" duties were not removed during these years with the exception of a reduction of the advertisement duty in 1833 and the repeal of the minor taxes on almanacs and pamphlets.

The Whig ministries of the 1830's were reluctant to appear in the guise of opponents of any measure that purportedly strengthened freedom of the press. They affirmed repeatedly the undesirability of the newspaper stamp in principle. But they also hoped to retain the sizable revenue accruing from this tax. Moreover, the "knowledge" imposts were a useful judicial weapon, an indirect form of "censorship," as Hume asserted, and one that could be employed subtly to dampen excessive criticism of the government.[38] Most significant perhaps was the fact that no interest group of substantial influence appeared in support of the radical demands for an untaxed press.

Leading members of the several Whig governments of the 1830's, including Althorp, Melbourne, Russell, and Spring Rice, shadow-boxed with their radical opponents. They frequently expressed private support for the principle of repeal but the exigencies of the budget, they contended, prevented substantial concessions. In a well-publicized letter written during 1832, Althorp stated that "the present state of the revenue" was the only consideration that prevented him from reducing the newspaper duty.[39] And two years later in a major speech to the Commons, he maintained that due to revenue considerations, he was compelled to submerge his private feelings in favor of repeal.[40]

In 1835, Spring Rice, the Chancellor of the Exchequer, went even further when he told the Commons: "I do not defend the [newspaper] tax. I repudiate it as to any protection it may be sup-

[38] *Ibid.*, p. 1082.
[39] Althorp, letter through W. H. Wickham to Robert Roberts, reprinted in *Midland Representative*, 21 April 1832.
[40] *Hansard*, H. of C., 22 May 1834, XXIII, 1213.

posed to afford to the diffusion of political information and of sound knowledge." [41] Three months earlier, in a letter to Brougham, he had proclaimed himself "quite willing to give his best attention to any proposed changes, by which the public revenues could be protected from loss." But like his predecessor Althorp he insisted upon retaining the duty on the ground that it was dangerous to "experiment" with the finances of the state.[42] Government supporters also implied that overwhelming popular support for repeal had not been demonstrated. Althorp told Hume privately in 1833: "I do not think the *people* care about it; when I mentioned it early in the session the *members* paid little attention to it." [43] These and other "moderate" arguments were employed effectively to thwart demands for repeal. Thus the parliamentary chapter of the taxes on knowledge agitation focusses largely upon a series of alleged promises and professions of agreement, paralleled by a corresponding absence of concrete concessions.

Except for Hume's abortive 1827 motion, the subject of the press duties was not raised substantively in the Commons until January 1831. During the preceding year, the Duke of Wellington's Tory government had attempted unsuccessfully to equalize the English and Irish stamp duties. Its objectives had been to increase the Irish newspaper tax from 2*d*. to 4*d*., thus bringing it into correspondence with that of England, and to tighten certain provisions of the "security system." [44] Reformers had viewed the proposed statute as no more than a gesture of defiance by a moribund Tory government and in January 1831, when Parlia-

[41] *Ibid.*, 21 Aug. 1835, XXX, 845.

[42] Spring Rice, letter to Brougham, 8 May 1835, Brougham Papers, No. 10,467.

[43] Hume, letter to Place, 28 July 1833, Place Papers, Add. MSS 35,149, f. 227.

[44] Place described the proposed act as "perhaps the most effective way to extinguish such publications that has ever been devised" (Place Diary, *ibid.*, Add. MSS 35,146, f. 110). Daniel O'Connell attacked the measure as "calculated" to extinguish the expression of Irish public opinion (*Hansard*, H. of C., 29 April 1830, XXIV, 237).

ment convened under the auspices of a Whig government for the first time in twenty-three years, a feeling of optimism was prevalent. Justifiably high hopes were expressed that the ministry would seek to secure "the confidence and support of the press and of the people," and that repeal of the newspaper duty would be undertaken in the immediate future.[45]

At least three members of the Grey ministry—Althorp, Russell, and Brougham, the Lord Chancellor—were correctly regarded as sympathetic to repeal. Each was a member of the executive committee of the Society for the Diffusion of Useful Knowledge, and each had been identified publicly with the movement to disseminate cheap literature.[46] In addition, Lord Durham, the Lord Privy Seal, despite his public silence on the issue, had been identified consistently with radical causes throughout his parliamentary career.[47] Lord Denman, the Attorney-General, was also popular with reformers, having amassed a considerable legal and political reputation in 1819 when he led the opposition to the Six Acts.[48] The presence in the government of so many persons favorable to an untaxed press, in conjunction with the rising crescendo of proreform sentiment in the country, seemed to portend rapid amendment or repeal of the taxes on knowledge. But disappointments were to underlie the reformers' efforts during the succeeding five years.

Althorp's unsatisfactory budget proposals of February 1831

[45] Hume, letter to Althorp, 11 Jan. 1831, Althorp Papers.

[46] *Official Kalendar for 1831*, pp. 541–542. The activities of Brougham and Althorp will be covered in the narrative. Russell never became involved actively in the question of the taxes on knowledge, but during 1834 he expressed full support for removal of the newspaper tax (letter to Brougham, 29 Aug. 1834, Brougham Papers, No. 14,414).

[47] The best account of Durham's political career is in Chester New, *Lord Durham: A Biography of John George Lambton, First Earl of Durham* (Oxford: Clarendon Press, 1929), chaps. 1–6.

[48] Sir Joseph Arnould, *Life of Thomas, First Lord Denman, Formerly Lord Chief Justice of England* (Boston: Estes and Lauriat, 1874), I, 96–98. At least one member of the government, Lord Lansdowne, the Lord President of the Council, was opposed to repeal or to a substantial reduction (Lansdowne, letter to Althrop, *c.* 1833?, Althorp Papers).

constituted the initial major setback. Instead of conceding demands for repeal of the advertisement and the newspaper duties or accepting a more moderate plan advocated by Charles Buller by which the newspaper stamp would be reduced to ½d., Althorp agreed to reduce the former tax to 1s. and to reduce the latter from 4d. to 2d.[49] But the value of this concession was diluted by his decision to terminate the 20 per cent bulk discount on cash payment of the newspaper tax. The net saving per newspaper offered to reformers was, therefore, only slightly in excess of 1d.

Reactions to Althorp's proposals were markedly unenthusiastic. John Cam Hobhouse, a critic of the government, spoke for many reformers when he affirmed that the proffered concessions were "good" so far as they went, but that they "might be better."[50] Place, reacting more negatively, tried to arouse a concerted opposition to the Chancellor's tepid proposals.[51] On the other hand, many stamped newspapers, including the *Times*, felt that even this modest concession was too extreme. Althorp, under substantial parliamentary attack for several other budgetary proposals including a controversial scheme for taxing the transfer of landed property, did not wish to alienate both reformers and conservatives. He thereupon quietly allowed the proposed reductions of the advertisement and newspaper duties to lapse, amidst the unparalleled political excitement following upon Russell's introduction of the first Reform Bill in March. Althorp's failure to implement his own suggested modification of the newspaper impost was of great importance since no further changes in this tax were

[49] *Hansard*, H. of C., 11 Feb. 1831, II, 403–418. R. K. D., *Letter to Viscount Althorp*, pp. 6–9. In January 1831, Hume wrote a letter to Althorp calling for reduction of the advertisement duty to 1s. and of the newspaper duty to 2d. or 1d. (letter to Althorp, 11 Jan. 1831, Althorp Papers).

[50] Broughton, *Recollections*, IV, 84.

[51] Place, letter to Hume, 16 Feb. 1831, Place Papers, Add. MSS 35,149, ff. 27a–30a. Hume defended Althorp for going "as far as he thought he could" (Hume, letter to Place, 12 Feb. 1831, *ibid.*, f. 26).

officially proposed until Spring Rice's reduction of the duty in 1836.

Althorp's abandonment of his own budgetary proposals together with the commencement of prosecutions against the working-class journalists Carpenter and Hetherington in the spring of 1831 infuriated reformers.[52] It was widely believed, though probably without justification, that the Whigs had reneged on a promise.[53] During the remainder of 1831 a stream of petitions was presented to the Commons, demanding repeal of the newspaper duty and termination of the governmental prosecutions. Simultaneously, parliamentary reformers led by Hume, Edward Bulwer, Daniel O'Connell, and Sir Francis Burdett announced plans to activate a full-scale movement for repeal as soon as the reform bill became law.[54] In November 1831, Bulwer waged psychological combat with the Grey government in the pages of his *New Monthly Magazine* by falsely reporting that the ministry was prepared to repeal the stamp duty the moment the Reform Bill was passed.[55]

The willingness of parliamentary reformers to wait until the question of the franchise was decided irritated working-class activists. The latter had already commenced an illegal journalistic struggle against the stamp duty, and while Hume and his colleagues patiently awaited the outcome of the agitation for parliamentary reform, dozens of illicit periodicals, nurtured into existence by the rising political excitement, began to circulate. The breach between the two segments of the radical movement was permanently and irremediably widening.

[52] "Taxes on Knowledge," *Examiner*, 31 July 1831.

[53] A prominent member of the Birmingham Political Union reported that Brougham had described repeal as a certainty by the beginning of 1832 (speech by Haynes at a meeting of the National Political Union, as reported in *Morning Chronicle*, 2 Dec. 1831).

[54] *Hansard*, H. of C., 28 July 1831, IV, 412–429; *ibid.*, 15 Sept. 1831, VII, 52–58.

[55] *New Monthly Magazine*, XXXII (1831), 487.

Subsequent developments on the parliamentary level were not conducive to meliorating this division. Bulwer's first motion for repeal of the newspaper duty in June 1832, coinciding as it did with the resolution of the political reform crisis, signified the recommencement of the middle-class campaign. The speech accompanying his motion was phrased in particularly eloquent language. Why, asked Bulwer, "is truth confined to the rich? . . . Is it not time to consider whether the printer and his types may not provide better for the peace and honor of a free state, than the gaoler and the hangman." He asserted that "if Knowledge was Power to its possessor, its diffusion was Wealth to a State," particularly inasmuch as a "free press," by generating a variety of opinions, assisted in extinguishing corruption. Over five thousand copies of his speech, together with explanatory comments appended by Place, were circulated by reformers.[56] But Bulwer's intemperate references to the illicit periodicals as "dangerous" and "pernicious and visionary" assured an icy reception for the motion in working-class journals.[57]

On the positive side, the national publicity that the motion received insured that the issue of repeal of the "taxes on knowledge" would be prominently discussed in the general election of 1832. This election, involving the selection of members to serve in the first Reformed Parliament, was one of the most important ones of the early nineteenth century. Attempts were made by numerous political unions to pledge every candidate to a specific program of reform and, in most instances, total repeal of the newspaper duty ranked foremost among the pledges sought. Several proreform candidates refused to make a specific commitment, and the issue of "pledging" became itself a major subject of controversy during the campaign. At least one reformer, John

[56] Proceedings of the National Political Union, Place Papers, Add. MSS 27,796, f. 34. The pamphlet was *Taxes on Knowledge*; see note 28 above. Copies of it are in Place Newspaper Collection, Set 63, ff. 148–149; Place Papers, Add. MSS 27,796, ff. 111–134. The quotations are from pages 14–15 of the tract.

[57] See the letter from a correspondent in *Poor Man's Guardian*, 30 June 1832.

Cam Hobhouse, was opposed by radicals at Westminster for his refusal to pledge himself to a program that included repeal of both the newspaper duty and the excise duty on paper.[58] Of the several hundred candidates who did give pledges to the electorate, however, an overwhelming majority seem to have committed themselves to support repeal of either the newspaper or advertisement duties in the new Parliament.[59]

The inability of parliamentary reformers to extract substantial concessions from the Whig ministry became evident at the commencement of the 1833 session. The moment for concessions on the newspaper issue seemed exceedingly propitious. Although there are contradictory contemporary estimates as to the strength of the "radical" contingent elected to the first Reformed Parliament, a safe calculation is that it probably numbered about one-hundred.[60] Thus the parliamentary radicals possessed a strength substantial enough to exert pressure on the Grey government. It was also known that Althorp had been conducting informal negotiations with Henry Warburton, the M.P. who was acting on behalf of a newly formed Society for the Diffusion of Political and Moral Knowledge. This association, which was sponsored by

[58] In the Westminster election Hobhouse was opposed by Colonel George Evans, who drew about 10 per cent of the vote (*Spectator*, 24 Nov. 1832).

[59] It is next to impossible to comb every electoral address issued during the period. For some typical statements of support, see Grote's speech to his constituents in the City of London, as reported in *ibid.*; Matthew D. Hill's address to his constituents in Birmingham, as reprinted in Davenport-Hill, *Recorder of Birmingham*, p. 114; William Brougham's "pledge," *Spectator*, 1 Dec. 1832. See also Francis Place, *On Pledges to Be Given by Candidates* (London: National Political Union, 1832).

[60] Tory estimates exaggerated radical strength. Lord Mahon, for example, stated that there were at least 190 "thick and thin Radicals, Repealers from Ireland, members or friends of the Political Unions, and so forth" (*Sir Robert Peel from His Private Papers*, ed. C. S. Parker [London: J. Murray, 1891–1899], II, 209–210). Whig estimates, on the other hand, tended to under-calculate the numbers of Radicals. Buckingham estimated that there were only ninety-six "Liberals" and four "Independents" in the Reformed Parliament (*Parliamentary Review*, I, 31, as cited in Maccoby, *English Radicalism*, p. 426). A number of estimates are given in Hamburger, *Intellectuals in Politics*, p. 115.

Place, Hume, Roebuck, and others, was seeking to procure repeal of the newspaper duty so that it might freely disseminate penny political tracts. Althorp had intimated strongly to Warburton and Bulwer, it was correctly reported, that the objectionable duty would be repealed in the immediate future.

The foundation for this report was an article that appeared in the *Town* newspaper on January 27 and was subsequently reprinted by the *Times,* the *Globe,* and other influential journals. Based upon extracts from a forthcoming issue of Bulwer's *New Monthly Magazine,* the article referred to conversations between Althorp and Bulwer in which the Chancellor had allegedly pledged himself to remove the newspaper tax. When Althorp read the article, he became furious at the presumed breach of confidence that underlay it. Admonishing Bulwer for the "leak," Althorp demanded "to know how the publication has taken place." In a private letter to Bulwer, written on January 28, he suggested that the incident had thrown "insuperable obstacles" in his path and that "after the occurrence of such a circumstance it will hardly be possible for me to carry into effect the measures which I had intended to bring before my colleagues." On the following day, the *Globe* printed a news item, "leaked" undoubtedly by Althorp, in which it was positively stated that the latter had met with Bulwer only in order to clarify his intention of *not repealing* the newspaper duty.[61]

Despite this unpromising background, only a portion of which could be suspected by the most industrious newspaper reader, an announcement affirming Althorp's decision either to repeal or to reduce substantially the stamp duty, was confidently awaited. It was within the context of such expectations that Warburton submitted a formal question to Althorp on February 5, the opening day of the new session, asking if the Chancellor planned to take

[61] Althorp, letter to Edward L. Bulwer, 28 Jan. 1833, Althorp Papers; *True Sun,* 28 and 29 Jan. 1833; *Spectator,* 6 Feb. 1833; *New Monthly Magazine,* XXXVII (1833), 141; *Tait's Edinburgh Magazine,* III (1833), 683. The controversial article was withdrawn from the *New Monthly Magazine* before publication.

any measures to repeal the newspaper duty. Althorp replied with an admission that the impost had a "disadvantageous effect" upon the extension of knowledge and that it was essentially a "bad tax." But he refused firmly to take any immediate steps, urging that the financial impact of such steps had to be evaluated more precisely.[62] This disappointing response again generated charges that Althorp had "betrayed" the radical cause. In spite of the Chancellor's vigorous disclaimer, such accusations may have had a more substantial basis in fact than many reformers suspected. During the previous summer the Chancellor had written a letter to Grey, the Prime Minister, in which he had alluded to discussions he had just concluded with his colleagues regarding "the three or four great questions to be brought forward next session." In this letter Althorp made no reference whatever to the newspaper duty, the conclusion being that six months prior to the convening of the new parliament he had already decided not to take action on this question.[63]

Notwithstanding the apparent strength of the radical contingent at Westminster, overt divisions existed within it, and these hindered an effective response to Althorp's unyielding position. The proreform *Glasgow Argus* aptly analyzed the plight of the radical movement at the outset of 1833: "There is not a Radical party. There are Radicals in plenty—rational and irrational, learned and illiterate, upon principle and from passion, honest and dishonest—still there is no Radical party." [64] Charles Greville drew a similar if considerably less sympathetic picture in his journal: "The Radicals are scattered up and down without a leader, numerous, restless, turbulent, and bold—Hume, Cobbett, and a multitude such as Roebuck, Faithfull, Buckingham, Major

[62] *Hansard*, H. of C., 5 Feb. 1833, XV, 136, 202.

[63] Althorp, letter to Grey, 6 Aug. 1832, Althorp Papers. In a later exchange of letters both Brougham and Spring Rice agreed that Althorp had at one point agreed to repeal the newspaper duty (Brougham, letter to Spring Rice, 7 May 1835, Monteagle Papers, No. 13,378 (1); Spring Rice, letter to Brougham, 8 May 1835, Brougham Papers, No. 10,647).

[64] *Glasgow Argus*, 15 April 1833.

Beauclerck, etc. (most of whom have totally failed in point of speaking)—bent upon doing all the mischief they can and incessantly active." [65]

The prolonged crisis over political reform had forged a temporary bond of unity among parliamentary reformers with differing interests. Variations in approach and temperament had been subsumed into the general agitation for extension of the franchise. With the passage of the Reform Act this fragile harmony received a severe buffeting. Many reformers, including Hume and Place, now expended most of their energies on promoting repeal of the newspaper duty.[66] But other reformers pursued different interests. George Grote, newly elected from the City of London, turned his considerable talents to the question of the ballot and sought unremittingly to gain parliamentary support for it during the remainder of the 1830's.[67] William Molesworth concentrated his abilities on colonial reform while Roebuck presented several important motions on behalf of a national system of education, his major consideration being to ensure that the people learn to use their political power responsibly.[68] Divisions among parliamentary reformers persisted up to and beyond 1836 and, during the final stages of the repeal agitation, Wakley futilely warned of the consequences of radicals "dividing among themselves upon half-a-dozen different points, each party refus-

[65] *The Greville Memoirs: A Journal of the Reigns of King George IV and King William IV*, ed. Henry Reeve (New York: D. Appleton, 1886), III, 149–150.

[66] In October 1832, Place considered repeal of the taxes on knowledge as one of the three most desirable reforms (Place, letter to John Nicholson, 20 Oct. 1832, Place Papers, Add. MSS 35,149, ff. 201a–202). By January 1834 he was convinced that newspaper reform was the most important change that could be effected and this remained his position for several years (letter to Thomas Young, 8 Jan. 1834, *ibid.*, f. 269).

[67] *Dictionary of National Biography*, XXIII, 284.

[68] *Hansard*, H. of C., 3 June 1834, XXIV, 127–130. Roebuck argued that education was necessary to "raise the mental and moral culture of the people" (*ibid.*, 30 July 1833, XX, 139–166; John A. Roebuck, *To the Electors of Bath* [London: W. Barnes, 1832], pp. 4–6).

ing, as to a deadly foe, to give the slightest way to the other." [69]

Thus while working-class radicals were demonstrating increasing enthusiasm for illegal journalism, the parliamentary reformers were simultaneously dissipating a position of strength. Althorp and other members of the government clearly were apprised of this situation, as a letter written by the Chancellor in February 1833 makes clear:

Such being the state of things, I feel very sanguine that the Radical party will be almost powerless. I do not mean to say that on certain questions Government may not be run hard, those for instance which involve Economy in which the House may be inclined to move too rapidly, but I begin to have great confidence that there will be no danger of an inroad being made upon the Institutions of the Country. [70]

Althorp's reduction of the advertisement duty in 1833 from 3s. 6d. to 1s. 6d. contributed paradoxically to a further weakening of the position of the parliamentary reformers since a minority of the latter accepted this concession as a sufficient one. Most, including Hume and O'Connell, remained embittered. Hume reminded Althorp acidly that "ignorance was the greatest bane of society," whereas O'Connell pleaded for "knowledge for the people." [71] The influential *Spectator* remonstrated: "Our sheet anchor has given way. The Reformed Parliament has proved unfaithful." [72]

The disappointments of the session of 1833 shaped profoundly the direction of the taxes on knowledge movement. Place and other influential reformers became convinced that extraparliamentary pressure tactics had to be resorted to on a larger scale to compensate for ministerial intransigence and parliamentary divisiveness. A committee for the repeal of the newspaper tax

[69] Speech at a London meeting, as reported in *Glasgow Argus*, 11 Feb. 1836.
[70] Althorp, letter to Sir Herbert Taylor, 9 Feb. 1833, Althorp Papers.
[71] *Hansard*, H. of C., 19 April 1833, XVII, 340, 349.
[72] *Spectator*, 18 May 1833.

organized by Place's London supporters in the spring of 1835 was a direct outgrowth of this disenchantment. For their part working-class radicals became doubly convinced, as a result of the negligible parliamentary developments of these years, that meaningful concessions could never be secured via conventional channels. They turned in increasing numbers after 1833 to the burgeoning unstamped press.

In 1834 the middle-class campaign for repeal of the newspaper duty received a temporary fillip as the result of the creation of a Select Committee on Libel Law. This committee was established in March in response to a government proposal by John Campbell, the Solicitor-General.[73] Although its terms of reference appertained solely to the laws of libel, the Committee was instructed subsequently to consider the effects of the stamp duty on the question of libel. During the 1830's the movement for rectification of the archaic libel laws was interwoven closely with the newspaper repeal agitation. The most stringent of the recent statutes affecting libel, that of 1819 which established a security system for publishers of newspapers, was still in effect. Demands for rationalization of the libel laws involved such proposed changes as the abolition of *ex officio* informations and the acceptance of the truth of a libel as a legal extenuation of it. These demands had been endorsed by Place and, more recently, by O'Connell.[74] Many reformers regarded the newspaper duty and the existence of restrictive libel laws as complementary obstructions to the establishment of a free press.

The Select Committee of 1834 represents a milestone toward a less antiquated libel structure. But it also performed an important, if less immediately fruitful, role in the concurrent agitation

[73] It may safely be assumed that Campbell was acting in an "official" capacity (*Hansard*, H. of C., 18 March 1834, XXII, 410–418).

[74] O'Connell had proposed the creation of a Select Committee on Libel in February 1834. His arguments were phrased moderately. (*ibid.*, 18 Feb. 1834, XXI, 468–478). He agreed fully with Place that "people ought to be allowed to attack anything in the abstract, and ought to be restricted only when the attack was personal" (*ibid.*, 18 March 1834, XXII, 421).

for repeal of the newspaper stamp. Brougham's widely-publicized testimony before the committee became the focal point of the parliamentary repealers' efforts during the spring and summer of 1834. Of potentially greater significance, however, was the attempt by Place and Hume to attach to the anticipated libel recommendations a provision for repeal of the newspaper duty. Roebuck, like Hume a member of the committee, acted in collaboration with them on this abortive scheme.[75]

During the meetings of the committee, Hume and Place tried unsuccessfully to duplicate the tactics that they had employed in 1824 to secure a repeal of the Combination Acts.[76] They entrusted Erskine Perry, a young barrister who had played a prominent role in the movement for political reform, to "ransack the Statute Book and pick out all that has ever been enacted respecting stamps on newspapers and other small publications." [77] Perry's prior investigations of this subject on behalf of the National Political Union had qualified him as an expert favorable witness. He had had several conversations with Althorp regarding the substitution of a small postal duty for the newspaper tax, and these conversations were to be related to the members of the committee.[78]

One major setback encountered by Place and Hume was their inability to locate the comprehensive statistical summaries that Perry had submitted to Althorp in 1832.[79] These charted relevant revenue statistics and elaborated several cogent arguments

[75] For a list of the original members of the Committee, see *Journals of the House of Commons*, 18 March 1834, LXXXIX, 135. Since the Committee never issued an official report, its activities must be reconstructed carefully from surviving MS sources.

[76] The repeal of the Combination Acts is comprehensively explored in Graham Wallas, *The Life of Francis Place, 1771–1854* (London: George Allen and Unwin, 1925), pp. 197–240.

[77] Place, letter to Erskine Perry, 6 June 1834, Place Papers, Add. MSS 35,149, f. 294. Perry later became prominent in the Indian judiciary and as a member of the Council of India.

[78] *Ibid.*, f. 294a.

[79] Perry, letter to Place, 9 June 1834, *ibid.*, f. 298.

in favor of repealing the newspaper duty. In the absence of these tables, Hume was compelled to rely upon a "useful" covering letter that Perry had written to Althorp in November 1832.[80]

During the committee sessions, Hume remained in constant contact with Place and Perry regarding the provisions of the proposed libel bill, as well as the arguments to be employed on behalf of repeal of the newspaper stamp. For use before the committee, Place sent Hume a copy of the pamphlet, constructed around Bulwer's 1832 repeal motion, that the National Political Union had published, as well as a copy of his own tract, *A Letter to a Minister of State*.[81] Despite the labors of Hume and Place and in spite of Perry's expert testimony, little of substance resulted from their efforts. The committee failed to report any proposals respecting either the antiquated libel system or the taxes on knowledge.

Brougham's testimony before the Select Committee on June 4 and 5 and the subsequent publicity given to it by reformers had a considerably more striking impact than the abortive maneuverings of Place and Hume. Since the commencement of his political career, the Lord Chancellor had demonstrated an acute interest in cheap literature. He had been a charter member of both the Society for the Diffusion of Useful Knowledge and the University of London. In his widely distributed pamphlet *Practical Observations upon the Education of the People*, written in 1825, he had urged the dissemination of cheap literature as "the most effectual method of bringing knowledge within the reach of a poor man's income." [82] Nonetheless, Brougham was strongly distrusted by working-class reformers who resented his patroniz-

[80] Place, letter to Hume, 11 June 1834, *ibid.*, ff. 297–299.

[81] A handwritten note to this effect is in Hume's personal copy of the N.P.U. pamphlet in University College, London.

[82] Brougham, "Practical Observation upon the Education of the People, Addressed to the Working Classes and Their Employers," in Brougham, *Works*, VIII, 424. The pamphlet ran through nineteen editions in three months and had a large readership (Chester W. New, *The Life of Henry Brougham to 1830* [Oxford: Clarendon Press, 1961], pp. 336–337).

ing approach to questions of literacy and his consistently erratic behavior.[83] Some had not forgotten his opposition in 1827 to Hume's attempts to repeal the Act of 1819. [84] In several articles written for the *Edinburgh Review* prior to 1834, Brougham had vigorously championed repeal of the newspaper duty.[85] But his reiterated condemnations of "the lovers of confusion, [and] the workmen of destruction" as well as his denunciations of political unions had vitiated the effect of these essays.[86]

In spite of Brougham's umpopularity in working-class quarters and the distrust felt for him by many parliamentary reformers, Hume and Place sought to give maximum publicity to his testimony. Although they justifiably regarded him as inconsistent and unreliable, particularly in his capacity as a member of the government, they were not averse to employing his name in a useful fashion.[87] It was rightly believed that the Lord Chancellor's energetic endorsement of repeal would create an impression of ministerial concurrence in the project.[88] And it was anticipated that a nationwide agitation for removal of the newspaper tax might be generated as a result of Brougham's testimony.

Place and Hume financed the reprinting of Brougham's evidence in a 1*d.* pamphlet, notwithstanding the technical breach of

[83] The *Poor Man's Guardian* described him as the "greatest and most deceitful enemy" of the people (15 Oct. 1831).

[84] There is no reference to his remarks on the subject in *Hansard*, H. of C., 31 May 1827, XVII, 1063–1083. Working-class journalists, however, attacked him continually for his opposition. Carlile described him as "half-drunk with liquor or rage for the occasion" (*Prompter*, 25 June 1834).

[85] Brougham, "Working and Prospects of the Reform," *Edinburgh Review*, LVI (1832), 245–260; [Brougham], "Progress of the People—the Periodical Press," *ibid.*, LVII (1833), 239–248. Two subsequent articles on the subject which Brougham wrote for the *Edinburgh Review* are of greater interest: "Newspaper Tax," *ibid.*, LXI (1835), 181–185; "Taxes on Knowledge," *ibid.*, LXII (1835), 126–132.

[86] Brougham, "First Session of the Reformed Parliament," *ibid.*, LVIII (1833), 223; Brougham, "Working and Prospects," pp. 254–56.

[87] Hume, letter to Place, [20 Sept. 1834], Place Papers, Add. MSS 35,149, ff. 313–314.

[88] See *Scotsman*, 3 Sept. 1834.

privilege that this involved since the evidence had not yet been officially reported to the Commons.[89] They distributed ten thousand copies of the tract and forwarded many of them to influential reformers in key sections of the country.[90] Other copies were supplied gratuitously to newspapers and periodicals, several of which, including the *Spectator*, republished substantial excerpts.[91]

By the end of 1834, however, the expectations of reformers had been dissipated. Despite the publicity given to Brougham's testimony and to the latter's further condemnations of the tax in the House of Lords and despite Bulwer's second motion for repeal in May 1834, followed by a series of public meetings during the summer, no substantive national agitation materialized.[92] To a great extent, Brougham was personally responsible for the disappointments that followed. He continued to demonstrate a measureless capacity for erratic political behavior, and his influence in the Melbourne government, negligible at the outset, further declined. His abortive Scottish "electioneering" junket during the autumn of 1834 culminating in an unseemly quarrel with Durham further reduced his public standing.[93] While journals

[89] The evidence was not officially reported to the Commons until 1843.

[90] Place, letter to Ebenezer Elliott, 9 July 1834, Place Papers, Add. MSS 35,149, ff. 304–307; Joseph Parkes, letter to Place, July 1834, *ibid.*, f. 309; Hume, letter to Brougham, 20 April 1835, Brougham Papers, No. 13,984.

[91] *Spectator*, 28 June 1834, 5 July 1834.

[92] In March 1835, Brougham presented a petition to the Lords and vigorously attacked the tax: "Nothing," he urged, "could be more effectually conservative, than the circulating through all classes of the people a perfect knowledge of what was doing, as well as of what was done, by the Government and the Legislature" (*Hansard*, H. of L., 23 March 1835, XXVII, 88). Richard Potter, a reformer, notes in his diary that he supported Bulwer's second motion for repeal but with "some degree of diffidence" since "its effects would probably be to injure the leading papers" (Parliamentary Diary, Potter Papers, IX, 155).

[93] Halévy, *Triumph of Reform, 1830–1841*, p. 188; *Glasgow Argus*, 15 Sept. 1834. Brougham's antics provided for a lively summer in London's social circles. See J. C. Lockhart, letter to William Blackwood, 18 Aug. 1834, cited in Margaret Oliphant, *Annals of a Publishing House: William Blackwood and His Sons: Their Magazine and Friends* (Edinburgh: William Blackwood and Sons, 1897–1898), I, 123–124.

such as the *Times* and the *Courier* castigated him unmercifully for his increasing "radicalism," reformers began to desert him. His unequivocal and reiterated professions of fidelity to the cause of repeal of the taxes on knowledge could not reverse this tendency.[94]

From 1834 on Brougham worked unceasingly, both publicly and in private, to secure repeal. In May 1835 he attacked Spring Rice's "*wet blanket* observations" and exhorted the government not to be "the slaves of a few men who are, at this very moment (*as I see*) about to bully some and wheedle others of you into the most ruinous measures, in order to gratify their own spite—and having succeeded partially, are resolved (naturally enough) to press their victory—the *Stamp* repeal must disown them." And two months later he urged repeal in order that "when the abominable taxes upon the knowledge which most concerns the people are removed . . . we shall have a universal diffusion of sound political knowledge among all classes of the community." [95] But these and similar observations were of no avail, and the attempt to engender a national campaign for repeal of the newspaper duty, with Brougham's 1834 testimony as the focus of the reformers' efforts, collapsed ignominiously. Meaningful governmental concessions were, if anything, further removed from reality as a result of these events.

The parliamentary repeal movement endured yet another set-

---

[94] *The History of the Times: "The Thunderer" in the Making, 1785–1841* (London: *The Times*, 1935), pp. 299–332. Notwithstanding his testimony, the *Spectator* urged all its readers "who call themselves Liberal, not to put faith in Henry Brougham" (30 Aug. 1834). John Campbell, the Attorney-General, thanked Brougham for enforcing "the distinction between mere *vituperation* and an *incitement to crime*" (letter to Brougham, [*c.* July 1834], Brougham Papers, No. 14,290).

[95] The references are to the proprietors of stamped newspapers (Brougham, letter to Spring Rice, 8 May 1835, Monteagle Papers, Folder 13,378 [1]; Brougham, Speech at the Liverpool Mechanics' Institute, July 1835, cited in Brougham, *Works*, I, 88). In July 1835 he asserted in Manchester: "The tax on bread is no more a tax on the staff of our natural lives than the taxes on knowledge are on our immortal lives" (*Manchester Advertiser*, 25 July 1835).

back during 1835. The prospects for reformers again seemed moderately hopeful at the outset of the session. The government formed by Melbourne in April 1835, succeeding a short-lived Tory ministry led by Peel, was intrinsically weak. Molesworth and other leading parliamentary reformers attempted to construct a "Radical Party . . . the commencement of . . . which will one day or another bring destruction upon both Whigs and Tories." [96] Though such a scheme remained a chimera, an informal agreement was concluded during the spring of 1835 between Irish radicals led by O'Connell and English reformers.[97] This circumstance created a temporarily advantageous political situation but no substantive concessions were extracted from the government on the subject of the taxes on knowledge.

This failure partially resulted from defective tactics. On the same day that the Melbourne ministry was officially organized, a small group of reformers met to discuss the best method for securing repeal of the newspaper impost. In the belief that the glaring weaknesses of the ministry would assure adoption of repeal, they decided to take no immediate action. As one participant later described the meeting: "Little doubt was entertained of success. It was therefore determined not to call a public meeting, or attempt to increase the excitement existing in the minds of the people upon this question, until it was ascertained, by personal application to the Chancellor of the Exchequer, what were his intentions upon the subject." [98]

In fact, since the political situation was in a state of flux, pressure could be exerted effectively upon the government only if the latter were kept in "a certain state of disquietude." [99] Some re-

[96] William Molesworth, 19 Feb. 1835, letter to his mother, cited in Millicent G. Fawcett, *Life of the Right Honourable Sir William Molesworth, Bart., M.P., F.R.S.* (London: Macmillan, 1901), p. 73.

[97] See Alan H. Graham, "The Lichfield House Compact—1835," *Irish Historical Studies*, XII (1961), 209–225.

[98] Hickson, *Taxes on Knowledge*, pp. 2–3.

[99] Henry Warburton, letter to Harriet Grote, 21 Dec. 1836, cited in Harriet Grote, *The Personal Life of George Grote: Compiled from Family Documents, Private Memoranda, and Original Letters to and from Various Friends* (London: John Murray, 1873), p. 110.

formers recognized this and hinted that their support for the government would be withdrawn if adequate concessions were not granted. Those who contemplated such a threat agreed that a minimal *quid pro quo* would involve concessions on Irish church reform, municipal corporation reform, and the taxes on knowledge.[100] Roebuck in his unstamped *Pamphlets for the People* specifically advocated a withdrawal of support from the Melbourne ministry on the Irish church question, so as to compel the removal of the taxes on knowledge and the establishment of a secret ballot. In a Commons speech, he warned that the existence of the ministry was at stake unless concessions were offered on the newspaper issue.[101] Place, in his prodigious correspondence with reformers in many sections of the country, staunchly endorsed Roebuck's proposal.

But in the final analysis, the prospect of another Tory government, led by Peel, was sufficiently alarming to Hume, Grote, and most other parliamentary reformers to induce them to reject all proposals of this nature.[102] O'Connell's unwillingness to support Roebuck's scheme and to sever his alliance with the government was of particular significance. Several working-class journalists, including John Cleave and John Bell, pleaded unavailingly with him *"to stake everything upon this question*—to make the real freedom of the press the condition of ministerial support."[103] He persistently refused to pursue such a course despite his assertion in July 1834 that repeal of the taxes on knowledge should be "the first object of all Reformers."[104]

The failure to employ effective political pressure against the

[100] *Glasgow Argus*, 23 and 27 April 1835.
[101] Roebuck, "Persecution of the Unstamped Press," (*R. Pamphlet*, No. 9), pp. 10–16, Roebuck, "Prospects of the Coming Session: Views of the Radical Party" (*R. Pamphlet*, No. 23), pp. 1–7; *Hansard*, H. of C., 10 Aug. 1835, XXX, 202–206.
[102] Hume, letter to Francis Place, 24 April 1835, Place Papers, Add. MSS 35,150, f. 35.
[103] *Cleave's Weekly Police Gazette*, 6 Feb. 1836; *New Weekly True Sun*, 19 March 1836.
[104] Daniel O'Connell, letter to Eagle, the radical candidate at Nottingham, reprinted in *Glasgow Argus*, 24 July 1834.

Melbourne government was crucial. No changes in the press laws were brought about during the session of 1835. The parliamentary reformers contented themselves instead with a verbal condemnation by the Chancellor, Spring Rice, of "the principle of this [newspaper] Tax," and a vague anticipation, expressed by Melbourne, that "the state of the revenue will enable us to settle the question next session." [105] Spring Rice's conciliatory demeanor and public commitment to the principle of repeal apparently placated many of them. Hickson described a delegation to the Chancellor in May 1835 as follows: "The effect of this interview was to produce an impression on the minds of many that the object was gained. The candid manner and apparent liberality of the Chancellor of the Exchequer lulled them into a false security." [106] In addition, reformers may have placed too much trust in an "authoritative" endorsement of repeal made by Russell during a campaign speech in Devonshire in April, 1835.

By their patent unwillingness to exert sufficient pressure upon the government, the parliamentary reformers unwittingly set the stage for the disappointing compromise of 1836. In spite of much ministerial verbiage, it was clear to many observers that they were no longer likely to secure their demands from Parliamentary activities alone. Working-class reformers became more disenchanted than ever with legal channels and turned in increasing numbers to illicit journalism. Many propertied reformers transferred their activities simultaneously to the extra-parliamentary level, a subject that will be explored in the next chapter.

[105] For Spring Rice's statement, see *Hansard*, H. of C., 21 Aug. 1835, XXX, 862. For Melbourne's statement, see Melbourne, letter to Bulwer, Aug. 1835, cited in Earl of Lytton, *The Life of Edward Bulwer, First Lord Lytton* (London: Macmillan, 1913), I, 503.

[106] Hickson, *Taxes on Knowledge*, p. 4. On the day following the meeting with the delegation, Spring Rice informed Brougham privately that "there is no possibility that a Stamp Bill can be introduced at present" (letter to Brougham, 8 May 1835, Brougham Papers, No. 10,467).

CHAPTER 4

Pressure from Without

Between 1830 and 1834 the energies of middle-class repealers were directed primarily into parliamentary channels. But by the spring of 1835 many of these reformers had become convinced of their inability to secure meaningful concessions from the Whigs unless they applied more direct methods of agitation. Thus a massive national movement for repeal of the newspaper duty was launched and conducted by middle-class reformers during 1835–1836. This campaign, which centered around the activities of a Westminster association directed by Place and his supporters, involved multiple activities in many spheres. In several sections of the country, its efforts complemented those of working-class journalists; hence, during the final phases of the newspaper agitation, some differences between the two types of reformers were resolved, and a tenuous semblance of radical unity was reestablished. This semblance did not, however, fundamentally meliorate the divisive split between middle- and working-class reformers that had been widening steadily since 1830.

The failure of parliamentary reformers to generate an effective "pressure from without"[1] on the newspaper issue between 1830

[1] This phrase is a standard one throughout the period. See Henry S. Chapman, "State of the Newspaper Stamp Question" (*R. Pamphlet*, No. 34), p. 13; Hickson, *Taxes on Knowledge*, p. 9.

and 1834 is traceable to ideological as well as political factors. The degree of emotional commitment by propertied reformers to the ideal of an untaxed press was limited, and so long as their immediate objective seemed attainable by parliamentary methods, there was, in their view, no pressing need to wage a massive extraparliamentary campaign. In addition, many reformers of a more conservative hue were still ruminating over the implications of the recent agitation for parliamentary reform. This movement had been strikingly successful in helping to secure passage of the Reform Act of 1832 but at the cost, it was maintained, of arousing unappeasable expectations and unrest.

Prior to the spring of 1835 several reformers sought to initiate a popular agitation for repeal of the taxes on knowledge. Fox, a persistent critic of both Whig and Tory governments, recommended a national petitioning movement in the pages of his influential *Monthly Repository*.[2] In April 1834 the *Sun*, a proreform London daily, urged a similar course upon its readers.[3] But in neither instance did a substantial popular movement materialize. The organizing abilities of a political genius such as Francis Place were needed. And Place, though disposed favorably to vigorous agitation on the subject, was temporarily satisfied to work through parliamentary channels as well as through the machinery of the existing political unions, particularly the National Political Union in London. Several meetings sponsored by middle-class reformers were held prior to 1835 to petition for repeal of the newspaper duty. But almost invariably they were conciliatory in tone and lacked the spontaneous enthusiasm of the weekly protest gatherings that were held at the Blackfriar's Rotunda and other working-class centers in London. These working-class meetings were convened for the purpose of denouncing Whig "persecution" of the radical press and of inducing popular support for the growing numbers of unstamped journals.

The first important meeting of middle-class reformers on the

---

[2] W. J. Fox, "Taxes on Knowledge," *Monthly Repository*, VI (1832), 271.
[3] *Glasgow Argus*, 10 April 1834.

subject of the taxes on knowledge took place in April 1830 at the City of London Literary and Scientific Institution. This was not the first time that (in the words of the *Examiner*) the offending duties had been "publicly discussed as a matter relating to the progress of civilization," but it represented an initial attempt to give publicity to the subject and to stimulate public interest in it.[4] Although the *Times* and most other London morning newspapers ignored the gathering, several reformers reprinted a comprehensive account of it in the form of a pamphlet entitled *Moral and Political Evils of the Taxes on Knowledge*. This tract sold for 3*d*. and was widely circulated.[5]

The meeting was convened by Edwin Chadwick, the Benthamite reformer, and among its prominent participants were Southwood Smith, the well-known lecturer in medical subjects and political economy, and William E. Hickson, the educational reformer.[6] After two consecutive evenings of concentrated debate those present drafted a petition calling for repeal of the newspaper, advertisement, and paper duties.[7] The tone and phraseology of this petition, and that of most of the recorded speeches, was predictably restrained. Commercial considerations were accorded priority over political ones, and statistical arguments, culled from recent articles in the *Scotsman* and the *Westminster Review*, were emphasized.[8] The egregious error of permitting

[4] "Taxes on Knowledge," *Examiner*, 16 May 1830.

[5] *The Moral and Political Evils of the Taxes on Knowledge* . . . (London: Effingham Wilson, 1830).

[6] For his part in convening this meeting, Hickson exaggeratedly stated that to Chadwick, "belongs the exclusive honour, and it is an enviable distinction, of having first directed the attention of the public to this important subject" (Hickson, *Taxes on Knowledge*, p. 10 n.).

[7] *Journals of the House of Commons*, 19 May 1830, LXXXV, 446. There are copies of the petition in Place Newspaper Collection, Set 57, ff. 97–98, 172.

[8] See, for example, *Scotsman*, 27 Sept. 1828, 1 Oct. 1828, 2 June 1830; [T. Perronet Thompson], "Taxes on Literature: 'The Six Acts,'" *Westminster Review*, XII (1830), 416–429 (this article was reprinted as a pamphlet); [Thompson], *The Article on the Six Acts, Especially Taxes on Literature: Reprinted (by Permission) from the Westminster Review, No. XXIV, for April, 1830* [London: William Strange, 1830]).

Henry Hunt, William Cobbett, and other working-class "demagogues" to increase their influence among the docile masses was condemned. As an effective counterresponse, it was suggested that moderate publicists should be encouraged to propagate their "ideas and modes of thinking . . . among the more ignorant." The best method for accomplishing this was to facilitate the removal of all obstacles to a free press.[9]

A second meeting was held at the same institution in January 1831, and its objectives were similar.[10] On this occasion, George Birkbeck, the pioneer of the Mechanics' Institute movement, was in the chair. Birkbeck, who was to play a significant role during the culminating phases of the newspaper agitation, was ably assisted by Hume, Warburton, Rowland Hill, and Erskine Perry.[11] The removal of all financial restrictions on the press was demanded by those present, and a deputation was selected to present this viewpoint to Althorp. But despite the warmth of several of the speeches, the tenor of the meeting, like that of the previous gathering, was noticeably moderate. Hume spoke restrainedly of the need to assure "safety to property and to life," while Hill, employing similar phraseology, stressed the necessity for security "to people and to property." [12] These statements were oblique references to the agricultural disturbances that had occurred recently in several southern counties. Birbeck's arguments were aimed particularly at this theme. He assured his listeners that these riots had taken place solely because "the schoolmaster has not been allowed to penetrate into [the] humble dwellings [of the rural labourers]" Had the newspaper stamp been removed, he asserted confidently, "it is quite impossible that

[9] *Moral and Political Evils*, p. 11.

[10] Much of the following account is based upon the report of the meeting printed in *Penny Papers for the People*, 4 Feb. 1831. There is also a full report in *Voice of the People*, 5 Feb. 1831.

[11] Thomas Kelly, *George Birkbeck: Pioneer of Adult Education* (Liverpool: Liverpool University Press, 1957), p. 168.

[12] *Penny Papers for the People*, 4 Feb. 1831.

in this place and in the adjoining counties, those outrages which have been committed, should have occurred." [13]

Neither of these meetings had a substantial national impact. But they served as a guideline for subsequent repeal meetings organized by parliamentary reformers between 1830 and 1834. The majority of these were chaired by less prominent persons, and they usually produced speeches and petitions of a moderate cast.

Such meetings were supplemented by the publication of a handful of tracts, including Place's *Letter to a Minister of State*, Chadwick's *On the Taxes on Knowledge*,[14] and a reprint of Thompson's *Westminster Review* article of April 1830. Middle-class extraparliamentary activity remained relatively sparse prior to 1835, however, and what did occur was confined largely to London.[15] No effective protest organization of national dimensions emerged during these years. Neither was there substantial undirected local activity commensurate with the working-class enthusiasm manifested for the unstamped press, a form of journalism that began to gain increasing adherents after the spring of 1831. A small number of reformers, including Hume and T. Perronet Thompson, contributed to subscriptions for imprisoned publishers and vendors, but only a minimal attempt was made to capitalize upon the feeling of public resentment and grievance. Hence a pattern of middle- and working-class division continued to make itself evident, a situation that was accentuated by the inconsistent activities of certain political unions.

[13] *Ibid.*

[14] The Chadwick tract, published by Robert Heward, was a reprint of an article that had appeared in the *Westminster Review*, No. XXIX, 1 July, 1831. Over five thousand copies of the pamphlet were distributed (Finer, *Chadwick*, p. 35).

[15] But provincial cities such as Glasgow, Birmingham, and Leeds did witness periodic protests against the taxes. For Glasgow, see *Herald to the Trades' Advocate*, 8 Jan. 1831; for Birmingham, see *Midland Representative*, 28 Jan. 1832.

The many extraparliamentary political associations that emerged during the years 1830–1832 played a part of some consequence in the movement to repeal the taxes on knowledge. These organizations were usually dominated by middle-class reformers, having been established initially to assist the Grey ministry with the passage of its measure of parliamentary reform. Being associations of disparate origins, they predictably reflected pressures of conflicting aims and internal tensions. When they sought gropingly to deal with the demands for an untaxed press, these pressures often became heightened. This effect was particularly the case at Birmingham and London, where the two most influential political unions existed.

The Birmingham Political Union was established in January 1830, under the aegis of Thomas Attwood. At the outset, it committed itself to supporting only two specific objectives—parliamentary reform and currency change.[16] No reference to repeal of the taxes on knowledge was incorporated into the Union's original declaration of objects, a situation that reflected the distinctly middle-class leadership of the Union's Executive Council, as well as the tight rein exercised by Attwood.[17]

The first overt challenge to this policy was launched in June 1831. A local branch of the British Association for Promoting Co-operative Knowledge, a predecessor of the ultra-radical National Union of the Working Classes, undertook a penny subscription for William Carpenter. Carpenter had been imprisoned recently for publishing an unstamped periodical known as the *Political Letters and Pamphlets*. Among the organizers of the Birmingham subscription for Carpenter were William Guest, the leading distributor of illegal journals in Birmingham, and James Morrison, the future editor of the *Pioneer*, an illicit trades union

---

[16] The currency issue was a particular favorite of Attwood (C. M. Wakefield, *Life of Thomas Attwood* [London: Harrison and Sons, 1885]). For a convincing defense of Attwood's inflationary currency proposals, see S. G. Checkland, "The Birmingham Economists, 1815–1850," *Economic History Review*, Ser. 2, I (1948), 1–19.

[17] Wakefield, *Attwood*, p. 134.

newspaper.[18] The Birmingham Political Union refused initially to countenance support for the subscription. Its leaders contended that if it endorsed the fund, it would be condoning "illegality." But discontented working-class members of the Union protested vehemently against this decision. The resulting controversy sparked an intra-organizational division along class lines.[19]

At the end of August 1831, after several rancorous debates, the Council acceded reluctantly to the working-class demands.[20] It unenthusiastically agreed to assist the "Victim Fund," which had been set up to aid all imprisoned vendors. The force of its assent was vitiated, however, by the stipulation that only Carpenter, the most moderate and "respectable" of the illicit journalists, was fully entitled to "public sympathy and protection." [21] As a result of this qualified position, only £4 11s. was collected by the end of 1831 when the subscription was terminated.[22]

Division of sentiment within the union was increased when M. P. Haynes, a working-class member, sought to secure the Council's endorsement of a petition calling for repeal of the taxes on knowledge. This petition was first offered by Haynes at the beginning of 1832, following upon an emotional Birmingham meeting on the subject at which James "Bronterre" O'Brien, the future Chartist leader, had spoken. At this gathering working-class activists had unrestrainedly denounced the imposts as "acts of positive despotism." [23]

The Council deliberately refused for three months to take ac-

---

[18] *Midland Representative*, 6 June 1831. The British Association for Promoting Co-operative Knowledge supported co-operative doctrines and initiated the first public working-class meetings on the subject of the newspaper duty, which it regarded as "the principal source of mental poverty and bodily degradation" (*Political Letters and Pamphlets*, 6 Nov. 1830; *Magazine of Useful Knowledge*, 13 Nov. 1830).

[19] *Midland Representative*, 20 Aug. 1831.   [20] *Ibid.*, 3 Sept. 1832.

[21] *Poor Man's Guardian*, 8 Oct. 1831. By this time local "Victim Funds" were being established to assist more aggressive working-class journalists, including Hetherington.

[22] See the letter from James Guest in *Midland Representative*, 26 Nov. 1831.

[23] *Ibid.*, 28 Jan. 1832.

tion on the Haynes petition. T. C. Salt, an influential middle-class leader, urged the Union to reject the petition as not of "immediate and pressing importance" and calculated only to embarrass the Whigs.[24] Parliamentary reform was, on the contrary, urged by Salt and others as "the one great national object" to be consummated.[25]

In the face of increasingly bitter assaults from O'Brien, who asserted that the primary interest of "the great body of the Unionists" was to insure "a free, honest, untaxed, and unshackled press," the Council finally adopted the petition.[26] It was then forwarded to the Commons as an aid to Bulwer in his first parliamentary motion on the subject of repeal in June 1832. Thus on two separate occasions, the middle-class Birmingham Political Union undertook meaningful action in support of the repeal campaign only after great initial reluctance and only in response to promptings from its more militant members.

Within the National Political Union, events took an analogous course, though the ensuing intra-union division was not demarcated as clearly along class lines. This was undoubtedly the case because much working-class sentiment in London had already gravitated toward the ultra-radical National Union of the Working Classes, which held weekly gatherings at the Rotunda. In Birmingham, on the contrary, no major working-class association was formed until August 1832, when the Midland Union of the Working Classes, an offshoot of the N.U.W.C., appeared on the scene.[27]

The National Political Union was established in October 1831, as a direct consequence of the rejection by the House of Lords of the first Reform Bill. The N.P.U.'s leading organizers were

---

[24] *Ibid.*, 4 Feb. 1832.   [25] *Ibid.*, 18 Feb. 1832.

[26] *Ibid.*, 17 March 1832; *Political Union Register*, April 1832.

[27] The Midland Union of the Working Classes was established by "non-electors" to agitate for radical reform, including repeal of "all taxes or duties preventing the attainment of political knowledge" (*Cobbett's Weekly Political Register*, 1 Sept. 1832; *Spectator*, 3 Nov. 1832). It had relatively little influence on Birmingham politics (Briggs, "Background of the Parliamentary Reform Movement," p. 297).

Erskine Perry, Major Aubrey Beauclerk, and a regular West-minster radical coterie that grouped itself around Place.[28] The venerable reformer Sir Francis Burdett, who was evidencing accelerating symptoms of conservatism, accepted the presidency of the Union, after Hume and several other parliamentary radicals had refused it.

The earliest meetings of the Union's Council, which were held in October 1831, sought to formulate its objectives. Several members of the Council proposed to convert it into a "permanent . . . political institution," whose objective would be "to effect the mental as well as political emancipation of the people." [29] Such a conception involved a concern with many issues that transcended the Reform Bill, and most immediately it meant involvement with the question of repeal of the taxes on knowledge. Rowland Detrosier, a nationally known lecturer of working-class origins, championed such a controversial position.[30] He maintained:

It was beyond the Bill that the Reformers of England should look for a cheap and efficient Government . . . and for that without which mere extension of suffrage might be an evil . . . the abolition of all taxes on the diffusion of knowledge; and it was beyond the Bill that they should look for a plan insuring the education of every poor man's child.[31]

[28] Place described Perry and Beauclerk contemptuously as members of the "half Whig, club men" class because of their upper-class backgrounds (Place Autobiography, Place Papers, Add. MSS 27,789, f. 337). For a provocative, if not entirely satisfactory, interpretation of the National Political Union, see Joseph Hamburger, *James Mill and the Art of Revolution* (New Haven, Conn.: Yale University Press, 1963), pp. 73–96.

[29] Detrosier, *Lecture on the Utility of Political Unions*, pp. 3, 22.

[30] Detrosier, a self-taught cotton spinner who had been active in the Mechanics' Institute movement in Lancashire, propounded a fusion of co-operative principles and orthodox Benthamism. For information on Detrosier, see his obituary in the *Manchester Times,* reprinted in *A Scourge for the Littleness of "Great" Men,* 31 Dec. 1834; Holyoake, *Sixty Years,* I, 188; Gwyn A. Williams, *Rowland Detrosier: A Working-Class Infidel, 1800–34* (York: St. Anthony's Press, 1965).

[31] Report of a meeting of the N.P.U. of 10 Nov. 1831, cited in *Spectator,* 12 Nov. 1831.

The acceptance of this position would have committed the Union to a substantial broadening of its activities and would have increased the organization's attractiveness for working-class radicals.

The opposing viewpoint was expounded most consistently by Burdett who envisaged the Union solely as a prop for the ministry. Its function would be to generate needed public endorsement of the government on the specific question of political reform. Although Burdett agreed that the taxes on knowledge were undesirable, he and his supporters emphasized that their removal should occur as a consequence of political change. Thus any agitation by the Union on the subject of the newspaper tax was premature and calculated to "embarass [*sic*] the King and Ministers." It was crucial, Burdett urged, to avoid "speechifying too many measures for [the Ministers] to consider simultaneously." Political reform "ought to be kept quite distinct, and to form the whole object." [32] Richard Lalor Sheil, an Irish radical M.P., strongly endorsed this approach. He emphasized the loss of strength entailed by any political movement when it overextended its resources. [33] The *Spectator* likewise articulated this viewpoint in a series of leaders. [34] Even W. J. Fox, a vociferous champion of "cheap bread . . . [and] cheap knowledge," accepted the need to concentrate all of the Union's immediate resources on the goal of parliamentary reform. [35]

The more conservative Burdett-Sheil faction gained temporary ascendancy within the Union. When the organization issued a conditional Declaration of Objects on October 24, just prior to its official formation, six demands were formulated. Five of these

[32] Burdett, letter to Rowland Detrosier, 28 Nov. 1831, Place Papers, Add. MSS 27,791, ff. 114–115. The letter is reprinted in M. W. Patterson, *Sir Francis Burdett and His Times (1770–1844)* (London: Macmillan, 1931), II, 599.

[33] Account of N.P.U. meeting of 31 Oct. 1831, as cited in *Morning Chronicle*, 1 Nov. 1831.

[34] *Spectator*, 24 Nov. 1831, 3 Dec. 1831.

[35] *Morning Chronicle*, 1 Nov. 1831. Fox worked subsequently for a more active repeal policy by the N.P.U.

related to the question of parliamentary reform. The sixth committed the Union to strive for the abolition of all "taxes on knowledge" and to assist in the diffusion of sound moral and political information.[36] But during the succeeding week Burdett became an official member of the Union. A series of further meetings was then held by the Provisional Council and several of the original objectives were heatedly debated. Some working-class members attempted to insert resolutions which supported the principles of universal suffrage and annual parliaments, and it is almost certain that the newspaper taxes were discussed.[37]

The crucial meeting probably took place on October 27, though there is no reference to a discussion of the newspaper duty either in the printed reports of the meeting or in the original minutes. On October 28, however, Perry vainly sought to "disabuse" Burdett of the notion that the N.P.U. was committed solely to parliamentary reform, and on October 31, when the N.P.U. was formally established at the Crown and Anchor Inn, all references to the taxes on knowledge had been deleted from the original Declaration of Objects. As a substitute for the latter, an innocuous platitude regarding the efficacy of frequent political meetings during times of stress had been inserted.[38]

This setback proved only marginally damaging to the repeal agitation since several of the later publications issued by the N.P.U. did reprint the original unamended Declaration of Objects, with its reference to the taxes on knowledge.[39] In addition, Burdett left the Union at the beginning of 1832, when he sensed that his conservative orientation was gradually losing support.[40] Most important, the association demonstrated repeat-

[36] *Ibid.*, 24 Oct. 1831; Place Papers, Add. MSS 27,822, f. 32.

[37] Place Papers, Add. MSS 27,822, ff. 38–40; Minutes of the N.P.U., Place Newspaper Collection, Set 63, f. 5.

[38] Place Papers, Add. MSS 27,822, ff. 39, 41–42; Minutes of the N.P.U., Place Newspaper Collection, Set 63, f. 5.

[39] See Bulwer, *Taxes on Knowledge.*

[40] See the report of the general meeting of the N.P.U. held on 2 Feb. 1832, in Place Papers, Add. MSS 27,791, f. 139; *Morning Chronicle,* 3 Feb. 1832.

edly by its actions that many of its members were committed to the removal of all restraints on the "diffusion of information." [41]

At the beginning of 1832 a period of temporary slack in the movement for parliamentary reform gave several members of the Union an opportunity to modify the official policy of exclusive concentration on political reform. Place, Perry, and Detrosier sought immediately to advance the question of the "knowledge" taxes. Under their guidance, a petition demanding total repeal of the "intolerable" duties was presented to the Council and officially adopted several weeks later.[42] In the interim, a small committee was appointed to undertake a detailed analysis of all aspects of the question.[43] Although the committee never issued a report, the statistical material that Perry accumulated as a result of conversations with Althorp and Brougham was employed usefully on subsequent occasions.[44] And as a corollary to these activities, the Union also published several "knowledge" tracts, notably the reprint of Bulwer's 1832 motion for repeal.

An important political union dominated by middle-class reformers had once again demonstrated its reluctance to become involved in the repeal agitation. But counsels of restraint were overcome more successfully within the N.P.U. than at Birmingham, and the former made a contribution of some substance to the newspaper agitation. This contribution represented primarily the efforts of a small group of dedicated reformers led by the indefatigable Francis Place. Neither within the N.P.U. nor in the country at large, however, was a middle-class commitment to newspaper repeal strikingly evident prior to 1835.

[41] Roebuck, *Report of the Council*, pp. 1–8.

[42] The petition was adopted at the first general meeting of the N.P.U., which was held on Feb. 2. It was at this meeting that Burdett offered his resignation (*Morning Chronicle*, 3 Feb. 1832; Place Papers, Add. MSS 27,791, ff. 135–143).

[43] Place Papers, Add. MSS 27,791, ff. 127a–128.

[44] Perry, letter to Brougham, 19 Nov. 1832, Brougham Papers, No. 44,147. This is the material that could not be located for use before the Select Committee on Libel Law (1834).

Closely related to the activities of the political unions was the formation in January 1833 of a Society for the Diffusion of Political and Moral Knowledge. Grote, Warburton, Molesworth, Roebuck, Fox, Place, and Hume were the leading personalities behind this association. Their objective was to publish inexpensive tracts, to agitate for popular instruction and, after repeal of the taxes on knowledge, to publish a radical daily newspaper.[45] The importance attached to these aims was underscored in the Society's circular which stated that "should convulsion take place [the middle classes] will be swept away—no matter which party conquers, if blind ignorance be paramount they must suffer. If, however, they at once go amongst the people—if they instruct— they may guide them." [46]

Negotiations with the Grey and Melbourne ministries for reduction or repeal of the newspaper impost proved abortive; as a result, the members of the Society abandoned plans for a variety of activities and concentrated instead upon the legal publication and dissemination of such radical tracts as Joseph Priestley's *Essay on the First Principles of Government* and Bentham's *Truth vs. Ashurst.*[47] Articles from the *Westminster Review*, the *London Review*, and other radical journals were reprinted, including several dealing with the taxes on knowledge. A new edition of Place's celebrated repeal tract, *A Letter to a Minister of State*, was also published by the Society, as well as a 1*d.* edition of

[45] Such a newspaper was conceived initially in 1830 and, at that time, Bentham recommended Chadwick as editor (Chadwick, letter to Albany Fonblanque, 1 Aug. 1830, cited in Finer, *Chadwick*, p. 35). For the objectives of the Society, see Place, letter to Roebuck, 27 Dec. 1832, Place Papers, Add. MSS 35,154, ff. 162–165; [John A. Roebuck], circular issued by the Society (Jan. 1833), Place Papers, Add. MSS 35,154, ff. 167–168. There is a discussion of the Society in Hamburger, *Intellectuals in Politics*, pp. 129–130.

[46] A preliminary circular that was issued by the Society in January 1830, is in Place Papers, Add. MSS 27,827, ff. 39–40.

[47] There is an inadequate summary of the work of the Society in Wallas, *Place*, pp. 337–339. The Society also reprinted several of the essays that James Mill had originally written for the *Encyclopaedia Britannica*.

Brougham's evidence before the 1834 Select Committee on Libel, ten thousand copies of which were printed.[48]

Commencing in June 1835, the Society undertook its most ambitious and controversial project. On at least three former occasions it had contemplated seriously the possibility of issuing a penny periodical, but in each instance it had decided not to transgress the stamp laws.[49] In 1835, however, it began to finance what was, in effect, an unstamped illegal weekly newspaper, the *Pamphlets for the People*.[50] This was edited by Roebuck, printed in an identical weekly format, although each number technically had a different title, and sold for $1\frac{1}{2}d$. per copy. Its sixteen octavo pages were crammed with signed articles, most of them written by Place, Roebuck, and Henry S. Chapman. Many were of a decidedly controversial nature, including several by Roebuck that denounced scathingly the "corrupt and base" activities of leading stamped journalists.[51]

Despite an introductory prospectus that was intended to mollify moderate thought, the opinions expressed in the pamphlets veered toward popular radicalism, particularly on the newspaper issue. Furthermore, the tracts were patently illegal. They were not dated but were published weekly without interruption for almost a year, and they featured a substantial quantity of news, much of it only thinly disguised as abstract "comment." Thus the *Pamphlets for the People*, despite its "respectable" paternity, discomfited many moderate reformers. The *Public Ledger*, a proreform journal, announced in June 1835 that it was opposed to repeal of the stamp duty on the ground

[48] Hume, letter to Brougham, 20 April 1835, Brougham Papers, No. 13,984.

[49] One such projected journal was to be called the *Penny Political Magazine* (MS note from Place to Hume, 1834?, in Hume's copy of the N.P.U. reprint of Bulwer's 1832 repeal motion, University College, London; Francis Place, "The Examiner and the Tax on Newspapers," *Radical*, 27 March 1836).

[50] The publication is usually bound together as *Pamphlets for the People*, though occasionally the tracts are catalogued separately.

[51] Roebuck, "The Stamped Press of London and Its Morality" (*R. Pamphlet*, No. 3), p. 4.

that "the Roebuck party" would subjugate the press.[52] When Place was soliciting support for a recently formed repeal association during the spring of 1836, he received at least one negative response accusing the *Pamphlets* of promoting "disunion" among reformers.[53] Although Place informed his correspondent that the *Pamphlets* were not officially sponsored by the association, he agreed reluctantly that Roebuck had been guilty of "inexcusable carelessness" in several of his articles.[54]

The extensive circulation of the *Pamphlets for the People* (often involving the printing of several editions) probably indicates a sizable working-class readership.[55] This seems to be further demonstrated by the fact that the advertisement columns of the *Pamphlets* were replete with tracts published by Cleave and other working-class journalists. If the supposition of a large working-class readership is correct, then the tracts served as one of the few points of contact between the middle- and working-class campaigns for repeal; in this area, at least, the activities of parliamentary reformers touched a response beyond the scope of their own ideology. But the *Pamphlets* survived for less than a year and no permanent union between reformers could be forged on the basis of them alone. Of far greater importance was the formation in the spring of 1835 of a national repeal association.

By April 1835, after the demise of Peel's brief Tory ministry and the return of the Whigs to power for a second time under Melbourne, the need for a national agitation on the newspaper issue had become clear. Place decided to establish an association that would devote itself entirely to securing repeal of the stamp duty. He had concluded that the "imbecile" Whigs could no longer be trusted, and that even radicals such as Hume were not

[52] *Public Ledger*, 23 June 1835. The pro-Whig *Morning Chronicle* described Roebuck as "an object deserving of our pity rather than of our indignation" (20 June 1835).

[53] John Taylor, letter to Place, 19 Jan. 1836, Place Newspaper Collection, Set 70, ff. 317–318.

[54] Place, letter to Taylor, 20 Jan. 1836, *ibid.*, ff. 319–320.

[55] Roebuck, "Address to Readers" (*R. Pamphlet*, No. 36), p. 16.

sufficiently aggressive on the more important issues.[56] The latter, in Place's opinion, had "neglected the means necessary to produce a feeling" on this as well as on other questions. As a result, neither press reform, Irish tithe legislation, nor municipal reform—the three most compelling issues—seemed even remotely assured of passage during the coming session of Parliament.[57]

The Association for the Abolition of the Stamp Duty on Newspapers, which Place organized, represents an important chain in the history of extraparliamentary pressure groups.[58] It derived several of its techniques from earlier associations and foreshadowed, on a smaller scale, many of the activities of the Anti-Corn Law League. Despite its importance, it has not received heretofore any significant attention from historians.

In April 1835 the Association was informally established with headquarters at Leicester Square. Place was its organizer, although Dr. James Robert Black, a Kentuckian, was technically the president of the organization. Black had emigrated to England in the early 1830's and had become involved in many of the reform activities of the period.[59] Described by Francis Place

[56] Place asserted: "I can do more good without [Radical M.P.'s] than with them" (Place, letter to Hume, 2 May 1835, Place Papers, Add. MSS 35,150, f. 36).

[57] *Ibid.*, ff. 38–38a. In much the same tenor, Place wrote of Hume on a later occasion: "His mode of thinking always makes him averse from entering into the projects of others until he sees, that he is sure to be countenanced by the public" (Place, letter to John S. Mill, 10 Feb. 1837, *ibid.*, f. 241a).

[58] An article by Samuel H. Beer, "The Representation of Interests in British Government: Historical Background," *American Political Science Review*, LI (1957), is the most suggestive essay on the subject of these early nineteenth-century organizations. He contends (p. 636) that these associations "conceived themselves to be formed and united by a meeting of individual minds. This . . . was what joined them, not tradition, personal loyalty, class, estate, vocation or some secret bond. Hence there was no reason to expect that once they had achieved the desired reform, they would have further common interests." See also Eugene C. Black, *The Association: British Extraparliamentary Political Organization, 1769–1793* (Cambridge, Mass: Harvard University Press, 1963).

[59] Dr. Black has been confused with John Black, editor of the *Morning Chronicle* (Hovell, *Chartist Movement*, pp. 59–60). Though a Benthamite

as "a discreet middle aged systematic man," and by the hostile
John Bell as "a man-of-all-work to his party—prudent and active
—active as a blue-bottle, secret as an earwig," Black played an
influential if unassuming role in several proreform political ventures.[60] Among those who most prominently assisted Black in
the work of the association were William E. Hickson, John
Travers, Henry S. Chapman, John Crawfurd, and George Birkbeck.

Hickson, the future proprietor of the *Westminster Review* and
a prominent educational reformer, played an especially active
role during the repeal campaign. In addition to his work within
the Association, he participated in several repeal meetings,
drafted a memorial that was submitted to Spring Rice in the
spring of 1835, and wrote at least two articles in 1836 on the subject of the newspaper duty, both of which were subsequently reprinted in pamphlet form.[61] Hickson's basic approach to the question of the newspaper duty was restrained and "middle class,"
but as parliamentary methods failed, he became increasingly
sympathetic to the unstamped press. Like Place, he rejected bit-

---

reformer, John Black was not active in the movement to repeal the taxes on
knowledge, nor was he connected in any way with the London Working Men's
Association.

[60] Place, letter to Brougham, 2 April 1835, Place Papers, Add. MSS 35,150,
f. 27; *London Mercury*, 2 April 1837. Black served William Molesworth as
private secretary and John T. Leader as agent. Both were prominent Radical
M.P.'s (James Grant, *The Newspaper Press: Its Origin, Progress and Present
Position* [London: Tinsley Bros., 1871], I, 373; J. T. Leader, letter to R. E.
Leader, 19 Feb. 1896, cited in Robert E. Leader, *Life and Letters of John
Arthur Roebuck with Chapters of Autobiography* [London: Edward Arnold,
1897], p. 107).

[61] William Hickson, letter to Place, 2 May 1835, Place Newspaper Collec-
tion, Set 70, f. 206; Hickson, letter to Place, 20 July 1835, *ibid.*, f. 239.
Hickson's article for the *London Review* was republished as a pamphlet; see
Chapter 2, note 84. It sold for 2*d.* but another edition published by C. and W.
Reynell was "printed for distribution." An article which Hickson wrote for the
Monthly Repository in April 1836 was reprinted as *Manifesto of the Chancellor
of the Exchequer Against the Moral Interests of the Productive Classes* (London: T. C. Hansard, 1836). For proof of Hickson's authorship, see Hickson,
letter to Place, April 1836, Place Newspaper Collection, Set 70, f. 561.

[99]

terly any compromise on the subject, arguing that a reduction of the duty would merely "rivet more firmly than before the chains by which the press would still remain bound."

Travers was an influential City of London reformer. Described by a contemporary as "discreet and energetic," he was closely identified with such City radicals as Samuel Crawford and George Grote.[62] Travers' chief task as a member of the Association was to raise subscriptions, since as president of the City of London Reform Club he possessed many important financial contacts.[63] Although he participated in an important repeal meeting held at the Guildhall in March 1836, Travers was more active in the organizing phase of the repeal campaign than in its public one.

Henry S. Chapman shared joint formal leadership of the Association with Black. He had previously edited a penny newspaper in Canada where he had lived for many years.[64] Chapman contributed several articles to the *Westminster Review,* and in 1837 provided Place and Brougham with relevant information about the Canadian Rebellion.[65] But his activities in connection with repeal of the newspaper duty were of particular importance. During the final stages of the agitation, he spoke at many repeal meetings and contributed forty-three articles to Roebuck's illegal *Pamphlets for the People.* A witty, sardonic writer possessed of a streak of "ultra-Liberalism," Chapman consistently championed municipal reform, the secret ballot, annual parliaments, and the abolition of tithes.[66] His primary interest during the 1830's,

[62] *Spectator,* 28 Feb. 1835.

[63] For his financial activities, see [Place], letter to Birkbeck, March 1836, Place Newspaper Collection, Set 70, ff. 429–432.

[64] Leader, *Roebuck,* p. 61.

[65] Place Papers, Add. MSS 35,151, ff. 45–46, cited in New, *Durham,* p. 319.

[66] Chapman himself used the phrase "ultra-Liberals" (Chapman, "Toryphobia" [*R. Pamphlet,* No. 26], p. 14). In 1835 he published *The Municipal Corporation Act* [*Text*] *With Notes, Practical and Explanatory.* This sold for 1*s.* 6*d.* and was advertised in radical journals as the "cheapest and most complete edition of the Corporation Reform Act." For his views on the ballot, see Chapman, "The American Ballot Box" (*R. Pamphlet,* No. 5), pp. 11–15 and

however, lay in securing repeal of the newspaper duty, which he described as "the most odious of the taxes ever imposed in this country." [67] To secure this objective, he vigorously endorsed the Roebuck-Place suggestion that parliamentary radicals withdraw support from the Melbourne government unless repeal was conceded.

Chapman possessed a tenuous ideological link with working-class thought on the newspaper issue. Although his primary goal was to increase the level of general intelligence by disseminating knowledge amongst the masses, his approach to the subject possessed an unorthodox "class" element. He contended that laws "were made by the rich for the rich, and there is not a day that justice is not denied to the poor." [68] A tax on newspapers was especially unjust, in his view, since newspapers were "one of the prime necessaries of [the poor man's life]." [69] He depicted poignantly the vendor of unstamped periodicals as a "miserable, defenceless, starving creature who was driven to sell an Unstamped Paper at the corner of the street, in order to get a pennyworth of taxed Bread for his famished wife and children." [70] By 1836, Chapman was openly defending the unstamped press and counseling resistance to the law, a position that few middle-class reformers were prepared to follow.

John Crawfurd, another important member of the Association, was a well-known surgeon and a former East India Company translator. Upon his return from abroad, Crawfurd had acquired influential contacts in London reforming circles and had married a sister of Erskine Perry. During 1832 he had worked closely

---

for his views on the subject of tithes, see Chapman, "A Tithe Case" (*R. Pamphlet*, No. 21), p. 15.

[67] Chapman, "State of the Newspaper Stamp Question" (*R. Pamphlet*, No. 34), p. 14.

[68] Chapman, "Crusade Against the Unstamped: Mr. Broughton's Decision" (*R. Pamphlet*, No. 30), p. 15.

[69] Chapman, "Mr. Rice and the Tax on Knowledge—A Few Words against Partial Reduction" (*R. Pamphlet*, No. 11), p. 10.

[70] Chapman, "Conduct of the Authorities towards the Unstamped Press" (*R. Pamphlet*, No. 18), p. 14.

with Hume to secure the termination of the East India Company's monopoly of the China trade.[71] Crawfurd contested several parliamentary elections as the candidate of the Westminster radicals and was only narrowly defeated at Glasgow in 1832 and at Paisley in 1834. During each of his electoral campaigns, he endorsed an unqualified middle-class reform program that featured household suffrage, the ballot, repeal of the Corn Laws, disestablishment of the Church of England and, most importantly, the immediate abolition of the "taxes on knowledge." [72] Crawfurd was a notably poor speaker, and there is no evidence that he participated actively in any of the major public meetings that were convened to promote newspaper reform.[73] But his analytical mind and his notable adeptness at marshalling statistical data made him a valuable asset to the Association. Two of his pamphlets, *Taxes on Knowledge: A Financial and Historical View of the Taxes Which Impede the Education of the People* and *The Newspaper Stamp, and the Newspaper Postage; Compared,* sold for 6*d*. and were among the most influential tracts issued during the repeal campaign.[74]

Crawfurd eschewed the educational approach in his advocacy of newspaper reform. He concentrated instead almost exclusively upon the free-trade aspects of the subject. He regarded a newspaper as essentially a "commodity" and felt that a superior literary product could be ensured only through "freedom and absence of taxation." [75] Possessing little of Chapman's popular radicalism and almost none of Hickson's overriding concern for the edu-

[71] The best summary of Crawfurd's early activities is in an obscure pamphlet entitled *Some Notices of John Crawfurd, Esq., One of the Candidates for the Representation of this City* (Glasgow: Privately publ., 1832). A copy is in the Mitchell Library, Glasgow.

[72] For his Marylebone address issued as a by-election candidate in 1834, see the *Spectator*, 11 Jan. 1834.

[73] On his oratorical deficiencies, see *Reformer's Gazette*, 20 Oct. 1832; letter from "A Glasgow Elector," *Cobbett's Weekly Political Register*, 27 Oct. 1832.

[74] See chapter 1, note 6, and chapter 2, note 85; Crawfurd, letter to Place, 9 April 1836, Place Newspaper Collection, Set 70, ff. 467–468.

[75] Crawfurd, *Taxes on Knowledge*, p. 34.

cational betterment of the poor, Crawfurd's perspective was entirely that of the undiluted political economist. The newspaper duties were particularly deplorable, he felt, because of their vagueness and indeterminacy. This ambiguity wrongly enabled the Stamp Office to exercise legal discretion which it could then use to prosecute working-class publishers such as Cleave and Hetherington while deliberately foregoing action against Lord Brougham and other "wholesale smugglers." [76]

A final important personality active in the Association was George Birkbeck, the founder of adult Mechanics' Institutes. Birkbeck, like Place, had some contacts with working-class radicals, particularly through the London Mechanics' Institution.[77] He was one of the few middle-class reformers who personally knew Hetherington, the "father" of illegal journalism. During the spring of 1836, Birkbeck and Place served as co-treasurers of a subscription fund established to pay off the fines of Cleave and Hetherington whose printing presses and types had been seized by the authorities for violation of the stamp laws.[78] By this action, Birkbeck and Place provided one of the few tangible links between the middle- and working-class repeal campaigns.[79] But despite this balancing role, Birkbeck's frequently reiterated views on the newspaper issue were more anathema to the working classes than those of Place. Pedagogically, his primary objective

[76] *Ibid.*, pp. 36–37. The reference is to the weekly appearance of the S.D.U.K.'s *Penny Magazine*, a periodical of questionable legality and one with which Brougham was associated.

[77] Kelly, *Birkbeck*, pp. 167–168.

[78] William Lovett, *Life and Struggles of William Lovett, in His Pursuit of Bread, Knowledge, and Freedom: With Some Short Account of the Different Associations He Belonged to and of the Opinions He Entertained* (London: G. Bell and Sons, 1920), p. 91. For a copy of the printed circular issued by the Birkbeck-Place committee, see Place Newspaper Collection, Set 70, f. 434; *Weekly True Sun*, 21 Feb. 1836.

[79] The initial circular of this committee, undoubtedly approved by Place and Birkbeck, solicited unqualified support for the unstamped press. But a later circular, written by Lovett, was more in line with their moderate views, and merely requested support for the "principle" of an unstamped press (Place Newspaper Collection, Set 70, ff. 438–439).

was to gain "access to the understandings of the [working class]," and the unobstructed dissemination of cheap newspapers provided, in his view, the most effective means for achieving this end.[80]

By 1835, Birkbeck had become increasingly concerned with repeated violations of the stamp laws by working-class journalists. He regarded this as a grave threat to the mechanism of government since public contempt for its processes would undoubtedly increase.[81] Thus for essentially conservative reasons, Birkbeck agreed to join the newly-formed London repeal association, apparently as the result of a letter of solicitation from Brougham.[82] He was initially reluctant to become a member of the Association, since he strongly believed that the Melbourne government would "readily give up an inconsiderable piece of revenue." He preferred to avoid public gatherings and to rely instead upon Brougham's influence with members of the government to secure repeal. As he told the former Lord Chancellor in April 1835, Brougham not being a member of the second Melbourne government: "You having *more power*, as unquestionably *you* will have, in consequence of having *no place*, will advocate the measure with unjustifiable energy. It is, as it appears to me, quite provided for by being in your own hands." [83] Birkbeck's early doubts were soon overborne, and he shortly afterwards wrote enthusiastically that "enough will soon be done to show that the Desire for the removal of the Tax is exceedingly extensive." [84]

Throughout 1835–1836 Birkbeck devoted a considerable proportion of his time to the cause of repeal. His value to the Asso-

[80] See his speech as a member of a delegation to Melbourne in Feb. 1836, reprinted in Kelly, *Birkbeck*, pp. 170–172.

[81] According to Birkbeck, Hetherington, "a mild, placid, sensible man, who was incapable of violating any other law . . . had been goaded into a disposition which nothing could change," as the result of a heavy-handed governmental prosecution (*ibid.*, p. 171).

[82] Brougham, letter to Birkbeck, April 1835, reprinted in *ibid.*, p. 169.

[83] Birkbeck, letter to Brougham, 20 April 1835, Brougham Papers, No. 22,872.

[84] *Ibid.*, 29 April 1835, No. 22,345.

ciation lay primarily in the respected public position which he commanded. He played a conspicuous role at meetings and also invariably headed repeal delegations to the government, including the well-publicized one of May 1835, at which Melbourne and Spring Rice committed themselves to the "principle" of repeal. In a general sense, Birkbeck provided a substantial measure of "respectability" for the middle-class agitation.

The Association's immediate objective was to arouse a national feeling on the subject of newspaper repeal. This was to be accomplished by a mass petitioning campaign and through the stimulus of numerous public meetings. Place undertook to procure funds for these purposes by means of his many contacts in Parliament and in reforming circles. In his correspondence he described the question of repeal as "of more national importance than any single measure in the power of the Legislature," and assured recipients of his letters that the Committee was determined "never to relinquish its [object] until it is obtained." [85]

Although the campaign was under the control of middle-class reformers and although most of those solicited for funds were persons of substance, the laborers were requested to contribute at least one farthing apiece to help finance the cost of the petitions. This request was necessary, in Place's opinion, since "there are men of character, wealth and influence who are willing enough to work for and with the people for their good, but they are not able to do much and never will be able to do much until the people will do their little." [86] But the response of the working classes to his request was not notably large. The total sum raised from both middle- and working-class sources during the thirty months of the Association's existence was only about £110, a phenomenon that provoked John Stuart Mill to a denunciation

[85] Place, letter to Brougham, 2 April 1835, Place Papers, Add. MSS 35,150, f. 27; Place, letter to Brougham, 1 April 1835, Brougham Papers, No. 10,041. For a general letter by Place soliciting funds dated 12 April 1835, see Place Newspaper Collection, Set 70, ff. 201–205.

[86] Place, letter to William Longson, 25 May 1835, Place Papers, Add. MSS 35,150, f. 50a.

of "the spiritless, heartless imbecility of the English Radicals." [87]

In April 1835 approximately twenty thousand circulars were lithographed and judiciously distributed by the Association. Most of them were transmitted through the Post Office free of charge under cover of the Parliamentary franking privilege. In addition to letters of solicitation, the circulars enclosed a moderately-phrased petition form calling for repeal of the restrictions on newspapers. Restrictions, in the words of the petition, were undesirable because they assertedly "prevent the spread of knowledge, impede the progress of morality, are obstacles to good order, and encourage ignorance, which is the parent of vice, of crime, and of misery." [88] Accompanying this form were precise instructions as to how the petitions could be utilized most effectively. Recipients were advised to affix two to three hundred signatures to each petition, since this was calculated to be the number which would have the greatest impact upon Parliament.[89]

Brougham, Bulwer, Warburton, Roebuck, Dr. John Bowring, and Charles Buller were among the more prominent reformers who agreed to receive the petitions and to present them to the Commons.[90] Hume's name also appeared on most of the circulars. He had initially opposed a national extraparliamentary campaign for repeal but was persuaded by Place that the Whigs contemplated no action on the subject during the 1835 session of Parliament. By the first week of May he had committed himself wholeheartedly to the movement and was even hinting indirectly to Spring Rice that he was the leading personality behind the Association.[91]

[87] Place, letter to Thomas Gibson, 29 Sept. 1840, *ibid.*, Add. MSS 35,151, f. 279; John S. Mill, letter to Albany Fonblanque, 1837?, cited in *Life and Labours of Fonblanque*, pp. 30–31. Mill himself contributed £4.

[88] Place Papers, Add. MSS 35,150, f. 32.

[89] A copy of the circular is in *ibid.*, f. 33. After receiving the circular, Ashton Yates of the Middlesex Registration Society offered to introduce the subject at the next meeting (letter to Place, April 1835?, *ibid.*, f. 34).

[90] Archibald Michie, Jr., letter to G. Faithfull, 28 April 1835, Place Newspaper Collection, Set 70, ff. 207–210.

[91] Hume had written to Place two weeks earlier that "nothing should be done" on the subject until the ministers have had a chance to act (letter to

The Association conducted a vigorous, effective campaign. During the 1835 session, an estimated 137 petitions demanding repeal were forwarded to Parliament as a result of the Association's activities.[92] The phraseology and emphasis of these petitions differed, but most bore similar marks of "respectable" paternity, including frequent allusions to the religious and social benefits derivable from repeal. No sense of class grievance informed these petitions and relatively little concern was demonstrated by them regarding the impact of the newspaper duty upon the laboring classes.[93]

Association-sponsored public meetings to demand repeal were also organized in increasing numbers, despite an apparent determination on the part of the stamped press not to publish accounts of them. One successful meeting held at the Guildhall in July 1835 was described by a participant as "crowded to overflowing," and another important protest meeting was held at Southwark with Brougham serving as chairman.[94] Of greatest significance, however, was a gathering held at the Crown and Anchor Inn on July 18. All of the leading parliamentary reformers including Hume and O'Connell were present, and supporters of the campaign estimated the attendance at six thousand. Brougham, who was continuing to play a conspicuous role in the agitation, chaired the gathering, and advocated "the total and absolute repeal of this obnoxious impost." The cause of an untaxed press, according to Brougham, was that "of knowledge, of public improvement, of good morals, of correct manners, of sound principles, of political improvement, and of every species of advance and important progress, which it most interested the people to

Place, 24 April 1835, Place Papers, Add. MSS 35,150, f. 35). Yet on May 8 he appeared surprisingly at the head of a delegation to the Chancellor (Place, postscript of letter to Hume, 2 May 1835, *ibid.*, f. 45).

[92] *Weekly Chronicle*, 18 Dec. 1836. The Association's own estimate of 300 petitions was probably exaggerated. There is a card printed by the Association with this estimate in Place Newspaper Collection, Set 70, f. 301.

[93] For a sampling of nine petition forms, all originating with the Association, see Place Newspaper Collection, Set 70, f. 299.

[94] Testimony of William E. Hickson before the *S.C. on Newspaper Stamps* (1851), p. 465, q. 3181; Brougham, "Taxes on Knowledge," p. 128.

make." [95] To counteract widely-circulated reports that the government was planning to reduce the duty, petitions demanding *total* repeal of the tax were drawn up and forwarded to both Houses of Parliament. A modest subscription campaign was also undertaken to defray the expenses of the Association.[96] The ultra-conservative *Courier,* not surprisingly, described the Crown and Anchor assemblage as "of the most revolutionary tendency" and warned the upper and middle classes that they "had better take their ground in time, they may lose their all." [97]

The committee also attempted to establish provincial branches in order to promote more effectively the growing agitation. Despite claims by Place that such branches were set up in Birmingham, Glasgow, and Coventry, this objective does not appear to have been successful.[98] In Brentford, preliminary meetings were held for the purpose of forming such an association but there is no evidence to indicate that such an organization was successfully established.[99] Likewise, although working-class representatives convened in Glasgow in order to endorse the activities of the Association, no Scottish repeal organizations appear to have been established during 1835.[100] Even in Newcastle-upon-Tyne, where a meeting was officially summoned by the Mayor to protest against this "obnoxious, political, ignorance-perpetrating tax," a repeal association does not seem to have been formed.[101] Thus in spite of scores of meetings in provincial urban centers,

[95] Hickson described the meeting as "the most effective one . . . yet held" (letter to Place, 20 July 1835, Place Newspaper Collection, Set 70, f. 239). For a report of Brougham's speech, see the *Times,* 20 July 1835. The *Courier,* a Tory journal, commented: "Except the little clique which has the ―――― for its head and Lord Brougham for its tail, no individual in the country wishes any change in the existing law" (18 July 1835).

[96] Place, "The Taxes on Knowledge" (*R. Pamphlet,* No. 8), pp. 8–11.

[97] *Courier,* 20 July 1835.

[98] *Manchester Advertiser,* 23 May 1835; Place, letter to Hume, 12 May 1835, Place Papers, Add. MSS 35,150 f. 49.

[99] *Glasgow Argus,* 8 June 1835.

[100] Speech of John Tait, as reported in *ibid.,* 4 June 1835.

[101] A posting bill advertising the Newcastle meeting is in Place Newspaper Collection, Set 70, f. 213.

the roots of the middle-class repeal agitation remained firmly grounded in the activities of London radicals. And within London working-class activists who agitated for repeal continued to give support to their own leaders and largely to ignore the middle-class campaign.

During 1836 the activities of the committee were expanded considerably. Although the same persons directed the movement, its scope was broadened and the public response was substantially larger.[102] Blank petition forms were again directed to leading reformers in London and the provinces, and the number of petitions forwarded to Parliament during 1836 was approximately four times greater than it had been in the preceding year.[103] The public meetings sponsored by the Association increased from an estimated thirty-five in 1835 to more than one hundred during the spring and summer of 1836.[104]

During the spring of 1836 several meetings of major importance were organized by the committee. The most publicized gathering took place at the Guildhall in March. A "respectable and orderly assemblage" of over five thousand persons, constituting in the words of one participant "the largest public meeting we remember in the City of London," gathered to hear Hume, O'Connell, Roebuck, Molesworth, Grote, Wakley, and other M.P.'s attack the record of the Melbourne government on the newspaper issue.[105] The unstamped press received some predictable censure, and the tone of several of the speeches was restrained. But on the whole, the occasion was conducive to emotional oratory. The recent conviction on dubious legal grounds of John Cleave, a working-class publisher, had aroused excitement,

[102] For a list of the committee of the Association, as of January 1836, see Hickson, *Taxes on Knowledge*, p. 2 n.

[103] Place, letter to [Birkbeck?], [March 1836?], Place Newspaper Collection, Set 70, ff. 429–432.

[104] *Weekly Chronicle*, 18 Dec. 1836. For an estimate of the number of signatures on petition forms during each of the two years, see Maccoby, *English Radicalism*, p. 147.

[105] *Spectator*, 12 March 1836; Hickson, *Mister Spring Rice*, p. 6; *Morning Chronicle*, 10 March 1836; *Weekly True Sun*, 13 March 1836.

and O'Connell, conciliatory heretofore on the issue of repeal, accused the whigs of "tyranny." The Irish leader declaimed: "I am a Radical, and shall have [the newspaper tax] out by the roots. . . . There is no spot on the face of the globe where tyranny now reigns triumphant that shall not, when knowledge is sent forth, be freed from the fell monster." [106] Hume and several other speakers orated in similar fashion causing the *Radical*, a stamped newspaper, to categorize the proceedings as "the first national convention of democracy." [107]

The impact of this and other London meetings during the early spring probably hastened Spring Rice's decision to reduce the newspaper tax, a decision that was announced officially on March 15. Such gatherings also helped to temper working-class resentment, as a leader from *Cleave's Weekly Police Gazette*, commenting on the Guildhall assemblage, makes clear: "A while ago, none but those who wanted cheap newspapers for themselves called out for the abolition of the tax; but their cry has been so loud and long, and withal so just and reasonable, that they have at length enlisted the sympathies of almost all classes in the community." [108]

Provincial activity was quickened as well during the spring of 1836. In January a vigorous demand for total repeal of the newspaper duty was made by Place in a widely-circulated essay entitled "A Repeal of the Stamp Duty on Newspapers" which appeared in Roebuck's *Pamphlets for the People*. Place castigated reformers for their apparent willingness to accept a partial reduction of the tax. The essay provided a focal point for the Association's provincial efforts.[109]

[106] *Radical*, 13 March 1836.   [107] *Ibid.*

[108] *Cleave's Weekly Police Gazette*, 5 March 1836.

[109] In the spring of 1836 Place also wrote a series of articles for the *Radical*, a newly established stamped newspaper. Several of these were reprinted as 2*d.* pamphlets and disseminated by the Association. See Francis Place, *The Stamp Tax Bill* (London: G. Morgan, 1836); Place, *The Stamp Duty on Newspapers* (London: G. Morgan, 1836). Copies of these pamphlets, originally in the possession of Hume, are in University College, London.

Shortly after the pamphlet was circulated, Place and his supporters commenced a correspondence with provincial reformers.
This was predictably unsuccessful in eliciting subscriptions, but it
did lead to the requisitioning of a large number of public meetings. In Nottingham local reformers persuaded the Mayor to
summon a meeting at which a repeal petition was circulated, and
in Kingston-upon-Hull the Town Clerk, responding to a similar
requisition, convened a gathering at which several repeal petitions were approved.[110] Newcastle-upon-Tyne reformers, at a
meeting summoned by the Mayor, petitioned for repeal on the
ground that the stamp duty "places the power of the Periodical
Press in the hands of a few Interested Persons supported by the
richer classes only, and interested, or supposing themselves to be
interested, in narrowing or distorting the Political Knowledge
and views of the great mass of the People of England." [111]

The approximately seven hundred reformers gathered at
Salford passed a resolution suggesting that the government, in
order to make repeal viable financially, agree "to abolish all un-
necessary offices and the sinecures in the state, to economise its
expenditure by rigid retrenchment, and thus lighten the heavy
burdens of the people." In Bradford an assemblage of workers
and propertied reformers, including the town constable, passed a
similar resolution endorsing repeal as the best means of eliminating "vice, crime, and misery." Although attendance at the meeting was reportedly small, an estimated six thousand signatures
were affixed to a repeal petition.[112] Petitions were likewise forwarded to Parliament from meetings held almost simultaneously
in Glasgow, Leeds, Leicester, Liverpool, Manchester, Edinburgh, and other major industrial and urban centers.[113]

[110] John Clayton, letter to Place, 20 Jan. 1836, Place Newspaper Collection,
Set 70, ff. 321–324; *ibid.*, 17 Feb. 1836, ff. 359–361; report from the *Hull
Advertiser*, as cited in the *Public Ledger*, 15 Feb. 1836.

[111] A handbill asking for signatures is in Place Newspaper Collection, Set 70,
f. 365; *Hetherington's Twopenny Dispatch*, 5 March 1836.

[112] *Leeds Times*, 5 March 1836.

[113] *Radical*, 13 March 1836; *Cleave's Weekly Police Gazette*, 20 Feb. 1836;
Leicester Corporation and Parochial Reformer, 29 Feb. 1836; *Manchester*

Almost invariably the civic officers of the town presided at these meetings and "respectable" elements predominated. But in several instances the latter were challenged by working-class radicals who sought unsuccessfully to carry "extreme" resolutions supporting the dissemination of illegal newspapers. In Leeds, for example, a tenuous unity on the issue was maintained only when working-class reformers agreed not to press for adoption of their resolutions.[114] In Lynn, Norfolk, such unity collapsed entirely when the presence of a vendor of unstamped newspapers at a repeal meeting provoked confusion. A reformer named Towell admitted, amidst shouts and protests, that "he should not have attended the meeting if he thought it connected with the dealers in unstamped papers, which he neither read nor purchased." [115]

Despite this accelerated outburst of activity by the Association, contact with working-class reformers in London, Scotland, and the provinces remained minimal. William Lovett, who was active in London working-class politics, implored his followers in January 1836, to assist the Association in the "holy cause" of repeal, but there is no evidence to indicate that this verbal exhortation was translated into meaningful political activity, either in the metropolis or in the provinces.[116] On the contrary, it is reasonably certain that the Association's influence remained limited to middle-class reformers. During February 1836, for example, two

Advertiser, 6 Feb. 1836. The conservative *New Monthly Magazine* sought to convince its readers that about a "half-dozen" persons were responsible for all this activity. Singling out Hume, Bowring, Wakley, Grote, Roebuck, Buckingham, and O'Connell for special censure, it claimed that "it is merely their power of ubiquity that gives the semblance of public sentiment" (XLVI [1836], 487–488).

[114] See the letter from "Bobadil" in *Cleave's Weekly Police Gazette*, 5 March 1836. The author maintains that "the unenfranchised have a right to break the laws made by force and against their will and interest, for the purpose of keeping them in ignorance and slavery."

[115] From an unidentified newsclipping [1836], Place Newspaper Collection, Set 70, f. 405.

[116] Lovett, letter to Place, 5 Jan. 1836, *ibid.*, ff. 305–307.

meetings were held in the Scottish town of Kilmarnock to demand repeal of the newspaper duty. According to an account in *Cleave's Weekly Police Gazette*, one meeting was attended by local operatives and the other by more affluent reformers who looked to Robert Wallace, the local radical M.P., for political leadership.[117] The London Association may have initiated the latter; it almost certainly had no more than a very tenuous connection with the former.

A similar pattern prevailed in other cities. In Manchester at least three repeal meetings were held during the spring of 1836. The chief magistrate presided at one, and prominent middle-class reformers, including Archibald Prentice, the future Corn Law reformer, attended. The other two meetings, however, were initiated by the Manchester Radical Association, a working-class organization, and by a group of carpenters.[118] In Greenock several propertied reformers established a committee to agitate for repeal of the taxes on knowledge. This committee probably had contact with Place's Association, but it almost certainly had no substantial working-class support.

Thus despite a large-scale campaign during the parliamentary sessions of 1835 and 1836 the extent of the Association's influence was considerably more limited than the scope of its activity would indicate. It made a substantial dent in public opinion and clearly stimulated some "pressure from without." And its activities represented undoubtedly the most effective contribution by parliamentary reformers to the entire repeal campaign. Middle-class apathy remained widespread, nonetheless, as the following analysis by Edward Rainford, a colleague of Place's, so amply demonstrates:

You recollect the story told by Richard Taylor of a man at a public meeting bawling "Taxes on Knowledge damned," (meaning that he did not care a damn about them)—there are few professing Radicals

[117] *Cleave's Weekly Police Gazette*, 6 Feb. 1836.
[118] *Radical*, 13 March 1836.

hereabouts tho' they are very noisy about comparative nothings, who would not say "ditto" to the fellow's damn.[119]

And unless the reserves of working-class enthusiasm could be tapped, a massive national agitation could not be launched successfully. This the Association failed to do. As a result, working-class repeal sentiment continued to gravitate further toward those who were directing the illegal war of the unstamped.

[119] Letter to Place, 6 Jan. 1836, Place Newspaper Collection, Set 70, f. 308.

CHAPTER 5

The Working-Class Ideology

The elements comprising the working-class repeal ideology differed significantly from those of the parliamentary reformers. The working-class ideological spectrum involved a much greater intensity of feeling and emotion and a deeper personalization of the newspaper issue. As one witness told a parliamentary committee, the working classes "regard the stamp on newspapers as something in the light of a personal enemy . . . the stamp is personified by them."[1] Thus for the committed amongst the laborers, newspaper repeal took on a near-messianic quality.

An analysis of working-class thought concerning repeal suggests a threefold division: cheap political knowledge viewed as a symbol, an intensity of "class" feeling, and the ideal of a free press. As suggested previously, support for the principle of violation of the law was the major presupposition that underlay the total range of working-class commitment on this issue. Although the degree of commitment to an illegal press varied, nearly all working-class reformers were in agreement with the sentiment, expressed by Carlile, that "the most virtuous patriotism of the present day is a resistance to bad laws. More good is

[1] Testimony of C. D. Collet, *S.C. on Newspaper Stamps* (1851), p. 156, q. 952.

likely to be worked through this medium than through any other." [2]

To most working-class radicals, the specific demands espoused by the illegal periodicals were less important than the fact of their existence. For by challenging overtly the "monopoly" possessed by the "unprincipled scribblers" of the stamped press, they were, in effect, serving as a "workingman's press." Their function, as the only valid "mirror of the opinions of the people," was to record "the movements of the mass towards that point in the education of the mind when the many will be emancipated from the rascality of the few." [3] Thus the twin assumptions that the law should be violated and that unstamped newspapers should be supported placed the consensus of working-class attitudes on the repeal issue in direct, unqualified opposition to the opinions held by parliamentary reformers.

THE SYMBOLIC SIGNIFICANCE OF CHEAP KNOWLEDGE

A distributor of unstamped newspapers, James Reeve, declared in 1835:

Were I to give over selling the Unstamped, *my customers declare that they will get them of some other person; as they were determined to have an Untaxed Newspaper, even if they subscribed among themselves to purchase the materials for printing, for cheap knowledge they would have.*[4]

Another vendor justified his violation of the stamp laws in the following terms:

[2] *Gauntlet*, 10 Feb. 1833, Thomas Macconnell, a working-class lecturer, asserted: "It was *resistance* mainly that had done the business—(cheers)—in Ireland, relative to tithes; and it would do it in England relative to the taxes on knowledge" (*Cleave's Weekly Police Gazette*, 16 May 1835).

[3] Rev. Dr. Wade speaking at a meeting held on 18 Jan. 1836, from a news-clipping in Place Newspaper Collection, Set 70, f. 337; George Edmonds, in the *Weekly Herald*, 14 Aug. 1836.

[4] As quoted in Chapman, " 'Cheap Knowledge They Will Have'—Reeve's Application" (*R. Pamphlet*, No. 35), p. 15.

I stands here, your worships, upon right and principle, on behalf of the poor working *unedicated* classes of the Country. They are called ignorant, but what is the cause of their ignorance? *Why, the tax which prevents them getting information.* Your Worships pretty well knows the reason them in power puts on the tax; it is to keep the poor from knowing their rights; for if poor working people knowed their rights, they would soon annihilate the corrupt institutions that oppress them.[5]

The statements of these obscure "victims" of the newspaper prosecutions help to illuminate a major motivation behind the working-class movement for repeal, namely, the passionate determination to attain "cheap knowledge" or "cheap information." [6] These phrases, and others of a similar nature, became shibboleths during the newspaper agitation.[7] On the one hand, such slogans had roots in a concrete series of changes that were broadening the intellectual horizons of the uneducated masses. But they also came to symbolize and articulate a host of ill-defined grievances; in this capacity, they provided a symbolic dimension to the newspaper agitation that gave it significance beyond its immediate scope.

The working-class demand for political knowledge reached unprecedented proportions during the 1830's. It produced and was in turn the product of increasing literacy, as well as of a host of related cultural phenomena. Reading rooms where newspapers could be read at a charge of 1*d.* per hour were opened, discussion clubs and mutual improvement societies formed, and well-known literary and political writings reprinted voluminously in weekly

[5] Report quoted in *Spectator*, 13 Aug. 1831.

[6] Louis James suggests perceptively that this demand resulted from the fragmentation of an older working-class culture impacting against newer urban values (*Fiction for the Working Man, 1830–1850* [London: Oxford University Press, 1963], pp. 28–29).

[7] The term "cheap knowledge" was employed, for example, in a working-class leader on the Manchester election of 1832 (*Poor Man's Advocate*, 8 Sept. 1832). Similarly, Scottish working-class radicals, meeting at Kirkintilloch, called for "cheaper instruction" (*Glasgow Argus*, 22 Dec. 1834).

[117]

numbers.[8] Of significance was the fact that working-class initiative was directly responsible for many of these cultural developments. An increased self-consciousness was rapidly spreading among the laboring population, and the publication of large numbers of illegal ultra-radical periodicals during the years 1830–1836 accelerated this process significantly.

Working-class reformers regarded penny newspapers as a "compensation" for their exclusion from the franchise and as the primary means by which a minimal degree of cheap knowledge could be communicated. The removal of all financial restrictions on the press was, therefore, particularly crucial to them. They felt that the illegal journals which were circulating in defiance of the law were contributing to the removal of "ignorance and misery" and that, so long as the newspaper stamp remained, great social transformations were unlikely to be consummated.[9] The removal of the taxes on knowledge would, in their view, generate a dramatic increase in the number of cheap journals, and desirable changes, many of a radical complexion, would necessarily follow.

The kinds of changes that were envisaged in the absence of press restrictions took on varied hues, depending upon the particular visions of the leading personalities in the campaign. Since the degree of personal vision was often so marked, the agitation for cheap knowledge came to possess symbolic as well as concrete attributes. Thus during the 1830's repeal of the taxes on knowledge performed a political function for many similar to that which adherence to the workingman's Charter did during the 1840's.

For large numbers of laborers an untaxed press came to represent abstractly the ideal of a better society, and it clearly transcended all other specific issues. Many reformers assumed

[8] For a penetrating analysis of the effects of expanding literacy see Williams, *Long Revolution;* Harrison, *Learning and Living,* pp. 18–19. The latter stresses the poor quality of much of this new literacy.

[9] Speech by James Watson to celebrate the anniversary of the French Revolution of 1830, as reported in *Poor Man's Guardian,* 6 Aug. 1831.

implicitly that the desiderata of an improved social system would
follow at once upon this change, since "the brutal tyranny of a
single man or of any set of men now-a-day could not possibly
exist a single week, under the omnipotent cannonade of the untaxed press." [10] In the words of one leading reformer:

An unstamped press was everything for the people. . . . Give them
this and they would ask nothing more in the shape of favour, either
from Whigs or Tories; the people with the possession of this would
themselves effect all that they desired . . . without an unstamped
press, they were slaves.[11]

A more radical reformer employed poetic license to express similar thoughts:

Ah! Sanguinary traitors, well ye know we want but knowledge to direct the blow! That taught by an unshackled honest press, the people
quietly would *command* redress for all their wrongs! [12]

In the narrowly political sphere, most working-class radicals
foresaw behind repeal of the newspaper stamp the prospect of a
democratic society based upon universal manhood suffrage, secret
ballot, and annual parliaments. Unstamped journals, such as the
Poor Man's Guardian, the *Cosmopolite,* and the *Man,* implied
that such a democratic utopia would be one of the initial fruits of
an unstamped press. It was suggested that the dissemination of
knowledge would, by itself, so drastically transform public opinion, that opposition to political equality would dissolve. The "two
grand props of all safe human government," universal suffrage
and a free press, would serve as complementary emancipatory
elements.

[10] George Edmonds, *The English Revolution . . . Addressed to My Unrepresented Fellow Millions* (London: William Strange, 1831), p. 6.

[11] Speech by John Bell at an Islington meeting, from an unidentified newsclipping, *c.* May 1836, Place Newspaper Collection, Set 70, f. 523.

[12] George Petrie, "Equality" in *The Works of George Petrie: Comprising
Equality, and Other Poems: Select Extracts from the Letters of Agrarius: With
a Biographical Memoir of the Author* (London: John Cleave, [1841]), p. 9.

R. E. Lee, the editor of the *Man,* articulated this viewpoint when he wrote that "Universal Liberty and Happiness" would follow automatically upon removal of the oppressive newspaper tax.[13] John Bell, linking repeal similarly to universal suffrage, urged that "the emancipation of the press involved the liberation of the whole human race," and with an air of seeming reasonableness, Bronterre O'Brien, the future Chartist leader and editor of several unstamped newspapers, traced a similar connection: "With representatives in the Press, we shall have representatives in the corporations and popular societies; and with representation in these, the transition will not be impossible as regards the House of Commons." [14] It was assumed unquestioningly by many laborers that, with the press liberated, a "reign of justice" would envelop British political institutions, and that the publishers of unstamped newspapers would be recognized universally as "the deliverers of the human mind from one of its greatest political difficulties." [15]

The tax on newspapers also acquired symbolic attributes in the social and economic spheres. "Let the stamp laws be once abolished . . . ," the editor of the *Man* intoned, "and internal discord, commotion, and strife, will disappear forever." [16] Similar sentiments were echoed repeatedly throughout the campaign. An

[13] R. E. Lee, *A Whisper to the Whigs, or, What Is Treason? Answered by Lords Grey, Brougham, and Company: His Majesty's Whig Tinkers of the "Glorious Constitution," and Military Law Makers to the People of Ireland* (London: R. E. Lee, 1833), p. 1.

[14] Speech by John Bell at a meeting of the Southwark Radical Association, as cited in *Cleave's Weekly Police Gazette,* 23 Jan. 1836; Thomas Potts, "Address to the Unemployed Artizans of London," *Radical Reformer,* 28 Oct. 1831; Bronterre's letter, No. 3, *Hetherington's Twopenny Dispatch,* Vol. II, No. 84.

[15] *Le Bonnet Rouge,* 16 Feb. 1833; "The London Scribe to His Friends in the Country," *Political Register,* 15 Aug. 1835.

[16] *Man,* intro. to Vol. I. Manchester operatives, petitioning the government in 1830 for removal of the taxes, claimed: "Give us knowledge, and we will answer for the peace of the country" (*Prompter,* 11 Dec. 1830). A working-class reformer named William Hoare maintained that an unstamped press "will emancipate the whole human family from the reign of ignorance and slavery in which they are now benighted" (*Radical,* 5 June 1836).

"Operatives Association" of Warrington petitioned for repeal in the conviction that "one great cause of the misery and crime prevailing among the working classes of these kingdoms, is the *want of useful, moral, and political knowledge.*" Employing similar phraseology, the Manchester Radical Association, a working-class association, declared in a petition that "national crime, poverty, and degradation" would be obliterated if the newspaper tax was removed." [17] Statements that were circulated by the National Union of the Working Classes in August 1831 demanded on behalf of the people, "a full, fair and free opportunity of a community of sentiment in the circulation of cheap knowledge, whereby the foundation of crime will be sapped by the removal of ignorance, and the extending of information." [18]

More specific social and economic changes were also anticipated. John Cleave, a leading publisher of unstamped journals and a disciple of Cobbett, envisaged an end to the national debt, to the speculative paper money system, and to all taxes that bore heavily upon the productive classes, when once the stamp duty was removed.[19] Feargus O'Connor, the future leader of "physical force" Chartism, predicted somewhat incoherently that an unstamped press would generate "the destruction of all corporate abuses, and all religious establishments and monopolies," as well as the permanent prosperity of the people.[20] One convicted journalist suggested that the illegal newspapers which he published gave the workers an insight into present social inequalities whereby "the whole working population . . . are made the daily victims of ignorance, and robbed of their wages by an

[17] *Cleave's Weekly Police Gazette,* 16 May 1835, 13 Feb. 1836; petition from "Manchester carpenters and joiners," *Manchester Advertiser,* 6 Feb. 1836.
[18] Quoted in *Poor Man's Guardian,* 20 Aug. 1831.
[19] Cleave's speech to the N.U.W.C., as reported in *Poor Man's Guardian,* 22 Feb. 1834. George Condy, a Manchester radical, foresaw an end to the national debt if the press was unshackled (speech at Stockport, as reported in *Manchester Advertiser,* 6 Feb. 1836).
[20] Newsclipping, Place Newspaper Collection, Set 70, f. 205; speech by Keene at the Rotunda, *Republican,* 28 May 1831.

innumerable host of legalized thieves and robbers." [21] Another prominent "victim" avowed that his objective in selling illicit journals was to demonstrate to the working classes how "they might extricate themselves from their degraded state of thral-dom, and place society upon a basis where every individual member of the social brotherhood, should enjoy his just rights and no more." [22]

The principles of economic co-operation were a part of working-class social thought, and they performed a "utopian" role that was comparable to the doctrines of political economy for middle-class reformers. Not surprisingly, many working-class radicals conceived of an end to the competitive economic system as soon as the newspaper duties were repealed. They tacitly assumed that only through the mechanism of an unstamped press could the "productive" or laboring classes, who generated the wealth of society, be made cognizant of their grievances, thus preparing the way for a substantive economic transformation. Bronterre O'Brien, the most articulate working-class publicist to emerge during the repeal agitation, documented this important theme:

Government have ultimately no other basis of support than public opinion. Be they ever so complicated or simple, be they monarchical or Republican, they stand or fall, move retrograde or forward, solely in obedience to Public Opinion. It is therefore of vital importance to gather up this Public Opinion . . . and make it bear irresistibly on the government, by the weight, unity of direction, and simultaneous action of all its parts.[23]

Thomas Macconnell, a well-known lecturer, invoked the virtues of an approaching co-operative millenium. He suggested that once the taxes on knowledge were removed:

[21] *Trial and Self-Defence of Alexander Campbell, Operative, before the Exchequer Court, Edinburgh, for Printing and Publishing "The Tradesman,"* *Contrary to the Infamous Gagging Act* (Glasgow: W. and W. Miller, 1835), p. 7.

[22] Account of Joshua Hobson's trial, as reported in *Voice of the West Riding,* 3 Aug. 1833.

[23] Bronterre O'Brien, letter to Robert Owen, 27 May 1832, cited in Frank Podmore, *Robert Owen: A Biography* (London: Hutchinson, 1906) II, 430.

Peace will follow with her olive, and plenty with her horn; profuse of comfort and prodigal good the arts and sciences will follow in their train. These universal facts when men are induced to walk in their light, will lead into community, in which the science of human nature, and the science of society will be developed, and the millenium, anticipations of which have floated in men's minds through all past times, will be realised. The dream of the ages will be broken.

This theme was echoed in varying degrees by Robert Hammersley, the Rev. Dr. Wade, and other working-class reformers. Hammersley situated the predicted social transformations within a context of worldwide conflict between the aristocracy and the "popular power." Wade believed that a new era was imminent but that "the most odious of all the numerous and hidden progeny," that is, the taxes on knowlege, had to be removed so that England could develop her "mental and physical resources to a very great extent." [24] William Lovett, the future Chartist leader, agitated similarly for repeal as the best means of bringing about a more just distribution of property along co-operative lines. "If cheap knowledge were universally distributed," he wrote, "it would work its way in effecting a more equitable and useful distribution of that property which now lay in great heaps." [25]

Thus several fundamental components of the working-class re-

[24] Thomas Macconnell, *A Lecture on the Signs of the Times: Delivered in the Great Lecture Room of Robert Owen's Institution, Gray's Inn Road, on the Morning of November 18, 1832* (London: Eamonson, 1832) pp. 1–3; Robert Hammersley, *Hints to the Young Men of Great Britain, on the Progress of Political Opinion* (London: Wakelin, 1836) pp. 1–2; Rev. Arthur S. Wade, *A Voice from the Church: or, a Sermon (with a Few Notes and Amplifications) on Church Reform, Pledges, Cheap Government—Cheap Justice—Cheap Food —Cheap Knowledge—and on a Cheap and Efficient Medium of Exchange . . .* (London: James Ridgway, 1832), pp. 20–21.

[25] *Cleave's Weekly Police Gazette*, 16 May 1835. See also Lovett, "What do the Millions Want?—and What Can They Do to Obtain It?" *"Destructive,"* 11 May 1833, 1 June 1833. Lovett urged abstinence from drinking and the purchase of unstamped newspapers in the absence of a free press (letter in *Poor Man's Guardian*, 2 March 1833). See also the Address published by the British Association for Promoting Co-operative Knowledge, as printed in *Poor Man's Guardian*, 30 July 1831.

peal ideology were at variance with middle-class radical assumptions. The apocalyptic social, political, and economic implications which the phrase "cheap knowledge" connoted to the former was virtually incomprehensible to the latter. Despite this sharp division, however, strong "class" feelings were largely absent from this aspect of the working-class intellectual syndrome. The abiding element was a faith in the power of the printed word, a conception that was to be channeled into "moral force" Chartism at the end of the decade.

CLASS FEELING GENERATED BY THE REPEAL MOVEMENT

The working-class movement for repeal of the taxes on knowledge also comprehended an increasingly sharp degree of class bitterness. In its most extreme manifestation, this class feeling occasionally assumed a near-revolutionary coloring. Thus many of its elements directly prefigured "physical force" Chartism. Not surprisingly, the presence of strong class antipathy reduced significantly the possibility of a coalescence between middle- and working-class reformers on the newspaper issue.

The basis of this intense approach to the question of press reform had its roots in previous "betrayals," notably the Reform Act of 1832, which had intensified class hostility by failing to meet the political demands of the laborers. As a result, working-class reformers felt increasingly isolated from the mainstream of governmental power. They believed that neither the Tory nor Whig parties were prepared to take any notice of their grievances.

This sense of class "alienation" was sharpened considerably by the frequent prosecutions of illegal newspapers from 1830 on, under circumstances that seemed discretionary and arbitrary. For example, although the *Penny Magazine* was illegal since it possessed an identical weekly format, consecutive dating and pagination, and news accounts of recent origins, it was never even threatened with prosecution. On the other hand, scores of un-

stamped journals of considerably humbler paternity were ha-
rassed by the Stamp Office, a situation that caused one reformer
to declare contemptuously that the law was interpreted "in a
favorable sense, when Brougham and Canterbury, and in a hostile [sense] when Cleave and Hetherington are offenders." [26]
Another repeal spokesman categorized more militantly this dis-
criminatory use of enforcement powers as involving "the brute
force of government against the working classes, who wish to obtain cheap knowledge." [27] Still another reformer who was active
in illegal journalism accused the Whigs of "treason" for their
discretionary approach to the law. He concluded that the people
had a responsibility to respond to this "subversion" of the constitution by violating not only the statutes affixing a duty on newspapers but all other parliamentary enactments.[28]

The accumulation of prior resentments, combined with hostility stimulated by the discretionary enforcement of the taxes on
knowledge, caused many reformers to view the question of the
newspaper duties in strident class terms. Some alluded to a direct
confrontation between the poor and "rich capitalists" who
monopolized covertly the instruments of economic and political
power. Others attacked the "stamped gentry" against whom their
untaxed journals were competing. The former, in the words of
one journalist, were "associates of noblemen's fat footmen, loiter-
ers at the inner doors of the Treasury, and pickers up of pro-

[26] Crawfurd, *Taxes on Knowledge*, p. 37; Crawfurd, *Newspaper Stamp*, p.
22. The invocation of the Archbishop of Canterbury's name was an allusion
to the *Saturday Magazine*, a 1*d.* journal published by the Society for the Propagation of Christian Knowledge and similar in format to the *Penny Magazine*.

[27] Speech by Macconnell at a meeting of the Southwark Radical Association,
Weekly Times, 28 Feb. 1836. The *Church Examiner and Ecclesiastical Record*,
a working-class journal that was prosecuted by the Stamp Office, queried: "Why
was not the same measure of justice or tyranny (whichever it may be called)
applied to the Society of Useful Knowledge? Why not to the rich and the
wealthy, as well as to the poor and unsupported?" (newscutting of September
1832, Place Newspaper Collection, Set 57, f. 217). The *True Sun*, a stamped
newspaper, maintained that "the administration of Justice is thus known to be
tainted at its source" (10 Sept. 1832).

[28] Lee, *Whisper to the Whigs*, pp. 7–8.

found secrets from the porters and 'menials' of the ministry." [29]

It was avowed by working-class opponents of the newspaper stamp that "the poor have as much right to knowledge as the rich have" and that retention of the taxes demonstrated that there was "one law for the rich and another for the poor." [30] Joshua Hobson, publisher of the unstamped *Voice of the West Riding* and a prominent factory reformer, propounded one version of this argument at his trial on charges of vending illegal newspapers. He contended that he was being prosecuted solely because "they are rich—I am poor." "The man that would tamely submit to such infamous enactments as these," Hobson stated, "ought to have the word 'slave' branded in his forehead, and a whip placed in the hand of every honest man to lash the rascal naked through the world." [31]

Deriving similar advantage from the publicity accorded to a governmental prosecution, Cleave addressed those present at his 1836 trial in the following manner:

The people were determined to be represented in the press as well as in the legislature, and to be no longer contented with a system which applied learning and intelligence to the worst of purposes, making the poor poorer, and the rich more rich.[32]

With greater bitterness, a fellow-reformer suggested that the revenue "problem" could be solved even if all of the taxes on knowledge were removed:

[29] *Cleave's Weekly Police Gazette,* 19 Dec. 1835.

[30] Speech by Cleave at an N.U.W.C. meeting, as reported in *Poor Man's Guardian,* 19 Nov. 1831; speech by Julian Hibbert at an N.U.W.C. meeting, as reported in *ibid.,* 10 Dec. 1831; *Working Man's Friend,* 22 Dec. 1832. A corollary of the above thesis was that "the poor have as much right to knowledge as the rich" (petition from the "mechanics and labourers" of Winchester, reprinted in *Poor Man's Guardian,* 21 Jan. 1832).

[31] For an account of Hobson's trial see the *Halifax Express,* a copy of which is in Place Newspaper Collection, Set 70, f. 304; *Leeds Times,* cited in *Cleave's Weekly Police Gazette,* 30 Jan. 1836; *Voice of the West Riding,* 10 Aug. 1833.

[32] From the report of Cleave's trial in *Cleave's Weekly Police Gazette,* 13 Feb. 1836.

Let [the government] apply to those for whom alone it exists; let it apply to the upper and middle classes, who alone have any interest in the institutions of the country. Let it apply to such fellows as Rothschild and Goldsmid—to the great commercial and manufacturing interests—to the lords and lordlings of the country.[33]

Such descriptive phrases for the 4*d.* stamp duty as "mark of the beast" and "that blood-mark, that knowledge prohibiting biped" entered the working-class political vocabulary.[34] And the extreme class bitterness engendered by the newspaper issue is also seen in the coruscating satire which the unstamped press employed at the expense of the Whig government. One illicit newspaper acclaimed: "It is not to be permitted to vulgar mortals like us to know or speak out what our rulers may be doing. Their sublime movements are wisely concealed from the public gaze, except to such as can pay *four pence* for every peep." [35] Another suggested that, as a consequence of the newspaper tax, politics had become "that sacred science, that inviolate subject, reserved for the exclusive consideration of the wealthy aristocrat." [36]

This class ingredient in the newspaper agitation frightened many parliamentary reformers and it imparted a deeper intensity to the working-class resistance to the stamp laws. Only a segment of the working-class support for the war of the unstamped remained grounded in a moderate, pragmatic temperament. Carlile, Lovett, James Watson, and several others, for example, reluctantly endorsed violation of the law *on this particular issue* only, in the absence of other effective means of expression.[37] But

[33] O'Brien, writing in *Hetherington's Twopenny Dispatch,* 26 March 1836.

[34] Letter from "A Friend to Liberty," *Poor Man's Guardian,* 20 Aug. 1831; letter from "A Man of Finsbury," *Political Register,* 22 Aug. 1835. See also Carlile's speech at the Rotunda, as reported in *Prompter,* 20 Aug. 1831. A poster entitled "BLACK LIST!! TAXES ON KNOWLEDGE!!!", which attempted to prevent any M.P.'s from voting to perpetuate "THE MARK OF THE BEAST" was circulated. A copy is in Place Newspaper Collection, Set 70, ff. 171–175.

[35] *Workman's Expositor,* 7 Jan. 1832.

[36] *United Trades' Co-operative Journal,* 18 Sept. 1830.

[37] See Lovett's article in the *Poor Man's Guardian,* 24 Dec. 1831 (incorrectly dated 25 Dec. 1831); for an expression of Watson's relatively "moderate"

more aggressive elements within the working-class spectrum pursued the theme of resistance to the law in strident class terms.

These elements interpreted their isolation from the sources of political power as a signification that "laws," particularly the newspaper enactments, were founded entirely upon "might" or "brute force." [38] By this view, a small, selfish minority had, through physical force and manipulation of the sources of propaganda and communication, imposed its demands upon the unrepresented majority. In the words of an extreme radical, the newspaper acts were merely the "impudent edicts of a mock-representative, defunct, condemned Legislature" and should be violated, since the offence would be "committed against the *arbitrary will* of *individuals,* or at most, of the 'society' whom such individuals profess to represent." [39] "The unenfranchised have a right," wrote a correspondent in *Cleave's Weekly Police Gazette,* "to break the laws made by force and against their will and interest, for the purpose of keeping them in ignorance and slavery," and another journalist, in defence of such behavior, proclaimed: "We laugh at men who can assume gravity of phiz, and taunt us with the shame of deeds wherein we glory." [40] William Benbow, one of the more radical participants in the repeal movement, advocated a massive violation of the laws, to be complemented by a "grand national holiday," or general strike:

views, see [James Watson], *An Address to the Members of Trade Unions, and the Working Classes Generally: Being an Exposition of the Relative Situation, Condition, and Future Prospects of Working People in England, Scotland, and Ireland* . . . (London: James Watson, 1833), pp. 42–43. A copy of this rare tract is in the Goldsmiths' Library, University of London.

[38] See the speech by Hetherington at his trial for publishing illegal newspapers, as reported in *Poor Man's Guardian,* 9 and 23 July 1831. Terms such as "law" and "authority" were often set off in quotation marks by the *Poor Man's Guardian,* the *Republican, Le Bonnet Rouge,* and other unstamped papers.

[39] J. H. B. Lorymer, in *Le Bonnet Rouge,* 23 Feb. 1833; *Penny Papers for the People,* 21 May 1831.

[40] Letter from "Bobadil," *Cleave's Weekly Police Gazette,* 5 March 1836; George Edmonds, in the *Weekly Herald,* 3 July 1836.

Our Lawgivers have kept us in ignorance, for if we had knowledge we would not obey laws framed for our own destruction. Our lords and masters are doing everything that our ignorance may continue, in order that they may continue, like the lawyers of old, "to load us with burdens too grievous to be borne, which they will not touch with one of their fingers.[41]

Thus total resistance to the taxes on knowledge was endorsed as the primary sanction against governmental abuse. The hallowed phrase "Taxation without Representation is Tyranny and Ought to be Resisted" was invoked, as were the theoretical justifications for revolution offered by Locke and Paine.[42] Resolutions were carried at numerous working-class meetings that openly urged violation of the newspaper acts since, in the words of one such resolution, "infinitely more moral disgrace attaches to those who enforce and execute such odious laws . . . than to those men who violate them." [43]

Most reformers who espoused such views did not actually favor a resort to physical force. They preferred to propagandize strongly for their opinions in the penny press. But the reiterated advocacy of such doctrines created a stituation in which class violence became at least theoretically acceptable as a means for the rectification of grievances. Thus despite the lack of an appeal to overt physical violence, the climate was decidedly unpropitious for any mutual accord between parliamentary and working-class reformers.

The class element in the press agitation reinforced strongly a sense of working-class consciousness. Publishers risked imprisonment in order (in the words of a leading martyr) "to support the rights and interests of the order and class to which it is [their]

[41] William Benbow, *Grand National Holiday, and Congress of the Productive Classes* (London: William Benbow, 1831), pp. 5-6.

[42] *Poor Man's Guardian*, 22 Oct. 1831; *Voice of the People*, 19 Feb. 1831; James H. B. Lorymer, *A National Convention, the Only Proper Remedy* (London: Henry Hetherington, 1833).

[43] Meeting at Hebden Bridge, Lancashire, as reported in *Cleave's Weekly Police Gazette*, 5 March 1836.

pride and boast to belong." [44] The *Poor Man's Guardian,* a journal that was in the vanguard of the working-class agitation, described itself as the spokesman for the "poor working and oppressed *millions.*" [45] Watson's *Working Man's Friend,* a popular penny newspaper, attacked similarly "the deadly hatred this
treacherous Whig oligarchy feel toward the *Working Man's
Press.*" [46] Countless assertions and protestations of this kind,
when buttressed by radical solutions to social and economic problems, helped to forge a unified working-class outlook. Those
who bore the brunt of the struggle against the "common
enemy"—the Hetheringtons, Watsons, and Cleaves—became
working-class folk heroes.[47] Hence the path toward a distinctive
working-class literary tradition, replete with popular culture-
heroes, was partially paved in the movement against the taxes on
knowledge.

THE IDEAL OF A FREE PRESS

Belief in a free press was a cardinal tenet of British reformism
throughout the nineteenth century. It was invoked repeatedly by
persons of every political persuasion. Conservatives were no more
averse than reformers to toasting the "Liberty of the Press and
all it Stands For" at countless political banquets and testimoni-
als.[48] Furthermore, the issue of press freedom was undeniably
related to the conflict over the taxes on knowledge because, in the
absence of direct press censorship, a prosecution for violation of

[44] Joshua Hobson, in *Voice of the West Riding,* 3 Aug. 1833.

[45] *Poor Man's Guardian,* 1 Oct. 1831.

[46] *Working Man's Friend,* 12 Jan. 1833.

[47] Hetherington was described by a contemporary as "a kind of knight errant"
in the eyes of the working class (W. B. Adams ["Junius Redivivus"], *What
the People Ought to Do, in Choosing Their Representatives at the General
Election, after the Passing of the Reform Bill: A Letter Addressed to the Electors of Great Britain* [London: Effingham Wilson, 1832], pp. 14–15).

[48] The precise phrase varied. Upon occasion it was "the Liberty of the Press,
and the Education of the People." See "Report of a Free Trade Banquet," in
Glasgow Argus, 22 Jan. 1835.

the Stamp Acts remained one of the most effective means for suppressing critical dissenting opinion.

Freedom of the press was injected into the repeal compaign in innumerable ways. Working-class political unions demanded "a full restoration of the Civil and Political Rights of the Working Classes," foremost among which was press freedom. John Cleave, a prominent journalist, posed the rhetorical question that was being asked by many working-class reformers: "When we shall have got a free press, who will dare to oppress us?" [49] Hetherington, who pioneered illicit journalism and with whom Cleave worked closely, affirmed eloquently his belief in "the free exercise of the right of inquiry," and supported his intellectual commitment to this principle to the extent of three prison sentences. Acting out of the conviction that a free press was the only "effectual mode of arriving at truth" and that "public opinion shall be the only censor," Hetherington attempted to sell every type of printed material other than obscenity or works "that cast aspersions upon private character." [50] And to increase the effectiveness of the verbal onslaught against press restrictions, a *6d.* edition of Milton's *Areopagitica* was reprinted in 1835 by Carpenter and Cleave with the probable support of Hetherington as a weapon in the war of the unstamped.[51]

But despite these examples and others that could be offered, the specific ideal of freedom of the press does not appear to have

[49] *Poor Man's Guardian*, 16 July 1831; Cleave's speech at a Rotunda meeting, in *ibid.*, 30 July 1831.

[50] *A Full Report of the Trial of Henry Hetherington, on an Indictment for Blasphemy . . . for Selling Haslam's Letters to the Clergy of All Denominations: With the Whole of the Authorities Cited in the Defence, at Full Length* (London: Henry Hetherington, 1840), pp. 7, 8.

[51] John Milton, *A Speech on the Liberty of Unlicensed Printing, to the Parliament of England* (London: John Cleave, 1834). See the advertisement in *Poor Man's Guardian*, 22 Nov. 1834; *Radical*, 17 April 1836. A copy is in the British Museum. Milton's name was invoked repeatedly by reformers. In a *6d.* biography, Carpenter declaimed: "Can it be doubted . . . that he would have poured forth his eloquence against this as fervently as he did against that" (*The Life and Times of John Milton* [London: Wakelin, 1836], p. 73).

been a principal motivating factor in the repeal movement. Irrespective of the numerous eloquent tributes offered by Hickson and other parliamentary reformers to "the spirit of liberty . . . that of a free press," it did not enter significantly into the middle-class frame of reference.[52] And as a component of working-class thought, its role was only slightly larger. For most laborers, the issue of liberty of the press remained a distant abstraction. It lacked a foundation of economic or political grievance. Neither did it attach to itself the symbolic connotations acquired by the phrase "cheap knowledge." Few reformers were prepared to undergo voluntarily lengthy prison terms and substantial fines merely to give substance to this abstract ideal. Two prominent exceptions, however, were Richard Carlile and William Lovett. The thought of each was related integrally to the question of freedom of the press, and their careers left a strong imprint upon the struggle against the taxes on knowledge.

Of Richard Carlile it has been justly claimed that he accomplished "more than any other Englishman in his day for the freedom of the press." [53] His efforts to reform the obsolete laws relating to seditious libel resulted in several terms of imprisonment totaling nine years and seven months. During the war of the unstamped he played an important role, though one that did not receive public attention even in radical journalistic circles. Carlile published openly a number of illegal journals, such as the *Prompter*, the *Gauntlet*, *A Scourge for the Littleness of "Great"*

---

[52] Hickson, *Mister Spring Rice*, pp. 1–2. Thomas Wakley wrote: "The good sense of the people tells them that a nation is *not free* if its press be shackled, or if the movements of that glorious engine be restrained by the whims of an Executive Government, or by the caprice of a contemptible knot of Commissioners of Stamps" (*A Letter to the People of England, on the New Project for Gagging the Press* [London: G. Churchill, 1836], p. 24).

[53] From the D.N.B. article on Carlile by George Jacob Holyoake. The best studies of Carlile are Theophila Carlile Campbell, *The Battle of the Press as Told in the Story of the Life of Richard Carlile* (London: A and H. B. Bonner, 1899); George Jacob Holyoake, *The Life and Character of Richard Carlile* (London: J. Watson, 1849); G. D. H. Cole, *Richard Carlile, 1790–1843* (London: Victor Gollancz, 1943).

Men, and the *Isis,* and published others covertly, including the *Cosmopolite* and the *Political Soldier.*[54]

All of Carlile's journalistic activities were concentrated upon giving effect to one central idea. This was the reiterated conception that "mind must precede union, and union without the necessary preceding mind will ever be abortive. . . . Public free discussion is the only system of purification in society—the only system that abates wrong bias, and strengthens right and wrong."[55] A free press "can injure no one but those panders who prey on the vitals of their country," and free discussion, most effectively carried on in print, was, in Carlile's view, "the grand panacea for all human ills—the source of education, and the pillar of social dignity. . . . Discussion cannot be too free; cannot be carried too far; cannot take up an improper subject."[56] This supreme individualist faith linked Carlile's thought to that of the Benthamites and political economists discussed in Chapter 2. Like them, Carlile also rejected resort to physical violence as a means of rectifying grievances. He condemned the Chartist movement subsequently on the ground that "preparation of mind is a necessary preceding point. Let the people be mentally qualified for the suffrage, and it will by that time be ready for their use."[57] Furthermore, class consciousness did not comprise any significant part of his approach to reform.

But the prospect of effectuating a union between middle- and working-class reformers, with Carlile as a pivotal figure, was

---

[54] The *Isis* printed the free thought discourses of Elija Sharples, the "Lady of the Rotunda." Alexander Sommerville, who edited the *Political Soldier,* resigned after one number, refusing to accept "dictation" from Carlile (*Political Soldier,* 14 Dec. 1833).

[55] *Gauntlet,* 16 March 1834.

[56] *Prompter,* 5 Nov. 1831; Richard Carlile, *A Letter to the Society for the Suppression of Vice, on Their Malignant Efforts to Prevent a Free Enquiry after Truth and Reason* (London: Richard Carlile, 1819), p. 5; Carlile, "What is Education?" *Cosmopolite,* 11 Aug. 1832. The press "will always be purifying itself, if free, and can only be corrupted by restraint" (*Prompter,* 2 July 1831).

[57] A letter from Carlile, in *Regenerator, and Advocate of the Unrepresented,* 2 Nov. 1839.

illusory. Carlile exemplified both the best and the worst aspects of the individualist in politics. He lacked a substantial following and quarreled time and again with nearly every other prominent working-class leader.[58] More important, his views were extremely personalized. He condemned, with all the journalistic power at his command, the glaring abuses of society, and vowed to champion "the rights, liberties, welfare, and progressive improvement of the people."[59] But neither the laissez-faire nostrums of the political economists nor the co-operative utopias envisaged by many of the working classes could eliminate, in his view, the bulk of these grievances. What was needed, declared Carlile, was the endlessly contending principles of "mind." Knowledge alone possessed "the moral and physical power necessary to the people for the overthrow of whatever tyranny moves over them."[60] Such knowledge was not the "useful knowledge" being disseminated by the S.D.U.K. Nor was it the vaguely articulated "cheap knowledge" being demanded by the masses. It was instead the true "knowledge" that emerges inevitably through a process of free communication, and, therefore, liberty of the press was the only lever that could effectively assure material and moral progress.[61]

Lovett, unlike Carlile, was not primarily a journalist, and he did not publish or edit any unstamped newspapers. His talents were employed largely on the organizational side of the working-class movement. He served as secretary of the "Victim Fund,"

[58] Carlile's periodical *A Scourge for the Littleness of "Great" Men* denounced Watson as "a viper, who has neither honour nor honourable memory, who can insult and rob the first and chief benefactor that he has had to put him in motion in his present business" (18 Oct. 1834). Hetherington was described as "a poor, vain, contemptible, and talentless fool" (*ibid.*, 22 Nov. 1834).

[59] *Gauntlet,* 18 Aug. 1833.   [60] *Ibid.,* 25 Aug. 1833.

[61] Progress was entirely empirical, according to Carlile. The conception of a Divine Being had no place in his thought. See his essay *An Address to Men of Science: Calling upon Them to Stand Forward, and Vindicate the Truth from the Foul Grasp and Persecution of Superstition; and Obtain for the Island of Great Britain the Noble Appellation of the Focus of Truth . . .* (London: Richard Carlile, 1822).

[134]

which supported the families of hundreds of imprisoned vendors, and in 1836 worked with Birkbeck and Place to raise subscriptions for Hetherington, Cleave, and other publishers who faced prosecution. By means of speeches and articles written for a number of the illicit journals, Lovett articulated a conception of the liberty of the press that become an important component of working-class thought.[62]

Up to the present, according to Lovett, "the power and monopoly of the few have enabled them to set their thousand schemes in action to brutalize and stultify the people—war, glory, splendour, fame, spectacles, songs, and every other brutalizing and degrading means the demon of evil could suggest." [63] A free press was, however, "a powerful instrument for the direction of the public mind" and could serve as a prerequisite to "THE COMING AGE OF FREEDOM, PEACE AND BROTHERHOOD." [64] But it could only perform its function efficiently under conditions of maximum freedom, inasmuch as the achievement of "moral and intellectual progress, the advance of trade, commerce, and the peaceful arts of life" were related integrally to the unobstructed communication of ideas.[65] Progress, by this conception, was intrinsically moral. It could not be artificially accelerated by governmental action. It had instead to evolve "naturally" from within the individual under the stimulus of knowledge, a knowledge that was freely and voluntarily acquired.

[62] Place condemned Lovett's adherence to Owenite doctrines but described him as an "honest sincere courageous man [*sic*]," a tribute vouchsafed by him to few working-class reformers (Place Papers, Add. MSS 27,791, ff. 241–242).

[63] Speech by Lovett to the London Working Men's Association, from a news-clipping in Lovett Papers, Vol. I, ff. 26–27.

[64] Speech by Lovett at a meeting of the British Association for Promoting Co-operative Knowledge, as reported in *Magazine of Useful Knowledge*, 13 Nov. 1830; Lovett, *Address to the French* (1848), reprinted in Lovett, *Life and Struggles*, II, 337; speech by Lovett to the N.U.W.C., as reported in *Poor Man's Guardian*, 3 March 1832; Lovett, *Address to the Working Classes of France on the Subject of War* (1844), reprinted in *Life and Struggles*, II, 313.

[65] Lovett, *Address to the Working Classes of America on the War Spirit to Be Created between the Two Countries*, reprinted in *Life and Struggles*, II, 321.

Lovett's views resembled those of the middle-class educational reformers and, partly for this reason, he was able to maintain ideological as well as political contacts with several of the latter, notably Birkbeck and Place. His conciliatory and restrained approach to the question of repeal prefigured his subsequent leadership of "moral force" Chartism. Lovett did not, however, establish a viable alliance with parliamentary reformers on the issue of the taxes on knowledge. His opinions were influential but not sufficiently so to imprint themselves upon the war of the unstamped.

Thus despite the influence of Carlile and Lovett, the syndrome of working-class thought on the newspaper issue was such as to widen the gap between moderate and "extreme" radicals. This widening lessened the pressure which reformers could exert effectively upon the government and helped to accentuate a polarization in British reform politics.

CHAPTER 6

The Unstamped Press

During the years from 1830 to 1836 hundreds of periodicals and newspapers circulated throughout England and Scotland, many without a government stamp. Their retail price usually fluctuated between 1*d*. and 3*d*., and because they possessed most of the attributes of newspapers, they were patently illegal. A large number of these weekly tracts attempted overtly to challenge the detested stamp duty, or, in the words proclaimed on its masthead by the *Poor Man's Guardian*, "to try the Powers of 'Might' against 'Right.'"

The publication and distribution of illegal journals, referred to by contemporaries as the "war of the unstamped," was undertaken almost exclusively by the working classes. It overshadowed in intensity and vigor the repeal agitation of the middle classes and proved to be the most creative and effective form of opposition to the taxes on knowledge to emerge during these years. The harshness of the ministerial counteroffensive accentuated this conflict since, as prosecutions were undertaken, illicit periodicals began to appear with increasing frequency, and many were tinged with near-revolutionary bitterness. Furthermore, techniques of defiance as embodied in the productive and distributive processes became more sophisticated, posing an additional challenge to the government.

During the 1820's there were few flagrant attempts to violate the stamp laws. Only a handful of publications were prosecuted, and no ministry faced the problem of pronounced resistance to the press laws. The first notable challenge was not launched until October 1830, when William Carpenter, a hitherto obscure journalist, published the first of his *Political Letters and Pamphlets*.

The *Political Letters* began to circulate in an atmosphere of increasing national excitement. France's second revolution within forty years had occurred during the previous July in the midst of a British general election. The result had been a decisive reactivation of the general demand for reform. As a corollary to these events, the Wellington government was in the final stages of disintegration during October 1830, and a more vigorous reform ministry was about to take office under Grey. Carpenter, a moderate working-class reformer, capitalized upon this situation. He issued thirty-three numbers of the *Political Letters*, with an estimated average circulation of ten thousand.[1] A ministerial prosecution in May 1831, alone sufficed to terminate its existence.

In October 1830, Hetherington, a London printer, likewise began to distribute a weekly periodical entitled *The Penny Papers for the People, Published by the Poor Man's Guardian*.[2] This journal did not purvey as much news as Carpenter's *Political Letters*, and its circulation was considerably smaller.[3] Nonetheless, its advocacy of radical doctrines made it worthy of governmental attention, and whereas Carpenter had accepted his prose-

---

[1] It is difficult to estimate the precise circulation. Carpenter's own claim of 19,000 per number is probably exaggerated (*Political Letters and Pamphlets*, 29 Oct. 1830). On the other hand, Hetherington, a political opponent, admitted that the *Political Letters* were "encouraged with the greatest zeal in every shop of London" (*Penny Papers for the People*, 25 Dec. 1830).

[2] The first number of Hetherington's journal appeared on 1 Oct. 1830, thus preceding Carpenter's *Political Letters* by several days. But *Penny Papers for the People* remained an obscure tract until its more famous successor, the *Poor Man's Guardian*, was born in July 1831.

[3] It barely circulated at all in the provinces, and its over-all sale could hardly pay expenses (*Penny Papers for the People*, 13 May 1831, 8 Nov. 1830).

cution resignedly, despite the fact that a group of fellow-reformers was prepared to continue publishing the *Political Letters* for him, Hetherington responded in starkly dramatic terms. He accused Carpenter of "weakness" and contended vociferously that "so long as our hand is able to wield a pen, the POOR MAN'S PRESS SHALL BE FREE!"[4] In July 1831, he began to issue an illegal penny newspaper entitled *The Poor Man's Guardian: A Weekly Newspaper for the People, Established Contrary to "Law" to Try the Powers of "Might" against "Right."* Thus by the summer of 1831, a conflict of major dimensions had been launched. It was not to be resolved even partially until the newspaper tax was reduced to 1*d.* in 1836.

LEADING PERSONALITIES

Of the myriad of journalistic participants in the "war of the unstamped," most of whom only transitorily escaped from obscurity, four implanted themselves into positions of leadership—William Carpenter, Henry Hetherington, James Watson, and John Cleave. All engaged actively in the manufacture and distribution of illegal newspapers and in other illicit activities, and with the partial exception of Carpenter, their careers were closely intertwined. Their public activities during the 1830's are, to a considerable degree, a microcosm of larger developments in the history of British radicalism.

Carpenter, the first journalist to secure national recognition through defiance of the stamp laws, was born in London in 1797. He became a journeyman printer who specialized in the popularization of Christian doctrines and became active subsequently in working-class reform circles. Like others who were to involve themselves in illicit journalism, he joined several of the nascent radical organizations that sprang up in London during the late 1820's and early 1830's. As a moderate exponent of co-operative doctrines, Carpenter took a particular interest in the activities of the Owenite-sponsored British Association for Promoting Co-

[4] *Ibid.,* 21 May 1831; *Poor Man's Guardian,* 3 Sept. 1831.

operative Knowledge, for which he edited the *Trades Weekly Free Press*, a stamped newspaper.[5]

Carpenter's decision to publish the *Political Letters* in October 1830, and thus to challenge openly the implicit censorship of the press, thrust him into the national spotlight.[6] After issuing thirty-three numbers of the *Letters* and making several vigorous pleas for a national agitation on the subject in order to eradicate what he described as "the lever of corruption," he was brought to trial in May 1831.[7] In a leader that appeared in his newspaper on the day of his trial he contended that:

The verdict of the jury, if against the Crown, will lay the basis for a wide and general diffusion of political knowledge among the poor, who are now deprived of the means of obtaining it; but if that verdict should be . . . in favour of the prosecution, then the existence of an untaxed press, applicable to any *purposes*—not merely political purposes —becomes impossible, except by an undoubted evasion of the law, and the constant *connivance of the law* officers of the crown.[8]

Notwithstanding the accuracy of this analysis and the seeming firmness of his position, Carpenter's trial before Lord Lyndhurst and a special jury in the Court of Exchequer proved to be the meridian of his influence in working-class politics. He defended unsuccessfully his violation of the law on technical grounds. After deliberating for one minute, the jury adjudged him guilty of having transgressed three separate statutes dealing with the newspaper duty, and he was sentenced to King's Bench Prison in lieu of payment of a heavy fine. He secured his release after several months' imprisonment but, in the interim, became firmly wedded to moderate, legal techniques of protest.[9]

[5] *Magazine of Useful Knowledge*, 30 Oct. 1830.

[6] For his view that the taxes on knowledge were more insidious than a direct censorship, see his speech to a Rotunda meeting, as reported in *Republican*, 21 May 1831.

[7] The phrase "lever of corruption" is in *Political Letters and Pamphlets*, 5 March 1831.

[8] *Ibid.*, 14 May 1831.

[9] Since he championed the Whig reform bill subsequently, several reformers, including Hetherington and Hunt, accused him of having concluded a secret

Beginning in September 1831, Carpenter issued a legal 6*d.* journal entitled *Carpenter's Monthly Political Magazine*. During the thirteen months of its existence this periodical unsuccessfully attempted through intellectual persuasion to mediate the chasm between middle- and working-class reformism. Such was likewise the objective of the *True Sun,* a stamped London evening newspaper, and of the *Weekly True Sun,* both of which Carpenter helped to edit.[10] Despite the fact that these journals and several tracts that Carpenter wrote and printed, including the *Political Alphabet* (1831), the *Political and Historical Tracts* (1831), *A Peerage for the People* (1837,) and the *Political Almanack for 1836,* secured substantial working-class support, he was increasingly regarded as a "traitor" by the latter. This reputation was a product of his failure to uphold the mantle of resistance against the government on the repeal question and of his strong endorsement of the Reform Bill.

Carpenter continued to play a peripheral role in the war of the unstamped. He edited, among other illicit periodicals, *A Slap at the Church* (1832), the *Political Anecdotist and Popular Instructor* (1831), and the *Political Letter* (1832), a revived 4*d.* version of the earlier *Political Letters and Pamphlets.* But none of these journals ventured beyond a moderate position on the question of repeal and all appeared anachronistic within the context of the more militant reformism that was shaping the tone of the war of the unstamped.

Carpenter's major commitment was to the principle of a unified reform movement. As an active member of both the National Union of the Working Classes and the National Political Union, he sought to mold a common approach to the social and political problems of the 1830's. On one occasion, in attempting to engender support for the Reform Bill, he presented an abortive motion to the N.P.U. to the effect that both organizations should

---

bargain with the government to gain his freedom. See the report of Popay, the informer, S.S. file, 26 Jan. 1832, H.O. 64/12.

[10] *New Political Register,* 17 Oct. 1836; Carpenter's testimony before *S.C. on the Cold Bath Fields Meeting* (1833), p. 69, q. 1419.

unite.[11] Similarly, he supported repeal of the taxes on knowledge in the conviction that free expression of opinion was essential to prevent "a violent convulsion in society," a convulsion that would render permanent the division between middle and working classes.[12] With more than a touch of the political economist, he urged that nothing can avert "the horrors of a civil war between the two great classes into which [the country] is unfortunately divided, but the instruction of the great body of the people in the real principles of social and political science." [13] Analogously, Carpenter propagandized on behalf of the Reform Bill in the belief that it would go far toward preparing the "basis for good legislation." [14] In a pamphlet addressed to the laboring classes, he postulated that "the middle classes of 1831 are not only *not* a class of persons having interests different from your own; but they *are not a different class from your own.*" [15]

This theme of reconciling the demands of middle- and working-class reformers proved to have little success in the 1830's, and Carpenter, partially because of his ineffectual attempt at "moderation," rapidly lost journalistic support. His editorships of the *London Journal* (1836–1837) and of the *Charter* (1839–1840), the official newspaper of the London Working Men's Association, proved to be notably short-lived and unhappy political experiences.[16] He died in relative obscurity in 1874.

Of greater importance than Carpenter in the working-class re-

[11] Carpenter's petition from the Kings Bench Prison, reprinted in *Carpenter's Monthly Political Magazine*, I (Oct. 1831), 61–62.

[12] *Poor Man's Guardian*, 2 June 1832.

[13] *Political Letters and Pamphlets*, 18 Feb. 1831.

[14] *Political Letter*, 18 June 1831.

[15] William Carpenter, *An Address to the Working Classes on the Reform Bill* (London: William Strange, 1831), p. 14.

[16] *Prospectus of a Weekly Newspaper, Entitled the Charter, Devoted to the Interests of the Working Classes, the Profits of Which Are to Be Placed at Their Disposal.* A copy of this is in Place Papers, Add. MSS 27,820, f. 381. Place, who was hostile both to Carpenter and to the *Charter*, described the former as "a particularly ill qualified man for his office" (Place Papers, Add. MSS 27,821, ff. 22–23).

peal movement was Henry Hetherington. If Holyoake's eulogistic assertion that "Hetherington represents the Unstamped agitation, and this is his great political and historical distinction" is an exaggeration, it is, nonetheless, a suggestive one.[17] Hetherington, more than any other single person, imposed his personal courage, his determination, and his intellectual commitments upon the war of the unstamped, and to the extent that it was successful, a large debt is owed to him.

Born into an impoverished London family, Hetherington was apprenticed to a printer at an early age, and it was as a printer that he rose to a recognized position in London's radical circles. During the 1820's he helped to establish several working-class organizations, including the Co-operative and Economical Society (1821), the London Mechanics' Institution, the British Association for Promoting Co-operative Knowledge (1829), the Metropolitan Political Union (1830), and, most importantly, the National Union of the Working Classes, a coalition of trades and radical associations that was formed in May 1831.[18] As an active member of these groups, he identified himself with Owenite and other co-operative economic theories, with a commitment to political equality, and with an increasingly passionate conviction of "the right of all men to freely publish their opinions upon every subject of general interest—whether SOCIAL, POLITICAL, OR RELIGIOUS, aye, or ANTI-RELIGIOUS."[19] It was within the framework of these political and social convictions that Hetherington

[17] George Jacob Holyoake, *The Life and Character of Henry Hetherington* (London: James Watson, 1849), p. 12. Holyoake (*ibid.*, p. 13) described Hetherington wittily as "a personification of good-humoured Democracy." W. J. Linton reminisced about him as "a leader of men, a ready and effective speaker, plain, pathetic, humourous, or sarcastic, as occasion required; a bold thinker and a good organizer, prompt, energetic, earnest, and devoted" (*Memories* [London: Laurence and Bullen, 1895], p. 37).

[18] George Jacob Holyoake, *The History of Co-operation* (London: T. Fisher Unwin, 1908), pp. 40, 72; Thomas Cooper, eloge, in *Reasoner*, VII (1849), 146–148; *Republican*, 23 April 1831.

[19] *Report on the Trial of Hetherington*, p. 24; Lovett, *Life and Struggles*, I, 55–56.

cast himself into the spotlight in October 1830, with a direct, unqualified challenge to the government on behalf of an untaxed
press. The public gaze was to remain rivetted upon him until his
premature death from cholera in 1849.[20]

Hetherington's leadership of the war of the unstamped was
achieved by virtue of his publication of the *Poor Man's Guardian*. This widely circulated journal which was the successor to his
earlier *Penny Papers for the People* was in the vanguard of resistance to the newspaper duty between 1831 and 1835.[21] Several
hundred of its vendors were imprisoned and Hetherington himself endured three terms of incarceration totaling almost a year.
Despite this harassment he refused steadfastly to compromise the
principle of an untaxed literature and, unlike Carpenter, he made
large personal sacrifices in an attempt to underwrite this determination. After his second conviction he wrote from Clerkenwell
Prison: "Had I 20,000 lives I would sacrifice them all rather than
succumb to such mean, such dastardly, such malignant reptiles." [22]

During his association with the *Poor Man's Guardian* Hetherington's involvement in radical politics deepened, and he came to
be regarded as a "martyr" in working-class circles. His extensive
recruiting trips into the North of England on behalf of the *Poor
Mans' Guardian* and of his other illicit periodicals, which included the *Radical* (1831–1832,), the *Republican; or, Voice of
the People* (1831–1832), the *"Destructive" and Poor Man's
Conservative* (1833–1834) and *Hetherington's Twopenny Dispatch, and People's Police Register* (1834–1836), were well

[20] According to Holyoake, Hetherington counted on temperance to ward off
the disease and would not consult a physician (*Life of Hetherington*, p. 12).

[21] In its final number, Hetherington described the journal accurately as "a
real pioneer in the cause of Political Justice, accelerating the establishment of
the Liberty of the Press, and clearing the way for the not-far-distant emancipation of the working classes" (*Poor Man's Guardian*, 26 Dec. 1835).

[22] Hetherington, letter to Henry Hunt, *c*. Jan. 1833, as reported in *Poor
Man's Guardian*, 19 Jan. 1833. One month later he asserted: "I will rather
sacrifice my life than pay one farthing to a gang of despicable villains who
sustain themselves by the plunder and oppression of the industrious classes"
(*Poor Man's Guardian*, 20 Feb. 1833).

publicized.[23] His frequent challenges to local police forces and to magistrates, challenges which often resulted in his being pursued over much of England, were reported regularly in the penny journals. Activities such as these and the flair for "heroic" publicity that Hetherington possessed made him a powerful political force in England. They more than counterbalanced the relative paucity of his own journalistic contributions, a situation that derived from his preference for hiring editors and correspondents to manage the technical side of his periodicals for him.

Hetherington believed strongly in the need to reconstruct England's economic system in accordance with co-operative principles. As was the case with many other working-class reformers during the 1830's, however, he came to devalue this theme temporarily at the expense of a commitment to universal suffrage and to "an unstamped and really free Poor Man's Paper." [24] In his view extension of the suffrage represented power for the dispossessed and propertyless masses whereas removal of the newspaper duty opened the avenues of knowledge to them.[25] Thus each demand effectively complemented the other, and both became critical prerequisites to the attainment of radical social changes and to the subverting of the "aristocratical spirit which . . . pervaded all ranks of British society." [26] This obsessive dual commitment remained the core of Hetherington's political commitment for the remainder of his life, and his attachment to "moral force" Chartism after 1836 was partially the product of disillusionment stemming from the failure to achieve either objective.

[23] According to Popay, the informer, when Hetherington traveled to the north of England, Cleave and Watson managed his publications for him (S.S. report, 26 July 1831, H.O. 64/11).

[24] *Poor Man's Guardian*, 24 Dec. 1831, 19 Jan. 1833; letter to A. Dallas, *ibid.*, 30 March 1833; speech to the Salford Political Union, as reported in *Manchester Advertiser*, 7 Sept. 1833.

[25] Speech at a meeting of the N.U.W.C., as reported in *Poor Man's Guardian*, 12 April 1834.

[26] Speech by Hetherington to the Metropolitan Political Union, as reported in *Republican*, 23 April 1831.

Unlike Carpenter, with whom he maintained a personal friendship, Hetherington perceived no necessary virtue in class cooperation. Such was likely, in his opinion, to prove a disheartening chimera, and so he preferred to champion unqualifiedly "the *disreputable* industrious producers of wealth against the *respectable* idle consumers of it." [27] Under his prodding and in accordance with the thinking of O'Brien who edited several journals for him, the *Poor Man's Guardian,* the *"Destructive" and Poor Man's Conservative,* and *Hetherington's Twopenny Dispatch* all launched strong attacks upon the "profit-hunters" and the "middleocracy." But none of these denunciations incorporated appeals to physical violence, and all three journals maintained a faith in the efficacy of free discussion, a commitment that remained central to Hetherington.

After the termination of the war of the unstamped, Hetherington continued to play a leading role in radical politics. He became the proprietor of the influential *London Dispatch* (1836–1839) and one of the active leaders of the London Working Men's Association, the Chartist organization formed by Lovett which opposed O'Connor's more militant policy of "physical force." [28] He also participated vigorously in the burgeoning secularist movement of the 1840's. Hetherington remained a formidable symbol of resistance to governmental oppression until his death and has since held a secure niche in the British working-class tradition.

Watson, who worked closely with Hetherington on all aspects of the repeal agitation, was born in Malton, Yorkshire, in 1799. In his youth he migrated to London and, under the influence of the free thought principles expounded by Carlile, became rapidly involved in radical activities. Having achieved a modicum of notoriety by serving as Carlile's shop assistant (a situation that

[27] Newsclipping of a Crown and Anchor meeting, *c.* July 1836, Lovett Papers, Vol. I, f. 5.

[28] R. G. Gammage, *History of the Chartist Movement, 1837–1854* (Newcastle-upon-Tyne: Browne and Browne, 1894), pp. 12–13; Lovett, *Life and Struggles,* I, 154.

led to a years' imprisonment), Watson thrust himself at the end of the 1820's into the same organizational and journalistic activities that preoccupied Hetherington.[29]

By 1830 he had become involved in the Owenite co-operative movement and in the proliferating working-class demands for political equality.[30] This involvement gave him personal contact with Hetherington, Carpenter, Lovett, Cleave, Julian Hibbert, and other radical journalists, and his printing and publishing activities began to increase considerably, largely within the framework of the National Union of the Working Classes, the organization with which he became most closely associated. His unassuming and relatively circumspect manner belied the skillfulness with which he promoted the dissemination of cheap literature.

From 1831 on, Watson collaborated with Hetherington, Cleave, and Lovett in the production and distribution of the *Poor Man's Guardian* and other unstamped journals.[31] In December 1832, though still continuing to work with Hetherington, he launched the *Working Man's Friend; and Political Magazine*, a 1*d.* periodical that ran for thirty-three numbers. As a result of its articulate advocacy of factory legislation, universal suffrage, and repeal of the newspaper duty, the *Working Man's Friend* became one of the better-known newspapers of the decade. Watson's public association with it led to his imprisonment for six months during 1833 and to a subsequent incarceration in 1834.[32] Unlike Carpenter and Hetherington, he never was

[29] Holyoake, *History of Co-operation*, pp. 96–97; Lovett, *Life and Struggles*, I, 55; *A Biographical Dictionary of Modern Rationalists*, ed. Joseph McCabe (London: Watts, 1920), pp. 872–873.

[30] He did missionary work for the Owenite British Association for Promoting Co-operative Knowledge and was an agent for the First London Co-operative Society (*British Co-operator*, April 1830; James Watson, letter to Robert Owen, 28 March 1830, Owen Papers, No. 216).

[31] He had contacts with reformers in the north of England and supervised the distribution of unstamped periodicals in that area (S.S. report, 13 Nov. 1830, H.O. 64/11).

[32] Watson was technically prosecuted in 1833 for vending the *Poor Man's Guardian* (*Working Man's Friend*, 16 Feb. 1833; *Gauntlet*, 17 Feb. 1833).

closely identified with a large number of unstamped journals, and his contributions to the war of the unstamped were in the form of organizational work, speechmaking, and the publication of a large number of radical tracts and broadsides.[33]

Watson's ideological commitments were nearly identical to those of Hetherington, though invariably his pronouncements were more temperately phrased. Like Hetherington he wrote comparatively little, preferring instead to rely upon the journalistic talents of others, notably Cleave. But his positions on major issues were expressed through numerous speeches and in occasional special addresses that appeared in the *Working Man's Friend* and other unstamped periodicals.

Watson strove tirelessly to achieve the "mental emancipation" of the working classes as a prerequisite to the overthrow of aristocratic and Whig predominance.[34] Such a task could best be accomplished, in his opinion, by "treading the obnoxious stamp act down to the dust" and by securing universal manhood suffrage.[35] What was required most urgently, he suggested, was "a storm which would shake to atoms the abominable system which held the people in ignorance under the lash of tyrants." [36] In his opinion, "the workers must become rich—the idle become poor"

In 1834 he was prosecuted for vending the *People's Conservative* (*Poor Man's Guardian*, 28 June 1834).

[33] Among the numerous tracts that Watson reprinted were a 3*s*. collection of Paine's major writings entitled the *Working Man's Political Companion*; a 1*s*. 6*d*. version of Volney's *Lectures on History*; Byron's *Cain*; a 2*d*. edition of Robert Dale Owen's *Influence of the Cleric Profession*; and John Lawless' *History of Ireland* issued in 3*d*. numbers (*Working Man's Friend*, 22 Dec. 1832).

[34] *Working Man's Friend*, 3 Aug. 1833.

[35] Speech to the National Association for Promoting Co-operative Knowledge, as reported in *Magazine of Useful Knowledge*, 13 Nov. 1830. The newspaper duty permitted "the bloated parson to 'pray and to cant,' the soldier to fight, and the lawyer to delude and cheat the unwary under a pretense of justice, nicknamed law" (Watson, "A Voice from the Bastille," *Working Man's Friend* 2 March 1833).

[36] Speech to a quarterly meeting of the N.U.W.C., as reported in *Poor Man's Guardian*, 19 Oct. 1833.

because under the existing system "the labourers are plundered at all ends; by the state; by the church; by the lawyers; by the doctors; by the fundholders; by the buyers cheap; sellers dear, in all departments of trade and commerce." [37] Economic co-operation, to which he remained more directly committed than Hetherington, was not, however, immediately necessary since it would follow assuredly upon the other changes.[38]

From 1837 on, as the result of profound disillusionment with British politics combined with an abiding attachment to the force of the printed word, Watson became an advocate of "moral force" Chartism. Along with Hetherington, he became prominent in the London Working Men's Association, and in the 1840's was perhaps the best-known London publisher of radical and free thought literature. He subsequently participated in such radical organizations as the People's International League, which was founded by Giuseppe Mazzini in 1847.

When Watson died in 1874, he left behind him a lifetime of personal dedication to working-class causes. Place, a vigorous political opponent who was often vindictive, described him as "a very remarkable man, quiet and mild in his manner and deportment, an honest well-meaning man, one who knows but little guile himself, and unapt to support it in others." [39] More striking was W. J. Linton's posthumous tribute: "[Watson was] a brave specimen of the intelligent and honest English workman . . . essentially a religious man, a believer in duty, though he bowed in neither church nor chapel, and only gave an honestly industrious life for freedom of thought and speech." [40] To a degree, both verdicts are probably sound.

The fourth member of the working-class quadrumvirate that dominated the war of the unstamped was John Cleave. Cleave remains less well known than the others, and to the extent that

---

[37] Watson, *Address to Trade Unions*, pp. 42–44.
[38] *Proceedings of the Third Co-operative Congress*, p. 71.
[39] Place Papers, Add. MSS 27,796, f. 304.
[40] Linton, *Memories*, pp. 38–39.

he has secured historical recognition it has been through the negative account of Place.[41] Yet he performed solidly during the repeal campaign, if occasionally with a surfeit of emotional vituperation, and his contributions to the history of penny literature loom large.

Little is known of Cleave's background other than that he was of Irish parentage, had served two apprenticeships in the navy, and had probably spent time in the United States.[42] By the late 1820's and early 1830's he had established himself as a printer in London and, along with Carpenter, Hetherington, and Watson, had become active in such organizations as the British Association for Promoting Co-operative Knowledge, the Metropolitan Political Union, and the National Union of the Working Classes.[43] After forming a close friendship with Carpenter and Watson, he emerged as a leader of the repeal campaign within the N.U.W.C. He organized public meetings, at which he and other speakers condemned the newspaper duty, raised subscriptions for imprisoned vendors, and assisted Hetherington and Watson in the publication of the *Poor Man's Guardian*.[44]

From 1832 onward, Cleave became even more active in the war of the unstamped. He collaborated with Carpenter in the production of two successful illicit journals, *A Slap at the Church*

[41] Place, in comparing him with Lovett, wrote: "He was not so well informed nor so placid a man as Lovett, he on the contrary was passionate and revengeful, and not at all scrupulous as to the use of any means of accomplishing his purpose the end of which was improving the condition of the working people" (Place Papers, Add. MSS 27,791, ff. 67–68).

[42] In an 1837 speech Cleave praised the United States on the basis of "personal observation" (*London Dispatch, c.* July 1837, Lovett Papers, newscutting in Vol. I, f. 100; Lovett, *Life and Struggles,* I, 55; *Poor Man's Guardian,* supp. 17 Dec. 1831; *People's Conservative,* 3 May 1834).

[43] According to one source, he assisted Carpenter in editing the *Weekly Free Press* during the 1820's (S.S. report, 23 Nov. 1831, H. O. 64/11).

[44] For his activity in collecting subscriptions, see *Man,* 10 Aug. 1834; *People's Hue and Cry,* 10 Aug. 1834. He organized meetings and framed resolutions, according to S.S. report, 31 Dec. 1832, H. O. 64/12; *Political Unionist,* 7 July 1832; *Poor Man's Guardian,* 29 Oct. 1831.

(1832) and the *Church Examiner and Ecclesiastical Record* (1832), edited the *Working Man's Friend* for Watson during 1833–1834, and published and edited a comprehensive 2*d.* news sheet entitled *Cleave's Weekly Police Gazette* from 1834 to 1836.[45] During these years he predictably incurred the wrath of the Stamp Office and of vigilant local magistrates. In April 1834, and again in March 1836, he was convicted for violating the stamp laws and on both occasions served brief prison terms.[46]

Cleave's ideological orientation was fundamentally similar to that of Hetherington and Watson though he issued stronger tirades against a variety of abuses. He repeatedly attacked royalty, factory abuses, and the union with Ireland but expended his primary energies upon the twin causes of "cheap political knowledge" and universal suffrage. His expectation was that these changes would provide a foundation for a noncompetitive economic system in which productive labor would be amply rewarded.[47]

Repeal of the stamp duty was particularly important, in Cleave's opinion, because:

Every prospect [the labouring poor] have of lessening their intolerable burdens—every chance of improving their physical and moral condition —every hope of escape from the fangs of famine, from the chilling miseries, the wasting sickness, the gnawing and ghastly destitution that now beset them on all sides—consists in the acquisition . . . of that

[45] Among his controversial collaborative efforts with Carpenter was a pirated abridged 1834 edition of William Howitt's *A Popular History of Priestcraft.* Howitt responded by publishing his own "authorized" abridgment (*A Scourge for the Littleness of "Great" Men*, 25 Oct. 1834; *Poor Man's Guardian*, 27 Sept. 1834). Cleave and Watson published an original tract of similar content entitled the *Poor Man's Book of the Church* that was widely circulated at 3*d.* (S.S. report, 16 Jan. 1832, H.O. 64/12).

[46] For a report of his trial in 1834 for publishing *Cleave's Weekly Police Gazette*, see *Weekly True Sun*, 27 April 1834. For a summary of his 1836 conviction, see *Radical*, 13 March 1836. He was released in April 1836, after intervention by Place and Dr. Black (*Radical*, 1 May 1836).

[47] See speech at the Rotunda, as reported in *Republican*, 18 June 1831.

knowledge of the laws and the legislature, which will enable them to comprehend the ruinous and fatal influence of both upon their own individual destinies.[48]

Universal suffrage was likewise of great significance because it would strengthen the laborer's ability to alter "those institutions, the direct tendency of which is to wring from those who create all the wealth by which they are surrounded, the produce of their misery." [49] But to a greater extent than was true of Hetherington and Watson, he harbored a vision that was agrarian and reactionary in the tradition of Cobbett. The paper money, Jew-dominated "system" had to be destroyed, he believed, before a new social structure could be established.

This complex of radical commitments led Cleave, as it did many others, to "moral force" Chartism after 1836.[50] He became active in the L.W.M.A. and achieved a continuing measure of journalistic renown as the creator of the popular illustrated weekly *Cleave's Gazette of Variety* and as the publisher of a number of original penny novels.[51] Thus, as was true of Watson and Hetherington, Cleave's career led successively through radical resistance, disillusionment, and the subsequent nurturing of new interests.

CHARACTERISTICS AND TECHNIQUES

The difficulties in legally defining a newspaper offered a choice opportunity for prospective illegal journalists. The Act of 1819 had established specific guidelines for determining what constituted an illicit publication. With minor exceptions, every periodi-

[48] *An Address to the Readers of Cleave's Weekly Police Gazette* (London: John Cleave, 1836), p. 2; speech to the N.U.W.C., as reported by *Poor Man's Guardian*, 10 Dec. 1831.

[49] *Working Man's Friend*, 27 April 1833. An "untaxed press," he believed, would help to inculcate in "the minds of the industrious multitude their unquestionable title to political equality" (*ibid.*, 6 July 1833).

[50] His daughter subsequently married Henry Vincent, the prominent Chartist leader (Holyoake, *History of Co-operation*, p. 84).

[51] James, *Fiction for the Working Man*, p. 26.

cal that sold for less than 6*d.* and was published more frequently than monthly, was legally a newspaper and liable for payment of the stamp duty. But it was difficult to apply such a definition in practice when successive numbers of a periodical lacked clear continuity. The publisher of such a journal might claim that it was a "pamphlet" and required, therefore, to pay only the insignificant pamphlet duty. And it was precisely on the technical point of continuity that both Carpenter and Hetherington launched their initial journalistic campaigns. Neither succeeded in countervailing the government's assertion that their publications were illegal, but they provided techniques of defiance that other reformers were to pursue during succeeding years.

The *Political Letters and Pamphlets* was probably intended merely to test the phraseology of the law. Carpenter was a conciliatory reformer who hoped to secure abolition of the newspaper duty by all means "short of an actual violation of the *law*."[52] He published the *Political Letters* at irregular intervals varying in length from three to eight days and affirmed that they were "isolated, or distinct and independent publications; they have no kind of connection with each other; they are written upon distinct and specific topics." Each number bore a different title page, and since these were in epistolary form, Carpenter contended that he was engaging merely in public correspondence with prominent political figures.[53]

This defense was legally unconvincing since each "letter" featured a sizable proportion of political debates, reports of public meetings, theatrical reviews, and accounts of Old Bailey proceedings. The *Political Letters* were, in fact, full-sized news-

[52] Carpenter, "National Union of the Working Classes and Others," *Carpenter's Monthly Political Magazine*, I (Jan. 1832), 178–184; *Political Letters and Pamphlets*, 7 Dec. 1830; *Carpenter's Monthly Political Magazine*, I (Oct. 1831), 42.

[53] *A Report of the Trial of Mr. William Carpenter . . . for Publishing a Number of Political Letters and Pamphlets, Charged to Be Newspapers, Within the Meaning of the Acts of Parliament* (London: William Carpenter, 1831), p. 4.

papers which sold for 4*d.* and contained as substantial a compilation of secondhand news as almost any periodical in England. Even the contention that they were "irregular" was untenable, for Carpenter invariably announced in advance the date on which the next number would appear. The columns of the *Political Letters* were also replete with advertisements, an indication that a regular readership was assumed. But the statute of 1819 was constructed with sufficient ambiguity so that a technically phrased argument could have some impact on a sympathetic jury. In order to increase the likelihood of Carpenter's conviction, therefore, the Stamp Office prosecuted him under an earlier newspaper act which did not make any reference to regularity of publication.[54]

Hetherington's argument that his *Penny Papers for the People* were "irregular" pamphlets was even less convincing. These tracts were almost always published on Saturday, and on the very few occasions when they appeared on the preceding Friday, this was done, as Hetherington admitted, to exploit ambiguities in the stamp law.[55] Furthermore, the subheading of the *Penny Papers for the People* proclaimed its intention to provide "a Comprehensive Digest of all the Political Occurrences of the Week," and this aim was pursued steadfastly. Though scathing political commentary was the paper's staple, both it and its successor, the *Poor Man's Guardian*, regularly printed substantial excerpts from Parliamentary debates, as well as accounts of domestic and international radical activities.

The *Republican; or Voice of the People*, a weekly journal for the publication of which Hetherington was prosecuted simultaneously in June 1831, was likewise illegal. It contained less

[54] See the testimony of J. Timm, a Stamp Office official, to the effect that under the Acts of 1798 and 1815 "the single publication of a paper containing news is a newspaper," *S.C. on Newspaper Stamps* (1851), p. 39, q. 223. See also the testimony of Keogh, *ibid.*, p. 39. The working-class *Voice of the People* admitted that the Whigs "might have found some colour of excuse in the existing laws" for the prosecution (16 July 1831).

[55] *Penny Papers for the People*, 25 Dec. 1830.

news than did the *Penny Papers,* but it appeared every Saturday without exception.[56] Hetherington's contention that the *Republican* was not a newspaper because it was not successively numbered was flagrantly specious.[57] His emphasis on the "irregularity" of publications seems, therefore, to have been a more deliberate attempt to defy the government than Carpenter's. In fact, Hetherington consistently affirmed that "LAW is only the will of the aristocratic *few*" and can be ignored—a position that was rejected vehemently by Carpenter.[58]

By the summer of 1831 penny newspapers began to issue regularly from presses throughout England and Scotland. A substantial proportion of these illicit journals were not identified by their projectors as illegal but were published under a variation of the "regularity" subterfuge.

Henry Hunt, for example, circulated a series of "occasional" *Addresses* during the winter of 1831–1832.[59] These were widely circulated at a price of 1*d.* in the industrial towns of Lancashire and the West Riding. They were patently illegal despite their appearance at unpredictable two- or three-day intervals because of the continuity of printer and publisher and because each number possessed an identical format and arrangement. Furthermore, the expressed intent of the *Addresses* was to provide a vehicle in which Hunt's opposition to the Reform Bill could be defended publicly. Thus the *Addresses* were replete with news of

[56] The *Republican; or Voice of the People* was more radical than Hetherington's other publications. It was commenced in March 1831 at ½*d.*, and its price was raised subsequently to 1*d.* and then 3*d.* The meetings held at the Rotunda by working-class reformers were reported extensively in its pages; see, for example, *Republican,* 21 May 1831.

[57] See the account of Hetherington's trial in *Penny Papers for the People,* 24 June 1831.

[58] *Ibid.* Hetherington contended that "robbery, injustice, and tyranny of the grossest description are perpetrated with impunity under the form of 'law' " (letter to A. Dallas, *Poor Man's Guardian,* 30 March 1833).

[59] The full title of these addresses was Henry Hunt, *An Address from H. Hunt, Esq. M. P. to the Radical Reformers of England, Ireland, and Scotland, on the Measures of the Whig Ministers Since They Have Been in Place and Power.*

his activities both in and out of Parliament.[60] In spite of the publication's illegal nature, no prosecution of Hunt was undertaken, an occurrence that is undoubtedly attributable to his standing as a member of Parliament and to the substantial popular support that he commanded rather than to the efficacy of the subterfuge that he employed.

In the Lancashire cotton towns of Preston and Bolton, working-class supporters of Hunt published, between December 1831 and the beginning of 1833, a 1*d.* weekly *Address from One of the 3730 Electors of Preston, to the Labouring Classes of Great Britain and Ireland*. This periodical had a weekly variation in its title and listed frequent changes of publishers. These technical exceptions notwithstanding, it possessed all the attributes of a newspaper as defined by the Act of 1819 and was flagrantly illegal though no prosecution appears to have been undertaken.[61]

Other instances of resort to the regularity device abound. In Manchester, the *Poor Man's Advocate, and People's Library*, one of the longest-lived of the unstamped periodicals, was published.[62] This 1*d.* factory journal, which was edited by the trade union leader John Doherty, appeared under such varied weekly titles as *A Penny Paper by a Poor Man's Advocate, A Poor Man's Advocate*, and *A Penny Poor Man's Advocate*, in an attempt to conceal its activities from the Stamp Office. In Edinburgh, a weekly proreform newspaper under the editorship of James Browne, was published in 1835. It likewise featured different title pages on successive weekly appearances. Since the titles possessed no obvious similarities, and since individual numbers were undated, only the name of the publisher and an identi-

---

[60] See, for example, *Address to the Radical Reformers*, 20 Oct. 1831, 3 Nov. 1831.

[61] The "3,730" electors were those who voted for Hunt in the general election of 1830. It reprinted addresses and resolutions carried by local radical societies, an important category of working-class news. See, for example, *Address from One of the 3730 Electors of Preston*, 21 April 1832.

[62] It commenced publication in January 1832 and, though forced out of circulation for a time, did not finally terminate its existence until December 1834.

cal journalistic format linked these "pamphlets" together.[63] Roebuck's *Pamphlets for the People* was another illicit newspaper that tenuously purported to be a series of isolated tracts. It was undated, unnumbered, and lacked a consistent weekly title page, but its format was always precisely identical, and the name of its editor, Roebuck, conspicuously graced each number.

Disguises of a more imaginative nature were sometimes employed in an attempt to evade the tentacles of the law. In Glasgow, local reformers published at least two numbers of a journal entitled the *New Political Dictionary*. It was probably a penny weekly though neither a date nor a price appeared on the periodical. Successive numbers were printed in lexicographical form. Words such as "abominable" and "aberration" were listed, and then defined so as to score satirically and with acerbity at the expense of the Church of England and other hated institutions.[64] The editor's expressed objective was to present to his readers "almost all that they require to know regarding the political maneuvres of the enemies to political regeneration." [65] The *New Political Dictionary* may have been suppressed by the Scottish Stamp Office together with a companion Glasgow periodical entitled the *Reformers' Pocket Companion,* though there is no certainty of this.[66]

Pseudonyms were commonly utilized by printers and publishers during the war of the unstamped. Although the authorities almost invariably prosecuted the vendors of illegal newspapers rather than the printers and publishers, the latter took substantial risks. Their printing presses, types, and related possessions were

[63] The titles of three of these tracts which survive in the Place Newspaper Collection are: *The Friend of the People; or, Political, Literary and Scientific Instructor; Dr. Browne's Publication, containing The People's Friend;* and *The People's Friend.* All were sold at 1½d.

[64] "Aberration" was defined as "going astray; wandering; a thing which clergymen seldom or never do, from the path of worldly interest" (*New Political Dictionary,* No. 1 [1832]).

[65] *Reformers' Pocket Companion,* 9 June 1832.

[66] Both periodicals were printed and published during the spring of 1832 by Muir, Gowans, a radical Glasgow publishing house.

liable to seizure by the authorities, and even if the parties were adjudged innocent ultimately, compensation was never paid. Thus the projectors of some unstamped newspapers sought to conceal their identities from the Stamp Office. The pseudonym "Benjamin Franklin" became especially popular in this regard. Both James H. B. Lorymer, a virulent working-class reformer, and B. D. Cousins, a publisher of free thought literature, participated in illegal press activities under cover of this name.[67]

It was sometimes also the practice to conceal one's identity behind a "dummy" publisher, one who was presumably willing to risk imprisonment. After Cleave's presses were confiscated by the Stamp Office in August 1835, most of his stock of penny literature began to be formally issued by "T. Wakelin." "Wakelin" was probably one of Cleave's shop assistants since the publisher's address remained unchanged, and Cleave almost certainly continued to exercise effective control over these publications.[68] After the reduction of the newspaper duty in September 1836, the possibility of further governmental action was lessened, and Cleave again assumed public responsibility for the publication of cheap tracts.

Carlile concealed even more successfully his relationship with at least one important unstamped newspaper. Having spent almost ten years in prison on charges of seditious libel (most recently during 1831 as the result of an article that appeared in the *Prompter*), Carlile preferred to play a less conspicuous role in the movement against the taxes on knowledge.[69] He did publish

---

[67] Lorymer published several journals, including the *Republican*, which he took over from Hetherington, and the *Reformer*. He also used the pseudonym "Benjamin Franklin" in a 2*d*. tract entitled *The Conservative-Reform Humbug* (1832). Cousins published the *Crisis, and National Co-operative Trades' Union and Equitable Labour Exchange Gazette* (1833–1834), *Antichrist, or Christianity Reformed* (1833), and the *Weekly Herald* (1836), one of the best unstamped newspapers of the decade.

[68] There is a small possibility that "T. Wakelin" was a pseudonym employed by Cleave. It is surprising that the name "Wakelin" does not appear in any other context during the entire repeal movement.

[69] *Reports of State Trials: New Ser. Vol. II, 1823 to 1831*, ed. John MacDonell (London: Her Majesty's Stationery Office, 1889), pp. 459–627.

several illegal periodicals openly, including the aforementioned
Prompter, Gauntlet, and *Isis,* and escaped prosecution by the
government; but his contribution to the *Cosmopolite, A London
Weekly Newspaper,* an important unstamped journal, was concealed deliberately. Though several "victims" of the Whig
prosecutions technically printed and published the periodical,
Carlile financed it and served as editor throughout most of its
existence.[70]

The most sensational subterfuge of the entire war of the unstamped was employed initially in September 1831. Henry
Berthold, a journalist from Saxony who acquired an unsavory
reputation in London's radical circles, began at that time to issue
Berthold's Political Handkerchief, a weekly unstamped newspaper that was printed on calico.[71] Berthold employed calico because he contended that the newspaper acts had reference either
to paper alone or to a closely related substance. With the repeal
of the excise duty on printed calico in March 1831, the publication of cotton newspapers seemed economically and journalisti-
cally feasible to him.[72]

Berthold's Political Handkerchief scored an instantaneous success, and several of its early numbers were reprinted. Carlile,
expressing the sentiments of other reformers, described the journal enthusiastically as "the best hit that has yet been made in
warring with the taxes on knowledge."[73] But once the initial
novelty had waned, the *Handkerchief* began to enjoy considerably less success. It provided a substantial compilation of secondhand news, including an unconventional emphasis upon continen-

[70] Joseph Walker and James Knight were among the "victims" who published the *Cosmopolite,* and both were imprisoned as a result. For Carlile's
influence see *Cosmopolite,* 14 July 1832. Carlile claimed to have written all of
the paper's leading articles (*Regenerator, and Advocate for the Unrepresented,*
2 Nov. 1839).

[71] For details of Berthold's activities see "*Destructive,*" 7 Dec. 1833; *Regenerator, or Guide to Happiness,* Aug. 1832. Many sections of the surviving copies
of *Berthold's Political Handkerchief* at Colindale are barely legible.

[72] *Berthold's Political Handkerchief,* 3 Sept. 1831.

[73] *Prompter,* 1 Oct. 1831.

tal politics.[74] Few working-class reformers could, however, afford to pay its price of 4*d*. Furthermore, Berthold antagonized many persons by his unorthodox amalgam of quasi-revolutionary fervor, financial theorizing, and concern with the excesses of "the property-destroying mob." [75] In October 1831 the Stamp Office declared the *Handkerchief* to be subject to all restrictions on periodicals and several hawkers were imprisoned by local magistrates for vending the periodical.[76] Thus Berthold's tract ceased publication after ten numbers, and the attempt to disseminate cheap literature on calico received a formidable setback. Carlile also attempted unsuccessfully to capitalize upon this method of defiance. He published on cotton an "untaxed general almanack" in 1831 and again in 1832 and a handful of radical broadsides, including *Cobbett's Spelling Book*, an attack upon the latter's use of "fables," and *Coronation Handkerchief*, a denunciation of the expenses entailed at William IV's coronation.[77]

Other journalistic maneuvers were resorted to in an attempt to circumvent the newspaper tax "legally." One device involved the "lending" of unstamped journals to prospective readers. Radical propagandists urged that the stamp acts merely prohibited the sale of untaxed newspapers and that a periodical could legally be "lent to read" for a limitless period. Many vendors proclaimed that they were lending periodicals rather than selling them, and

---

[74] There are extensive extracts from French political journals in *Berthold's Political Handkerchief*, 24 Sept. 1831, 1 Oct. 1831.

[75] *Ibid.*, 15 Oct. 1831. Berthold's all-consuming passion was for an ill-defined "system of Common-Wealth, aided and secured by a new medium as inexhaustible as the means of production, and yet obtainable only by he that produces" (*Regenerator, or Guide to Happiness*, Aug. 1832). His irrationalism (if not insanity) is indicated by the following letter written to Robert Owen: "Luther could not succeed without a Melanchton [*sic*], nor Christ without his Apostles [*sic*]—nor Moses without his brother Aaron—nor will ever Owen succeed without Berthold" (24 Dec. 1831, Owen Papers, No. 347).

[76] *Berthold's Political Handkerchief*, 24 Sept. 1831.

[77] *Poor Man's Guardian*, 26 Nov. 1831; *Cosmopolite*, 24 Nov. 1832. Copies of Carlile's tracts are in H. O. 64/17. Carlile also published a 6*d*. cotton edition of the *Union* (1831–1832), a 2*d*. unstamped weekly (S.S. report, 28 Nov. 1831, H.O. 64/11).

several newspapers sought to give substance to this fiction. The mastheads of these journals asserted defiantly that they were being "lent to read" for periods which varied in length from six months to two years.[78] Both the Stamp Office and local magistrates predictably ignored these pronouncements and continued to prosecute the publishers and vendors of such journals.

A comparable stratagem evolving from the fiction that an illegal act was committed only when unstamped periodicals were actually sold was employed by several vendors, including Alexander Campbell, the publisher of the *Tradesman,* and P. T. Bready. Campbell maintained a special box at his printing shop in Glasgow, the alleged purpose of which was "to receive donations of all those who wish for copies" of the *Tradesman.* Ignoring this deception, the Scottish authorities prosecuted Campbell successfully in June 1834.[79] Bready operated a "silent" shop in Sheffield. Illegal newspapers were placed on the counter, customers took them, deposited their money in a receptacle, and departed. The entire transaction was reportedly completed without a single word being exchanged.[80]

The unstamped newspapers that inundated England and Scotland during the years 1830–1836 were exceedingly fertile in scope and content. The majority of these journals were of an ephemeral nature, a substantial proportion not surviving even beyond a single number.[81] During periods of political excitement, as in the spring of 1832, the quantity of such publications accelerated dramatically. The tribulations of an established stamped journal could then be satirized effectively: "Sleep sel-

---

[78] For an example of a six months' period, see *Bath Elector,* 6 Oct. 1832. Lorymer's *Republican* proclaimed that it was "lent to read" for two years. The *Radical* stated: "Lent to Read for the Year for one Penny."

[79] *Trial of Alexander Campbell,* p. 11.

[80] Alexander Paterson, *Yorkshire Journalism: Past and Present* (Barnsley: *The Institute of Journalists,* 1901), p. 9.

[81] William Chambers, *Memoir of William and Robert Chambers* (Edinburgh: W. and R. Chambers, 1884), p. 234; Charles Knight, as quoted in *Chambers' Edinburgh Journal,* 1 Feb. 1834.

dom visits the editor [of the *Times*]; and when he dozes, he seems to be enveloped by a mass of three-halfpenny journals, which press upon him, and he awakes in danger of suffocation." [82]

Amidst the multiplicity of illicit journals, political publications garnered the largest degree of support. Most were of working-class origin, and their prime objective was frequently to disseminate radical political and economic ideas. In journalistic terms, many of these penny and twopenny newspapers, grounded as they were in a realistic assessment of working-class demands, were creditable endeavors. Some contained a substantial proportion of actual news, with comment being relegated to a column or two on the leader page. Parliamentary accounts and reports of working-class political gatherings often formed the staple of a journal's weekly offering. These were supplemented by summaries of police cases, by columns of opinions and letters from correspondents, and by advertisements. Names and dates were omitted occasionally from news accounts in an attempt to "conform" with the stamp laws, and one or two periodicals couched their reports in the prophetical or future tense (a practice that was allegedly advised by Brougham [83]) in order to evade the law.

Hetherington and Watson worked closely together to disseminate political news in the unstamped press.[84] The former's *Poor Man's Guardian* and the latter's *Working Man's Friend* sought to provide parallel comprehensive coverage of "ultra-radical"

---

[82] *Magician,* 24 March 1832.

[83] This omission of names and dates was followed by the *Artizan's Miscellany, or Journal of Politics and Literature,* an Edinburgh reform journal. It is doubtful that such a practice was endorsed by Brougham but a report to this effect was carried in the *Comet; or, Falvey's Liverpool Observer,* 4 Aug. 1832.

[84] The two men worked closely together in all phases of the newspaper movement, and as a token of their friendship, Hetherington dedicated the report of his 1840 trial for blasphemy to Watson: "The Friend of Truth, the Infidel to Error, and the Lover of Liberty, This Trial Is Dedicated, in Proof of the Affectionate Attachment That Subsists between Two Friends . . . and as a Tribute of Esteem, to God's Noblest Work—An Honest Man!" *Report of the Trial of Hetherington.*

activities. News accounts were not duplicated in either periodical; rather, they aimed deliberately to complement each other. Hetherington's journal often concentrated on general political summaries, whereas the *Working Man's Friend*, reflecting Cleave's association with it, tended to stress Irish news.[85] It featured detailed accounts of meetings held to agitate for repeal of the Union with Ireland, particularly during the spring of 1833 when the Coercion Bill proposed by the Grey government was being discussed by Parliament.

From 1834 onward, trade union activities began increasingly to dominate the columns of many unstamped journals. Several illegal periodicals, such as the *Pioneer; or Grand National Consolidated Trades Union Magazine*, and the *"Destructive" and Poor Man's Conservative*, specialized in trade union news. And in the northern industrial districts, the *United Trades' Cooperative Journal* and the *Poor Man's Advocate*, published in Manchester, and the *Voice of the West Riding*, published in Huddersfield, were only three among scores of journals that concentrated on extensive summaries of factory news.

Almost invariably the unstamped journals, including those of relatively high quality, reprinted news reports from the pages of the stamped dailies. For example, *Cleave's Weekly Police Gazette*, one of the most comprehensive illegal news sheets of the decade, extracted the bulk of its material from the *True Sun*, a radical evening newspaper. *Hetherington's Twopenny Dispatch*, a competitor, pursued a similar policy, as did the *Weekly Times* (1835–1836), a 2d. journal that boldly advertised itself as "the largest and best unstamped paper."

Accreditation was sometimes given to the newspaper from which the stories were taken, but more often it was not. News accounts were pilfered freely from the *Times*, the *Weekly Dis-*

---

[85] Cleave wrote many leaders for the *Working Man's Friend*. See, for example, the issues for 22 June and 6 July 1833. Cleave urged repeatedly that "the cause of Ireland [is] . . . the cause of England" (*Poor Man's Guardian*, 27 April 1833).

patch, and the *Morning Chronicle* and reprinted occasionally within two hours of their initial appearance. As a result, the proprietors of the stamped newspapers insistently, though unavailingly, demanded an effective copyright law, one that would provide them with at least one day's protection. The unstamped publishers retorted, in defense of their action, that the daily newspapers frequently appropriated news from each other without permission and that legal Sunday weeklies, including the *Examiner* and the *Spectator,* indulged in this practice at the expense of the dailies.

The better-quality illicit newspapers attempted to supplement the pilfered news accounts with reports submitted by their own correspondents. Such supplementation was often a necessity since the established journals did not usually cover "ultra-radical" activities.[86] When correspondents were employed by the unstamped newspapers, they were themselves oftentimes participants in the events about which they were writing. Members of the N.U.W.C., for example, were chosen at local meetings to forward accounts to the *Poor Man's Guardian.* Such correspondents generally received no monetary compensation, but the prospect of publicizing their hitherto obscure activities served as a sufficient inducement to many of them. During its early years, the *Poor Man's Guardian* relied on this psychological stimulus and, as a result, its news columns were replete with fascinating accounts of obscure radical meetings.

When circulation lagged, this voluntary spur sometimes proved insufficient. The *United Trades' Co-operative Journal* warned its readers that unless reformers in Ashton-under-Lyne and other South Lancashire towns forwarded reports of their meetings, the periodical could never be "as valuable and interest-

---

[86] On one occasion John Black of the *Morning Chronicle* refused to print a report of an N.U.W.C. meeting on the ground that it was "too revolutionary" (S.S. report, 26 Oct. 1831, H.O. 64/11). Few stamped journals printed accounts of the newspaper repeal meetings, a source of continual irritation to reformers.

ing as it otherwise might be:" [87] But this admonition had little effect, and paid reporters were assigned subsequently by the *United Trades' Co-operative Journal* to cover radical activities in nearby towns such as Ashton, Stockport, and Haslindon.[88] The use of paid reporters was infrequent, however, because the operating costs of the illegal journals had to be pared to a minimum. Not surprisingly, correspondents performed a more crucial function in provincial areas, where there were fewer news reports available to be pilfered. John Doherty admitted this when he sought in September 1831, to transfer his stamped *Voice of the People* from Manchester to London, partially on the ground that "in Manchester . . . a reporter is indispensible [*sic*], while in London the daily papers supply all the news." [89]

Columns of opinion were also expropriated wholesale from many of the stamped journals. The numerous articles written by an ex-naval lieutenant named John Williams under the pseudonym "Publicola" were especially popular.[90] These weekly exhortations for reform appeared initially in the *Weekly Dispatch*, a proreform stamped journal. Within hours of their appearance, they were re-copied into several unstamped periodicals, including the *Man*, the *Working Man's Friend*, and the *Political Register*.[91] The weekly comments of "O.P.Q." which appeared regularly in the *Morning Chronicle* were made similarly available to working-class readers. Illegal journals, such as *Berthold's Political Handkerchief*, featured these columns on a regular basis.

At the commencement of the war of the unstamped, many illicit penny periodicals were produced by a single person. Car-

[87] *United Trades' Co-operative Journal*, 24 April 1830.

[88] *Ibid.*, 22 and 29 May 1830.

[89] Doherty, *Letter to the Members*, p. 13.

[90] For information about Williams, described as "one of the noblest warriors that ever yet appeared in the Cause of the liberties of man," see "Private History of the London Newspaper Press," *Tait's Edinburgh Magazine*, supp., new ser. I (1834), 792. *Letters of Publicola*, 1st ser. (London, 1840) is a collection of many of "Publicola's" columns.

[91] Hickson, *Taxes on Knowledge*, p. 9; *Political Register*, 15 Aug. 1835.

penter, for example, printed, published, and edited the *Political Letters and Pamphlets* without assistance for approximately the first two months of its existence. Carlile performed similarly with respect to at least three of the illegal periodicals which he issued, the *Prompter, Gauntlet,* and *A Scourge for the Littleness of "Great" Men.* Berthold likewise managed his *Handkerchief* without any assistance whatever.[92]

But as the circulation of the illegal journals increased, there developed a rising demand for a better-quality product. Even talented writers of the caliber of Carpenter and Carlile began to feel the need for assistance. They sought regular contributors for their journals. Once acquired, these additions would often be advertised as a mark of distinctive quality for the journal. In this way O'Brien first achieved journalistic renown as a contributor to Carpenter's *Political Letters and Pamphlets.* The series of articles which he wrote for that journal during 1831 under the signature "Bronterre," brought him the editorship of the *Midland Representative and Birmingham Herald,* a stamped newspaper published in Birmingham, and subsequently that of the *Poor Man's Guardian* and *Hetherington's Twopenny Dispatch.*[93]

Watson was not as successful as Carpenter in his search for literary contributors. He solicited assistance vainly from the Irish M.P.'s Daniel O'Connell and Richard Lalor Sheil in order to increase the appeal of his *Working Man's Friend.* When this effort failed he turned to John Lawless, a minor Irish publicist, and gave prominence to a series of addresses by him in which repeal of the Union with Ireland was propounded vigorously.[94]

[92] The publisher of an unstamped journal had occasionally to acquire his own press and types because no regular printer was willing to undertake the work (Carlile, letters to Thomas Turton, 19 Nov. 1835, 10 Dec. 1835, as quoted in Campbell, *Battle of the Press,* pp. 203–204).

[93] Cole, *Chartist Portraits,* pp. 242–244.

[94] Lawless' *History of Ireland* was published in 3*d.* numbers during the war of the unstamped and became a staple of the cheap literature of the 1830's (*Poor Man's Guardian,* 29 Sept. 1832).

The *Poor Man's Guardian,* during most of its existence, solicited contributions from a variety of correspondents who represented a broad spectrum of radical thought.

As a result of this search for contributors, the illicit periodicals began increasingly to be the product of joint enterprise. The *Man,* for example, was edited, printed, and published by Richard E. Lee, an enthusiastic young radical who continually agitated for a National Convention.[95] Yet the better-known Spencean propagandist, George Petrie, writing regularly under the nom de plume "Agrarius," was the effective mainstay of that paper during the greater part of its existence, and when Lee was imprisoned in August 1834, Peter Baume, an eccentric and prosperous London reformer, maintained that journal temporarily until a committee could be established to continue it.[96] The *Working Man's Friend* was published and financed by Watson, both before and during his term of imprisonment in 1833 for publication of an illegal newspaper. But John Cleave was almost certainly the editor of the journal during much of its existence and the author of many of its leaders.[97] Even Carlile, who epitomized individualism, accepted financial and technical assistance willingly from Julian Hibbert and others for the publication of the *Prompter* after being imprisoned for seditious libel in 1831.

Hetherington relied even more unhesitatingly upon the support of colleagues. He admitted freely that his successes were dependent upon the efforts of more talented co-workers, and that the major literary activities connected with his publications were

[95] Lee played a prominent role in the Calthorpe St. incident during the spring of 1833. See *S.C. on Cold Bath Fields* (1833), p. 36, q. 534. For further information about Lee see Lovett's account of the N.U.W.C. in Place Papers, Add. MSS 27,791, ff. 256–257; Lee, *Whisper to the Whigs,* pp. 12–15.

[96] *Man,* 10 Aug. 1834; S.S. report, 8 Aug. 1834, H.O. 64/11.

[97] The evidence for Cleave's editorship seems conclusive. Although he is not identified by name, the residence listed for the editor, 27 King St., Snow Hill, is that of Cleave. Also, the style and tenor of many of the leaders is redolent of Cleave's oratory and, in a speech to the N.U.W.C., he referred to his participation in the journal along with Watson (*Poor Man's Guardian,* 27 April 1833).

borne by others. O'Brien, who edited the *Poor Man's Guardian* for him, wrote that journal's commentary upon events and during 1835–1836 performed similarly for *Hetherington's Twopenny Dispatch*.[98] In an unusual demonstration of political ambivalence, Hetherington employed Lorymer, a reformer possessed of a much more revolutionary temperament, to edit two of his other journals, the *Radical* and the *Republican; or, Voice of the People*. According to a police informant, Lorymer agreed to write gratuitously for Hetherington, to turn all profits from the journals over to him, and to insure him against financial loss.[99] A culmination of this tendency toward collective publication of illegal newspapers was reached in 1834 when a group of "St. Simonians" proposed that a trades union of unstamped editors be organized. This association would attempt to regulate standard literary forms, prices, and advertisements and would seek to assure the production of a different unstamped newspaper each day. The scheme, so far as is known, proved abortive.[100]

Due to the increasing reliance upon correspondents, a number of persons began to contribute regularly to many unstamped journals. Allen Davenport, a moderate Spencean socialist, who played a minor role in the activities of the N.U.W.C., was one of the most productive of these proletarian free-lance journalists.[101] He furnished poems and articles to at least four of the more important illegal journals—the *Man*, the *Poor Man's Guardian*, the *Prompter*, and Lorymer's *Le Bonnet Rouge*. Davenport propounded the theme of an alliance between the working classes and the lower middle class in order to secure political concessions from the Whigs. Once such concessions were

---

[98] O'Brien broke with Hetherington in 1837 and claimed at that time that the latter had imitated his style and that he had written most of Hetherington's articles for him (Bronterre O'Brien, "Is Henry Hetherington an Honest Man?," from newsclipping, 1837, in Lovett Papers, Vol. I, ff. 72–73).

[99] S.S. report, 2 July 1831, H.O. 64/11.   [100] *Gauntlet*, 19 Jan. 1834.

[101] For Davenport's activities in the N.U.W.C., see *Poor Man's Guardian*, 7 Sept. 1833, 9 Nov. 1833.

obtained, a more humane society could be developed through the nationalization of all land by the parishes.[102]

George Edmonds, one of the most extreme radicals involved in the repeal campaign, was another writer who contributed regular signed articles to many unstamped newspapers, including *Le Bonnet Rouge* the *People's Weekly Police Gazette,* and the *Weekly Herald*.[103] Edmonds also edited the final four numbers of the *Cab,* a halfpenny radical journal which circulated in London during the summer of 1832 and which proclaimed on its masthead: "England shall never know Peace till Six Hours Hard Labor is, by Law on Demand, exchangeable for Twenty-Four Hours good Food." [104] Edmonds advocated a "social revolution" in coruscating language. He regularly depicted Parliament as a "Gang of Housebreakers" and "a great lubberly, insolent, political union" and the nation's churches as "tithe-traps," and his essays bore such titles as "the Things in Office" and "the Butchers in the Lords." [105] These stylistic excesses when linked to his endorsement of class conflict, identified Edmonds' articles to the public even when they were unsigned. Other regular contributors to the unstamped press included the Owenite lecturer Thomas Macconnell, who composed poems, co-operative essays, and radical leaders, and Richard Oastler, the factory and poor law reformer who wrote scathing articles for the *Poor Man's Guardian, Cleave's*

[102] See his letter in *ibid.,* 24 Aug. 1833; *Man,* 28 July 1833.

[103] Thompson, *Making of the English Working Class,* p. 811, incorrectly confuses Edmonds with a Birmingham radical of the same name. Edmonds was a Cornishman who came to London initially in 1832 and then became active in London journalism. See the clipping from the *Morning Chronicle, c.* 1832, Place Newspaper Collection, Set 57, f. 214.

[104] *Cab,* 23 June 1832. The *Cab,* which commenced publication in March 1832, became noticeably more extreme after Edmonds became editor.

[105] *Weekly Herald,* 7 Aug. 1836; *People's Weekly Police Gazette,* 7 May 1836; *Le Bonnet Rouge,* 23 and 30 March 1833. In a letter which circulated in one of the unstamped journals, Edmonds asserted: "We are civilized cannibals. We eat each other by *law*" (*Appeal to the Labourers of England, an Exposure of Aristocrat Spies, and the Infernal Machinery of the Poor Law Muder Bill* . . . [London: S. Wilson, 1835?], p. 12).

[169]

Weekly Police Gazette, and *Hetherington's Twopenny Dispatch*.[106] Thus one by-product of the journalistic war of the unstamped was the nurturing into existence of many free-lance journalists of working-class origins and outlook.

Many illicit political journals performed an important function in addition to disseminating news and comment. Their advertising columns served as media of communication for radical associations. Foremost among the latter was the N.U.W.C., and resolutions passed by its local chapters were forwarded regularly to the *Poor Man's Guardian* and to other unstamped journals for insertion. Similarly, the British Association for the Promotion of Co-operative Knowledge, which played an active role in support of the untaxed newspapers, employed the columns of Carpenter's *Political Letters* in order to communicate more effectively with its members. These advertisements and notices helped to forge a greater degree of working-class solidarity since they were widely read by the laborers.

In return for the right to advertise either gratis or for a nominal fee, the branches of the N.U.W.C. and other associations all but took the illegal journals under their protection.[107] Copies of the *Poor Man's Guardian*, for example, were hawked and distributed at weekly meetings of the N.U.W.C. held at the Rotunda and at meetings of the organization's district classes. One member of the organization even recalled that Popay, a notorious police spy, had "frequently" read the *Poor Man's Guardian* to him at such gatherings.[108]

Conversely, the control of advertising columns by the illicit journals was sometimes employed to exert pressure upon political

[106] *"Destructive,"* 26 Oct. 1833; *Poor Man's Guardian*, 27 Sept. 1834; Cecil Driver, *Tory Radical: The Life of Richard Oastler* (New York: Oxford University Press, 1946), pp. 286, 301–304, 535.

[107] The *Radical Reformer* accepted gratis advertisements of a political content that were "promotive of radical reform" (17 Dec. 1831).

[108] Testimony of William Woodford, *S.C. on the Petition of Frederick Young and Others* (1833), p. 41, qq. 908–912; *Working Man's Friend*, 19 Jan. 1833.

opponents. It was reported that in 1832 Hetherington refused to accept advertisements from the Spitalfields and East End branch of the N.U.W.C. because it was in the process of severing its relationship with the parent organization. The branch unavailingly threatened in turn to cease selling the *Poor Man's Guardian* to its members unless the order was rescinded.[109]

Despite the widespread interest in politics, a phenomenon attested to by greater support for illegal journalism during periods of political excitement, many illicit penny periodicals were of lighter content. The spectacular success of the Society for the Diffusion of Useful Knowledge's *Penny Magazine,* which commenced publication in March 1832, generated an initially hostile response from working-class reformers. Angered by the journal's failure to deal with politics, they condemned the "mere pabulum which the Education and Improvement-of-Society mongers" sought to foist upon them in the form of "useless" knowledge and engravings.[110] But when the circulation of the *Penny Magazine* began to attain unprecedented proportions, possibly to the extent of 200,000 weekly by the end of 1832, working-class imitators took their cue.[111] The result was a spate of "useful knowledge" penny journals, many of which terminated their existence even more quickly than did their political counterparts.

The "useful" penny periodicals which circulated illegally be-

---

[109] This situation assertedly led to friction between the *Cosmopolite,* edited by Carlile, and the *Poor Man's Guardian* because the former was willing to accept advertisements from the organization (S.S. report, 13 Aug. 1832, H.O. 64/12).

[110] *Political Penny Magazine,* 10 Sept. 1836. Lorymer described the *Penny Magazine* as "a pennyworth of nauseous literary garbage—the very offals of literary slaughter-houses—such as the history of beetles, kangaroos, and all sorts of beasts (except Whigs)!" (*Le Bonnet Rouge,* 16 Feb. 1833). John Bell depicted the S.D.U.K. as "A Society for the Confusion of Useful Knowledge" (*True Sun,* 25 Aug. 1832).

[111] For an estimated circulation of 200,000, see Knight, *Passages,* II, 184. The *Penny Magazine* itself claimed a sale of 160,000 (supp., Sept. 1833, II, 378).

tween 1830 and 1836 featured a mixture of anecdotes, poems, reviews, essays, and extracted descriptive passages. Innocuous political comments were interspersed occasionally in the guise of a book review or of a poem, but few of these periodicals, whether of working- or middle-class paternity, provided penetrating criticism of the government. One miscellany entitled the *Patriot*, for example, offered an assortment of "useful knowledge" articles and also deplored "the lamentable and wretched and heart-rending condition of the working classes." But its proffered endorsement of "a real radical reform" was too ambiguously phrased to arouse governmental concern.[112] Another "useful knowledge" miscellany entitled the *Halfpenny Magazine* which was published in London during 1832 featured some reprinted proreform political material, most of it aimed at prominent Tories, such as the Duke of Wellington. Of far greater impact, however, was the journal's variegated compilation of biographical and literary sketches, poems, descriptive accounts, "useful" information, and anecdotes.[113]

Thus the objective of these "useful knowledge" journals was primarily to titillate the fancy and the intellect, or, as one periodical expressed it, "to unite the *utile et dolce*." [114] Avoidance of political controversy often insured a more permanent though smaller readership, one less likely to dissolve during periods of general excitement. An additional factor was that the discretionary implementation of the stamp laws meant that nonpolitical periodicals were unlikely to be prosecuted. The *Penny Magazine*, the Society for the Propagation of Christian Knowledge's *Saturday Magazine, Chambers' Edinburgh Journal*, and the numerous other penny miscellanies that circulated, both middle- and

[112] *Patriot*, 27 Aug. 1831.

[113] *Halfpenny Magazine*, 19 May 1832, 26 May 1832.

[114] *Half-Penny Magazine, or, Cheap Repository of Amusement and Instruction*, No. 1 (1832). This was an undated biweekly published in Edinburgh by "a Gentleman who was many years connected with the London Cheap Periodicals."

working-class in origin, were as illegal as the controversial publications of Hetherington, Watson, Lorymer, and Carpenter. But they were rarely prosecuted, an indication that the newspaper tax was manipulated indirectly to dampen excessive criticism of the government.

With political content excluded, a diet of "instructive" essays, poems, and anecdotes, even when profusely complemented by illustrations, was not likely to prove sufficiently popular. Imaginative literature, often of a poor quality, was requisite to securing a larger circulation, and those journals which ignored this fact did so at their own peril. As one successful journal observed, with reference to the rising demand for popular tales and narratives: "Nothing but what is new can go down now-a-days." [115]

The *Antiquarian*, an illegal journal that survived for only one number, exemplifies the difficulties experienced by penny miscellanies that eschewed both fiction and political controversy. It sought to generate an appreciation among the working classes for the Fine Arts and Architecture. One article was devoted to this subject in its initial number but its other contributions, including selections from the *Old Oxford Guide* and a secondhand description of the resinous substance gum-lac, were not likely to wean politically conscious readers away from the *Poor Man's Guardian*.[116] The *Argus*, a penny weekly that was also published in 1832, endured a similar fate. It likewise eschewed political subjects and refused to compromise with the literary demands of its working-class readership. Its "useful knowledge" offerings made insufficient concessions to popular taste in terms of imaginative fiction or novelty, and it survived for only two numbers.[117] The *Magazine of Interest*, still another amongst the scores of short-lived "useful knowledge" miscellanies that circulated between 1830 and 1836, was slightly more popular in for-

---

[115] *Parrot*, 2 June 1832.   [116] *Antiquarian*, 26 May 1832.

[117] A weekly section entitled "Hints to the Instructors of Youth" was the only concession to public taste (*Argus*, 13 Oct. 1832).

mat. Its articles possessed only a few minor political references, however, and its pages lacked a substantive degree of imaginative content. It proved to be as unsuccessful as the *Antiquarian* and the *Argus*.[118]

The *Half-Penny Magazine*, published in Edinburgh during 1832, was one of the few working-class "useful knowledge" miscellanies of the decade to achieve success. It made fifty biweekly appearances and thus survived for over six months, a considerable journalistic achievement. But the relative success of the *Half-Penny Magazine* was attributable to the simplicity of its format and to its stress upon fictional and imaginative literature. None of its selections was original, and all were sufficiently "popular," that is, lacking in intellectual demands upon the readers. The bulk of its weekly fare consisted of simple tales, often dealing with criminals.[119]

Thus, a decided preference for the *dulce* over the *utile* appears to have been expressed by working-class readers. Only a relatively small number of illegal periodicals of any kind survived beyond a few weeks, but of those that did prosper, most were either political in content or possessed of a substantial proportion of purely entertaining matter. The longevity of such crude literary productions as the *Annals of Crime and New Newgate Calendar*, a weekly that circulated for more than a year, and the *Calendar of Horrors! A Weekly Register of the Terrific, Wonderful, Instructive, Legendary, Extraordinary, and Fictitious*, edited by the prolific Thomas Prest, attests to this. Both eschewed political analysis, but their regular staple of ghost stories, horror tales, and narratives of criminals enabled each of them to prosper for more than a year.[120] Other successful illustrated

---

[118] For an example of the *Magazine of Interest's* "radical" tone, see the account of the trial of Thomas Wentworth, Earl of Strafford, 31 Aug. 1833.

[119] See the tale entitled "MacVarich the Murderer," *Half-Penny Magazine*, No. 1 (1832).

[120] The *Annals of Crime* (1833–1834) ran for fifty-three weekly numbers and the *Calendar of Horrors!* (1835–36) survived for ninety-one numbers. Thomas Prest, who engaged in many cheap publishing ventures during the

weeklies, such as the *Tales of the Wars; or, Naval and Military Chronicle* (1836–1840) and *Tales of All Nations; or, Popular Legends and Romances* (1836), both of which were published and compiled by William M. Clark, provided a steady outpouring of adventurous narrative.

The survival of the penny chapbook tradition into the 1830's also facilitated the dissemination of unstamped literature. This literary genre, which had provided the staple reading matter of the poor and of the lower middle class during the eighteenth century, embodied a mixture of crude local radicalism and poor-quality fiction.[121] William Smith, an Edinburgh stationer, was one of the most active publishers of chapbooks during the 1830's. In addition to a prodigious output of poems, broadsides, and tracts, all embellished with woodcuts, Smith published at least two illegal journals, the *Bawbee Bagpipe* (1833) which survived for twelve numbers, and the *Advocate; A Half-Penny Periodical* (1834) which expired after six numbers. Both periodicals furnished a judicious compound of Scottish tales and anecdotes and ill-defined radical complaints. The *Advocate*, in particular, aimed satirical shafts at the local police and at other Edinburgh institutions.[122] Thus Smith and a few other publishers of chapbooks achieved minor success during the war of the unstamped by catering to working-class demands for political and imaginative offerings.

Police gazettes formed another category of unstamped newspapers, buttressing the political and "useful knowledge" journals. They were frequently successful since they often fused popular radicalism with crude fiction. Many of the police journals placed heavy emphasis upon political news, and the majority that circu-

---

1830's, is accurately described by Louis James as "a general literary hack" (*Fiction for the Working Man,* p. 25).

[121] John Ashton, ed., *Chap-Books of the Eighteenth Century* (London: Chatto and Windus, 1882), pp. vii–ix.

[122] *Advocate,* No. 4 (1834). For an introduction to Smith's multiple literary activities, see the bound volumes in the British Museum entitled *Smithiana* (840 m. 33, 34).

lated between 1830 and 1836 were strongly radical in tone. This radical content was a partial response to the official police gazettes, such as the *Hue and Cry,* which, although technically illegal, circulated without fear of prosecution.

Imaginative fiction was an important component of these unstamped police journals since the borderline between police "news" and sensational crime and adventure narratives was often razor thin. For example, the *Calendar of Crime, and General Advertiser,* a London penny weekly, featured lurid descriptions of brutal crimes, both historical and contemporary. Much of its content was obviously fictional; however, portions of it could be validly described as constituting legitimate "news." [123] Its professed aim was to plead the cause of "innocence, poverty, misery" by reporting every type of crime, an objective that closely aligned it with the official police sheets.[124] Another police journal, the biweekly *Life in Edinburgh, or, the Police Intelligencer, and Dramatic Review,* was far more akin to Smith's *Bawbee Bagpipe* in tenor than to conventional police journals. But despite its atrocious literary quality, it consisted mostly of popularized accounts of cases actually before the Edinburgh police courts.[125]

During the spring and summer of 1833, working-class police gazettes began to play a major role in the war of the unstamped. Charles Penny's *People's Police Gazette, and Tradesman's Advertiser,* a folio-sized amalgam of crime reports and accounts of trades union activities, was one of the earliest in existence, and it remained extant for about a year despite repeated Stamp Office harassments.[126] Its longevity is probably attributable to its marked tendency toward sensationalism.[127] But the persistence of its publisher was undoubtedly a crucial factor in keeping it alive, since according to Penny's own testimony, he spent nearly

[123] See, for example, *Calendar of Crime,* 24 March 1832.

[124] *Ibid.,* 17 March 1832. [125] *Life in Edinburgh,* 29 May 1833.

[126] See *People's Conservative* (formerly the *"Destructive"*), 15 Feb. 1834.

[127] One reforming middle-class journal (*Tait's Edinburgh Magazine,* new ser. I (1834), 734) described it as "a most disgusting mass of trash and depravity."

£700 in defending himself against repeated governmental prosecutions.[128]

In March 1834 the *People's Hue and Cry, or Weekly Police Register* appeared. This was similar in format to the *People's Police Gazette* and was not noticeably superior to it in literary quality. It was much more radical in outlook, however, reflecting the views of its proprietors, Lee and Petrie, the organizers of the *Man*.[129] Despite a substantial circulation, it seems to have been out of existence by the summer of 1834, possibly as the result of a Stamp Office prosecution.[130] *Cleave's Weekly Police Gazette*, which began publication in January 1834, then supplanted it in public estimation and went on to become unquestionably the most influential of the decade's illegal police journals. Rapidly outpacing its original conception, *Cleave's Weekly Police Gazette* became a full-sized comprehensive newspaper, one that provided a surfeit of news accounts and radical political commentary. By the end of 1835, it had amassed an estimated weekly circulation of thirty to forty thousand. [131]

A final class of illegal penny periodicals was the illustrated satirical miscellany. Like the chapbooks and the police gazettes, these journals, which included such productions as *Figaro in London* (1831–1839), the *Devil's Memorandum Book* (1832), *Punch in London* (1832), and *Punchinello! or Sharps, Flats, and Naturals! A Family Gazette of Fun, Fashion, Literature, and the Drama* (1832), blended radical political analysis with lit-

---

[128] *People's Police Gazette*, 3 May 1834; *Poor Man's Guardian*, 3 May 1834. Penny produced several other untaxed journals of a nonpolitical nature, including the *Doctor: A Medical Penny Magazine* (1832–1837) and the *Penny Story-Teller* (1832–1836).

[129] *People's Hue and Cry*, 13 July 1834; *Man*, 13 April 1834.

[130] *Tait's Edinburgh Magazine*, new ser. I (1834), 622–625.

[131] For this estimated circulation, see Buller's speech in the Commons, *Hansard*, H. of C., 18 Aug. 1835, XXX, 624. See also Place's statement in Place Papers, Add. MSS 27,791, f. 290. Place is an unreliable source for the circulation of illegal newspapers since his information was secondhand. In this instance the estimate may be sound since Place helped Cleave publish the *Gazette* from King's Bench Prison (Place, letter to Hume, 12 May 1835, Place Papers, Add. MSS 35,150, f. 49a).

erary extracts. But for the most part they were more sophisticated in style and execution than the aforementioned and were more exclusively "middle class" in orientation.[132] Their main ploy was a steady concentration of subtle wit at the expense of the Church of England, the aristocracy, the monarchy, and other conservative institutions. Much of this wit was cleverly capsuled in the form of mock births, deaths, and advertisements, a technique that had been originated by William Hone in the 1820's. The coruscating engravings of George Cruikshank, Robert Seymour, and other popular illustrators graced the pages of the satirical weeklies while prominent literary personalities such as Douglas Jerrold, Thomas Hood, and Henry Mayhew conducted them. Working-class journalists were, as a consequence, unable to compete successfully in this phase of the war of the unstamped.[133]

The overriding aim of the satirical sheets was to ridicule the forces of conservatism and reaction and to assist in the cause of moderate reform. They were not regarded specifically by their projectors as auxiliary weapons in the agitation for an untaxed press, though the latter was accepted as a laudable goal. But the large quantity and variety of these periodicals contributed to the effectiveness of the working-class repeal campaign, particularly during the spring of 1832 when satire became a popular weapon as the result of emotions generated by the controversy over parliamentary reform. In London alone more than eighteen satirical penny periodicals were circulating during the spring of 1832, a situation that impelled one of these journals to report humorously: "The town is overrun with devils! . . . two hundred in the publishers' shops in Regent Street, and a large assortment of every size and shape at all the newspaper printing offices and

[132] This point is also stressed by James, *Fiction for the Working Man,* p. 21.
[133] Mayhew edited the celebrated *Figaro in London,* and Jerrold edited *Punch in London,* a rival weekly (E. E. Kellett, "The Press," in G. M. Young, ed., *Early Victorian England* [London: Oxford University Press, 1934], p. 86). Hood was the editor of a third competitor, the less successful *Punchinello! or Sharps, Flats, and Naturals! A Family Gazette of Fun, Fashion, Literature, and the Drama.*

minor theatres." [134] Satirical miscellanies likewise appeared in provincial cities, including Liverpool, Glasgow, and Sheffield, and though most of these journals failed to survive beyond a few numbers, their impact was pronounced.

Only a bare indication has been given of the scope of the many hundreds of cheap journals that inundated England and Scotland during the years 1830–1836. Periodicals were published that catered to every level of social and individual taste—legal, scientific, historical, political, religious, and literary. Such journals as the *Evangelical Penny Magazine, and Bible Illustrator* (1832), the *Graphic and Historical Illustrator: An Original Miscellany of Literary, Antiquarian, and Typographical Information* (1832–1834), the *Lawyer: A Legal Penny Magazine* (1833), the *Physician* (1832), and the *Sporting Courier* (1832?) are representative to a far greater extent than they are inclusive.

Although those unstamped journals that espoused controversial political and social themes left the greatest imprint on the repeal movement, the majority of the illegal journals that appeared were politically innocuous. But even amongst these, the prevalent tendency, as in other aspects of the war of the unstamped, was in the direction of increasing radicalism. *Punchinello! or Sharps, Flats, and Naturals!,* for example, featured literary satire in its initial number but by its third appearance, as competition increased perceptibly, it began to attack the "full-fed cormorants of the Church of England and other institutions." [135] This general tendency of the unstamped toward greater militancy, which was paralleled by shifts in the commitments of leading journalists and by more sophisticated techniques of defiance, alienated many moderate reformers and reduced the possibility of a viable radical coalition. The severe response of the government to the war of the unstamped exacerbated this situation further.

[134] *Punchinello,* 24 Feb. 1832; *Figaro in London,* 17 March 1832.
[135] *Punchinello,* 20 Jan. 1832, 3 Feb. 1832.

CHAPTER 7

Governmental Response

The unstamped working-class newspapers published between 1830 and 1836 generally attained spectacular success in terms of circulation. Throughout England and Scotland radical penny journals poured forth in defiance of the stamp laws. These periodicals were extensively disseminated, both in London and in leading urban provincial centers. Only rural areas remained relatively unaffected by the war of the unstamped.

Precise circulation figures are difficult to establish. Both supporters and opponents of the unstamped press frequently exaggerated its potency. The latter hoped to arouse a substantial conservative counteroffensive, and the committed were often tempted to exaggerate the influence of their activities. Furthermore, illicit journalism became increasingly competitive as the agitation against the newspaper duty developed momentum, and financial rewards, in the form of advertising revenue and increased sales, might accrue to those periodicals that purported to have the largest circulations. The paucity of surviving contemporary accounts of the war of the unstamped presents another obstacle in pinpointing the numbers of illegal newspapers circulated. Several of these accounts (including that of Place) shed

[180]

valuable light on the repeal agitation, but few were written by persons who were in a position to know exactly how many copies of the illegal journals were being disseminated.

Place's impressionistic estimate that several hundred unstamped newspapers were published in Great Britain in the years between 1830–1836 is, if anything, too modest.[1] At any moment during these years between thirty and forty illegal journals were probably circulating in London alone, and with provincial publications added, the projected total of illicit periodicals is considerably larger.[2] And during periods of widespread political excitement, as in the spring of 1832, the number of untaxed periodicals in circulation was increased further.

Between 1830 and 1836 illegal journals were openly hawked at radical meeting places, coffee shops and news rooms, in London and in the provinces.[3] Placards boldly displayed these journals in shop windows, often within hailing distance of Somerset House, the headquarters of the Commissioners of Stamps.[4] Hand-printed posters announced almost weekly the appearance of fresh entrants in the journalistic competition. Not surprisingly, demands for the destruction of the "desperate trash" that was

---

[1] Place Papers, Add. MSS 27,819, f. 26. Without citing her reference, Lucy M. Salmon quotes Place as suggesting that only about 150 unstamped newspapers were published (*Newspaper and Authority*, p. 197). This estimate is ridiculously low. Over five hundred unstamped periodicals are described in Wiener, *A Descriptive Finding List*.

[2] According to Halévy, thirty-two were circulating in London during July 1831. (*Triumph of Reform*, p. 18). According to C. H. Timperley, thirty to forty were circulating in London during the spring and summer of 1833. (*An Encyclopaedia of Literary and Typographical Anecdotes* [London: Henry G. Bohn, 1842], p. 929 n.).

[3] Popay, the police spy, has vividly described the vending of such journals in the Rotunda: "[There are] two stalls in the passage where all the Weekly Pamphlets and Papers may be bought by any person, one in the theatre and there is generally about 10 men and youths who hawk them about the theatre among the persons" (S.S. report, 22 Nov. 1831, H.O. 64/11).

[4] The "Western Republican Repository" where Lorymer sold unstamped newspapers and almanacs was located next to Somerset House (*Poor Man's Guardian*, 2 Nov. 1833).

inundating Britain provoked only renewed efforts from working-class journalists.[5]

The circulation of individual journals is particularly difficult to determine. One contemporary estimated that a penny publication required a sale of four to five thousand in order to remain viable financially.[6] This is a convincing estimate for pamphlets but it is probably too high to be applicable to unstamped weeklies since they were printed on a single sheet and their operating costs were minimal. Unstamped periodicals could also expect to earn more profit from advertisements than could the pamphlets. Many of the journals simply ignored the advertisement duty, and the low rates that they charged for advertising represented a clear profit. For these reasons, it is more likely that a weekly circulation of three to four thousand was sufficient to enable a penny journal to break even. The *Literary Test; a Liberal Moral and Independent Weekly Review*, a 2*d.* periodical, estimated that it needed a sale of eight thousand to avoid financial loss whereas Carlile's *Prompter* survived for an entire year with a weekly sale of one thousand at a retail price of 3*d.*[7] The *Devil's Pulpit*, a 2*d.* journal that reprinted the free thought lectures of Carlile's associate, the Rev. Robert Taylor, ran for forty-six numbers with a circulation that probably did not substantially exceed two thousand.[8]

But even if only three thousand copies had to be sold to avoid financial loss, the overwhelming majority of illicit periodicals could not approach this minimal amount, and most terminated

[5] *Chambers' Edinburgh Journal*, 2 Feb. 1833, 28 April 1832.

[6] Chadwick, *On the Taxes on Knowledge*, p. 29. Charles Knight estimated that a 2*d.* newspaper had to sell 10,000 copies in order to break even. (*Newspaper Stamp*, p. 11).

[7] *State Trials*, II, 610, as cited in Wickwar, *Struggle for the Freedom of the Press*, p. 296 n. George Pilgrim, one of the publishers of the *Cosmopolite*, claimed exaggeratedly that a sale of 10,000 copies was required to show a profit on a 1*d.* newspaper (*Cosmopolite*, 6 Oct. 1832).

[8] S.S. report, 17 May 1831, H.O. 64/11.

their existence within a month. The *Literary Test*, for example, which expired after five numbers, claimed to have suffered losses of twenty to thirty pounds per week during its final weeks.[9] Those journals that remained in circulation for a longer period of time were often compelled to do this on a readership of under one thousand, thus enduring substantial economic losses. Such losses were especially severe during the final months of the war of the unstamped when the government substantially accelerated its policy of repression, forcing one participant to admit that "the struggle has become ruinous to the proprietors of the Unstamped." [10]

Hence in most instances political idealism and a pronounced sense of grievance, rather than a projection of financial gain, were the motivating elements behind the working-class journalism of the 1830's. The profit motive was not an entirely negligible factor, particularly in the case of the "useful knowledge" miscellanies; a reasonable profit, however, could not ordinarily be anticipated from illegal journalism, even when circulation exceeded expectations. Many journalists, therefore, including Carpenter and Hetherington, participated in the campaign at a weekly loss while others contented themselves with a negligible profit.[11] R. E. Lee, who published and edited the *Man*, one of the more successful journals of the decade with an estimated circulation of twelve thousand, had to settle for a maximum profit of five pounds weekly.[12]

Some publishers depended upon wealthy sympathizers, such as

[9] *Literary Test*, 21 Jan. 1832.

[10] *Hetherington's Twopenny Dispatch*, 19 March 1836. During one week in the spring of 1836, Cleave lost 2,500 newspapers due to governmental seizures and Hetherington lost twice that (Cleave, letter to Place, 15 May 1836, Place Newspaper Collection, Set 70, f. 514).

[11] According to Cleave, Carpenter suffered heavy losses in each of his early journalistic ventures, culminating in *Carpenter's Monthly Political Magazine* (*Proceedings of the Third Co-operative Congress*, p. 40).

[12] *Man*, 25 Aug. 1833. The profit on Number 28 of the *Man* was £3 9s. 5¼d. (*ibid.*, 10 Aug. 1834).

Julian Hibbert, for necessary financial support. Hibbert, a gradu-
ate of Eton and Oxford and a classical scholar of some note, gave
assistance to Carlile's publishing enterprises and was almost certainly the "truly noble friend to the cause of freedom and Hu-
manity" who kept Lee's *People's Hue and Cry* afloat financially
during 1834.[13] Another wealthy reformer, Peter Baume,
claimed to have financed the publication of Lee's *Man* to the extent of £27 during the latter's imprisonment in 1834, and yet
another patron, the phrenologist Dr. John Epps, pledged himself to purchase twenty-five numbers per month of the radical
Church Examiner and Ecclesiastical Record, in order to help underwrite that periodical.[14]

Only a handful of the more successful working-class journals
achieved weekly sales in excess of ten thousand. The *Poor Man's
Guardian* probably attained a circulation slightly in excess of this
during the first two years of its existence when it was vended
widely among London's working-class radicals, and *Cleave's
Weekly Police Gazette,* a news sheet of considerably higher quality, attained a weekly circulation in the range of forty thousand
during 1835–1836.[15] Despite their militant reformism, the circulation of some journals was enhanced because they were purchased by persons of middle- or upper-class background. As their
quality improved and the amount of news that they printed increased, so did their appeal to readers who would otherwise have
to spend 7*d.* per day to purchase a "respectable" stamped journal.[16] By 1834 the total number of subscribers probably approxi-
mated one hundred thousand weekly, and two years later, on the

[13] *People's Hue and Cry,* 13 July 1834. Hibbert left substantial sums of
money to Carlile, Watson, and Hetherington when he died. For a copy of his
will, see *A Scourge for the Littleness of "Great" Men,* 21 Feb. 1835. For further information on Hibbert's financial assistance to the repeal campaign, see
Linton, *Memories,* p. 36.

[14] *Man,* 10 Aug. 1834; *Church Examiner,* 1 Oct. 1832.

[15] A disputed figure for the peak circulation of the *Poor Man's Guardian* is
16,000 (Cole, *Chartist Portraits,* p. 244). The *"Destructive,"* also owned by
Hetherington, estimated its circulation at 15,000 (6 July 1833).

[16] See *Examiner,* 19 Jan. 1834.

eve of reduction of the stamp duty to 1*d*., the number of regular purchasers had probably doubled.[17]

The provinces played a striking role in the war of the unstamped. Manchester and its surrounding area purchased consistently about 10 per cent of the total number of illegal journals, a development that partially reflected the pronounced class consciousness of the Lancashire cotton districts.[18] Since the impetus behind illicit journalism was primarily working-class, it derived much of its support from those regions in which class antagonisms flourished. Thus industrial centers such as Newcastle-upon-Tyne, Leeds, Glasgow, Sheffield, and Huddersfield gave substantial support to the radical penny press.

Birmingham, in closer proximity to London, rivaled Manchester as a distribution center for the untaxed periodicals. Its workers lacked a strong sense of class grievance due to the moderating influence of Thomas Attwood and, more importantly, to the failure of the factory system to take root.[19] But a tradition of aggressive radicalism had emerged by the 1830's, and this strengthened considerably the repeal movement. Carpenter reported in April 1831 that approximately nine hundred copies of his *Political Letters and Pamphlets* were being disseminated weekly in

[17] Two inaccurate estimates are available for the year 1834. A proreform journal calculated a readership of only one hundred thousand monthly ("Fatherhood of the Unstamped," *Tait's Edinburgh Magazine*, new ser. I [1834], 733–734). The hostile *Morning Chronicle* reported the circulation of illegal journals to be 300,000 monthly in London alone, a seemingly exaggerated estimate (*Scotsman*, 4 Oct. 1834). For the 1836 estimate see the testimony of Hickson, *S.C. on Newspaper Stamps* (1851), p. 465, q. 3182.

[18] See Carlile's testimony concerning the *Prompter* in *State Trials*, II, 60, as cited in Wickwar, *Struggle for the Freedom of the Press*, p. 296 n.; Abel Heywood's testimony before the *S.C. on Newspaper Stamps* (1851), p. 381, qq. 2532–2535. Briggs has described Manchester as "a city of cleavages, of social separation and often of open class antagonism" ("Background of the Parliamentary Reform Movement," p. 302).

[19] Briggs, "Background of the Parliamentary Reform Movement," p. 300; Briggs, "Thomas Attwood and the Economic Background of the Birmingham Political Union," *Cambridge Historical Journal*, IX (1948), 191, 199–201; Briggs, "Social Structure and Politics in Birmingham and Lyons (1825–48)," *British Journal of Sociology*, I (1950), 67–76.

Birmingham, a figure constituting a substantial proportion of the total circulation.[20] As the agitation increased in intensity, Birmingham's working-class leaders, notably James Guest who operated a "Cheap Book Repository," made pronounced efforts on behalf of the "Great Unstamped." [21] By 1836 as many as seven thousand illicit newspapers were being vended weekly in the streets of Birmingham.[22]

Other sections of the Midlands responded with similar ardor. In Leicester supporters of the newspaper duty complained that illegal journals were being distributed in large quantities, and that "some . . . quite profligate and blasphemous, [were] calculated to set the lower orders against all that is decent and orderly in the land." [23] In Derby reformers were likewise able to purchase a variety of unstamped newspapers, some of them being vended by the seventeen-year old George Julian Harney, the future Chartist leader.[24]

The spectacular success of illegal journalism both in London and in the provinces was facilitated by sophisticated techniques of distribution. These were refined in order to hamper governmental interference with circulation. Journalists who engaged in illegal activities lacked access to the post and had to obviate the likelihood of confiscation of their stock if intercepted by the authorities during transmission. In spite of this enormous difficulty, major gains were made in the distributive process. In 1820 Cobbett had been compelled to introduce a 1s. stamped edition of his *Weekly Political Register* because adequate private deliveries, even in the absence of governmental interception, were unavail-

[20] *Ballot*, 4 Dec. 1831; Guest, "A Free Press," p. 495.

[21] Guest's "Cheap Book Repository" was the leading distribution center for illegal newspapers in the Birmingham area, and he and other local reformers suffered imprisonment for vending unstamped journals (*Poor Man's Guardian*, 26 May 1832, 18 May 1833).

[22] Chapman, "Victims of the Unstamped Press" (*R. Pamphlet*, No. 8), p. 12.

[23] *Leicester Journal*, 3 Aug. 1832, cited in Patterson, *Radical Leicester*, p. 290.

[24] *Weekly Herald*, 7 Aug. 1836; Place Autobiography, Place Papers, Add. MSS 27, 821, f. 4a; Cole, *Chartist Portraits*, p. 271.

able in rural areas. By 1832 this situation had been dramatically reversed. Unstamped penny journals could now be privately forwarded to remote corners of the British Isles, often within two days of publication.[25] In the relatively few areas of the country where transmission could not be assured, four weekly numbers were stitched together to form a monthly part, and this was forwarded legally through the Post Office.

The distributive process initially involved the transmission of illegal newspapers from the source of publication to primary agents in major urban centers. The journals were then subclassified by these agents and forwarded by coach to secondary vendors who worked in smaller local centers. Manchester, for example, served as the major distribution point for the South Lancashire towns of Oldham, Rochdale, and Bolton, and Leeds performed a similar function for the manufacturing towns of the West Riding.[26]

During periods of governmental prosecutions, when coaches were intercepted regularly, this complex system was put to its most severe test. Packages of unstamped newspapers became liable to arbitrary confiscation by industrious Stamp Office officials. To avoid this, numerous stratagems were developed. Dummy parcels were occasionally shipped by coach. If uncovered, the persons transmitting them deliberately resisted the authorities, in order to facilitate distribution of the real package. In some instances, illegal journals were transmitted in shoes, tea chests, fruit baskets, and other common household items so as to hamper detection.[27] Despite their apparent crudeness, such strat-

[25] *Penny Magazine*, preface to Vol. I, 18 Dec. 1832. One reformer, as if to demonstrate the efficacy of the distributive system, personally delivered a copy of the *Poor Man's Guardian* to the Duke of Bedford at his Woburn estate with a note recommending a "perusal of the same by the Duke" (S.S. report, 6 Nov. 1832, H.O. 64/12).

[26] Testimony of Abel Heywood, *S.C. on Newspaper Stamps* (1851), p. 371, q. 2478. Heywood was the chief distributor of illegal periodicals in the Manchester area during the 1830's.

[27] Linton, *Memories*, pp. 28–29; Holyoake, *Sixty Years*, II, 265. A shipment of illegal newspapers was seized while being transmitted to Bath in a fruit

agems often proved effective. Notwithstanding repeated seizures, which sometimes necessitated an increase in price in response to this "brigand tax," the distribution of illegal tracts flowed with comparative smoothness.[28]

Much of the success of the unstamped press resulted from the large numbers of journals that were published locally, a phenomenon reflecting the sectional interests of working-class reformers. These local unstamped journals often competed against illegal London news sheets, a process that brought growing numbers provincial reformers into the war of the unstamped. This circumstance effectually accelerated the long-term development of provincial journalism and enabled the Chartist movement, which emerged at the end of the 1830's, to draw upon a stronger base of provincial support.

Class-conscious Manchester and its surrounding industrial satellites led other provincial areas in the publication of illegal journals. John Doherty, the leader of the Lancashire cotton spinners, was responsible for several important journalistic ventures. The *United Trades' Co-operative Journal*, an illegal 2*d*. Manchester periodical, appeared initially in March 1830, predating by several months the more important *Penny Papers for the People* and *Political Letters and Pamphlets*. It was suppressed in October of the same year by the Grey government.[29] The *United Trades' Co-operative Journal* consistently bewailed the evils of economic competition and concentrated its energies upon the exposure of factory abuses. Although it possessed few stylistic virtues, it sought to uphold "the cause of the poor, defenseless and

basket (*Radical*, 1 May 1836). According to one account, *Cleave's Weekly Police Gazette* was regularly smuggled out of the printer's shop in a coffin (Grant, *Newspaper Press*, II, 308–309).

[28] A slight charge of ½*d*. was sometimes added to the price of the newspaper by the vendor (*Radical*, 1 May 1836).

[29] See Bowring's account of the suppression of the journal in *Penny Papers for the People*, 4 Feb. 1831. Place denounced the suppression as "a wanton and aggressive act of power" (*Letter to a Minister of State*, pp. 6–10).

unprotected labourer," and, as a result, it probably attained a respectable circulation.[30] Though not revolutionary in tone, it laid the groundwork for class bitterness by repeated attacks upon the aristocracy and the factory owners, as when it warned in one number that "the might and irresistible power of acquired and accumulating knowledge, will speedily overwhelm [the master-manufacturers], and may eventually sweep their cherished order from all but our recollections." [31]

After editing a short-lived stamped newspaper, the *Voice of the People,* Doherty turned again to illegal journalism. In January 1831 he published the *Workman's Expositor, and Weekly Review of Literature, Science and the Arts,* the first of two unstamped journals. This survived for only two numbers, but its successor, the *Poor Man's Advocate,* was one of the best-known illicit periodicals of the decade. The professed aim of both periodicals was to protect the industrial workers against "the merciless fangs of the innumerable host of mercenary despots which the manufacturing system has called into existence in every part of this country." [32] They denounced factory abuses in quasi-revolutionary terms, notably in a weekly column sardonically entitled "Beauties of a Cotton Factory." Though both newspapers gave ambiguous endorsement to co-operative ideas, the range of their constructive criticism was noticeably limited, and both engaged regularly in vituperation and invective. In spite of a national reputation as a trade union leader, Doherty never demonstrated more than minor competence in journalism. But he strengthened considerably the repeal movement in South Lancashire by harnessing it to the powerful local demand for factory reform.

A similar link between the factory and newspaper issues was forged in Huddersfield. Joshua Hobson, the West Riding's leading distributor of illegal journals, began to publish the *Voice of*

---

[30] *United Trades' Co-operative Journal,* 6 March 1830.
[31] *Ibid.,* 18 Sept. 1830.   [32] *Workman's Expositor,* 7 Jan. 1832.

the West Riding in June 1833.[33] This Huddersfield factory journal remained in existence for over a year and became one of the liveliest and most controversial of the illicit provincial journals. Its tone was one of extreme class animosity. In passages such as the following, it eschewed all association with the middle classes: "Here is conscience: The conscience of political economists, christians, and whigs . . . when ye hear of a Grey administration, curse it; you can do no other, their villiany [*sic*] is unparalleled."[34] Semirevolutionary invective was expended continually upon the evils of the factory system, though in deference to the omnipresent libel laws, firsthand descriptive accounts were omitted. And in the area of political and social criticism, the *Voice* anticipated "physical force" Chartism, as in its exhortation to the working classes to "organize a provisional directory of incipient force . . . to be in readiness to act in such emergency as is anticipated."[35]

Glasgow was a center of trade union and co-operative agitation during the 1830's and, as in the case of Manchester, much of this activity was linked to journalistic protest. Local trade unionists supported the *Liberator*, a stamped working-class weekly under the control of John Tait, to an estimated sum of one thousand pounds.[36] Many illegal periodicals, including the *Tradesman* (1833–1834), the *Loyal Reformers' Gazette* (1831–1838), the *News of the World* (1834–1835?), and the *Scottish Trades'*

[33] Hobson headed the Short Time Committee in Huddersfield, which championed factory reform, and he advocated a monthly general strike to protest the imprisonment of the Dorchester laborers. He later published and edited the *Northern Star*. For information on Hobson, see Ward, *Factory Movement*; *Voice of the West Riding*, 12 April 1834. The Tolson Memorial Museum, Huddersfield, has several newsclippings that contain biographical information about Hobson.

[34] *Voice of the West Riding*, 3 Aug. 1833.

[35] On several occasions it recommended exclusive trading and repudiation of the debt (*ibid.*, 29 June 1833).

[36] Henry Cockburn, *Journal* . . . *Being a Continuation of the Memorials of His Time, 1831–1854* (Edinburgh: Edmonston and Douglas, 1874), I, 159. Tait was head of the Glasgow Trades Union, and the most active person in the Glasgow newspaper agitation (*Glasgow Argus*, 4 June 1835, 24 Sept. 1835).

Union Gazette (1833) were published in Glasgow, and several were prosecuted at the instigation of local magistrates. Though Peter Mackenzie, a member of the middle-class Glasgow Political Union, was particularly active in the repeal campaign, the bulk of the illegal journals were of working-class origin.[37]

A penny periodical entitled the *Agitator* (1833) was perhaps the most radical working-class journal published in Glasgow. Under the control of John Sharp, a Greenock printer, it advocated universal suffrage, annual parliaments, the communal ownership of land, and a working day limited to six hours.[38] It condemned the middle-class "shopocracy" in unqualifiedly harsh terms. But the *Agitator's* most vehement criticism was leveled against the Church of England and its clergy. In a passage that was as virulent as any published during the war of the unstamped, it described a parson in the following terms: "You see his fat, beastly carcase stuffed with good meat, and sanctimoniously clothed in a sheep's garment,—meek, pious, good souls,— all for the good of religion." [39] Similar themes were articulated by other Glasgow penny journals. The effect of this outpouring of illegal periodicals in Scotland's largest industrial city was to assist markedly the working-class repeal campaign.

Other sections of Scotland and the provinces also contributed to the dissemination of illegal newspapers. In Preston, William P. Staines, a primary distributor of unstamped periodicals, joined with other local radicals to produce *An Address from One of the 3730 Electors of Preston*, a weekly that echoed the political views of Henry Hunt by championing ardently universal

[37] Mackenzie's best-known periodical was the 2*d. Loyal Reformers' Gazette*, which was compelled to become a monthly in May 1832 in order to avoid a Stamp Office prosecution. Hume assertedly intervened to save Mackenzie from a heavy fine (R. M. W. Cowan, *The Newspaper in Scotland: A Study of Its First Expansion, 1815–1860* [Glasgow: G. Outram, 1946], p. 40; J. Stewart, letter to C. Wood, 24 Jan. 1833, Treasury Papers, 22/20 ff. 224–225).

[38] *Agitator*, 9 March 1833, 13 April 1833. Sharp published simultaneously cheap weekly editions of Paine's *Rights of Man* and *Common Sense* (*Radical Reformer's Gazette*, 19 Jan. 1833).

[39] *Agitator*, 9 March 1833.

suffrage and complete political equality. In Edinburgh and Liverpool illegal journalism flourished as well during these years.[40] Many of Edinburgh's illicit publications were moderate in tone, reflecting the absence of a discontented industrial proletariat. Several of them, including the *Edinburgh Echo; or Weekly Register of Remarkable Events, and Repository of Wit* (1831), the *Edinburgh Magazine* (1833), and the *Edinburgh Saturday Register* (1831–1832), concentrated on literary subjects and sought assiduously to avoid discussion of controversial matters. Others featured restrained political analysis as, for example, the *Artizan's Miscellany, or Journal of Politics and Literature* (1831) which described the first Reform Bill as "a full, a generous, and almost faultless measure for the extension of political privileges to a great and influential body of the people."[41]

Liverpool was the birthplace of a number of Owenite cooperative miscellanies, and of unstamped literary and political journals. M. J. Falvey, described by one contemporary as "the best public speaker in Liverpool," and John Finch, an Owenite propagandist who adhered to an orthodox religious position, published several journals including the *Bee* (1832) and the *Comet; or, Falvey's Liverpool Observer* (1832).[42] These endorsed political reform but concentrated almost exclusively upon such Owenite proposals as the creation of Labor Exchange Banks.

In Birmingham several local penny journals demonstrated a similar tendency toward moderate reformism. The *Pioneer; or Trades' Union Magazine* (1833–1834), with a weekly circula-

---

[40] An interesting contemporary description of Edinburgh survives: "For these last six months Edinburgh has been swarming with newspapers of all forms, sizes, and titles, published at the small charge of one penny. On a Saturday, whithersoever you went, along Princes' Street or across the Bridges, huge placards stared you in the face, announcing the contents and publication of Registers, Miscellanies, Cornucopias, etc." (*Aberdeen Magazine*, II [1832], 161).

[41] *Artizan's Miscellany*, 28 May 1831.

[42] For the description of Falvey, see *Liverpool Examiner*, 2 Dec. 1832.

tion that may have approached twenty thousand, was by far the most important unstamped weekly.[43] As the organ of the Operative Builders Union, it played an effective role in the advocacy of trades unionist and co-operative proposals, and it served as a decisive link between these Midlands movements and the national agitation for repeal of the newspaper duty. The *Birmingham Labour Exchange Gazette* (1833) edited by William Pare was another "moderate" illegal Birmingham periodical that strongly championed Owenite social theories.

Most sections of England and Scotland were affected to some degree by the large-scale distribution of illegal newspapers that occurred between 1830 and 1836. There is evidence to demonstrate that some of these radical news sheets had an impact in remote weaving villages and in obscure country towns, as well as in the larger industrial centers.[44] But agricultural areas were considerably less affected by the war of the unstamped than other sections of the country. The major reason for this was a lower literacy rate in rural districts, where an estimated 50 per cent of the workers could read as opposed to 66 to 75 per cent in the towns.[45] A corollary factor was that the habit of reading was less pervasive in the countryside.

It may be validly assumed that all those who could meet certain minimal standards of literacy were capable of reading at least some of the illegal penny newspapers. Most of the latter, includ-

---

[43] *Tait's Edinburgh Magazine*, new ser. I (1834), 662.

[44] See Samuel Kydd's testimony in the *Northern Star*, cited in Simon, *Studies in the History of Education*, p. 257; Chambers, *Story of a Long and Busy Life*, p. 35. A contemporary study of a depressed weaving area in Norwich disclosed that "there is a shop in the district where the writings of Paine, Carlile, Voltaire, and Volney, as well as many publications of a deleterious kind, are sold, and which are very extensively read" (W. Felkin, "Moral Statistics of a Section of the City of Norwich," *Journal of the Statistical Society of London*, I [1838], 541).

[45] R. K. Webb, "Working Class Readers in Victorian England," *English Historical Review*, LXV (1950), 337–339; "Literacy among the Working Classes in Nineteenth Century Scotland," *Scottish Historical Review*, XXXIII (1954), 100–114.

[193]

ing the more sophisticated productions, were simple in conception and execution. Many workers, however, in both urban and rural areas, possessed the skills of literacy but did not acquire the habit of reading newspapers until later in the century. A study made in 1843 of a portion of St. George's parish, London, revealed that only 42 per cent of the inhabitants of that unusually "moral" district read newspapers regularly.[46] And in agricultural areas the situation was unqualifiedly bleaker. A "typical" rural parish near Woburn yielded a comparable statistic of only 7 per cent, according to an investigation made in the same year.[47] Thus even if the factors of political stimulation and rising class consciousness in the towns are ignored, it is not surprising that agricultural districts were less implicated in the newspaper repeal campaign than urban areas.

The Whig governments of the 1830's, however, affected public and private concern that the illegal tracts were penetrating into isolated agricultural districts, and both Carlile and Cobbett were prosecuted for seditious libel on the assumption that their journals, the *Prompter* and *Cobbett's Weekly Political Register*, were being heavily subscribed to by disaffected agricultural laborers.[48] This ministerial "concern" had no substantive foundation. G. J. Holyoake reported that none of the persons whom he encountered in a rural district near Stockbridge in 1843 had ever heard of Hetherington's *Poor Man's Guardian*, and other contemporary observers support the substance of this testimony.[49] Furthermore, during the 1830's radical journalists themselves

---

[46] C. R. Weld, "On the Condition of the Working Classes in the Inner Ward of St. George's Parish, Hanover Square," *Journal of the Statistical Society of London*, VI (1843), 19, 21.

[47] Out of more than two hundred families in the district, fourteen read newspapers regularly (John E. Martin, "Statistics of an Agricultural Parish in Bedfordshire," *Journal of the Statistical Society of London*, VI [1843], 255).

[48] For an expression of ministerial concern, see Duke of Wellington, letter to Melbourne, 7 Nov. 1832, cited in *Lord Melbourne's Papers*, ed. Charles Sanders (London: Longmans, Green, 1889), p. 151.

[49] Holyoake, *Sixty Years*, I, 199–200.

constantly lamented their lack of support in rural districts.[50]
Several of them attempted to attract rural inhabitants to their
periodicals by popularizing demands for the nationalization of
land, and others contemplated the distribution of surplus free
copies of their tracts in agricultural sections to stimulate interest
in the repeal agitation.[51] Neither approach had a perceptible impact. The working-class war of the unstamped, successful in so
many other ways, failed noticeably to secure a foothold among
the rural populace.

To a large measure the success of the illegal press campaign is
attributable to the sheer good fortune of repeated Stamp Office
prosecutions. As the chief distributor of unstamped publications
in Coventry stated: "Prosecution is the best advertiser of good
books." [52] The psychological response generated by a prosecution complemented and strengthened previous commitments.
The sense of satisfaction to be derived from the well-publicized
defiance of a detested governmental authority induced hundreds
of poor laborers to risk imprisonment on behalf of an untaxed
press; on the other hand, the comparative humaneness and ineffi-
ciency of the British political tradition assured that the physical
rigors of incarceration would be bearable. Thus, a powerful radical campaign attuned to the emotions of the working classes could
be mounted for the removal of what some reformers referred to
as the "blood-coloured seal of mischief and demoralization." [53]

The decision taken by the Grey and Melbourne ministries to
suppress opposition to the newspaper duty was not easily predicted in view of its willingness to make important concessions in
other areas. Few, if any, members of the government favored abstractly a policy of repression. Grey, more conservative than

---

[50] See the testimony of Henry Watkinson, owner of the *Spalding Free Press*,
S.C. on Newspaper Stamps (1851), pp. 396–398, qq. 2673–2690; Cassell's
testimony, *ibid.*, p. 234, q. 1429.

[51] *Man*, 25 Aug. 1833; *Working Man's Friend*, 29 June 1833, 3 Aug. 1833.

[52] Letter from Jesse Stokes in *Poor Man's Guardian*, 3 March 1832.

[53] *Ibid.*, 20 April 1833. This reference to the red color of the stamp was
popular among working-class radicals.

many of his colleagues, questioned seriously the "prudence" of such a policy.[54] Althorp, the Chancellor of the Exchequer, asserted continually both in public and in private that his sole objective was to guarantee an adequate revenue.[55] His successor, Spring Rice, publicly declared previous to and again after taking office that he was opposed to "all restrictions on the free circulation of opinion." [56]

Lords Denman and Campbell, the two Attorneys-General during the Whig ministries and thus responsible for several prosecutions initiated under the newspaper statutes were sympathetic to the cause of reform. Denman told the Commons in May 1832, that "a libeller thirsted for nothing more than the valuable advertisement of a public trial in a Court of Justice," and he substantially reaffirmed these sentiments in his private correspondence.[57] Even Melbourne, despite his conservative record as Home Secretary and his hostility to the war of the unstamped, was not anxious to indulge in press prosecutions and by 1835 was prepared to make concessions to the reformers.[58]

Nonetheless, the Whig governments of Grey and Melbourne, as well as the brief Tory ministry of Peel, sanctioned a harshly repressive policy that was heavily weighted against the poor. The fear of extreme radicalism, underpinned as it was by financial considerations, overcame legal and political scruples. It was believed that persons "incapable of thought or discrimination"

[54] Grey, letter to Thomas Denman, 6 May 1831, cited in Arnould, *Denman*, I, 263.

[55] See Althorp's speech as reported in *Hansard*, H. of C., 5 Feb. 1833, XV, 202–205. Althorp told William IV in May 1832 that "the result of prosecutions in times of high political excitement is very doubtful" (letter to William IV, 22 May 1832, Althorp Papers).

[56] *Hansard*, H. of C., 6 May 1830, XXIV, 449.

[57] *Ibid.*, 21 May 1832, XII, 1148; Denman, letter to Althorp, 24 May 1832, Althorp Papers.

[58] Melbourne, private letter to the Duke of Wellington, 10 Nov. 1832, cited in *Melbourne's Papers*, p. 152. For his more conciliatory approach, see *Newspaper Stamps: Deputation*, p. 16; Melbourne, letter to Brougham, 18 June 1832, Brougham Papers, No. 48,487.

could not be exposed safely to illegal penny newspapers.[59] The latter were, in the opinion of leading Whigs, devoted to "the circulation of the most abominable matter—morally, scandalous and obscene; religiously, not simply infidel, but scoffing and ribald; politically, preaching anarchy hardly even confined to the crazy dreams of socialism." [60] Pressure from William the Fourth, particularly during the spring of 1832 when the parliamentary reform crisis was approaching its culmination, further inclined the Whigs toward a policy of repression. In May 1832, the king wrote a letter to Althorp in which he deplored this "unfortunately Press-ridden Country" and urged prosecutions of journalists, whenever necessary, to assure "the preservation of the Constitution and its Monarchical feature." [61] An additional factor was the continual pressure exerted upon successive governments by the proprietors of stamped journals such as the *Times* and the *Morning Chronicle*. These newspapers using the fulcrum of public opinion as a means of applying political pressure worked diligently for a policy of suppression of the unstamped journals.

Defenders of the Whigs affirmed that the large majority of prosecutions initiated during the years 1830–1836 under the Hawkers' Act (1743) and the several newspaper statutes were the product of private or magisterial initiative and not that of the Stamp Office. It was accepted practice prior to 1835 for common informers, who received twenty shillings per conviction and who therefore provoked incidents by purchasing illegal newspapers, to initiate prosecutions under the Hawkers' Act.[62] The procedure

---

[59] Statement by the Whig Attorney General, cited in *Report of the Trial of Hetherington*, pp. 20–21.

[60] Brougham, "On the Diffusion of Knowledge," pp. 34–35.

[61] William IV, letter to Althorp, 23 May 1832, Althorp Papers; William IV, letter to Althorp, 26 May 1832, cited in Arnould, *Denman*, I, 293. This letter is reprinted in Henry Brougham, *Life and Times: Written by Himself* (New York: Harper and Bros., 1871), III, 144. William IV also pressed for a prosecution of the *Hull Portfolio*, an unstamped journal edited by James Acland (Melbourne, letter to Brougham, 18 June 1832, Brougham Papers, No. 48,487).

[62] See the *True Sun*, 12 Sept. 1832.

was terminated in March 1835, and local Stamp Office personnel and police officers subsequently took over the burden of enforcing the law effectively. In either event, Althorp and other members of the government, when questioned in Parliament, could plausibly disavow complicity in unpopular prosecutions. But the repressive tone which successive governments set, based partly upon the confidential reports of Secret Service informants, made itself felt on all levels. The Whigs, to this extent at least, bear considerable responsibility for the vigorous enforcement of the taxes on knowledge undertaken during these years.

The policy of repression led to the imprisonment of almost eight hundred persons for violation of the stamp laws. It is difficult to be more precise than this due to the unevenness of parliamentary returns and to the difficulties in correlating provincial police records with those of the London courts. On the basis of parliamentary returns for the period January 1831 to March 1834, a minimum of over five hundred vendors and publishers of illegal journals were convicted in England alone. A subsequent return for 1835 lists an additional 219 prosecutions. Since these documents include no Scottish statistics and contain no information for 1836, a year in which prosecutions continued, the overall number of those imprisoned is unquestionably in the area of eight hundred.[63]

Watson, Hetherington, Carpenter, Charles Penny, Alexander Campbell, R. E. Lee, and other well-known publishers of illegal journals were formally tried and convicted in the Court of Exchequer or in one of the magistrates' courts under the provisions of the newspaper statutes of 1798 (38 Geo. III, c. 78), 1815 (55

[63] Great Britain, Sessional Papers, *Return of the Number of Persons Who Have Been Committed by the Magistrates of the Metropolis, within the Last Year, for Selling Unstamped Publications* . . . (1831–1832), XXXIV (40), p. 103; *Return of the Number of Persons Who Have Been Committed by the Magistrates for Selling Unstamped Publications, from 10th and 12th December 1831* . . . (1831–1832), XXXIV (711), p. 107; *Returns of Persons Committed by Magistrates for the Sale of Unstamped Publications* (1836), XLI (21), p. 427. Hume claimed that 728 vendors had been convicted as of Feb. 1836 (*Newspaper Stamps: Deputation*, p. 7).

Geo. III, c. 185), or 1819 (60 Geo. III, c. 19). But this was a costly, time-consuming process and one that was likely to generate far too much unfavorable publicity.[64] As a result, the overwhelming proportion of persons accused of vending or publishing illegal newspapers were tried summarily before one or two magistrates, usually in the presence of agents from the Stamp Office. They were not charged under any of the statutes that affixed a duty on newspapers but rather under the Hawkers' Act of 1743 (16 Geo. II, c. 26) which forbade, irrespective of price, the unlicensed sale of newspapers and which did not allow for an appeal. According to a parliamentary return for 1831, of seventy-seven persons tried and convicted in London police courts for selling illegal newspapers during that year, seventy-five were prosecuted under the act of 1743.[65] Although subsequent returns are incomplete with respect to the statutory provisions by which vendors and publishers were convicted, this pattern was broadly representative. Occasionally, even important journalists were tried under the Hawkers' Act as, for example, Cleave who in 1836 was sentenced summarily to three months' imprisonment for "carrying about" copies of *Cleave's Weekly Police Gazette*.[66]

The financial penalties established by the Hawkers' Act were moderate but invariably beyond the ability of working-class vendors to pay. In default of payment, prison sentences ranging from seven days to three months were meted out, depending upon the inclinations of particular magistrates.[67] Some magis-

[64] The practice of printing lengthy accounts of these trials, often in the form of separate pamphlets, was commenced by Carlile in the 1820's. It was followed in the 1830's by several of the more prominent journalists. See, for example, the account of Carpenter's trial (1831) and that of Alexander Campbell (1835).

[65] *Return of the Number of Persons*, (1831–1832), XXXIV (40), p. 103. Several vendors were convicted for selling unstamped almanacs and were prosecuted under 30 Geo. II, c. 19, a similar statute.

[66] Cleave's legal advisers attempted unsuccessfully to secure his release from prison on the ground that he had not been "carrying about" such newspapers for "sale" (*Radical*, 27 March 1836).

[67] George Edmonds expressed the sentiments of many reformers when he referred to the magistrates as "people-hating agents of the rich and rascally men of England" (*People's Weekly Dispatch*, 23 April 1836).

trates were notably more zealous in enforcing the law than Stamp Office officials. At one London police court a justice of the peace sentenced an obscure vendor to one month in prison in June 1832, after telling the defendant that he would have liked to annex hard labor to the sentence. The latter punishment in the opinion of the magistrate "would soon put a stop to the *Poor Man's Guardian*, as it was erroneously called." With becoming illogicality he implored the vendor to sell the equally illegal *Penny Magazine* or "other useful and cheap works which contained none of the inflammatory trash of which the *Poor Man's Guardian* was chiefly distinguished." [68] Another magistrate, after rejecting an appeal from the *Church Examiner and Ecclesiastical Record*, declared that it was his responsibility to "teach these deluded people how vain was their reliance upon numbers and popular will, in attempting to set the laws at defiance." [69] Still another justice, Sir Peter Laurie, a former Lord Mayor of London, reportedly sentenced a ten-year-old boy to one month of silence in prison on the ground that "the evil was increasing daily." [70]

Vendors were sometimes freed by well-intentioned magistrates, several of whom demanded legal proof of actual sale or intent to sell rather than the mere "carrying about" of illegal newspapers. Others refused to take any judicial action in the absence of a Stamp Office representative. But even when the magistrates demonstrated leniency, the vendor's stock of unstamped journals, representing a sizable investment, was usually impounded.[71] Few magistrates were as generous as Alderman Kelly, who freed a young hawker in November 1832 and returned his newspapers, affirming that "it was a disgrace to the Stamp-office not to go to the fountain-head instead of seizing upon such victims as this unfortunate person, and cramming the gaols with them." [72] And

[68] Newsclipping, 16 June 1832, Place Newspaper Collection, Set 57, f. 216.
[69] Newsclipping, *c.* Sept. 1832, *ibid.*, f. 217.
[70] *Public Ledger*, 12 Jan. 1836; *Spectator*, 16 Jan. 1836.
[71] *Poor Man's Guardian*, 27 Aug. 1831.   [72] *Ibid.*, 3 Nov. 1832.

when important journalists were prosecuted, either by the terms of the Hawkers' Act or one of the newspaper statutes, their printing presses and types were frequently confiscated on the ground that the registration procedure required by an act of 1799 had not been complied with.

The Whig policy of repression produced inverse effects from those intended. The circulation of periodicals under governmental attack increased predictably as working-class reformers rallied to their support. So effective an advertisement did a prosecution become that Lee, the editor of the *Man*, hoped ardently for one in the final days of that newspaper's existence. With scarcely more than a few hundred readers remaining, his foremost hope for financial solvency lay in an attempt by the Stamp Office to suppress his journal.[73] In Glasgow, efforts by local magistrates to suppress the *News of the World* and the *Tradesman*, two leading unstamped journals, only induced additional news sheets to enter the competition.[74] Similarly, the sale of illegal publications in Birmingham reportedly increased by about one third during 1835, in direct proportion to the increase of provincial prosecutions.

The policy of repression was even more self-defeating in terms of the psychological effects that it had upon the distributors of illicit journals. Hetherington maximized the potential of the situation with a famous advertisement that was printed initially in the *Poor Man's Guardian:*

WANTED. Some hundreds of Poor Men out of employ, *who have* NOTHING TO RISK, some of those *unfortunate beings* to whom DISTRESS occasioned by a *tyrannical government* has made a PRISON a desirable *home.* An HONEST and moral way of finding *gaol bread and shelter,* and moreover, of EARNING THE THANKS of their FELLOW-COUNTRY-MEN, now presents itself to such *patriotic* ENGLISHMEN as will, in *defiance* of the most ODIOUS "Laws" of a most ODIOUS TYRANNY,

---

[73] *Man,* 13 April 1834.
[74] *Glasgow Argus,* 19 Jan. 1835, 17 Nov. 1834.

imposed on an *enslaved and oppressed people,* sell to the poor and the ignorant the *Poor Man's Guardian.*[75]

As a result of this appeal and in response to the prosecutions of the initial "victims," a surplus of vendors of illegal newspapers became available. At least two persons and probably more were prepared to "take the pledge" to distribute the illegal tracts in place of every one who was incarcerated. Once such a situation had developed, the destruction of the unstamped press through a policy of repression became physically impossible. The government, as one magistrate confessed in 1835, was "totally powerless" to enforce the law.[76]

Most of the vendors who risked imprisonment were of the class of the "forlorn poor." [77] They were the "decently dressed mechanics" who attended diligently the "seditious" gatherings held at the Rotunda, the Optimist's Chapel in Finsbury Square, and other working-class centers, who joined associations such as the N.U.W.C., and who frequented the radical news rooms of Carlile, Hetherington, Cleave, Watson, and Carpenter.[78] To such persons, the prospect of averting starvation while at the same time participating in a virtuous cause was an attractive one. Furthermore, the profit that accrued to a vendor was ordinarily about 25 per cent of the price of the journal. This price meant a margin of one farthing per penny newspaper, though occasionally it ranged higher. According to one report, a hawker earned 4s. 10d. for every 100 1d. newspapers and 2s. 6d. for every 100 ½d. newspapers that he sold.[79] And if a vendor promptly reimbursed

[75] *Poor Man's Guardian,* 30 July 1831. This appeal was also reprinted as a broadside. There is a copy in H.O. 64/17. Another placard read: "WANTED 1000 Unemployed Men, To SELL AN unstamped Almanack for 1833." H.O. 64/12 has a copy.

[76] Newsclipping, *c.* May 1835, Place Newspaper Collection, Set 70, f. 211.

[77] An expression employed by George Barber, an imprisoned vendor (*Gauntlet,* 28 April 1833).

[78] The phrase "decently dressed mechanics" is that of Popay, the informer (S.S. report, 10 June 1831, H.O. 64/11).

[79] *Ibid.,* 13 Nov. 1830. *Punchinello* gave 24 extra free numbers to hawkers who purchased 144 copies (3 Feb. 1832). The legal police gazettes often outbid

the publisher upon receipt of the newspapers, the money paid was usually refundable on unsold copies.

During periods of political excitement, therefore, an income that was respectable within the context of working-class expectations could be earned. And although prison conditions were atrocious, the offenders being treated as felons rather than as "gentleman debtors," imprisonment did not always represent the most disagreeable alternative for the very poor.[80] A "Victim Fund," organized in 1831 and financed by Cleave, Lovett, Julian Hibbert, and W. D. Saull and supported by the N.U.W.C. and by reformers in many sections of the country, provided small sums of money to the families of imprisoned vendors. It also undertook to re-establish the incomes of vendors upon their release which, in some instances, meant providing them with several dozen copies of illegal newspapers to sell. The "Victim Fund" also distributed penny tracts requesting financial assistance for the "Victims to Whig Tyranny and Knowledge Suppressing Laws" on the ground that "the conflict has commenced, the struggle is begun, and the issue depends upon those for whom the peril of the unequal encounter has been incurred."[81]

---

illicit journals by giving vendors a profit of 10*d*. per dozen copies sold (*Man*, 13 April 1834).

[80] For complaints about prison conditions, see the case of Ed Wastneys, *Poor Man's Guardian*, 1 Feb. 1834, 15 March 1834; letter from J. Herbert in *Man*, 8 Dec. 1833. The *Brighton Patriot* claimed exaggeratedly that Hetherington had been subjected while in prison to "the most cruel privations, under circumstances that would have disgraced the Spanish Inquisition" (12 May 1835). Hetherington denounced the "petty meanness—the execrable malignity" of those responsible for his treatment while in prison in 1832 (*Cheap Salvation; or, An Antidote to Priestcraft: Being a Succinct, Practical, Essential, and Rational Religion, Deduced from the New Testament* . . . [London: Henry Hetherington, 1838?], pp. iii–vi). See also Cleave, "A Cry from Warwick Gaol to the Men of Birmingham," *Cleave's Weekly Police Gazette*, 18 Oct. 1835.

[81] Copies of the "victim tracts" are in Place Newspaper Collection, Set 70, f. 147; Set 57, f. 214; and in H.O. 64/11. The Home Office was an unwilling subsidizer of the "Victim Fund" since its informer, a member of the N.U.W.C., billed it regularly for contributions to aid the vendors (S.S. report, 24 Feb. 1832, H.O. 64/12). Several vendors offered their bodies for dissection when

Despite this financial incentive, militant idealism was clearly the significant motivating factor for a majority of vendors. Many of the poor, viewing the newspaper stamp as an omnipresent symbol of oppression, voluntarily sought to become "martyrs" in "the sacred cause of freedom." [82] Otherwise consigned to an existence of grinding poverty, life became momentarily purposeful for them through active participation in the movement for an untaxed press. An obscure vendor named Robert Anderson succinctly expressed this feeling: "I rejoiced that I was counted worthy to suffer in so sacred a cause, and will never cease to agitate whilst I live, until the whole of that obnoxious impost is swept away." [83] Other "victims" similarly pledged themselves to pursue unremittingly the struggle to eradicate "starvation among mankind," "the grasping monopolizers of wealth and aristocracy," and "robbers . . . [who] live and grow fat on the toil of a miserable half-starved and priest-ridden people." [84] Cleave captured the essence of this sense of sacrifice in the following verse:

> Ourselves have been in durance vile
> For selling wholesome mental food;
> And yet we live & yet we smile,
> *At having done some public good.*
>
> . . . . .
>
> Your friends are here and everywhere
> Moving in your good behalf,
> So bye and bye you all will share
> *In triumph's merry social laugh.*

---

they died with the proceeds to go to the "Victim Fund" (*Cosmopolite*, 9 June 1832).

[82] From an N.U.W.C. petition, *Poor Man's Guardian*, 20 Aug. 1831.

[83] Letter from Robert Anderson, as reprinted in *London Mercury*, 19 Feb. 1837.

[84] *Cosmopolite*, 28 April 1832; Forster, *Rejected Address*, pp. 6, 11; letter from P. T. Bready, in *Voice of the West Riding*, 30 Nov. 1833.

A short good bye, dear brother slaves,
Let sorry take a lasting leave,
And Freedom's flag will proudly wave
O'er all good men—Your friend John Cleave.[85]

Much of the fervor exuded by the vendors was semirevolutionary in tone because the dissemination of illegal journals was to many the initial skirmish in a developing class conflict. One "victim" asserted that *"idle drones* and *usurious leeches"* would shortly be eliminated from society by physical force if necessary, and another admonished members of the Whig government that "the victims of your tyranny shall rise up against you and demand reparation for the wrongs wherewith your privileged crew have so unmercifully scourged them." [86] Others, operating on the assumption that "all bad laws must be broken before they can be mended," called for violent measures against the authorities and for a forcible "grand national holiday," in order to compel repeal of the stamp duty.[87]

A smaller number of vendors regarded their roles in educative terms and conceived of an imminent "moral revolution." Several, including Abel Heywood of Manchester, founded penny reading rooms and discussion clubs in order to accelerate the distribution of illegal periodicals. Some engaged in publishing ventures. P. T. Bready, a Sheffield hawker, reprinted several of Carlile's lectures and assisted the latter in publishing the *Gauntlet.*[88] George Pilgrim, a better-known "victim," became a publisher of unstamped almanacs with the pecuniary assistance of Carlile.[89] Still

[85] Cleave, "Dear Brother Navigators on the Road to Knowledge," *Cleave's Weekly Police Gazette,* 18 Oct. 1835.

[86] Letter by James Knight in *Herald of the Rights of Industry,* 12 April 1834; *Man,* 8 Dec. 1833.

[87] Guest, "A Free Press," p. 493.

[88] *Gauntlet,* 13 Oct. 1833. Bready also played a part in the establishment of a working-class political union in Sheffield (*Man,* 18 May 1834).

[89] *A Scourge for the Littleness of "Great" Men,* 4 Oct. 1834; *Gauntlet,* 31 March 1832, 10 Nov. 1833.

another vendor, Joseph Walker, who described himself as the "Victim General of the Six Acts," wrote and published on timber a radical tract known as the *Political Touchwood,* in which he advocated universal suffrage, the ballot, the sale of all crown lands, and abolition of hereditary peerages.[90]

A handful of "victims" achieved prominence during and after the war of the unstamped. Among these were several who had aided Carlile in his defiance of the libel laws during the 1820's. In Leicester the veteran "martyr" Thomas Riley Perry again led the local agitation. He lectured to radical organizations, assisted in the formation of a local Mechanics' Institution, and spent several months in prison for vending illicit newspapers.[91] Joseph Swann, another of Carlile's former shop assistants, performed a similar role in the repeal agitation at Stockport.[92] The future Chartist leader, George Julian Harney, began his career in obscurity during the 1830's as one of Hetherington's shopboys. After serving two brief prison sentences in London for selling the *Poor Man's Guardian,* he transferred his activities to Derby, where he underwent further incarceration for hawking illegal newspapers.[93]

Abel Heywood was undoubtedly the best-known "victim" of the entire agitation. As the leading distributor of cheap periodicals in South Lancashire, Heywood secured almost as much notoriety and fame in the provinces as Hetherington did in London. A future police commissioner and mayor of Manchester, Heywood described himself subsequently as a "fierce rebel against the condition of things which prevailed." In order that the "stronghold of tyranny" might be permanently breached, he

[90] *Cosmopolite,* 10 and 31 March 1832. The *Political Touchwood* was reprinted in the *Christian Corrector,* 7 March 1832. There are two original splintered copies in H.O. 59/31. I am indebted for this reference to Patricia Hollis of the University of East Anglia.

[91] Holyoake, *Carlile,* p. 13; *Gauntlet,* 15 Dec. 1833, 16 March 1834.

[92] *Poor Man's Guardian,* 12 Nov. 1831; Thompson, *Making of the English Working Class,* pp. 731–32.

[93] A. R. Schoyen, *The Chartist Challenge: A Portrait of George Julian Harney* (London: Heinemann, 1958), pp. 6–10; William E. Adams, *Memoirs of a Social Atom* (London: Hutchinson, 1903), I, 219.

worked assiduously to disseminate untaxed literature. As a result of his activities during the war of the unstamped, he suffered imprisonment for four months.[94]

In June 1834, after three years of prosecutions, Lord Lyndhurst ruled in the Court of Exchequer that the *Poor Man's Guardian* was too insignificant a publication to be defined as a newspaper.[95] This unexpected decision had strong political overtones. Inasmuch as Lyndhurst was a leader of the Tory party, the decision may have been intended deliberately to embarrass the Whigs.[96] Its immediate effect was to invalidate technically a large majority of the previous convictions, and several vendors were subsequently freed by order of the Consolidated Board of Commissioners, though none received compensation.[97] But the judicial ruling was a narrow one, as attested to by Lyndhurst's simultaneous pronouncement that Hetherington's other publication, the *People's Conservative; and Trade's Union Gazette,* was an illicit "newspaper." The prosecution of vendors continued, therefore, with the government maintaining that the decision affected only one publication and that the other penny journals in circulation were still illegal.

Thus, an additional tinge of bitterness was injected into the working-class agitation during its final two years. The authorities

[94] See Heywood's speech of Oct. 1891, reprinted in George B. Heywood, *Abel Heywood, Abel Heywood and Son, Abel Heywood and Son Ltd., 1832–1932* (Manchester: Abel Heywood and Son, 1932), p. 4; Heywood, letter to his future wife, 17 March 1832, reprinted in *ibid.,* p. 6; Holyoake, *Sixty Years,* I, 102–103; *The Mayor of Manchester and His Slanderers* (Manchester: Tubbs and Brook, 1877), pp. 7–14; *Poor Man's Guardian,* 17 March 1832.

[95] By June 1834 the *Poor Man's Guardian* was relatively innocuous both in terms of circulation and content. The verdict, according to the *Poor Man's Guardian,* signified that the "victims were innocent in law, as in justice, that the persecutions were, therefore, wanton, as well as cruel acts of tyranny" (21 June 1834).

[96] Lyndhurst was an unorthodox Tory, one who compiled a liberal record in press cases (Sir Theodore Martin, *A Life of Lord Lyndhurst* [London: John Murray, 1833], pp. 205–206).

[97] Consolidated Board, letter to Commissioners of Stamps, 16 July 1834, Treasury Papers, 22/26, f. 116; *ibid.,* 31 July 1834, f. 120.

increased their efforts to destroy illegal journalism, and in December 1835 the Stamp Office issued a circular to local distributors of stamps in which it pledged its support for the conviction of unlicensed vendors and advised the distributors to purchase copies of the illegal newspapers. According to the circular: "If due diligence be used purchases might be effected within a fortnight." Upon the Stamp Office's receiving details of the alleged sale from its distributors, "the necessary instruction will be sent down, so that Proceedings may be taken before Magistrates against all the parties with regards to whom evidence shall be obtained."[98]

This circular, by its suggestion for "entrapment" of vendors, gave considerable impetus to a series of press prosecutions in many sections of England and Scotland during the spring and summer of 1836, a phenomenon that was described by one reformer as "a campaign of increasing terror" and by another as "this last and most deadly crusade against the Press."[99] Publishers and hawkers were prosecuted in London, Manchester, Oldham, Ashton-under-Lyne, the Potteries, Bath, and other areas of the country on the basis of informations initiated by the Stamp Office. Thousands of unstamped newspapers were seized by the authorities as they were being transmitted in coaches, and the financial losses were ruinous to many journalists.

Class tensions increased and several incidents of near-violence occurred.[100] In London and Manchester police officers were attacked in working-class districts as they attempted to arrest distributors of unstamped newspapers.[101] Even as the Chancellor

[98] *Hetherington's Twopenny Dispatch*, 19 Dec. 1835; *Cleave's Weekly Police Gazette*, 19 Dec. 1835.

[99] *Radical*, 1 May 1836; John Bell, in *New Weekly True Sun*, 19 March 1836.

[100] In Newcastle-upon-Tyne an inflammatory tract entitled "Hurrah for the Unstamped!! Beware of Informers!" was circulated during the spring of 1836. It requested financial assistance for the most recent "victims." A copy is in Place Newspaper Collection, Set 70, f. 438.

[101] *People's Weekly Police Gazette*, 27 Dec. 1835. At least one incident of a similar nature occurred in 1834 when an angry mob attacked Stamp Office

of the Exchequer was announcing in the spring of 1836 his plans for a reduction of the stamp duty, vendors were being sentenced to terms of imprisonment that ranged up to three months.[102] As late as August 1836, large numbers of unstamped journals were being seized arbitrarily, and a "victim" was able to describe his "martyrdom" as a necessary sacrifice in the general movement to root out "ignorance and bigotry . . . [and] priest-craft, and all their concomitant evils." [103]

The working-class repeal agitation reached its climax in September with the reduction of the newspaper duty from 4*d*. to 1*d*. As it did, the quality and popularity of many of the unstamped periodicals was increasing; but at the same time, many of the doctrines propounded by the penny periodicals were acquiring an additional degree of asperity. These developments forestalled an eleventh-hour rapprochement with parliamentary reformers, and as a result Spring Rice's reduction of the newspaper duty to 1*d*., though an unsatisfactory alternative to total repeal, could not be effectively resisted. Both middle- and working-class reformers contributed to this ineffectual sequel to six years of agitation. Thus, the war of the unstamped approached its termination amid mutual recriminations and in an atmosphere of accelerating class tensions.

---

informers in London (Forster, *Rejected Address*, p. 5; Great Britain, Sessional Papers, *Copy of the Information, Evidence, and Conviction of Joseph Forster, for Selling Unstamped Publications, etc.* [1835], XXXV [555], 243). For a similar manifestation of violence that occurred in 1832 see *True Sun*, 21 July 1832; *Cosmopolite*, 9 Nov. 1832.

[102] See *New Weekly True Sun*, 2 April 1836; *Radical*, 13 March 1836.

[103] Letter from J. Riches, in *Weekly Herald*, 14 Aug. 1836.

CHAPTER 8

Ideas of the Unstamped Press

The multiplicity of illegal penny tracts generated a corresponding fertility of ideas. Most journals expressed the views of their
projectors and the latter mirrored the contradictions inherent in
British working-class radicalism. Trade unionists, co-operators,
factory reformers, advocates of universal suffrage, secularists, and
Spencean socialists vied for reader support in the pages of the unstamped press. The laissez-faire republicanism of Richard Carlile
had relatively little in common with the nascent socialism expounded by O'Brien in the pages of the *Poor Man's Guardian*.
Violent disagreements with respect to the merits of the Reform
Act of 1832 were also aired in the penny journals. William Carpenter urged acceptance of the Whig measure in his *Political
Letters and Pamphlets*, despite his belief that the bill was "a
very partial, defective, anomalous, and therefore, on the whole,
unsatisfactory measure of reform," whereas Hobson, Hetherington, Lee, and other working-class writers rejected it in the conviction that it was "intended to crush [the people] forever—to be
final." [1] The treatment of religious themes provoked similarly

---

[1] See Carpenter, *Address to the Working Classes*, p. 5; *Political Letters and
Pamphlets*, 26 March 1831, 30 April 1831. For Hobson's opposition see *Voice
of the West Riding*, 26 Oct. 1833.

incompatible expressions of opinion. Many illicit journals attacked the Church of England and the dissenting bodies, and several expressed considerable hostility toward Christianity itself. But other periodicals including the *Political Letters and Pamphlets* and Watson's *Working Man's Friend* treated religion in a much more conventional fashion.[2]

In spite of this bewildering crosscurrent of opinion, certain consistent themes were enunciated by the unstamped press. Although loosely defined, these themes sharpened an emergent sense of class consciousness and helped to shape the working-class ethos of this and the succeeding decade. By their stridency, however, they reduced significantly the feasibility of an alliance with parliamentary reformers on the repeal issue.

POLITICAL THEMES

Politically, the major themes revolved around the ideals enunciated by Tom Paine, particularly the twin conceptions of a prepolitical state of harmony and equality and of the existence of universal "natural" rights. These ideas became translated into concrete demands for universal manhood suffrage, the ballot, and annual parliaments, and, in a few instances, into an attempt to justify revolution as a means of rectifying the absence of political democracy.

The Painite conception of a natural state of equality was intertwined frequently with a variation of the "Norman Yoke" theory, that is, with the notion that an Edenic native egalitarian society had been permanently destroyed as the result of foreign invasion in the eleventh century.[3] One variant of this doctrine propounded by Cobbert and others was that it was the sixteenth-

[2] Carpenter, in a debate on the validity of Christian doctrine with Carlile and the Rev. Robert Taylor at the Rotunda, affirmed a positive view (*Prompter*, 25 Dec. 1830, 1 Jan. 1831).

[3] *Man*, 14 and 21 July 1833; an article by "Swing" in *ibid.*, 20 Oct. 1833. For a discussion of the "Norman Yoke" theory see Christopher Hill, "The Norman Yoke," in John Saville, ed., *Democracy and the Labour Movement* (London: Lawrence and Wishart, 1954), pp. 11–66.

century church reformation led by Henry the Eighth that had fastened this "yoke" upon England.[4] Whichever historical event was focussed upon, the conclusion was identical. Landed property had been expropriated unjustly in the past, and a vicious system of private profit instituted. A cruel form of political inequality based upon the unnatural institutions of monarchy and aristocracy had been likewise fastened upon England. The pristine "state of nature" had been irremediably destroyed.

Several illegal journals drew further political implications from these alleged events. They maintained that history itself was a vast charade and that England's unwritten constitution was merely a "disgusting piece of chicanery." In the opinion of one writer, history was "one continuous scene of legalised plunder and butchery."[5] Occurrences such as the Glorious Revolution of 1688 were regarded as conspiracies perpetrated by privileged groups in order to consolidate their economic and political powers.[6] Wars, particularly the recent conflicts against France, were assertedly initiated by well-to-do capitalists for purposes of personal aggrandizement. The workers whose "blood and treasure" was being frivolously squandered could effectively demonstrate their resentment by repudiating the national debt with its weighted profits to creditors.[7]

Conservatives and moderate reformers were repelled by yet another application of the Painite doctrine of natural equality. This was the thesis, underwritten by many illicit journals, that the

[4] Henry VIII was described by the *Political Penny Magazine* (17 Sept. 1836) as "the most remorseless and cruel tyrant that England ever beheld."

[5] Lee, *Whisper to the Whigs*, p. 11.

[6] *Republican*, 4 June 1831, 2 April 1831; *Reformer*, 5 Jan. 1834. An interesting exception to this interpretation of history was the consistently favorable view offered of Cromwell. The radical *Political Penny Magazine* said of him: "He crushed a tyrant, and he has left us a noble example" (10 Sept. 1836). See also Henry Hunt, *An Appeal to the People of England by the Council of the Metropolitan Political Union: Reprinted from a Monitory Letter to Sir Robert Peel* (London: Metropolitan Political Union, 1830), p. 5.

[7] See the articles by "Agrarius" (George Petrie) in *Man*, 14 and 21 July 1833; *Church and State*, 16 Jan. 1836.

laws themselves had no binding effect upon the unrepresented majority. The *Poor Man's Guardian,* the *Reformer,* and other journals affirmed that political institutions were artificial media of aggrandizement, grounded on unjust foundations, and that government had become "an expensive incumbrance; an impediment to the public good." [8] In the absence of a working-class suffrage, even a pretence of justice was lacking, and the attempt to enforce "laws" represented, therefore, an arbitrary act of power. The ultimate position to be derived from this contention was stated by the *Republican,* a leading unstamped newspaper: "We will treat [laws] as mere nullities, honour them with every species of due contempt, and oppose them by every rational, and, if necessary, physical method, within our power." [9] Similarly, O'Brien's more restrained *"Destructive" and Poor Man's Conservative* asserted: "Where a small knot of villains usurp to themselves the privilege of law-making, with a view to plunder the rest of the community, they have no right to make *their* laws the standard of right and wrong, or the measure of innocence and criminality." [10]

Other of Paine's doctrines were employed to bolster this invalidation of "law." It was avowed that each generation had the right to renew the social contract. Statutes were not, therefore, binding upon those individuals whose representatives had not specifically had an opportunity to pass upon them. Several radical journalists even concluded that persons who were not alive at the time a law was passed need not obey it.[11]

As a means of rectifying the ill effects of historical injustice and preparing the basis for a more equitable political system, some

[8] *Poor Man's Guardian,* 23 Nov. 1833; *Reformer,* 5 Jan. 1834.

[9] *Republican,* 2 July 1831.

[10] *"Destructive,"* 23 March 1833. O'Brien wrote subsequently that the people "know that the lawmakers are their natural enemies, that all their schemes and enactments are made to enable the rich to rob, brutalise and keep the poor under foot" (Bronterre's letter, No. 7, *Hetherington's Twopenny Dispatch,* 26 March 1836).

[11] *Republican,* 13 Aug. 1831. See the view of Edward Handcock, a vendor, as reported in the *Poor Man's Guardian,* 13 Oct. 1832.

influential working-class reformers began to call for a national convention. This panacea was most strongly urged during the spring of 1833 as disillusionment with the Reform Act of 1832 increased. A few illegal periodicals endorsed the demand, including the two edited by O'Brien, the *Poor Man's Guardian* and the *"Destructive" and Poor Man's Conservative,* and Lee's *Man.*[12] And James H. B. Lorymer, publisher and editor of several of the more extreme periodicals, advocated repeatedly the assembling of a convention in order that the unrepresented masses could "TAKE THE MANAGEMENT OF THE NATIONAL AFFAIRS INTO THEIR OWN HANDS." [13]

Not all of the penny periodicals helped to nurture a quasi-revolutionary popular temper in their readers. Carlile refused steadfastly to endorse any action beyond "moral" resistance to tyranny, and Carpenter avowed that "knowledge and moral power and not violence or brute force [are] the only means [the working classes] could successfully employ in the pursuit of political and social happiness." [14] Even O'Brien, in a number of forceful leaders, suggested that "moral agencies" such as newspapers were ultimately the most efficacious means of ameliorating abuses. "Blood," he cautioned, "ought [not] to be shed for any purpose, however legitimate or praiseworthy, unless rendered inevitable by wanton aggression or the necessities of self-defence." [15]

But despite these and other exceptions, the unstamped news-

[12] Lee, "The Wrongs of Man," *Man,* 7 July 1833. The Calthorpe Street incident of April 1833 was an abortive attempt by a handful of London radicals to establish a national convention. For Lee's participation see *S. C. on Cold Bath Fields* (1833), p. 207.

[13] *Radical Reformer,* 21 and 28 Oct. 1831. Lorymer reiterated these views in a handbill entitled *A National Convention, the Only Proper Remedy,* which was reprinted in the *Republican,* No. 38 (n.d.).

[14] Carlile refused to print several articles written by "Ichneumon Scrutator" (James H. B. Lorymer) due to their provocative content (*Prompter,* 9 July 1831); letter from Carpenter printed in *Spectator,* 17 March 1832. See Carpenter's petition from Kings Bench Prison in which he urged the primacy of "sound and wholesome knowledge" over "brute force" (*Carpenter's Monthly Political Magazine,* I [Oct. 1831], 61–62).

[15] *"Destructive,"* 13 July 1833.

papers as a whole placed a revolutionary imprint upon working-class political thought. This effect was partly inevitable since the very act of disseminating large numbers of illegal periodicals involved defiance of the established fabric of law. Furthermore, working-class frustrations and resentments in other areas were siphoned off into illicit journalism, the single effective channel of expression available to the unrepresented masses during the 1830's. Hence the temper of this decade, as articulated in its popular political literature, was near-revolutionary. An implied determination to achieve social change by "physical force" surged beneath the surface of political activity.

Only a small number of illegal newspapers unqualifiedly endorsed revolution. One journal that did was the *Christian Corrector,* a 2*d.* periodical that circulated in the greater London area for approximately one year. Thomas Parkin, its editor and publisher, utilized the Scriptures to buttress his weekly endorsement of a violent social conflagration. He stated his views in passages such as the following:

If the Aristocracy are so wickedly infatuated as to brave the people . . . no mercy will be shown to them, their wives, or their children, and their houses will be made a dunghill! I tell the government that if the just rights of the people are longer withheld, revolution will ensue. . . . Let the oppressors touch a hair of my head, or of any other real friend of the people, and I here proclaim that for every such sacrifice, fifty families of the oppressors will be cut off without mercy from the land of the living.[16]

The journals edited by Lorymer, who became an active "physical force" Chartist at the end of the decade, were only slightly less threatening in tone.[17] They unceasingly demanded "Radicalism and Republicanism" and condemned such institutions as the standing army ("man-butchers"), Parliament (the "tax-

[16] *Christian Corrector,* 25 Jan. 1832, 29 Feb. 1832. For information about Parkin, see *Poor Man's Guardian,* 27 April 1833.

[17] *Radical,* 8 Oct. 1831. For Lorymer's activities in the East London Democratic Association, see *London Democrat,* 4 May 1839.

trap"), and the aristocracy ("titled cattle").[18] Lorymer's vehement linguistic assault was tempered initially by a latent faith in the efficacy of a free press. Readers of the *Republican* and of his other journals—the *Radical* (1831–1832), *Le Bonnet Rouge* (1833), the *Laughing Philosopher* (1832), and the *Reformer* (1833–1834)—were adjured *"to annihilate the aristocracy, but spare the men."* [19] But the failure to secure repeal of the newspaper duty impelled him to turn to more overt methods of protest. By 1834 he was imploring his subscribers to retaliate against the authorities "blow by blow—BLOOD FOR BLOOD." He proclaimed that:

The cries of the tortured, half-murdered, crippled, emaciated, demoralized, infant slave, forced to labor sixteen hours per day, amidst the din and dust of machinery, has made itself heard, and has excited the execration of the operative class against the rich who profit by the blood and sweat of their fellow creatures.[20]

The oppressed, he concluded, have never secured a redress of grievances "by any other means than intimidation, menaces, and coercion," a viewpoint that caused O'Brien to denounce him as "dangerous and untrustworthy." [21]

For every penny journal that advocated overt physical violence, several prepared the public mind for this eventuality by less direct means. Under Hobson's editorship, the *Voice of the West Riding* refrained from the direct emotional appeal

[18] These expressions are sprinkled liberally throughout the *Radical*, the *Republican*, *Le Bonnet Rouge*, the *Laughing Philosopher*, and the *Reformer*. Lorymer described William IV as "a puppet made of bran, white leather, and wire" (*Laughing Philosopher*, 11 Aug. 1832).

[19] *Republican*, 4 June 1831.

[20] *Reformer*, 12 May 1833. Lorymer contended that if a "moral" revolution did not occur in the near future, then "a bloody convulsion would follow, the issue of which would be the immediate extermination of the aggressors" (*ibid.*, 5 Jan. 1834).

[21] *Republican*, 13 and 27 April 1834; *"Destructive,"* 31 May 1834. Hume, appalled by the intensity of Lorymer's views, ineptly and erroneously denounced him as a "person in the enemy's camp" (*Hansard*, H. of C., 29 June 1831, IV, 469).

proffered by Parkin or Lorymer. But its approach to most issues was one of class bitterness. Hints of revolutionary activity were disseminated in its pages to receptive West Riding readers. Leaders such as the following on the conviction of the Dorchester laborers were not untypical:

Will this fresh indignity—this *one lash more*, be borne with patience? Curse of the slavish soul, the coward leach, the grovelling mind that dares to *think* of such a *crime as patience*! PATIENCE?—What, when the assassin's knife is at our throat—when our very existence is at stake.[22]

The weekly articles contributed to the *Voice* by William Rider of Leeds, a subsequent proponent of "physical force" Chartism, were even more suggestive. These demanded adequate retribution for such abuses as the "MURDER of childhood by the avaricious Millocracy." [23]

The *Poor Man's Guardian* and the *Cosmopolite* had an analogous effect upon the thought of thousands of working-class readers. Both journals theoretically eschewed physical violence and reaffirmed the necessity for a moral transformation of society, a transformation that was to be consummated by means of universal suffrage and "a free people's press." [24] And unlike the *Cosmopolite*, the *Poor Man's Guardian* became increasingly moderate under the editorship of O'Brien, which began in November 1832. The "socialism" that it propounded was democratic in conception, and it invariably emphasized the effectiveness of nonviolent political change. But like many other unstamped journals, the leaders of the *Poor Man's Guardian* contained statements such as the following: "We had rather see our countrymen up to their ears in blood, than see them die by inches the despised outcast victims of your cannibal legislation." [25] References to the Church of England, the monarchy, the aristocracy, and other detested institutions, were phrased similarly. Private property was savagely condemned.

[22] *Voice of the West Riding*, 12 April 1834. [23] *Ibid.*, 17 Aug. 1833.
[24] *Poor Man's Guardian*, 21 June 1834. [25] *Ibid.*, 22 June 1833.

The *Cosmopolite* featured a less "moderate" editorial policy than did the *Poor Man's Guardian*. Control of the former journal fluctuated between Carlile and several of the more radical "victims." Despite its disavowal of physical force and notwithstanding Carlile's editorship during much of its existence, it employed bitter political invective and frequently came close to endorsing revolution. One front-page leader, written during the spring of 1833, advised readers that "it is an armed people only that a tyrannical government fears." [26] Another leader avowed menacingly: "There is no sympathy between the rulers of the people and the people, no link, no tie, no responsibility, beyond the abstract and now vague idea of physical force, no moral control over the rulers by the people." [27]

Though references to violence were often diluted, many of the illegal journals publicized specific proposals for implementing radical reform. William Benbow's plan for a general strike or "annual holiday" of one month's duration, for example, earned widespread endorsement by the unstamped press.[28] Benbow himself advocated the plan vigorously in the short-lived *Agitator and Political Anatomist*, his only known venture into illegal journalism, and Doherty's *Poor Man's Advocate* urged the "annual holiday" upon its readers as the best means to enforce a reduction of factory hours.[29] But the *Man* gave the scheme its most concrete formulation. George Petrie, that journal's leading contributor, envisaged a "rational commonwealth" to be constructed in the aftermath of the general strike. He advocated the immediate establishment of a Grand Union of Trades to give effect to

[26] *Cosmopolite*, new ser., 1 June 1833.   [27] *Ibid.*, new ser., 31 Aug. 1833.

[28] The monthly holiday was presented initially in Benbow's 2d. tract, *Grand National Holiday, and Congress of the Productive Classes*. The original pamphlet has been reproduced in *International Review for Social History*, I (1936), 237–252. For a useful summary of Benbow's main ideas, see Niles Carpenter, "William Benbow and the Origin of the General Strike," *Quarterly Journal of Economics*, XXXV (1920–1921), 491–499; M. Beer, *A History of British Socialism* (London: George Allen and Unwin, 1953) I, 314–318.

[29] *Agitator, and Political Anatomist*, Dec. 1833. The *Herald of the Rights of Industry* endorsed a general strike "against the idlers" (5 April 1834).

the proposal.[30] No substantive action developed in response to Benbow's suggestion. The fervor with which Petrie, Doherty, and other radical journalists espoused the idea, however, exacerbated tensions between middle- and working-class reformers and thus reduced further the possibility of a union with middle-class reformers on the issue of the newspaper duty.

Two additional proposals that were advocated by the penny journals as a means of securing fundamental changes were repudiation of the national debt and the systematic withdrawal of funds from savings banks. The former proposal was conceived as a means of rectifying the historical inequities accruing from the Napoleonic Wars and as an effective technique to counteract the "public robbery" that had been perpetrated by wealthy creditors upon the defenseless poor.[31] The threatened run on the banks had a less "moderate" aura since it was linked invariably with foreshadowings of a new political system to replace the present one. One illicit periodical suggested to its readers that *"the whole of this game* will be overthrown within a year from this date" if all savings banks and public companies were financially destroyed.[32] Several journalists counselled nonpayment of taxes as a useful technique to achieve desirable reforms, and others advocated nonpayment of rent and a system of "exclusive dealing" by the poor to enforce political and social objectives.[33]

Thus, with reference to political changes, the subsequent Chartist demands for a democratic utopia were prefigured by the il-

---

[30] *Man,* 13 Oct. 1833.

[31] *Cosmopolite,* new ser., 11 May 1833. Even Carpenter called for a vague "adjustment" of the debt (*Political Letters and Pamphlets,* 9 Dec. 1830, 12 Feb. 1831).

[32] *Cosmopolite,* new ser., 4 May 1833. The tone of this leader was so unequivocally bitter that the liberal pencilings of a government official are still visible on the Home Office copy (H.O. 64/19).

[33] See Lorymer's letter in the *Poor Man's Guardian,* 13 April 1833; *"Destructive,"* 31 Aug. 1833. The *Poor Man's Guardian, Poor Man's Advocate,* and *Voice of the West Riding* endorsed exclusive trading. See the articles by Allen Davenport in *Poor Man's Guardian,* 7 and 28 Sept. 1833; Lovett, in *"Destructive,"* 11 May 1833.

legal journals. "Physical force" methods for achieving this desired transformation were envisaged if not always specifically advocated. Parliamentary reformers were, not surprisingly, alarmed and, as a result, the divergence within reforming circles was widened.

ECONOMIC AND SOCIAL THEMES

In the realm of economic and social relations, many illegal newspapers combined criticism of the institution of private property with an advocacy of co-operative schemes. But again, the salient fact about the unstamped press was its diversity of response; thus, Carlile consistently rejected co-operative proposals as "circles in the air." Man's environment was capable of vast improvement, he admitted, since under the present system

so much is extracted by those who do not labour from the produce of those who do labour, that the one side is overwhelmed with the luxuries of life—I should even go so far as to say rendered vicious by the luxuries of life—while the other side is rendered vicious from the want of the necessaries of life.[34]

Human nature itself was, however, impervious to new circumstances, and hence for Carlile the Owenite conception of a modification of human behavior as the result of a transformed environment had no validity.[35] The state could neither artificially "create employment" nor establish a utopian system of "economic equality." [36] Carpenter expressed similar confidence in voluntary political and moral changes as opposed to underlying institutional reforms and concentrated most of his energies upon securing repeal of the taxes on knowledge. But neither Carpenter nor Carlile possessed substantial journalistic support after 1832 and much

[34] *State Trials* (1823–1831), p. 515.
[35] "The Creed of Richard Carlile," *Prompter*, 12 Feb. 1831.
[36] *Ibid.*, 16 April 1831, 4 June 1831. Carlile did advocate a system of national education based upon the proceeds of property confiscated from the Crown, the aristocracy and the Church (*ibid.*, 1 Jan. 1831).

working-class sentiment gravitated toward those writers who offered a more militant economic and social analysis.

A prevalent theme during the war of the unstamped was that of the evils of economic individualism, of the "profit-hunting system," and of the institution of private property. According to the *Poor Man's Guardian:* "Not one ounce more food—not one thread more clothing will [middle-class capitalists] give you for your labour; depend on it they will let you—make you starve and slave, as much as ever, under what they will call 'good and cheap government.' " [37] In the view of many writers the origins of these evils were traceable to England's perverted historical development. At a given moment in the past, it was asserted, property had been inequitably and unjustly expropriated from the public domain, "in ninety-nine instances out of a hundred, by direct and palpable robbery, unblushingly perpetrated under the forms of law." As a result of this monopolization of property the laboring classes were taxed unjustly and treated as a "marketable commodity." [38]

Furthermore, the evils of private property were considered more glaring than ever because the inequalities of the social system were widening due to the advance of industrialization. O'Brien, the most challenging thinker to emerge during the war of the unstamped, did not advocate the abolition of private property under all circumstances but only when, as at present, it was employed as "a sort of sucking-pump or thumbscrew for sucking and screwing other people's produce into [its] possession." [39] He denounced time and again the "middlocracy," whom he referred

[37] *Poor Man's Guardian,* 3 Dec. 1831.

[38] *"Destructive,"* 2 Feb. 1833. The United States, which lacked a long history, became from the working-class perspective a land of "peace, happiness, and prosperity," devoid entirely of the "want, wretchedness, crime, and discontent" so prevalent in England (speech of Benjamin Warden, as reported in *Poor Man's Guardian,* 16 July 1831; *Address from One of the 3730 Electors of Preston,* 21 April 1832; *Address to the Radical Reformers,* 9 Jan. 1832). C. D. Lillibridge, *Beacon of Freedom: The Impact of American Democracy upon Great Britain, 1830–1870* (New York: A. S. Barnes, 1961), pp. 1–39.

[39] *Hetherington's Twopenny Dispatch,* 26 March 1836.

[221]

to on one occasion as "the sham-liberal pauper-starving Malthusian crew." [40] In his view this class was the most aggressive, property-conscious, selfish element in society, comparable to a gangrenous body that responded invariably from egoistic motives. [41] He wrote in *Hetherington's Twopenny Dispatch:*

We know the middle class will encourage nothing which tends to make the productive class believe that they were born to a better state of things. Above all they must not discuss the question of Labour and Capital. The mysterious services rendered by capital for its assumed right to seize all the wealth of nearly all produce in the Kingdom could never be systematically obtruded with impunity. [42]

On another occasion, O'Brien affirmed that he preferred "the despotism that is tempered by education, and softened by urbane manners . . . [to] the griping remorseless despotism of the quill and the ledger." [43]

Most working-class journalists declared that private property, the fundament of the "system," had to be transformed substantially or totally destroyed. It represented the principle of "individual aggrandizement" and was the foremost impediment in the path of true co-operative development. [44] Lorymer's *Republican* concluded that:

Every priest, every great land-holder, every cut throat or soldier, every pensioner, and every other vulture, who had been gnawing the vitals of the nation—every sloth, every glutton, and every aristocrat who has been battening on the produce of the wealth-producers—every bloated hog who has been feeding on the fruits of the labour of the operatives and the peasantry, shall be made to restore the ill-gotten prey to the insulted, plundered owners—the industrious many. [45]

Few other illicit newspapers would have unqualifiedly endorsed

[40] Bronterre's letter, No. 6, *Hetherington's Twopenny Dispatch*, Vol. II, No. 91.

[41] *Poor Man's Guardian*, 5 April 1834.

[42] *Hetherington's Twopenny Dispatch*, 9 April 1836.

[43] Bronterre's letter, No. 5, *Hetherington's Twopenny Dispatch*, Vol. II, No. 90.

[44] *Poor Man's Guardian*, 16 and 30 July 1831.

[45] *Republican*, 2 July 1831.

such a threat, but nearly all accepted the principle that a better relationship had to be established between the state and the institution of property and that individuals should no longer be "slaves to the money-mongers." [46]

There was little agreement as to the precise nature of the anticipated economic and social changes. The more "moderate" working-class journalists concerned themselves largely with denigrating the inequities of the prevailing system and offered few concrete proposals. Several penny newspapers suggested a slight modification of the debt in order to align funded income with the shifting value of money, and Carpenter proposed a graduated property tax and a vaguely-defined system of social control as the best solution.[47] John Bell, who edited several unstamped journals including the *New Weekly True Sun* (1836), the *New Political Register* (1835–1836) and the *Mirror for Magistrates, A Strictly Legal Publication* (1836), offered the panacea of a property tax which would be substituted for all other imposts. This would eliminate indirect taxes upon labor and assist perceptibly in the redistribution of property.[48]

Others advocated factory legislation and repeal of the New Poor Law of 1834 as key stages in creating a more equitable economic structure. The latter statute was especially condemned as a flagrant manifestation of the power wielded by influential capitalists. The *Political Penny Magazine*, a journal that was devoted primarily to securing repeal of this law, proclaimed:

The Cotton Lords of Manchester, the Iron Lords of Birmingham, the Sugar Lords of Liverpool, and the Monied Lords of the whole Kingdom, want to have the power placed in their own hands to enable them to still grind and subdue the poor through their accursed machinery and commercial wealth.[49]

[46] *New Political Register*, 7 Nov. 1835.
[47] *Political Letter*, 18 June 1831; *Political Letters and Pamphlets*, 23 Dec. 1830.
[48] *New Weekly True Sun*, 2 April 1836.
[49] "A Real Radical," *Penny Political Magazine*, 17 Sept. 1836. For assertedly helping to draft the measure, Brougham was described as "the Poor Law Murder Bill Man" (Edmonds, *Appeal to the Labourers of England*, p. 12).

John Bell denounced the statute for presenting the laborers with the unenviable choice of "perpetually lowering wages on the one hand, or, on the other, imprisonment, half starvation, and a forfeiture of the domestic charities of life." [50] Still another journalist described the act as having "pronounced sentence of death on poverty." [51]

But the consensus of the unstamped periodicals (if such a mythical point can be charted accurately) was more decisively aimed toward a total transformation in the institution of property. In accordance with Ricardian theories as substantially modified and popularized in Thomas Hodgskin's *Labour Defended Against the Claims of Capital, or the Unproductiveness of Capital Proved* (1825), the value of capital and thus property was determined by the amount of labor that went into it. Inasmuch as most property owners had not earned their title through labor, justice demanded the forcible collectivization of many forms of property. Lovett, for example, demanded that all land revert to the people unless the landowners agreed to undertake the full fiscal responsibility of government. [52]

Even when collectivization of private property was not advocated openly, the employment of violent literary imagery was often conducive to drawing such implications. O'Brien, for example, affirmed that universal suffrage was a necessary prerequisite to massive economic and social reconstruction and that the act of forcible "confiscation," in the absence of political agreement, was anathema. [53] Yet he simultaneously impressed upon his readers that "rent and profits . . . are all so many subtractions from the wages of labour—all part and parcel of the same cannibal system, which sacrifices the many to the avarice and ambition of the few." [54]

The *Working Man's Friend,* despite its "moderateness,"

[50] *Political Mirror*, 23 Sept. 1837.
[51] Bronterre's letter, No. 5, *Hetherington's Twopenny Dispatch*, Vol. II, No. 90.
[52] Petition by Lovett in *Poor Man's Guardian*, 21 Feb. 1835.
[53] *Ibid.*, 23 Nov. 1833.   [54] *Ibid.*, 22 Jan. 1834.

hinted occasionally at social revolution. On one occasion it denounced the members of the reformed Parliament for being "greedy wretches who fatten on the miseries of their fellow-countrymen." [55] Lovett, ordinarily a nonviolent proponent of Owenite views, sometimes suggested forcible remedies, as when he wrote:

If, therefore, in spite of our reasoning and petitioning, the possessors of property turn from us with indifference or treat us with contempt, even the multitude will be fully justified in undermining and destroying a system productive of such mischief, *as is the system of private property.*[56]

And even Carpenter sometimes expressed restrained opinions in a context laden with social threats. Thus, when he said that if the national debt was not immediately adjusted "the renovated power and excited indignation of the people shall level the rotten fabric into the dust," a parliamentary reformer accused him and other working-class writers of advocating the "destruction of all property." [57]

For every column that appeared in the unstamped press that suggested legislative remedies to transform the economic system, there were probably several that hinted at violent measures. The *Cosmopolite* advocated repudiation of the national debt (by force if necessary) as a preliminary skirmish in an approaching social conflagration. "Prepare," it adjured its readers, "in every possible way, for a great change" once the "robbery" symbolized by the debt was destroyed.[58] Several of Lorymer's publications declaimed menacingly against the "ill-gotten" wealth of the privileged minority and advocated forcible nationalization of property in order to restore the "natural rights" of the masses to the soil.[59] Hobson's *Voice of the West Riding* also endorsed vigor-

[55] *Working Man's Friend,* 9 Feb. 1833.
[56] *"Destructive,"* 1 June 1833.
[57] *Political Letters and Pamphlets,* 9 and 23 Dec. 1830.
[58] *Cosmopolite,* 4 May 1833.
[59] *Republican,* 2 July 1831. Lorymer's revolutionary cast of mind is well expressed in the following observation: "We eagerly hope that we shall see

ously the panacea of nationalization. Its columns amalgamated demands for factory reform, universal suffrage, and radical social change with a championship of "The Rights of Man against the 'exclusives,' the rights of labour against the competatives [*sic*]." [60] George Edmonds, a prolific contributor to the unstamped press, warned of an impending conflict that would place "excessive wealth against excessive poverty." [61]

Foremost among the illegal periodicals that advocated outright nationalization of property was the *Agitator*, a Glasgow penny weekly. This journal favored the forcible collectivization of all land, since public control of land could alone rectify the "usurpation" of property which had taken place over a period of several hundred years.[62] George Petrie, writing in the *Man*, similarly drafted in uncompromising terms the blueprint of the "rational commonwealth" which he and other Spencean socialists favored. The "desolating, barbarous and unnatural institution" of private property was to be compulsorily abolished. When this took place, the social system could be restored to its pristine, noncompetitive framework. In the interim absentee landholdings were to be restricted to one-half square mile.[63]

The radical *Political Penny Magazine*, though describing these Spencean schemes as "visionary," reached similar conclusions. It averred that commercial and manufacturing property owners ("this MOLOCH of STEAM") had replaced landholders in positions of dominance. But the laborers were still deprived of their rightful share of the product, and since "the conquered have the same right to be conquerors in their turn—if they can," it endorsed

---

the day of Vengeance. We trust that all the living tyrants, high or low, who have insulted, plundered and enslaved the Many, of late years, will live to be punished" (F. Lamennais, *The Book of the People*, trans. with notes by James H. B. Lorymer [London: Henry Hetherington, 1838], pp. 79–80 n.).

[60] "Address," *Voice of the West Riding*, 6 Jan. 1833.

[61] *Le Bonnet Rouge*, 6 April 1833.

[62] *Agitator*, 30 March 1833, 13 April 1833.

[63] *Man*, 18 Aug. 1833, 22 Sept. 1833, 24 Nov. 1833.

compulsory nationalization of property.[64] The *Radical Reform-er's Gazette,* a Glasgow periodical that sought primarily to secure the abolition of paper money, likewise endorsed a forcible ex-propriation of land.[65] Thus, demands for collectivization of property oftentimes couched in militant terms and embodying fragments of developing socialist theory were an important con-stituent of illegal journalism. These demands linked this aspect of the war of the unstamped with the emergence of "physical force" Chartism at the end of the decade.

A predictable by-product of the repeated denunciations of "property" and "profit" was the nurturing of antisemitic feeling by the illegal press. In the tradition of Cobbett, the Jew was identified frequently with the desolating forces of individualism and speculation. *Hetherington's Twopenny Dispatch,* for exam-ple, assured its readers that the bankers Rothschild and Goldsmid were among the foremost possessors of "an unlimited power of robbing, pauperizing, and driving their fellow-creatures to de-struction." [66] O'Brien, who along with many other radical jour-nalists advocated Jewish political emancipation, observed that the avaricious, property-minded Jews "cannot even sell a bunch of oranges without first filching half the juice out of them." [67] The editor of the *Political Penny Magazine,* another unstamped journal, scathingly berated the "circumcised and Christ-denying" Jews for their alleged rapacity and repudiation of co-operative principles.[68]

The most positive economic theme enunciated by the working-class press was the endorsement of co-operative principles. These principles took varied forms but involved a fundamental commit-

---

[64] *Political Penny Magazine,* 10 Sept. 1836.

[65] *Radical Reformer's Gazette,* 24 Nov. 1832, 15 Dec. 1832.

[66] *Hetherington's Twopenny Dispatch,* 26 March 1836.

[67] *"Destructive,"* 16 March 1833.

[68] *Political Penny Magazine,* 3 Sept. 1836. For a further example of anti-semitism, see Thomas Macconnell's poem, "Two Hebrew Melodies," *Poor Man's Guardian,* 18 Oct. 1834.

ment to an economic system reconstituted along noncompetitive lines. Nearly every illegal periodical that dealt with social or political questions (with the exception of Carlile's several journals) gave at least partial support to such views. Even the *Political Letters and Pamphlets* printed excerpts from the writings of William Pare and other disciples of Owen, notwithstanding Carpenter's personal conviction that the laborers could more effectively advance through individual effort.[69]

A number of journals endorsed the principles of economic cooperation unqualifiedly, most specifically the notion that a reform of the system of property was much more critical than shifts of political power. Owen's disciples founded the *Crisis, or the Change from Error and Misery, to Truth and Happiness* (1832–1834) and the *Pioneer, or, Trades' Union Magazine* (1833–1834), two of the leading illegal journals, and Owen himself edited the former for a time. In Birmingham at least one penny weekly, the *Birmingham Labour Exchange Gazette,* was devoted solely to elucidating the principles that underlay the Owenite Labour Exchanges.[70] The Owenite British Association for Promoting Co-operative Knowledge, which included Hetherington, Cleave, Watson, and Lovett among its members, became a leading force in the war of the unstamped through its meetings on the subject and the active part that it played in soliciting subscriptions for the "victims." It published a short-lived 2*d.* sheet entitled the *Magazine of Useful Knowledge, and Cooperative Miscellany* (1830).[71] This journal eschewed political controversy, expounding instead the virtues of a regenerated social system based upon a redistribution of income and property. Unlike other journals, it made no references, even by indirection, to "physical force" as a means of achieving its social objectives.[72]

[69] *Political Letters and Pamphlets,* 28 Jan. 1831, 12 Feb. 1831.
[70] *Birmingham Labour Exchange Gazette,* 9 Feb. 1833.
[71] *Magazine of Useful Knowledge,* 13 Nov. 1830, 30 Oct. 1830.
[72] "Address," *ibid.,* 1 and 15 Oct. 1830.

Most of the journalists who participated in the working-class repeal agitation regarded themselves as co-operators, though many reached the conclusion that the achievement of political power, that is, universal suffrage, had to precede the economic restructuring of society. Hetherington strongly propounded co-operative ideas and gave force to these in his journals. He accepted the Ricardian-socialist thesis that "*labour* was the source of wealth" and believed that private property, as an artificial construct, was far less meaningful than the productive labor of individuals.[73] Whenever the two conflicted at any point, the institution of private property had to give way. Hetherington always considered himself a disciple of Owen, but his illicit journals increasingly predicated the theme that universal suffrage and an untaxed press rather than economic changes were the necessary prerequisites to a transformation of the social structure.[74] Even his strictures on property came to have reference to "existing circumstances only—the INSTITUTIONS by which property is acquired—and not to previously accumulated property." [75]

Watson and Cleave also enunciated co-operative principles. Watson believed that "base, selfish, dishonest" competition was responsible for economic inequality.[76] He offered no specific remedy but the *Working Man's Friend* vigorously urged social change along noncompetitive lines. Cleave repeatedly attacked "that system which looked calmly on a brave nation, starving in the midst of plenty . . . while they could find sufficient leisure to vote away the industry of the people, to support State paupers, and a £100,000 a year to the Queen." [77] A society organized

---

[73] Report of Hetherington's Rotunda speech in *Republican*, 18 June 1831; *Poor Man's Guardian*, 30 March 1833.

[74] *Poor Man's Guardian*, 13 April 1833. G. D. H. Cole's description of Hetherington as an "ardent Owenite" is not supported by the evidence (*A Short History of the British Working-Class Movement, 1789–1947* [London: George Allen and Unwin, 1948] p. 95).

[75] *Poor Man's Guardian*, 27 Dec. 1834.

[76] *Working Man's Friend*, 13 April 1833, 9 March 1833.

[77] *Republican*, 6 Aug. 1831.

upon co-operative principles was, in his view, the best alternative to this situation. But his analysis of economic problems was essentially negative. He expended much journalistic energy in attacking the "locusts" who were sponging parasitically on the poor, asserting on one occasion that "within five miles of St. James's, several men died in ditches, and when they were dissected nought but grass was found in their stomachs." [78] Yet his own periodicals, including *A Slap at the Church* and *Cleave's Weekly Police Gazette*, offered few concrete solutions to England's economic ills.

Co-operative ideas, irrespective of the vigor and emotion with which they were articulated, often served as a deterrent to political extremism. Those most uncompromisingly committed to co-operation rejected political action as time-consuming and irrelevant. Furthermore, co-operative principles, even when vaguely defined, represented the positive ideal of a shared society. Adherence to this ideal enabled many reformers to transcend negative criticism and personal animosity.

But co-operative principles, like the entire spectrum of thought unleashed by the war of the unstamped, were articulated within an increasingly radical context. The views of O'Brien illustrate this point. O'Brien enunciated frequently the moral and other virtues inherent in a system of social and economic co-operation.[79] At the same time he denounced the present system as "a mass of wrong and rottenness from top to bottom" and advocated "a radical change in the whole social system, embracing an entirely new and utter change in the laws of property, and establishing new relations between man and man, quite different from what exist now." [80] Such a change could be secured most efficiently through trade unions, which would gradually assist in the

---

[78] Speech to the British Association for Promoting Co-operative Knowledge as quoted in *Magazine of Useful Knowledge*, 30 Oct. 1830; *People's Conservative*, 3 May 1834.

[79] *"Destructive,"* 29 March 1834.

[80] Bronterre's letter, No. 1, *Hetherington's Twopenny Dispatch*, 2 Jan. 1836; Bronterre's letter, No. 2, *Hetherington's Twopenny Dispatch*, Vol. II, No. 83.

transformation of the forms of production. Universal suffrage was a necessary constituent of this process, as was the publication and dissemination of cheap literature. But physical violence was, in O'Brien's opinion, theoretically undesirable, although it remained a constant element in his thought. He wrote in the *Poor Man's Guardian* that "England will think twice before she suffers her middlocracy to HIRE FOUR HUNDRED AND TWENTY THOUSAND CUT-THROATS TO MURDER HER LABOURERS, FOR REFUSING TO LIVE ON GARBAGE AND POTATOES." Trade unions were urged to subvert England's institutions deliberately in order to redress the "source of all abuses." [81]

Thus, in the social and economic spheres as in the political, the ideas propagated by the unstamped press appeared dangerous to propertied reformers. Hume, Place, James Mill, and others spoke for the latter when they deplored the "virulent and ridiculous trash" being disseminated by these journals.[82] The possibility of achieving a meaningful rapport between middle- and working-class reformers was once again severely reduced.

RELIGIOUS THEMES

In the area of religion, the unstamped periodicals energetically denounced the temporal abuses of both the Church of England and dissenting churches. The Church of England was, in particular, equated with unyielding opposition to all proposals for political and social change. Its clergy were, in the words of one journal, "spiritual wolves, who are only qualified to mediate, intercede, and do business with the devil." [83]

The conservatism of the Anglican hierarchy gave force to these anticlerical sentiments. By voting against the Reform Bill, the Bishops had, according to one writer, "disgraced their holy calling, forfeited the respect of the people, and done more injury

[81] *Poor Man's Guardian*, 9 Nov. 1833. For an attack by O'Brien on "visionary" schemes, see *ibid.*, 1 March 1834.
[82] Parliamentary proceedings of 27 June 1831 as reported in *Penny Papers for the People*, 2 July 1831.
[83] *Cosmopolite*, 20 Oct. 1832.

to the Church of England than all the infidels that ever scribbled." [84] As the Church of England identified itself publicly with a negative position on other proposed reforms, this anticlerical feeling began to intensify.

Scores of illegal journals attacked the temporal evils of "Priestcraft." [85] George Cruikshank and other illustrators satirized the clergy repeatedly and effectively in such illicit periodicals as the *Devil's Walk! Edited by a Member of Parliament* (1832), *A Slap at the Church, Punch in London* (1832), *Punchinello! or Sharps, Flats, and Naturals! A Family Gazette of Fun, Fashion, Literature, and the Drama* (1832), the *Church Examiner and Ecclesiastical Record* and the *Squib* (1832). William Howitt's *A Popular History of Priestcraft*, a tract that proffered an unmitigated indictment of the Church of England, became a staple item in the untaxed literature of the decade.[86] Excerpts from it and other anticlerical pamphlets appeared in the unstamped journals. Howitt's depiction of the Church of England as "one of the greatest curses which has afflicted the earth," received widespread endorsement,[87] though most other working-class journalists went beyond his dissenting position and denounced the noncomformist bodies with equivalent fervor.

The wealth possessed by the Church of England was a particular source of discontent. The compulsory payment of tithes, referred to in working-class circles as "tithe-traps," was felt to be the greatest abuse. The *Church Examiner and Ecclesiastical Record*, for example, bewailed "the monstrous injustice of compelling the people of one faith to support in pomp, or at all, the enormously numerous clergy of a very small fraction of pro-

---

[84] *Church Examiner*, 26 May 1832. This was an ironic position to adopt since many working-class journals also opposed the Reform Bill, though for contrary reasons.

[85] See *Man*, 1 and 22 Sept. 1833.

[86] It ran through at least eight editions between 1834 and 1846, including the unauthorized abridgement by Carpenter and Cleave.

[87] William Howitt, *A Popular History of Priestcraft in All Ages and Nations* (London: Effingham Wilson, 1833), p. v.

fessors of another creed." [88] Other sources of dissatisfaction, as discussed in the unstamped press, included the enforced payment of church rates, and the administrative practices of simony or the buying and selling of church offices and of nepotism. The complacency of both Anglican and nonconforming clergy, in the face of these seemingly widespread abuses, was a constant irritant. "The mass of the people already hate it," asserted one unstamped newspaper, "true religion abhors the [Anglican] Church, and will rejoice in its downfall." [89] The *Christian Corrector* castigated "ecclesiastical robbery, villainy, plunder, and oppression." [90] Similarly, the *Trades Examiner; or, Political and Literary Review,* an Edinburgh periodical, petitioned for the liquidation of the Church of Scotland's property to meet the municipal debt. [91]

Of the numerous illicit journals published during the years 1830–1836, several were devoted exclusively to the subject of church reform. Thomas Parkin's *Christian Corrector,* a weekly that was the object of several Stamp Office prosecutions, was of particular importance. Parkin's radical views were grounded upon doctrines of primitive Christianity. On the basis of his Scriptural interpretations, he proposed the use of "physical force" to overturn the present social and political structure which was based upon the power of "black-clothed and black-hearted" clergymen. [92] In his view, "twenty years of immolation of millions and millions of the poor on the altar of lords and priests is quite sufficient." The basis of a better society would be established only when the abuses of a compulsory state church were forcibly rooted out and a state of "natural" morality restored. [93]

The basic tenets of Christian doctrine were only occasionally called into question by the illegal journals. Carlile, Lorymer, Watson, and others criticized in varying degrees the fundamental

[88] *Church Examiner,* 19 May 1832. [89] *Weekly Herald,* 31 July 1836.
[90] *Christian Corrector,* 25 Jan. 1832.
[91] *Trades Examiner,* 17 Nov. 1832.
[92] *Christian Corrector,* 18 Jan. 1832. [93] *Ibid.,* 2 May 1832.

beliefs of organized religion. Lorymer affirmed that Christianity was "the religion of slaves and idiots" and "the strongest ally of tyranny, both mental and physical." Thus, in his opinion, "until priests be swept from the face of the earth they pollute and degrade, we shall not be able to crush kings, lords, soldiers, and pulpit-mongers." [94] Carlile (who first attracted attention in 1818 when he began to reprint the anticlerical writings of Paine) was a materialist who attacked Christianity as "morally, historically, and metaphorically defective" and who propagandized on behalf of a system of pure rationalism or "atheism." [95] Likewise, Watson contended that Christianity was "like every other human system, defective, and required reformation to be made conformable to the wisdom of the age and the improvement of intellect." [96]

Notwithstanding this criticism of orthodox religious tenets, the exposition of such themes comprised only a small fraction of the total comment about religion in the working-class press. Of those journalists who played a prominent role in the war of the unstamped, only Carlile unhesitatingly publicized his antireligious views. And even his efforts during the 1830's were concentrated primarily upon political journals such as the *Gauntlet* and the *Prompter*.

Lorymer penned thousands of words of radical commentary during the repeal agitation, but only rarely did he attest publicly to his deep-rooted rejection of Christianity. The *Laughing Philosopher*, a bitterly satirical penny journal that was published and edited by Lorymer, contained only one deflationary religious dialogue in its five numbers.[97] Neither the *Poor Man's Guard-*

[94] Lamennais, *Book of the People*, pp. 72–73 n.

[95] *Prompter*, 19 Feb. 1831, 19 March 1831.

[96] *A Report of the Trial of James Watson, for Having Sold a Copy of Palmer's Principles of Nature, at the Shop of Mr. Carlile* . . . (London: Richard Carlile, 1825), p. 21.

[97] A divinity student is asked: "Where did Adam procure the needles with which he sewed his fig-leaf breeches? Did his breeches fit tight? Were they fashionably made?" (*Laughing Philosopher*, 4 Aug. 1832).

ian, the *Working Man's Friend,* nor most of the other illicit periodicals that inundated England, dealt with religion in a truly
iconoclastic or controversial manner. And in one instance Carpenter purportedly refused to print an account of a Rotunda debate
on the subject of Christianity in his *Political Letters and Pamphlets.* Despite the fact that, as a participant in the debate, he
endorsed the proposition that the truth of Christianity can be
confirmed historically, he refused to juxtapose political and religious subjects in his journal.[98]

This absence of penetrating critical comment about religion almost certainly was a concession to working-class sensibilities. The
reform of temporal church abuses was an issue upon which a
working-class consensus was derivable, as were the demands for
political change and a co-operative social and economic system.
But no comparable agreement could be assured in the more controversial realm of fundamental religious commitment. Thus, as
O'Brien perceptively wrote when requesting that Owen soften
his "peculiar" religious tenets:

I beg you to understand me not as pleading indulgence for my own
prejudice, but for those of others. If I mistake not, your ideas and my
own are the same or nearly so, on these subjects—but the people, the
unhappy, the ignorant, the debasingly superstitious people are *fright-
fully sensitive* and, if you like, *insane* on these points.[99]

The *Cosmopolite* made this even more explicit. After rejecting a
contribution from a correspondent because of its antipathy to religion, it informed its readers: "The great bulk of mankind is yet
priest-ridden. . . . We must deal cautiously; we must go a little
with the stream, and endeavour, whenever opportunity occurs, to
turn its current into the right track." [100]

Thus, in the area of religion, the themes developed by the unstamped press were not too unsettling to parliamentary reform-

[98] S.S. report, n.d. [1830?], H.O. 64/11.
[99] O'Brien, letter to Robert Owen, 27 May 1832, cited in Podmore, *Owen,*
II, 431.
[100] *Cosmopolite,* 15 Sept. 1832.

ers. An emotional assault upon Christianity itself would have generated a hostile response from middle-class reformers, who were otherwise agreed both in principle and in substantial detail upon the necessity for institutional reform of the church structure. The disunity within reforming circles was not, therefore, exacerbated as a result of the religious ideas propagated during the war of the unstamped. But the overall impact of the political, social, and religious discontents articulated by the illegal journalists was to inflame intra-radical tensions. The political tenets of the Chartist movement, and of many of the economic and religious frustrations that underlay it, were distinctly prefigured in the penny newspapers of the 1830's.

CHAPTER 9

Working-Class Resistance

The energies of working-class repealers between 1830 and 1836 were channeled primarily into the publication and distribution of hundreds of illegal newspapers; but as a complement to this illicit journalism, working-class radicals also participated in a miscellany of activities that created an effective national opposition to the newspaper duty. These activities included protest meetings, the drafting and forwarding of petitions to Parliament, and agitation by a variety of organizations. This aspect of the campaign for removal of the newspaper duty became increasingly militant and class conscious, and one of its unintended effects, like that of working-class journalism, was to exacerbate differences with parliamentary reformers.

The working-class agitation for repeal of the taxes on knowledge paralleled, to some extent, the extraparliamentary activities engaged in by middle-class reformers. And like the latter it comprehended a volatile though relatively ineffectual phase that lasted from 1830 until the middle of 1834, and a more aggressive phase that began in the summer of 1834 and continued for almost two years.

The earlier aspect of the working-class "pressure from without" began in 1830 within an atmosphere of revived and accelerating reformism. During the summer and autumn of 1830, coffee shops, public houses, and reading rooms were transformed into debating centers and, as one observer noted, "the general theme of conversation everywhere [was] of the present state of Government." [1] Small radical associations were established such as the British Association for Promoting Co-operative Knowledge, founded in May 1829, the Metropolitan Political Union which was founded by Henry Hunt in March 1830, and the National Union of the Working Classes, formed in the spring of 1831. These and like organizations had Huntite, Owenite, or Carlilean affiliations and possessed numerous contacts in London's obscure working-class circles. That this resurgent radical movement was in a state of flux and disharmony is indicated by the statement of a police informer who had a firsthand knowledge of these organizations:

The whole of the leaders of these and many of the followers are in opposition to each other and are all disagreeing as to their ways of thinking and obtaining redress, but the whole of which have begun to be more anxious to be known and continue to do so since the French Revolution and have had a good many extra followers. [2]

Within this context of discordant demands for change the movement to secure an untaxed press was launched in both its political and journalistic aspects.

During the years 1830–1831 numerous reformers began to bewail the horrors of the "blood-red" stamp, and the *Poor Man's Guardian* which stood in the vanguard of the working-class agitation proclaimed:

We will try, step by step, the power of RIGHT against MIGHT, and we will begin by protecting and upholding this grand bulwark and defence of all our rights—this key to all our liberties—the FREEDOM OF THE PRESS—*the press*, too, of the IGNORANT and the POOR! we have taken upon ourselves its protection, and we will never abandon our post: we will *die* rather. [3]

[1] S.S. report, 20 Nov. 1830, H.O. 64/11. [2] *Ibid., c.* 1830?.
[3] *Poor Man's Guardian,* 9 July 1831.

And during the succeeding three years many protest meetings, accounts of which received substantial publicity in the columns of the illegal newspapers, were convened to give maximum vent to these feelings. Subscriptions for imprisoned "victims" were commenced and inflammatory posters, including the following, were hawked in London and the streets of northern industrial towns:

DESPOTIC GOVERNMENTS are those in which the People are kept in Darkness by a Privileged and Servile Press, and in which the most generous Citizens are thrown into UNWHOLESOME DUNGEONS! Let, then, all True Friends to Civil and Religious Liberty; all who feel a profound HATRED of TYRANNY!! express it publicly and undisguisedly, by Posting up this Placard (which may be had of all the Vendors of the Unstamped, free of expense) against the Shutters of their windows, or in some safe place, to prevent its destruction during the night; and keep it up until the termination of sufferings of the noble-minded Editors and Vendors of A FREE PRESS!!! [4]

This growing agitation, which linked its activities to support for the burgeoning penny press, involved appeals to working-class self-consciousness. Pledges were given to continue "to fight the battle until prisons are crowded with martyrs, and millions shall be expended in idle and fruitless persecutions." [5] Hostility was expressed with equal vehemence against the Whig and Tory "aristocratic factions," though the latter was thought to possess at least the virtue of honest "perfidy." "So long as the people will suffer themselves to be deluded by the press," affirmed one repealer in addressing a sympathetic audience, "first crying up the Whig faction, then the Tory faction, so long will one or both of them, have their hands in your pockets [loud applause]." [6]

[4] A copy of this placard, printed by R. E. Lee in Aug. 1834, is in H.O. 64/15.

[5] Speech by John Lawless as reported in *Man*, 10 Aug. 1834; *People's Hue and Cry*, 10 Aug. 1834.

[6] Henry Hunt, *Lecture on the Conduct of the Whigs, to the Working Classes, Delivered at Laurence Street Chapel, Birmingham, on Wednesday, October 31st, 1832* (London: William Strange, 1832), p. 5. Augustus Beaumont wrote: "Our war is against both factions. The Whigs are, as much as the Tories, our

Devices by which economic pressure could be exerted upon the government were oftentimes suggested though rarely, if ever, applied. For example, in April 1833 the *Cosmopolite* issued an appeal for a boycott of all legal literature: *"Touch not a stamped paper;* the mark on it is the mark of your blood, your slavery, your degradation, the signet of your subjugation, and the warranty of your weakness." [7] Resolutions endorsing similar proposals were passed at many subsequent repeal meetings. At one gathering in January 1835, working-class supporters of the war of the unstamped were exhorted to boycott all public houses that subscribed to stamped newspapers other than the *True Sun.* In an attempt to make this plea effective, a boldly-printed placard was distributed which was addressed to the "WORKING MEN OF ENGLAND!!!" In provocative terms it urged:

If you wish for a Free Press, refuse to enter a coffee-shop, cook-shop, hairdresser's, beer-shop, or public-house where a STAMPED PAPER is taken in. By so doing, you will make the rascally proprietors of the Stamped Press wince, and induce them either to come out without a Stamp, or to fall to their slavish knees, and pray the Chancellor of the Exchequer to remove the obnoxious blood-mark from the tree of knowledge. [8]

Cleave and other repealers made similarly emotional pleas for a system of "exclusive dealing" as a means of securing repeal. "It is the duty of all honest men to do this," proclaimed Cleave. "It will be disgraceful to any friend of the Unstamped to omit the smallest opportunity of carrying [it] into effect." [9]

---

natural enemies" (*Whig Nullities; or, a Review of a Pamphlet . . . Entitled, "Domestic Policy of the Country under the New Parliament"* [London: Henry Hetherington, 1837], p. 11).

[7] *Cosmopolite,* 22 April 1833. *Le Bonnet Rouge* reported that several publicans in Hereford had been induced to stop taking in the *Globe* and to take in, as a substitute, the *True Sun,* a radical stamped evening newspaper (23 Feb. 1833).

[8] *Political Register,* 22 Aug. 1835.

[9] *Cleave's Weekly Police Gazette,* 6 Feb. 1836. Stockport reformers urged a boycott of all stamped newspapers (*Radical,* 13 March 1836). Hetherington

The widespread prosecution of vendors and publishers, and particularly the imprisonment of prominent journalists, invariably generated a flurry of meetings and protests. The prosecution and imprisonment of Carpenter in May 1831 touched off a wave of "liberty of the press" meetings at the Rotunda and other radical centers that culminated in the formation of the initial "Victim Funds." [10] Hetherington's apprehension in October 1831, after a previous conviction for publishing an illegal newspaper, even more significantly increased the tempo of working-class activity. During the four months that elapsed between his conviction in July 1831 and his capture, Hetherington traveled throughout northern England, addressing radical associations in Coventry, Blackburn, Manchester, and other industrial urban centers and arousing resistance to the stamp laws.[11] According to the account of Popay, the informer, a "great confusion" occurred within the N.U.W.C. when Hetherington was seized. Hurried conferences were held and proposals were tentatively discussed to convey "a mob of persons" to the House of Lords to protest the government's action. Although these proposals failed to materialize, the N.U.W.C. and other working-class organizations held protest meetings during the succeeding weeks.[12] When a subsequent prosecution of Hetherington was initiated in December 1832, the event generated even greater turmoil in working-class circles and was described by one illicit newspaper as the commencement of a "Reign of Terror." [13]

Unlike the middle-class extraparliamentary movement, the

---

asserted that he and his wife "frequently trudged 2 or 3 miles, to the shop of a real Radical, rather than spend their money with the shopkeepers around them, who were either opposed, or indifferent to the interests of the workmen" (Hunt, *Lecture on the Conduct of the Whigs*, p. 6).

[10] See the S.S. report, *c.* May 1831?, H.O. 64/11.

[11] *Poor Man's Guardian*, 30 July 1831, 3 Sept. 1831.

[12] S.S. report, 3 Oct. 1831, H.O. 64/11.

[13] *Working Man's Friend*, 29 Dec. 1832. The *True Sun* predicted, in connection with the prosecution, that "the labouring men of England will assemble, and assert their claims to be heard in reprobation of the infamous Taxes which Mr. Hetherington has resisted the payment of" (10 Jan. 1833).

first phase of the working-class agitation was closely connected with other radical activities. Trade union organizers, co-operators, Owenites, poor law and factory reformers, and advocates of universal suffrage became involved actively in the taxes on knowledge movement. Most reformers regarded an untaxed press as an indispensable prerequisite to a desired cluster of reforms. Thus, speakers at one repeal meeting after another placed removal of the stamp duties within a programmatic framework that also comprised universal suffrage, the ballot, annual parliaments, repeal of the New Poor Law of 1834 and of the Union with Ireland, and a more equitable distribution of property.[14]

Factory agitators in the West Riding and Lancashire and trade unionists in Birmingham and London played active roles in the repeal movement. They subscribed to the unstamped journals with regularity and occasionally edited or published them, attended local meetings to protest Stamp Office prosecutions, and served frequently on committees that supervised the "Victim Funds." The activities of working-class leaders such as Joshua Hobson and George Petrie illustrate the nature of these intertwined radical interests. Hobson, a Huddersfield handloom weaver and carpenter, was an active participant in several West Riding reform activities. As an influential member of the Political Union of Ashton-under-Lyne he vigorously agitated for political reforms. Simultaneously, he participated energetically in the Short Time factory movement alongside such better-known personalities as Richard Oastler, "Parson" Bull, and John Fielden. Finally, and of greatest significance for the war of the unstamped, Hobson published, edited, and vended the *Voice of the West Riding*, an illegal penny journal, for which he suffered six months' imprisonment.[15]

[14] Report of an N.U.W.C. meeting in *Poor Man's Guardian*, 23 July 1831; report of a Norwich repeal meeting, *Cleave's Weekly Police Gazette*, 30 Jan. 1836; speech by John Lawless at a Southwark repeal meeting, *People's Hue and Cry*, 10 Aug. 1834.

[15] Driver, *Tory Radical*, pp. 81–82; *Cosmopolite*, 13 Oct. 1832; "Destructive," 14 July 1832.

Petrie was a former tailor and soldier from Leicester who migrated to London in the early 1830's and became prodigiously active in working-class reform organizations. According to Richard Lee, an admirer and colleague, he joined several radical and cooperative associations and became a popular lecturer. Beginning in 1833, Petrie played an active role in the abortive Owenite-inspired attempt to establish a Grand National Consolidated Trades Union. He appears to have been preoccupied with the provincial side of this movement, despite the fact that his political base was in London.[16] As a complement to his trade union interests, he thrust himself consequentially into the taxes on knowledge agitation. He contributed numerous articles to the unstamped press, notably to the *Man* and to the *People's Weekly Police Gazette,* spoke at repeal gatherings, and served on the committee of management of the principal "Victim Fund." [17]

The provincial base of the first phase of the working-class repeal movement was strong. Repeal activities including meetings at which subscriptions were raised and petitions forwarded to Parliament were firmly rooted in industrial areas of northern England and the Scottish Lowlands, and some provincial repealers achieved prominence during these years. Abram Duncan, a factory reformer and future Chartist leader, played an important part in the Scottish repeal movement. He was active in the Glasgow-Ayrshire district, where he assisted in the circulation of unstamped newspapers and participated in a number of repeal meetings.[18] On one occasion, he represented Glasgow's working classes at a prominently attended reform banquet in honor of Lord Durham. In his toast on behalf of repeal of the taxes on

[16] See Ball, letter to Sir Francis Roe, 17 March 1834, H.O. 64/19.

[17] There is a wealth of material on Petrie, the best source being *Works of George Petrie,* pp. 17–25. See *Man,* 24 Nov. 1833, 1 Dec. 1833; *Poor Man's Guardian,* 2 March 1833.

[18] See report of a Johnstone repeal meeting in *Liberator,* 5 March 1836; J. T. Ward, "The Factory Movement in Scotland," *Scottish Historical Review,* XLI (1962), 110; Alex Wilson, "Chartism in Glasgow," in *Chartist Studies,* ed. Asa Briggs (London: Macmillan, 1960), p. 256 n.

knowledge, Duncan asserted that "the operatives were unable to pay for knowledge at the expensive scale charged through the newspapers, and that it would be eminently creditable to all parties, were they to apply their united exertions in removing that tax." [19]

George Condy, barrister, factory agitator, and editor of the radical *Manchester and Salford Advertiser*, was another provincial reformer active in the newspaper movement. Despite wealth and a prestigious position in Manchester, he identified his public fortunes with those of the laboring classes. He spoke at several local meetings, including one convened in Manchester in August 1835 to protest the seizure of Hetherington's and Cleave's presses, and another held at Salford in February 1836. On these and similar occasions Condy affirmed his intellectual commitment to the doctrines of Paine and Cobbett and denounced vehemently the repressive policies of the government.[20]

and 1834 were undertaken by associations rather than by individ-
Many of the activities of working-class repealers between 1830 uals acting singly or in small groups. Of the score or more of working-class organizations that played an active role in the movement, the British Association for Promoting Co-operative Knowledge (1829–1833) and the National Union of the Working Classes (1831–1835) were by far the most important. A large proportion of the leaders of the war of the unstamped, both those involved in journalism and those with political interests, were members of at least one of these associations. Cleave, Hetherington, Carpenter, Lovett, Watson, and Lee were all active members, as were many lesser personalities who spoke at meetings and engaged in clandestine literary activities. Much of the financial and emotional underpinning that the repeal move-

[19] *Report of the Public Reception, and the Speeches Delivered at the Dinner to Lord Durham . . . on Wednesday, 29th October 1834* (Glasgow: W. R. M'Phun, 1834), p. 32.

[20] *Manchester Advertiser*, 6 Feb. 1836; *Voice of the West Riding*, 15 March 1834; Read, *Press and People*, pp. 96–97; Place, letter to Parkes, 21 April 1834, Place Papers, Add. MSS 35,154, f. 193.

ment depended upon came from the hundreds of members who comprised these organizations and who filled the weekly meeting rooms at Blackfriar's Rotunda and other "seditious" centers. These organizations, whose multifaceted activities were often supported financially by wealthy sympathizers such as Julian Hibbert, collected subscriptions for imprisoned "victims," hawked copies of the *Poor Man's Guardian* and other penny journals at their weekly meetings, and initiated the first well-publicized protest meetings on the subject of repeal.

The British Association for Promoting Co-operative Knowledge was the predecessor of the N.U.W.C. It was established in May 1829, with the declared objective of diffusing "co-operative knowledge" in order to "secure the permanent happiness of the people at large," and within a year an estimated two to four hundred local co-operative societies were established under its aegis.[21] Notwithstanding its primary concern with securing a more equitable system of property holding, the Association began in October 1830 to agitate regularly on the subject of taxes on knowledge. During 1830–1831 it sponsored a series of meetings at the Mechanics' Institution and at the Rotunda, at which Cleave, Hetherington, Lovett, Watson, Carpenter, Petrie, Hibbert, and other activists played prominent roles. Resolutions were adopted denouncing "aristocratical misrule" and "the apostate and malignant traducers of the industrious and insulted poor," and petitions embodying these sentiments were forwarded to Parliament.[22] At one such meeting Hetherington, who had recently commenced the publication of his *Penny Papers for the People*,

---

[21] *Penny Papers for the People*, 31 Dec. 1830. For details about the Association, see Lovett's account in Place Papers, Add. MSS 27,791, ff. 237–248. Lovett estimated that two hundred branches were established, but the Association itself claimed four to five hundred (*Magazine of Useful Knowledge*, 30 Oct. 1830; *British Co-operator*, August 1830, pp. 101–102). See also G. D. H. Cole, *A Century of Co-operation* (Manchester: Co-operative Union, 1944), pp. 26–27.

[22] *Political Letters and Pamphlets*, 6 Nov. 1830; *Journals of the House of Commons*, 19 March 1831, LXXXVI, 408.

proclaimed that he would "rather spend his days in a prison than those obnoxious laws should be perpetuated," and Watson requested thousands of volunteers to prepare to consecrate themselves to the cause of a free press.[23] The Association also participated, through the activities of Lovett, its secretary, in the initial collection of subscriptions for Carpenter and Hetherington, and it established the first "Victim Funds" in Birmingham and in other major cities.[24]

Of greater importance than the British Association was the National Union of the Working Classes which was officially established in May 1831. The latter took over the defunct organization and personnel of the British Association and of the Metropolitan Political Union and amassed a probable membership of fifteen hundred by 1833.[25] Unlike the British Association, it stressed "Equal Rights" and "Radical Reform," that is, political democracy, rather than economic co-operation. And from the outset, although nearly all of its leading members described themselves as "co-operators" and "Owenites" and were antipathetic to capitalism, it concentrated most of its energies on the achievement of universal suffrage and an unstamped press.[26] Thus, the N.U.W.C. played a leading role in the war of the unstamped and its leadership provided much of the intellectual dynamic behind this protest movement.

The N.U.W.C. was implicated in the taxes on knowledge campaign in several ways. Its active participation stemmed from the

[23] *Political Letters and Pamphlets,* 11 Nov. 1830; *Magazine of Useful Knowledge,* 13 Nov. 1830.

[24] *Political Letter,* 16 July 1831; *Voice of the West Riding,* 20 Aug. 1831.

[25] In a preliminary circular, it predicted a membership of one to two hundred thousand (*Penny Papers for the People,* 26 March 1831).

[26] The appeal of the N.U.W.C. on a practical level was made in simpler terms. A carpenter, who belonged to the Union, described its success as follows: "Work being scarce and so on, brings people together; if there had been plenty of work I dare say there never would have been anything of it. If every man could keep the wolf from his door there would be no meeting of any sort. It is poverty that has brought the people together" (Testimony of Shem Shelley, *S.C. on Petition of Frederick Young* [1833], p. 39, q. 368).

first prosecution of Hetherington in June 1831. A succession of meetings was organized to pledge support for the "victims," and in the weeks and months that followed numerous verbal denunciations of the government were issued by the Union. At one of its meetings a petition was drafted which implored the Commons to refuse to grant supply until all "victims" were released.[27] And at a subsequent assemblage one speaker hinted at an insurrection if the government did not cease its prosecutions, while another urged "the necessity of taking the management of their affairs into their own hands" in the absence of governmental concessions.[28] Despite these allusions to violence the leadership of the N.U.W.C., with a few exceptions, was committed to voluntary change. In the words of an informer who scrutinized its activities closely for the Home Office, its principal objectives were "to recommend Reading all Pamphlets, abstinence from Liquours and Beer and drink Coffee and subscribe to pay expences of Placards etc. [*sic*]." [29]

From May 1831 until its effective demise in 1834, the N.U.W.C. arranged for numerous "debates" on the subject of the "tyrannical conduct" of the Whigs with respect to the taxes on knowledge. At these gatherings the Union's leaders, supported by the venerable and loquacious reformer Gale Jones, harangued the Stamp Office for its unyielding position and demanded a free press. Coruscating petitions and remonstrances were forwarded to Parliament on several occasions. Larger public repeal meetings were also sponsored periodically, and the Union propagandized for an untaxed press through the correspondence columns of the illegal journals and within its local thirty-to-forty member sections.[30] So firmly committed was the N.U.W.C. to

[27] *Penny Papers for the People*, 24 June 1831.

[28] *Ibid.*, 2 July 1831. The second speaker was Cleave.

[29] S.S. report, 19 Oct. 1831, H.O. 64/11.

[30] For information about the activities of the N.U.W.C., see the relevant numbers of the *Penny Papers for the People* and the *Poor Man's Guardian;* also R. F. Wearmouth, *Some Working Class Movements of the Nineteenth Century* (London: Epworth Press, 1948), pp. 66–84.

the cause of repeal that it was even suggested by one member that the terms "Union" and "untaxed press" were synonymous.[31]

Many smaller working-class political unions that were established in London and in the larger towns, frequently as offshoots of the N.U.W.C., played important if lesser roles in the repeal agitation. In Birmingham, the Midland Union of the Working Classes which was formed as a branch of the N.U.W.C. in October 1832 due to increasing dissatisfaction with the Birmingham Political Union worked vigorously on behalf of an untaxed press.[32] Likewise, the Manchester and Salford Political Union of the Working Classes and another organization, the Manchester Working Men's Association, propagandized consistently on behalf of untaxed literature. On one occasion the former pledged support to the *Poor Man's Guardian* and to Hetherington, its proprietor, "EVEN TO DEATH, as long as it advocates the doctrine of universal liberty." [33] The Dartford and Crayford Political Union of the Working Classes was similarly responsible for much of the agitation in Kent. During 1833 it held several meetings at which repeal of the taxes on knowledge was demanded. Petitions were forwarded to Parliament and subscriptions were commenced on behalf of Watson and other imprisoned vendors and publishers.[34] The Political Union of the Working Classes and Others of Great Yarmouth, the Hebden Bridge Political Union, the Leeds Radical Political Union, the Oldham Political Union of the Working Classes, the National Union of the Working Classes of Bristol, and the Norwich Union of the Working Classes were among the scores of other working-class associations that partici-

[31] *Political Unionist*, 7 July 1832.

[32] See the declaration of the Midland Union of the Working Classes in *Cobbett's Weekly Political Register*, 1 Sept. 1832. According to Briggs, it had "little influence" on Birmingham politics ("Background of the Parliamentary Reform Movement," p. 297).

[33] *Poor Man's Guardian*, 27 Aug. 1831.

[34] *Working Man's Friend*, 2 March 1833, 27 April 1833; *Cobbett's Weekly Political Register*, 18 May 1833.

pated actively in the repeal campaign by means of petitions, meetings, and patronage of the unstamped press.[35]

Many prominent provincial repealers and several London ones —including vendors, printers, publishers, and speakers—were affiliated with these smaller political unions. Thomas Parkin, the publisher and editor of the radical *Christian Corrector* and the author of several tracts that attacked church abuses, was Secretary of the Dudley Political Union of the Working Classes. Under his direction the Union, which was undoubtedly a branch of the N.U.W.C., denounced bitterly the "barbarous and tyrannical" prosecution of vendors and assailed the "hypocritical" Whigs for enforcing the stamp acts.[36] P. T. Bready, a well-known "victim" and collaborator with Carlile on several literary projects, played a correspondingly active role in the Sheffield Political Union of the Working Classes which was formed in May 1833 after a disagreement with the political union that dominated town politics. Bready's persistent attempts to enroll volunteers for Carlile and other publishers of unstamped newspapers exacerbated this division.[37] Joshua Hobson, whose activities have been discussed, was a leading member of the Political Union of Ashton-under-Lyne.

The more militant and critical phase of the working-class agitation began in the summer of 1834 and lasted for approximately two years. The incidence of meetings, petitions, and denunciations of governmental policies was substantially greater during these two years than earlier. Points of contact with middle-class reformers, rare prior to 1834 due to a paucity of extraparliamentary activity by the latter, increased slightly. Paradoxically, those events which touched off a major working-class response were Brougham's testimony before the Select Committee on Libel Law of 1834 and the formation in 1835 of Place's Association for the Abolition of the Stamp Duty.

[35] *Journals of the House of Commons*, 20 May 1833, LXXXVIII, 411; *Poor Man's Guardian*, 28 June 1835; *Cobbett's Weekly Political Register*, 22 Sept. 1832.

[36] *Working Man's Friend*, 6 July 1833; *Christian Corrector*, 25 Jan. 1832.

[37] *Sheffield Independent*, 25 May 1833, cited in *Gauntlet*, 2 June 1833.

In spite of the hostility felt for Brougham and Place by most working-class leaders, the activities of these men struck a sympathetic response in many sections of the country. Lee, the editor of the *Man*, reacted to Brougham's testimony by issuing a "PROCLAMATION" that called upon the proprietors of unstamped journals to "continue publishing, and meet any charges manfully and nobly!" "Sooner or later," he declared, "the unstamped will overthrow the government; the government never can overthrow the unstamped." [38] Other working-class spokesmen expressed similar sentiments notwithstanding murmurings of dislike for the Chancellor. And within the context of the national excitement created by Brougham's testimony, middle-class reformers appeared to become momentarily less fearful of the "seditious" doctrines uttered by the unstamped press. Hume, Harvey, Roebuck, O'Connell, and other M.P.'s ventured more frequently before working-class audiences to discuss repeal of the newspaper duty. During the remainder of 1834 and the early months of 1835 a unified commitment to the cause of an untaxed press seemed closer than ever.

The impact of Place's repeal association on the working-class "pressure from without" is less easy to discern, primarily because it was diffused over a two-year period. There is little direct evidence to indicate that its influence was other than peripheral. But a far greater number of working-class repeal meetings were convened during 1835–1836, and "mixed" repeal gatherings, that is, assemblages at which different types of reformers participated, increased substantially. Most of this increase is probably attributable to the climate of excitement generated by the activities of Place's organization.

The problem of defining the composition of a meeting poses formidable obstacles for the historian. Tenuous clues rather than concrete evidence must often be relied upon, and such clues include the tone and imagery of the recorded speeches, the identity

[38] *Man*, 10 Aug. 1834; *People's Hue and Cry*, 10 Aug. 1834.

of the orators and of their sponsoring organizations, and occasional references in newspaper accounts to the presence of persons of "respectable appearance" or to "mechanics."[39] On the basis of this type of evidence, it seems to be the case that laborers predominated at a large number of meetings held during 1835–1836 and that at some of these gatherings middle-class representation was marginal. Many of these meetings were credited by the Association for the Abolition of the Stamp Duty as having originated under its sponsorship, but it is more likely that they were initiated by working-class political unions and local reform associations.

A large number of the meetings held by working-class reformers during 1835 were stimulated by the intense legal and political controversy that simmered around the actions taken by the authorities against Cleave and Hetherington. In August of that year the Stamp Office, with seeming arbitrariness, confiscated printing presses and types in the possession of the two men in lieu of their asserted nonpayment of fines imposed for violation of the stamp laws. The presses were technically the property of Lovett and Watson, nonoffending third parties, to whose possession they had been recently transferred.[40] The seizure was, in fact, deliberately conceived as a means of undermining resistance to the law. One day prior to the actual confiscation the Stamp Office justified its subsequent behavior in these terms:

No such opportunity at the present is likely to occur, of breaking up two establishments by which our revenue has suffered very much, and

[39] For example, at a meeting held in Southwark in March 1836, few "respectable" persons spoke; the leading speakers were the Rev. Dr. Arthur Wade and Thomas Macconnell (*Radical,* 13 May 1836).

[40] While his premises were being searched, Watson tacked up the following sign: "Robbery and Oppression. A gang of thieves, pretending to act by the authority of the King, the father of his people, has entered these premises with intent to steal goods to a large amount. Englishmen! Your support is earnestly solicited to assist the proprietor in bringing these plundering villains to justice" (*Globe,* 31 July 1835, as reprinted in *Poor Man's Guardian,* 8 Aug. 1835).

[251]

must continue to suffer, so long as the law continues in its present unsatisfactory state.[41]

Cleave, with the support of many other working-class journalists, denounced the seizures as a "monstrous and incredible . . . offence against justice and equity" and contended that the Whigs:

have thrown Castlereagh and his Six Acts into the shade, and so completely out-heroded every attempt of even that celebrated worthy against the liberty of the press, that their names will henceforth be associated with all that is base and treacherous and tyrannical in the crusade against freedom.[42]

And during the first two weeks of August, a fortnight described by one newspaper as "the late emergency in the Unstamped press," a series of public meetings was convened, and numerous petitions and memorials were forwarded to the government.[43] At a Marylebone gathering resolutions were passed denouncing the Whigs as "tyrants under the mask of liberality . . . and . . . worse than Tories, because the latter make no pretensions to liberality." [44] In Manchester a protest gathering that was convoked two days after the confiscation of the presses nearly produced a riot when "pro-government" participants protested vigorously against the "strong" resolutions passed at the meeting.[45]

Amid rising excitement, the issue was raised ineffectually in the Commons by Hume and Roebuck, and shortly afterward a "Committee of Friends of Liberty of Discussion" consisting of prominent reformers was organized for the purpose of collecting

[41] John Wood, letter to Spring Rice, 31 July 1835, Monteagle Papers, No. 13,378 (1).

[42] *Address to the Readers of Cleave's Weekly Police Gazette; Supplement to Hetherington's Twopenny Dispatch*, 1 Aug. 1835. Copies are in Place Newspaper Collection, Set 70, ff. 243–54.

[43] *Cleave's Weekly Police Gazette*, c. Aug. 1835, Place Newspaper Collection, Set 70, f. 262. Thomas Macconnell described the incident as producing a "critical emergency" (*Cleave's Weekly Police Gazette*, 15 Aug. 1835).

[44] *True Sun*, 4 Aug. 1835.

[45] Newscutting, c. Aug. 1835, Place Newspaper Collection, Set 70, f. 259.

subscriptions for Hetherington and Cleave. According to the Committee, whose joint treasurers were Place and Birkbeck and whose membership included such influential parliamentary reformers as Dr. Black, Dr. John Epps the surgeon and phrenologist, Thomas Falconer, Hickson, and John Travers, the efforts of Cleave and Hetherington had been of "incalculable benefit in the struggle to obtain a FREE PRESS." [46] The Committee succeeded in paying the fines of the two men and in securing the release of Cleave from prison, and it attempted subsequently to raise subscriptions for less prominent "victims." [47] Thus the Hetherington-Cleave controversy aroused considerable national excitement and represented one of the few concrete instances in which the working-class agitation received substantial middle-class support.

The renewed wave of prosecutions undertaken by the government during the winter and spring of 1835–1836 as a prelude to its decision to reduce the newspaper duty was an even more potent factor in accelerating working-class discontent. Reformers in the provinces and Scotland as well as in London spoke repeatedly of a "crisis" and denounced acrimoniously the seeming vindictiveness of the government.[48] Support for the unstamped press was pledged as well as endorsements of all parliamentary candidates who committed themselves to vote for repeal. In an atmosphere of increasing vituperation and animosity, predictions were made that the true objective of the government was to crush the penny press.[49]

[46] Printed appeal from the Committee Collecting Subscriptions for Hetherington and Cleave; a copy is in Lovett Papers, Vol. 1, f. 1; Lovett, letter to Owen, 3 March 1836, Owen Papers, No. 779.

[47] *Radical*, 8 May 1836. John Bell, who quarreled subsequently with Hetherington and Cleave, accused them of having enriched themselves from the incident (*London Mercury*, 9 April 1837).

[48] See reports of a Wandsworth repeal meeting, newsclipping, *c*. Feb. 1836, Place Newspaper Collection, Set 70, f. 387.

[49] Even during these final months Cleave, Hetherington, Hobson, and others bewailed the fact that the "great multitude was not doing enough and that only a few were enlisted in the good cause" (*Cleave's Weekly Police Gazette*, 23 Jan. 1836).

As in the earlier phase of the working-class agitation, associations in London and the provinces played critical roles in underwriting a multiplicity of activities. The Great Radical Association of Marylebone and the Southwark Radical Association were two of the more important working-class organizations that were active in the final stages of the repeal movement. They sponsored large numbers of protest meetings during 1835–1836. Feargus O'Connor, the future "physical force" Chartist leader, and the Rev. Dr. Wade, a militant reformer, participated in these gatherings, along with Thomas Macconnell, John Bell, Lovett, Cleave, Watson, and the usual phalanx of London's working-class radicals. Several of these meetings were attended by Wakley, Roebuck, Harvey, and other M.P.'s, who attempted to channel the mounting popular protests into an effective source of parliamentary pressure. On a few occasions threats were made by parliamentary reformers at these meetings to withdraw support from the Melbourne ministry if repeal was not granted immediately.[50]

The Great Radical Association of Marylebone, which was founded in September 1835, was particularly active in the final stages of the agitation. It held a series of meetings at the Mechanics' Institution of Marylebone and carried several resolutions that supported the unstamped press and urged continued resistance to the "criminal" Whig policies.[51] With almost single-minded fervor it sought to initiate a petitioning campaign in order to compel radical M.P.'s to reject any Whig concession that fell short of total repeal. At its weekly meetings and at larger public assemblages held at Primrose Hill, White Conduit House, Islington, and elsewhere, its spokesmen, notably Maccon-

[50] See the report of an N.U.W.C. meeting of April 1835, in newsclipping, Place Newspaper Collection, Set 70, f. 205. Harvey denounced the government at a meeting of the Southwark Radical Association but did not specifically tender such a threat (*Weekly Times*, 24 Jan. 1836).

[51] Report of a Primrose Hill meeting in *Spectator*, 9 April 1836; meeting at the National Labour Exchange Bazaar, *Weekly True Sun*, 17 Jan. 1836.

nell, urged all radical associations to petition for repeal.[52] And after the provisions of the Whig "Gagging Bill" were made public in April 1836, it assisted in the establishment of a Central Committee of the Radical Associations whose purpose was to mobilize opposition to the measure.[53] On at least one occasion, in April 1836, this committee sent a delegation to Spring Rice to plead unsuccessfully the cause of total repeal.[54]

The Great Radical Association engaged in considerable verbal pyrotechnics at its repeal meetings. It described its support for the unstamped press as not a "crime" but rather a "virtue," and Macconnell, its leading spokesman, avowed that the supporters of the press "had lived fighting, and would die fighting, for the full freedom of a shackled press, to which there [*sic*] were attached with an idolatrous devotion." [55] Most striking were the animated speeches of James Savage, a leading member of the Association. Savage contended that the "dirty laws" passed by Parliament existed "only by suffrance" and that Spring Rice, by his refusal to repeal the stamp duty, was "a puny, pettifogging, sneaking, crawling slave." [56]

With comparable zest and organizational efficiency the Southwark Radical Association, founded in October 1835 and led by several of the same reformers, played an important role in the final year of the repeal agitation.[57] It sponsored frequent repeal meetings in 1836, including one of particular significance in Jan-

[52] Estimates as to the number of persons present at the Primrose Hill meeting in March 1836 range from three hundred (*Morning Herald*, 5 April 1836) to three thousand (*Cleave's Weekly Police Gazette*, 9 April 1836).

[53] *Weekly True Sun*, 8 May 1836.

[54] *Cleave's Weekly Police Gazette*, 23 April 1836.

[55] *Ibid.*, 30 Jan. 1836; report of a meeting at the Chapel, Chapel Court, *ibid.*, 15 Aug. 1835; meeting at the Mechanics' Institute, *Weekly True Sun*, 24 Jan. 1836.

[56] *Morning Herald*, 5 April 1836. Concerning the proposed reduction of the newspaper duty, Savage said: "If they pass this law . . . we, the working classes, shall be justified in taking arms into our hands against the useless ones" (*Hetherington's Twopenny Dispatch*, 7 May 1836).

[57] See *Cleave's Weekly Police Gazette*, 5 March 1836.

uary which was chaired by D. W. Harvey and addressed in volatile language by O'Connor, Cleave, Carpenter, Macconnell, and Henry S. Chapman, who still remained active in Place's organization.[58] Another large public gathering sponsored by the Southwark Association was chaired by John Sharp, a well-known "victim" and the printer of a halfpenny edition of Oliver Cromwell's *Speech on Dissolving the Long Parliament*. Like the Great Radical Association, the Southwark Radical Association sought to arouse a substantial national agitation by forwarding petitions and memorials to Parliament.[59]

A number of other London working-class organizations which were formed during 1835–1836 and were linked to the Marylebone and Southwark Associations participated in the repeal movement. These included the City of Westminster Radical Association, the Greenwich Radical Association, the Tower Hamlets Radical Association, the Finsbury Radical Association, and the Surrey Radical Association, all of which attempted strenuously to achieve a program of universal suffrage, annual parliaments, secret ballot, and a free and untaxed press.[60] The Surrey Radical Association was particularly active in the repeal campaign. Led by Macconnell and James Brown, its Secretary, it memorialized the Melbourne government on behalf of the publishers of unstamped periodicals, convened several meetings including one chaired by D. W. Harvey, and on one occasion passed a resolution imploring radical M.P.'s "to make the total repeal of the stamp duty on newspapers *a condition on which they will support the present government.*" [61]

[58] *Ibid.*, 23 Jan. 1836. Chapman said: "If after having used all exertions to recover their rights by tranquil and peaceable means their cause still proved hopeless, he . . . would vie with the bravest man in drawing the first sword in defence of the people's birthrights" (*Weekly True Sun*, 5 Jan. 1836).

[59] See *Radical*, 26 June 1836.

[60] For the City of Westminster Radical Association, see *Radical*, 20 March 1836. For the Surrey Radical Association, see *Weekly True Sun*, 5 June 1836.

[61] *Cleave's Weekly Police Gazette*, 30 Jan. 1836; *New Weekly True Sun*, 2 April 1836. In the meeting that he chaired Harvey endorsed resistance to the

Of those reformers who played notable roles during the latter phase of the working-class agitation, Feargus O'Connor was to become the best known. He had been active in the repeal campaign since 1831, but it was not until the final two years that he secured public recognition, if not within a context of maximum effectiveness. O'Connor made a number of well-publicized and frequently witty speeches during 1835–1836. On one occasion he depicted the House of Lords as "bloated old fools" and on another denounced the "tyrannical, unjust, and disgusting" suppression of the penny journals by the Whigs.[62] He believed that repeal could be gained only by illicit means and suggested to his receptive audiences that "any further application to the government would be an insult to the people as they had the remedy in their own power."[63] Of greater substance than his speeches were O'Connor's attempts, as a member of the Central Committee of the Great Radical Association, to weld various of the local working-class unions into a unified position on the repeal question.

In the final two years of the working-class agitation, much discontent was manifested in the English provinces and in Scotland, and as was true between 1830 and 1834, many meetings were summoned at the behest of local political unions and working-class organizations. In Norwich the Radical Association convened a meeting in January 1836 which drafted a memorial demanding repeal of the "cruel, unjust, and oppressive" newspaper duty and the liberation of all imprisoned vendors and publishers.[64] A well-attended repeal gathering took place in John-

---

law (*Weekly Times*, 24 Jan. 1836; *Cleave's Weekly Police Gazette*, 23 Jan. 1836).

[62] Report of an N.U.W.C. meeting of April 1835, in newsclipping, Place Newspaper Collection, Set 70, f. 205; meeting of Marylebone Radical Association, *Morning Chronicle*, 21 Oct. 1835. O'Connor contended that the Whigs still held the "balance of knowledge" (*Weekly True Sun*, 17 April 1836).

[63] *Cleave's Weekly Police Gazette*, 23 Jan. 1836.

[64] *Ibid.*, 30 Jan. 1836. An earlier working-class meeting at Norwich had been held at the reading room of Riches, a convicted vendor (*ibid.*, 16 May 1835).

stone, Scotland, at which acrid sarcasm was resorted to by one reformer in his attacks upon the government:

You have heard of a window tax, a smoke tax, and even a urine tax
[laughter], and a host of other taxes, equally ludicrous, oppressive, and
unjust; but a more iniquitous, a more oppressive, a more unjust tax was
never imposed by any Government than that on newspapers.[65]

Handbills that were circulated prior to a working-class repeal
meeting in Newcastle-upon-Tyne categorized recent developments as "our last struggle for a free and enlightened Press." [66]
And in Cambridgeshire the repeal agitation was led during the
spring of 1836 by the Association for the Protection and Diffusion of Moral and Political Knowledge, recently established at
Wisbeach. The speakers at one of this organization's meetings
described the unstamped press as articulating "the will of the nation" and asserted that memories of the imprisoned "victims"
would "float down the stream of time." At another gathering
convened by the Association, the newspaper duty was denounced
as "nothing short of robbery." [67]

Similar protest meetings usually dominated by working-class
reformers but occasionally of a "mixed" composition were held
during 1835–1836 at Kendal, Carlisle, Bristol, Glasgow, Dudley, Greenock, Keighley, Birmingham, Sheffield, Huddersfield,
Dundee, Plymouth, and in other provincial urban areas.[68] Lancashire remained a focal point of agitation. An assemblage of
Manchester carpenters and joiners drafted a repeal petition in
February 1836, and at Colne an even more forceful document
was drafted by working-class "Friends of the Freedom of the

[65] *Liberator*, 5 March 1836.

[66] A copy of this handbill is in Place Newspaper Collection, Set 70, f. 213.

[67] *Monthly Political Register*, 2 April 1836; unidentified newsclipping,
Place Newspaper Collection, Set 70, f. 519.

[68] *Kendal Mercury*, 30 May 1835; *Journals of the House of Commons*, 3
June and 4 Sept. 1835, XC, 310, 648; 27 April and 8 Feb. 1836, XCI, 296,
13.

Press." [69] Similar meetings were convened in Warrington, Ashton-under-Lyne, Bury, Liverpool, Halifax, Salford, and other Lancashire districts during 1835–1836.[70] In Hebden Bridge a petition inspired by working-class reformers and calling for open defiance of the stamp laws was circulated.

Thus, in a crescendo of verbal bitterness marked by numerous references to the success of resistance in Ireland and elsewhere, the working-class agitation rose to a climax in the spring of 1836. A sense of class consciousness was increasing, and denunciations of the "middlocracy" became more frequent, not only in the pages of the unstamped press but at repeal meetings. But some degree of harmony between middle- and working-class reformers was achieved, particularly during the early months of 1836. This harmony was due largely to the circumstance of increased governmental prosecutions and to the widespread belief that an unsatisfactory legislative compromise was pending. It was also due to the activities of such parliamentary reformers as Wakley and Roebuck, who sought deliberately to bridge the chasm between reformers by participating in "disreputable" meetings. The unity achieved was fragile, however, and it was to be shattered permanently by the decision of the Whigs to reduce the newspaper duty to 1*d*.

[69] *Manchester Advertiser*, 6 Feb. 1836; *Cleave's Weekly Police Gazette*, 13 Feb. 1836, which also contains a memorial from the Manchester Radical Association.

[70] *Cleave's Weekly Police Gazette*, 16 May 1835; *Journals of the House of Commons*, 14 Aug. 1835, XC, 547; 29 April and 6 May 1836, XCI, 304, 329.

CHAPTER 10

Conclusion: An Unsatisfactory Compromise

In the spring of 1836 the Melbourne government made the critical decision to reduce the newspaper tax to 1*d*. This led to the termination of the war of the unstamped, and it also brought the activities of parliamentary reformers to a conclusion, though these were to emerge again in the 1850's under the leadership of Richard Cobden and Milner Gibson.

The reduction of the stamp duty by the pronounced impetus that it gave to the dissemination of legal newspapers earned for itself an important niche in the history of journalism. During the two years that followed upon the lowering of the duty, the total circulation of stamped newspapers increased by approximately 50 per cent, rising from thirty-five and one half million copies in 1836 to over fifty-three million in 1838. This rate of increase, which was not equaled in the first half of the nineteenth century, tapered off in succeeding years; but newspapers continued to gain markedly in circulation, and from 1836 on, the foundation of a mass circulation press was laid.[1] It was in the

[1] Statistics submitted by C. D. Collet to the *S.C. on Newspaper Stamps* (1851), pp. 166–167, q. 1,021. There was more than a 70 per cent increase

realm of political and social relationships, however, that the reduction was of largest immediate significance. By accentuating a working-class sense of alienation and giving further vent to the latter's feeling of "betrayal," it helped prepare the way for the Chartist movement.

Spring Rice's decision to reduce the newspaper duty in 1836 was primarily due to the success of the war of the unstamped. The illegal periodicals had achieved widespread support by the spring of 1835, when the Chancellor had committed himself informally to take mediatory action during the next session of Parliament. By the early months of 1836, these journals were posing an ever more formidable challenge to the government both in terms of circulation and of content. There was a growing conviction (not supported by the facts) that the illegal journals were on the verge of economically undermining their stamped competitors.[2] But such alarm seemed understandable, particularly after the appearance of a short-lived daily unstamped journal in July 1835.

This newspaper, known as the *Daily National Gazette*, expired within a week. But during its brief existence it aroused an intense reaction from the legal dailies.[3] The *Times* and the *Morning Post* demanded governmental action, with the latter asking whether "extensive newspaper properties, some of which have

---

between 1836–1842 (Aspinall, *Politics and the Press*, p. 23). Technological changes and "lively" journalism were also stimulated by the reduction (Morison, *English Newspaper*, pp. 265–267). James states exaggeratedly that with the large increase in the number of newspapers, "the whole way of enthusiasm for learning and political self-betterment subsided" and literary sensationalism became dominant (*Fiction for the Working Man*, p. 22).

[2] In 1832 two and a half million fewer newspaper stamps were issued by the government than in 1831. This fact seems to demonstrate that the unstamped press was reducing the circulation of stamped journals. But the subsidence of political excitement after the resolution of the Reform Bill crisis could account for the decline. See the statistics submitted by Collet to the *S.C. on Newspaper Stamps* (1851), pp. 166–167, q. 1021.

[3] A prospectus of the *Daily National Gazette* is in Place Newspaper Collection, Set 70, ff. 592–593.

existed nearly a century, are to be left, by the callous indifference and shameful negligence of a Whig Government, at the mercy of every ruffian who chooses to defy the law." The *Sun,* a pro-Whig daily, threatened to "smuggle in self-defense" if Melbourne and his colleagues did not take adequate measures to halt the publication.[4] This threat was endorsed implicitly by the *Times* and given even more direct countenance by *Bell's New Weekly Messenger,* which maintained that the stamped press "will soon have no alternative but either to submit to the gradual destruction which . . . they have succeeded in establishing for themselves; or at once to . . . defy the laws which oppress, without defending them from the assaults of the scorners of the law, become themselves rebels to the stamp laws, and forthwith issue their journals with a stamp." [5]

The episode proved extremely unsettling to the stamped proprietors. During the remainder of 1835 and the early months of 1836, they maintained constant pressure upon the government to undertake a "moderate" reduction of the duty and to pursue effective legal action in defense of the newspaper stamp. Total repeal of the impost coupled with substitution of a postal duty was unacceptable since, in the words of Charles Knight, "it is better to have comparatively few national journals, than an immense multitude of merely local newspapers." [6] Led by the *Times,* the owners of the more influential London newspapers held meetings, established a committee to "watch" events, and sent delegates to the Chancellor to urge immediate action. This continu-

---

[4] *Morning Post,* 22 July 1835; a *Sun* leader quoted in *Public Ledger,* 25 July 1835. The Stamp Office contemplated a prosecution though it seemingly did not take action (Treasury, letter to the Commissioner of Stamps and Taxes, 18 July 1835, Treasury Papers, 22/27, f. 193).

[5] Leader from *Bell's New Weekly Messenger* as reprinted in *Poor Man's Guardian,* 18 July 1835. The *Spectator* hinted at "passive resistance" by the stamped proprietors (25 July 1835). The *Public Ledger* proclaimed: "Either put all on an equal footing by abolishing the tax, or protect me against the smuggler. If you will not do this I must smuggle in self-defense. I will publish without a stamp, and set you at defiance" (25 July 1835).

[6] Knight, *Newspaper Stamp,* pp. 38–40.

ous and effective pressure from the stamped proprietors was undoubtedly a factor in shaping Spring Rice's decision to reduce the newspaper duty.[7]

Reinforcing the pressure for reduction rather than repeal was that exerted by proprietors of many unstamped nonpolitical miscellanies which, although illegal, never faced the threat of prosecution. Knight, the publisher of the successful *Penny Magazine,* was especially influential. In the spring of 1836 he issued a tract entitled *The Newspaper Stamp and the Duty on Paper, Viewed in Relation to Their Effects upon the Diffusion of Knowledge,* in which he forcefully urged repeal of the paper duty and retention of at least a 1*d.* tax on newspapers. The necessity for a reduction was demonstrated, in Knight's opinion, by the fact that "financial regulations which oppose the education of the people, and their consequent advance in prosperity, as well as their consequent capacity for being orderly and quietly disposed in all their public relations, cannot be maintained by a Government which is essentially representative." Outright repeal would, on the other hand, produce a diminution of quality and a "degradation of journalism." He contended that a small stamp duty, when coupled with removal of the tax on paper, would effectively "prevent a total revolution of the present newspaper interests, and, by preserving those interests entire, preserve a standard that might be improved upon, but which would be very difficult to restore if once destroyed." [8] Knight subsequently admitted that his position was motivated partially by self-interest, inasmuch as he feared the competition of inexpensive, legal political journals.[9]

Action by the Chancellor, when once decided upon, could take several forms. The policy of repression and "no compromise"

---

[7] *Public Ledger,* 5 March 1836; *Courier,* 9 May 1836. C. M. Westmacott, the publisher of the *Age,* opposed any reduction in the belief that the people had to be protected against "the designs of the enemies of social order" (*The Stamp Duties: Serious Considerations on the Proposed Alteration of the Stamp Duty on Newspapers. . . .* [London: *Age,* 1836], pp. 13–15).

[8] Knight, *Newspaper Stamp,* pp. 56, 40.

[9] Knight, *Passages,* II, 250–252.

might be strengthened in the expectation that the illicit press would be undermined financially in the near future. Such an expectation was increasingly illusory by the spring of 1836, since repeated governmental prosecutions seemed only more likely to activate effective resistance. But the Stamp Office, nonetheless, substantially accelerated its prosecutions of vendors and publishers during the final months of the repeal agitation.

At the same time, the policy of outright negativism was abandoned by the government and an alternate course of action was pursued, that is, a reduction of the stamp duty to 1*d*. This represented considerably less of a concession than total repeal, and it was the course of action supported by the preponderant majority of the proprietors of the daily and weekly legal newspapers.[10] It had the seeming advantage of weakening decisively the illicit "smugglers" by enabling their legal competitors to reduce the price of their journals, and thus outbid them for the patronage of an expanding readership. Whereas a reduction of the duty would "facilitate the diffusion of sound principles, combined with the requisites for forming calm judgments on important questions," total repeal would produce "violent and sudden innovations" and might generate a "bloody rebellion." [11] Hence the Melbourne government, responding to disparate pressures arising from the war of the unstamped, resolved to reduce the stamp duty.[12]

The decision to reduce rather than to abolish the duty was taken by Spring Rice on his own initiative but with general con-

---

[10] According to Augustus Beaumont, who owned the *Radical*, only he and the proprietors of the *True Sun* and the *Public Ledger* campaigned privately for total repeal (*Radical*, 12 June 1836).

[11] *Bell's Weekly Messenger*, 20 March 1836; Martin, *Taxation of the British Empire*, p. 22. Unfounded rumors continued to circulate during the spring of 1836 that the government contemplated repeal (*Hetherington's Twopenny Dispatch*, 19 March 1836).

[12] With little validity Maccoby states that the reduction was effectuated by "pressure from the Parliamentary Radicals" (*English Radicalism, 1832–1852*, p. 415). Place did not subscribe to such an interpretation of events (Place Autobiography, Place Papers, Add. MSS 27,791, f. 290).

currence from the cabinet. At least three members of the government—Lord Holland, Lord Howick, and Poulett Thompson—privately preferred abolition. But there is no evidence to indicate that a serious disagreement took place within the cabinet over the issue. Few ministers comprehended the larger implications of repeal, and to many politicians the question never transcended revenue considerations.[13]

Spring Rice's reduction of the newspaper tax was initially proffered in nonpolitical terms, that is, as part of a general measure consolidating the various stamp duties. The proposed change, according to the Chancellor, would have the fivefold advantage of preserving the revenue from further losses, helping to defeat "the existing Combination against the law," putting an end to "vexatious prosecutions against the public," assisting "to shelter the law and the Government from odium and contempt," and protecting "the fair trader from the encroachments of the smuggler." He urged conservatives to support the measure "for the sake of the good order of society," stressing that total repeal was "entirely impracticable."[14]

But any hope that Spring Rice may have had of avoiding political controversy evaporated when he made clear his resolve to strengthen the enforcement provisions of the consolidating statute. Future attempts to publish or distribute illicit journals were

[13] Hickson, *Manifesto of the Chancellor*, p. 4; "Theta," *Monthly Repository*, X (1836), 259; Lord Howick, letter to Spring Rice, 12 Aug. 1835, Monteagle Papers, No. 13,378 (1). Hickson reported a false rumor to the effect that Russell was the major obstacle to repeal within the Cabinet (*Taxes on Knowledge*, p. 9). Russell actually favored a reduction (letter to Spring Rice, c. Dec. 1835, Monteagle Papers, No. 13,381 (7); Lord Holland, letter to Spring Rice, 26 July 1835, Monteagle Papers, No. 13,378 [1]).

[14] *Hansard*, H. of C., 15 March 1836, XXXII, 335–351; *ibid.*, 6 May 1836, XXXIII, 668–671. J. Wood, a Treasury official, submitted an eighteen-page memorandum to Rice in 1835 which purported to show that revenue from the newspaper duty would increase by £70,000 if it were reduced to 1d. (J. W. Ord, memorandum to Spring Rice, 1835?, Monteagle Papers, No. 13,378 [1]). A Stamp Office memorandum admitted a probable loss of £100,000 (John Wood, memorandum to Spring Rice, 24 July 1835, Monteagle Papers, No. 13,378 [1]).

to be dealt with harshly. As adopted subsequently into law, the measure sharpened the prevailing security system that regulated the registration of printers and publishers, defined newspapers broadly enough so as to include most tracts published periodically, and increased the penalty for mere possession of an unstamped newspaper. The statute also sanctioned the search of private houses and the seizure of materials connected with the publication of illegal papers, when such steps were deemed necessary to enforce the law.[15]

These enforcement provisions made the measure nearly as unacceptable to parliamentary reformers as to working-class journalists. The *Spectator*, a periodical that had favored only a reduction of the duty and so was in general agreement with the purported objectives of the bill, described it as an "inquisitorial" invasion of recognized legal rights.[16] Hickson denounced the measure as "the gravest insult that has ever been offered to a body of intelligent and deserving men" and as "the foulest and deepest blot by which the character of the present administration has been stained." [17] Place's reaction was even more unyielding. He condemned the "stultifying and debasing" provisions of the bill which, in his opinion, were intended to declare "war with the working people." [18] He now endorsed a policy of overt violation of the law: "The penny law will not be obeyed, it is so very partial and unjust, it is made so exclusively to apply to one portion of the public, and not to another, that it OUGHT NOT to be

[15] For a clause-by-clause analysis of the Stamp Bill prior to its enactment into law, see Fox, "Mr. Spring Rice and the Newspaper Press," *Monthly Repository*, X (1836), 278–280; *Voice from the Commons*, 23 April 1836; Wakley, *Letter to the People of England*, pp. 11–20.

[16] *Spectator*, 30 April 1836.

[17] Hickson, *Manifesto of the Chancellor*, p. 4. In Wakley's view the bill was "a newly fabricated instrument of oppression . . . *tyrannical, odious, infamous*" (*Letter to the People of England*, pp. 3–4).

[18] Place, letter to Hume, 10 April 1836, Place Papers, Add. MSS 35,150, f. 121; Place, letter to Spring Rice, 10 Aug. 1836, *ibid.*, ff. 135–137. Hume, who abstained on the measure, described it as "odious" (letter to Peter Mackenzie in *Spectator*, 17 June 1837).

obeyed." [19] And in a series of vituperative leaders written for the *Radical* and other newspapers, he alleged that the legal provisions of the bill had been drawn up "by some diabolical wretch of a parchment-hearted, technical-headed lawyer, equally ignorant of the state of society, and careless of consequences to both king and people." [20]

Working-class reformers were even more caustic as to the merits of the legislation. They castigated not only the government but also the large number of radical members of Parliament who offered no consequential opposition to the measure. Their anger was justified. During the preceding summer approximately forty proreform M.P.'s had pledged themselves to work for total repeal and, according to one report, a similar pledge had been taken by a smaller number of representatives at the outset of the 1836 session.[21] Despite the fact that many prominent members of Parliament had participated in these meetings and that several, including Hume, Harvey, and Roebuck, had threatened to withdraw support from the government if repeal was not forthcoming, only Thomas Wakley and T. Perronet Thompson unqualifiedly opposed the Whig measure and sought persistently to dilute the rigor of its provisions.[22] When the Commons rejected by sixty-nine to one Wakley's suggestion that the word "pamphlet" be deleted from the measure so as to prevent every type of publication from being subjected to the stamp duty, Thompson cast the lone dissenting vote.[23] Roebuck, another pro-

[19] Francis Place, *The Examiner and the Tax on Newspapers* (London: G. Morgan, 1836), p. 13.

[20] *Radical*, 24 April 1836.   [21] Hickson, *Mr. Spring Rice*, p. 5.

[22] *Newspaper Stamps: Deputation*, pp. 6–7. Thompson advocated continued resistance to the 1*d.* stamp: "It must be the business of reformers, to play their game according to the cards, and if they cannot make the best use of the repeal, *make the best use they can of the refusal*" (*Letters of a Representative* [1837] in Thompson, *Exercises*, V, 240). More typically, J. S. Buckingham favored repeal privately but publicly compromised with the ministry (letter to Place, 31 March 1836?, Place Newspaper Collection, Set 70, ff. 433–434).

[23] Parliamentary Diary, Potter Papers, X, 165–166. Even Wakley was criticized mildly for his strategy of trying to defeat the measure in committee rather than on the floor of the Commons.

nounced opponent of the bill, was unable to attend any of the debates on the subject due to illness. But in light of the vacillating tendencies demonstrated by most of his radical colleagues, it cannot be assumed that he would have added a third voice of protest to the bill.[24]

Though ineffectual politically, Wakley's strong opposition to the proposed reduction was significant. As a member of Parliament for the populous working-class constituency of Finsbury, he had acquired a reputation as the most "ultra-radical" spokesman in the Commons. In consonance with this reputation, repeal of the newspaper duty was of special concern to him, and he participated in the war of the unstamped both as a journalist and as a public speaker. In each capacity, he served as one of the few important political links between middle- and working-class reformers.[25] Some of the latter were sceptical of his motives, but were won over by *A Voice from the Commons*, his 2*d.* venture into illegal journalism in the spring of 1836, and by his numerous expressions of sympathy and support for the imprisoned vendors. By his aggressive leadership of the small parliamentary resistance to Spring Rice's "Gagging Bill," he secured support from working-class radicals and helped to prevent a total rupture with parliamentary reformers.

Thompson's unwillingness to compromise was likewise important. Though possessing fewer contacts in working-class circles than Wakley, Thompson attempted to reduce the disharmony within the repeal movement. As proprietor of the influential *Westminster Review* during the period from 1828–1836 he encouraged the reprinting at nominal prices of many of that journal's articles, in the conviction that "the powerful, the represented classes, the 'interests,' can afford to pay for whatever flat-

[24] For the final vote on the measure, see *Hansard*, H. of C., 25 July 1836, XXXV, 567–568.

[25] In *A Voice from the Commons*, a 2*d.* weekly journal, Wakley condemned the measure as "A GAG FOR THE POOR MAN'S PRESS" (1 May 1836). For his participation in public meetings, see *Radical*, 13 March 1836; *Poor Man's Guardian*, 30 Aug. 1834.

ters or supports them; but the *people* whom these combinations have made poor, must be furnished with cheap literature, if they are to be reached by literature at all." [26] And as the representative for Kingston-upon-Hull in the years 1835–1837, he thrust himself into the repeal agitation. He visited Cleave and other imprisoned "victims" and gave financial support to several of them. When Spring Rice proposed a reduction of the duty in March 1836, Thompson advised his constituents to agitate the question and urged his Parliamentary colleagues "to try the case —*they can never have a prettier quarrel;* and above all things not to give in, till they have got off the whole of the stamp." [27] When the latter ignored his counsel he perceptively prophesied the implications of that refusal: "Everything which makes one division of the Liberal Party view another as having turned round upon them after having had their assistance at the expense of great sacrifices in the common cause, is a violation of that prudence by which the ordinary affairs of men in society are conducted." [28]

The full dimension of working-class bitterness engendered by the 1836 statute exceeded even the most dire predictions. The unstamped journals denounced the "Gagging Bill," as it came to be known, in unexampled language. O'Brien led the journalistic onslaught in several widely circulated leaders written for *Hetherington's Twopenny Dispatch.* He described the measure as "a declaration of war against the working classes" and proclaimed that it was rooted inextricably in class privilege. Whereas the "capitalists and commercial speculators" were to be given de facto journalistic predominance as a result of the reduced duty, the "most useful" element in society had again been deprived of access to the sources of power. "An admirable constitution it is," exclaimed O'Brien, "for those who have the entree, but none can

[26] Flyer dated 31 Jan. 1830, cited in Frank W. Fetter, "Economic Articles in the Westminster Review and Their Authors, 1824–51," *Journal of Political Economy,* LXX (1962), 574.

[27] Thompson, *Exercises,* 30 April 1836, V, iii.

[28] Thompson, *Letter from a Representative* (*1836*), in *ibid.,* V, 133.

enter without the silver key—*ergo*, capital is admitted and protected. Labour has got no silver key—*ergo*, labour must stand shivering outside." [29] Cleave, after pronouncing reduction of the duty to be "an evil quite as deadly—a bar to knowledge equally as inseparable—as a four-penny stamp," told the working classes: "You, the toilworn, the trampled, the unrepresented, *will have no legal newspaper* under the new system, any more than you have had under the old one!" [30] In a subsequent leader he depicted the measure as:

thoroughly imbued with that vicious principle of partiality and exclusiveness which benefit the more wealthy classes of society at the expenses of the poorer—which places the burden of taxation where there is the least strength to sustain it, and suffers those who are alone justly amenable to the obligation, to escape scot-free.[31]

Working-class reformers drew invidious comparisons between the £10 Parliamentary franchise of 1832 which had electorally disenfranchised the laborers, and the 1*d.* stamp which sought to deprive them of effective means of political and economic expression. The stamped proprietors were described as "boroughmongers," who were desperately and uncompromisingly seeking to preserve a privileged journalistic franchise.[32] According to John Bell who edited several illegal journals and who subsequently became a "physical force" Chartist: "The people of England will lose the only political representation which they have ever enjoyed—representation in the columns of the unstamped." [33] As one working-class organization expressed it:

[29] *Hetherington's Twopenny Dispatch*, 7 May 1836, 26 March 1836. In a further leader O'Brien denounced the proposed statute as "a monster of tyrannic legislation, as against the oppressed classes" (*ibid.*, 3 July 1836).

[30] *Cleave's Weekly Police Gazette*, 20 Feb. 1836, 19 March 1836.

[31] *Cleave's Picture Gallery*, [Aug. 1836?], No. 1.

[32] *Cleave's Weekly Police Gazette*, 19 March 1836.

[33] *Mirror for Magistrates*, 16 April 1836. John Bell also stated: "The press is interwoven with the extension of the popular franchise. The principles of the thing are alike" (*Report of an Address . . . in the Music Hall, Blackett Street, Newcastle-upon-Tyne, on Tuesday Evening, September 6, 1836 . . .* [Newcastle-upon-Tyne: Joseph Harris, 1836], p. 14).

The stamp duty is to be reduced to a point which will permit newspapers to circulate as freely among the middle classes, as if the press were actually free; while so much of the stamp duty is to be retained, and such an inquisitorial law is to be enacted, in addition to all those now in force, as shall utterly prohibit the circulation of newspapers among the working classes.[34]

Parliamentary reformers who had accepted the measure were particularly reprehensible in the view of these radical journalists, since they had demonstrated again their willingness "to accept [a ministerial] bribe and to desert our cause, leaving us to the unscrupulous opposition of offended power." [35] As succinctly stated by a leading repealer: "The productive classes of England have been once more betrayed by their leaders . . . To free the press . . . is to give being, and form, and voice to the now still-born emotions and sentiments of countless millions." [36] "The Crown-and-Anchor is less than the London-tavern," asserted another reformer, "you may dine cheaper there—but they do not serve dinners for the poor. As far as the working man's pocket is concerned, the two houses are the same." [37]

Thus, reduction of the stamp duty was carried in the spring of 1836 amid rising hostility and bitterness. Even the stamped proprietors were not satisfied with its provisions. Though gratified that the "fair principle" of reduction rather than total repeal had been decided upon, they strongly opposed an amendment that was introduced successfully by Charles Buller. This amendment stipulated that in future all proprietors rather than a selected few had to be registered with the Stamp Office.[38] Other

---

[34] Association of Working Men, *Address.*

[35] Association of Working Men to Produce a Cheap and Honest Press, "Prospectus and Resolutions," in *Cleave's Weekly Police Gazette,* 23 April 1836.

[36] John Bell in *New Weekly True Sun,* 19 March 1836.

[37] *Cleave's Weekly Police Gazette,* 2 April 1836. The Crown and Anchor Tavern, located on the Strand, was a leading center of middle-class reform activity during the 1830's.

[38] *Hansard,* H. of C., 11 July 1836, XXXV, 118–125. A motion to delete the Buller amendment was defeated, 58–15 (Parliamentary Diary, Potter Papers, X, 167).

technical aspects of the statute irritated the stamped proprietors, such as the provision that a supplement to a regular edition, even one containing only advertisements, had to pay an additional stamp duty of $\frac{1}{2}d$. Whenever the number of square inches of letterpress in the regular edition exceeded 1530 a supplement was required.[39]

Although most radical M.P.s' and their supporters in London and the countryside gave reluctant assent to the measure, few were content with its provisions. It was universally admitted that the positive features of the bill had been vitiated by its stringent enforcement provisions. And many reformers recognized that the remaining $1d$. duty was a formidable obstacle to "the wider diffusion of knowledge." William Molesworth, who had voted for the measure, asserted in January 1837 that the penny stamp "falls almost entirely upon the industrious portions of the community who do not receive their newspapers by the post, whilst to the richer classes it is simply a cheap postage."[40] As if to validate this objection, the number of new journals that prospered was exceedingly modest, despite the considerable increase in the total circulation of newspapers after 1836. According to the official stamp returns, only sixty-two new newspapers were commenced in the immediate aftermath of the reduction of the stamp.[41] Thus, the real benefits of reduction, as was foreseen by

[39] The original bill had established a size limitation of 1,066 superficial square inches. This was modified due to considerable pressure from the stamped proprietors (*Sun*, 13 May 1836). Relations between the Chancellor and the stamped proprietors were poor (Spring Rice, letter to Thomas Barnes, 6 May 1836, Monteagle Papers, No. 13,378 [1]; Barnes, letter to Spring Rice, 6 May 1836, *ibid*.

[40] *Spectator*, 21 Jan. 1837. Six months later George Grote referred to the reduction more positively as "a measure imperfect in point of extent, yet tending towards the best and highest of all ends—the diffusion of knowledge and active discussion among the people (*ibid.*, 15 July 1837). See also the views of Joseph Parkes: "We have carried many strong outworks of Toryism—such as Corporations Self-Elect, the Municipal Charities, the reduction of newspaper stamp—and kept all patronage in Liberal hands" (letter to Durham, 30 May 1837, as cited in Buckley, *Parkes*, p. 155).

[41] Of the sixty-two newspapers, fourteen had been discontinued by April 1837

some parliamentary reformers, accrued to the established dailies which offered "better value for money." The *Times,* for example, purportedly doubled its readership between 1836 and 1842.[42]

Attempts by parliamentary reformers to capitalize upon reduction of the duty as a means of challenging the dominance of the more conservative London dailies were not notably successful. The major journalistic effort in this regard was the *Constitutional [and Public Ledger]*, a 4½d. London morning newspaper that commenced publication in September 1836 and never amassed a circulation of more than one thousand.[43] It collapsed within a year notwithstanding a surfeit of journalistic talent that included Laman Blanchard, Thornton Hunt, and William Makepeace Thackeray, as well as Place, Hume, and several other reformers. Thus the "first-fruit of the Penny Stamp—the eldest-born of Reduction," as the *Constitutional* described itself, could not overcome the obstacle of a 1d. duty.[44] Many other attempts by parliamentary reformers to secure a large proportion of the journalistic market met with failure. New journals were started, including several of a radical complexion, but so long as the 1d. duty remained, the viable selling price of a daily newspaper could not be reduced below 3d. This represented a considerable reduction from the previous price of 7d. but it nevertheless hindered the development of a journal that lacked a substantial reservoir of available support. This was particularly true in the provinces where most weekly newspapers sold for 5d. after 1836 and no successful daily newspaper was established prior to the total repeal of the newspaper duty in 1855.[45] By the 1840's, therefore, many middle-class reformers had become completely

---

(Great Britain, Sessional Papers, *Account of Effect upon the Revenue, by Reduction of Stamp Duty on Newspapers* . . . (*1837*), XXXIX, (291), p. 303.

[42] Williams, *Dangerous Estate,* p. 82; Kellet, "The Press," pp. 8–9.

[43] *Spectator,* 8 July 1837.   [44] *Constitutional,* 15 Sept. 1836.

[45] Read, *Press and People,* p. 67; "The Liberal Newspapers—Effects of the Reduction of Stamp Duty," *Tait's Edinburgh Magazine,* new ser. III (1836), 685–692, 799–808.

disillusioned with the remaining duty and began to describe it as "the worst penny of all." [46] Though Corn Law repeal became the focal point of reforming efforts during the 1840's, the pathway was being tentatively prepared for the second and more successful movement to repeal the taxes on knowledge which commenced in 1849 with the establishment of a Newspaper Stamp Abolition Committee headed by Place and Watson.

But of all those dissatisfied with the act of 1836, the attitude of working-class reformers was most critical. They had waged a remarkable journalistic campaign, one that had lasted for six years. Their efforts were largely responsible for impelling the government to reduce the duty. Yet the benefits of reduction accrued to established proprietorial interests and to the most articulate, influential segment of the middle classes. The latter had seemingly seized what advantage it could from the events of 1836, after conducting its own vigorous extraparliamentary campaign against the law. Thus, the pervasive feeling of political and social alienation, a mood that was already widespread prior to the war of the unstamped, received a powerful reinforcement. As in the precedents of electoral, poor law, and factory reform, the laborers perceived themselves again to be isolated and unable to secure meaningful concessions.

As a culminating reaction to this increasing sense of frustration, working-class reformers began to search for all-encompassing political panaceas. The mood that became dominant is exemplified in the following Chartist manifesto:

Fellow men! do not be led away by promises of repealing the detested Poor Law, or any of the other infamous laws which Whig and Tory have united to enact, and to laud the excellence, *unless* the promise be

[46] W. J. Fox, *Lectures Addressed Chiefly to the Working Classes* (London: Charles Fox, 1845–1849), III, 6. This disillusionment was not universal. Grote, deeply absorbed in the question of the ballot, refused to make even a small contribution to a newspaper repeal committee being organized in 1837 (Harriet Grote, letter to Place, 12 Nov. 1837, Place Papers, Add. MSS 35,151, ff. 29–30.

accompanied by the pledge of universal suffrage, and all the other great essentials of self-government.[47]

Thus during 1836–1837, individual reformers and local working-class associations began to transfer their energies from the newspaper repeal agitation to the nascent Chartist movement. For example, Joshua Hobson and William Rider who had participated actively in the working-class repeal movement in the West Riding became leading members of the Leeds Working Men's Association, a Chartist organization that was established in the autumn of 1837.[48] Abram Duncan and John Fraser, who had been responsible for much of the repeal agitation in central Scotland, became leaders of the Chartist movement in Glasgow. And throughout England and Scotland the existence of the remaining penny stamp with its deleterious effects upon "cheap knowledge" became a prime component of Chartist grievances.

In London the most important direct transition from the newspaper repeal agitation to Chartism occurred. In 1835 Dr. James R. Black, who was president of Place's repeal association, established a small workingmen's organization for educational purposes. This group's origins and activities are obscure, but from the summer of 1835 on it became directly involved in the war of the unstamped. It broadened its membership and, with Lovett serving as secretary and Place and Birkbeck as temporary cotreasurers, it took the lead in collecting subscriptions for Cleave and Hetherington. In April 1836, under equally obscure circumstances it re-formed itself as the Association of Working Men to Procure a Cheap and Honest Press. The membership of this new

[47] "Address of the Working Men's Association to the Radical Reformers of England, Ireland, and Scotland on the forthcoming Elections, 1837," reprinted in *Weekly True Sun*, 2 July 1837. In the same year Lovett urged: "Give, I would say, to the millions their political rights, and they will soon open every avenue to knowledge, will soon emancipate the press, and thus protect themselves against all their malignant influences" (speech to L.W.M.A., 28 Feb. 1837, newsclipping, Lovett Papers, Vol. I, ff. 26–27).

[48] Harrison, "Chartism in Leeds," in *Chartist Studies*, p. 67.

group was entirely working class and, though it accomplished
little of substance during its two months' existence, its proclaimed
objective was "to stimulate our own class, in every possible way,
to continual efforts in the holy cause of a free press." This Association of Working Men became the London Working Men's
Association in June 1836. Under the leadership of Lovett,
Cleave, Hetherington, and Watson (the latter three not having
been members of the preceding Association), the L.W.M.A.
played a foremost role in "moral force" Chartism.[49] The removal of "those cruel laws that prevent the free circulation of
thought through the medium of a cheap and honest press" became a prime desideratum of the L.W.M.A. but, as was true of
other working-class demands, it was increasingly subsumed under
the general banner of the Six Points.[50]

With the exception of Carlile, nearly all of those who participated prominently in the working-class war of the unstamped became Chartists during the late 1830's and many, including
Cleave, Hetherington, Lovett, Watson, and O'Brien, rose to positions of leadership. Most of those previously connected with
illegal journalism espoused "moral force" doctrines, but several,
including O'Brien, Lorymer, John Bell, and William Benbow,
became identified with the more aggressive "physical force" phase
of the movement.

The prevailing working-class temper after 1836 was, in either
case, one of defiance and protest, a situation that derived to a con-

[49] For an accurate summary of these events, see D. J. Rowe, "The London
Working Men's Association and the 'People's Charter,'" *Past and Present*, No.
36 (April 1967), pp. 74–81. Unfortunately, Rowe's contention that Chartism
was the product of a "radical middle-class element" rather than "working-class
consciousness" cannot be trusted. For Place's account see Place Newspaper Collection, Set 56, Vol. I, ff. 1–3; Place, letter to Perry, 4 Oct. 1838, Place
Papers, Add. MSS 35,151, ff. 100–105a. For Dr. Black's version see Place
Papers, Add. MSS 35,154, ff. 209–222; Place Papers, Add. MSS 27,819, ff.
1–40. For Lovett's narrative see Lovett, *Life and Struggles*, I, 91; letter from
Lovett dated 15 Jan. 1838 in *Leeds Times*, c. Jan. 1838, Lovett Papers, Vol. I,
f. 175.
[50] London Working Men's Association, *Prospectus and Rules*, 1836.

siderable extent from the recent journalistic frustrations. The penny stamp ("this hell born instrument, with which they mean to lay prostrate the liberties of England, and of mankind" in the words of an obscure member of the L.W.M.A.) remained.[51] And though several stamped working-class periodicals such as the *Northern Star* gained substantial influence during the succeeding years, the illicit radical penny press was temporarily prostrated by the act of 1836. When the reduction of the duty became effective in September 1836, all of the major unstamped newspapers either terminated their existence or, in the manner of *Hetherington's Twopenny Dispatch, Cleave's Weekly Police Gazette,* and the *Weekly Times,* transformed themselves into short-lived higher-priced stamped journals.

Thus, attention was focussed upon the Six Points of the Charter as the symbolic expression of the deep-rooted aspirations of millions. The chasm between middle and working classes was irremediably widened.

[51] *Radical,* 5 June 1836.

Bibliography

UNPUBLISHED SOURCES

Birmingham Central Reference Library
William Lovett Papers.

British Museum
Ellis Collection (Society for the Diffusion of Useful Knowledge).
Place Papers: Additional MSS 27,789; 27,790; 27,791; 27,796; 27,809; 27,819; 27,822; 27,827; 35,146; 35,149; 35,150; 35,151; 35,154.
Place Newspaper Collection: Set 57 (Statistics, Machinery, Improvement, Education, Press, Church, 1826–1840); Set 63 (Minutes of the National Political Union, 2 vols.); Set 65 (Newspapers, Specimens of Unstamped Illegal Newspapers, 1831–1836); Set 70 (Newspapers, Specimens, 1770–1837).

Co-operative Union Institute, Manchester
Robert Owen Papers.

The Huntington Library, San Marino, California
Richard Carlile Papers.

London School of Economics (British Library of Political and Economic Science)
Richard Potter Papers.

National Library of Ireland

Monteagle Papers (Thomas Spring Rice, 1st Baron Monteagle).

Private Collection

Althorp Papers (John Charles Viscount Althorp and 3rd Earl Spencer).

Public Record Office

Home Office. Files on Seditious Activities, 64/17; 64/18; 64/19.
———. Secret Service Reports, 64/11; 64/12; 64/13; 64/14; 64/15; 64/16.
Treasury Department Records. Outletters—Taxes, T. 22/20; T. 22/26; T. 22/27.

University College, London

Brougham Papers.

PUBLISHED SOURCES

Official Sources

Great Britain, House of Commons. *Report from the Select Committee on the Cold Bath Fields Meeting.* . . . Parliamentary Papers, 1833, XIII.
———. *Report from the Select Committee on the Petition of Frederick Young and Others . . . Complaining That Policemen Are Employed as Spies, and Praying That the People May Not Be Taxed to Maintain These Spies.* Parliamentary Papers, 1833, XIII.
———. *Report from the Select Committee on the Inquiry into Drunkenness.* . . . Parliamentary Papers, 1834, VIII.
———. *Report from the Select Committee on Newspaper Stamps; Together with the Proceedings of the Committee, Minutes of Evidence, Appendix and Index.* Parliamentary Papers, 1851, XVII.
Great Britain, Sessional Papers.
———. *Return of the Number of Persons Who Have Been Committed by the Magistrates of the Metropolis, within the Last Year, for Selling Unstamped Publications.* . . . 1831–1832, XXXIV (40), 103.
———. *Return of the Number of Persons Who Have Been Committed by the Magistrates for Selling Unstamped Publications, from 10th and 12th December 1831.* . . . 1831–1832, XXXIV (711), 107.
———. *Copy of the Information, Evidence, and Conviction of Joseph Forster,*

for Selling Unstamped Publications, etc. 1835, XXXV (555), 243.

——. *Returns of Persons Committed by Magistrates for the Sale of Unstamped Publications.* 1836, XLI (21), 427.

——. *Account of Effect upon the Revenue, by Reduction of Stamp Duty on Newspapers.* . . . 1837, XXXIX (291), 303.

Hansard's Parliamentary Debates.

Journals of the House of Commons.

Journals of the House of Lords.

Reports of State Trials: New Ser. Vol. II, 1823 to 1831, ed. John MacDonell. London: Her Majesty's Stationery Office, 1889.

Periodicals and Newspapers

An asterisk indicates that the periodical is unstamped.

The Aberdeen Magazine. 1831–1832.

*An Address from H. Hunt, Esq. M. P. to the Radical Reformers of England, Ireland, and Scotland. . . . London, 1831–1832.

*An Address from One of the 3730 Electors of Preston, to the Labouring Classes of Great Britain and Ireland. Preston, Bolton, 1831–1833.

*The Advocate: A Half-Penny Periodical. Edinburgh, 1834.

*The Agitator. Glasgow, 1833.

*The Agitator, and Political Anatomist. London, 1833.

*The Annals of Crime, and New Newgate Calendar. London, 1833–1834.

*The Antiquarian. London, 1832.

*The Argus. London, 1832.

*The Artizan's Miscellany, or Journal of Politics and Literature. Edinburgh, 1831.

The Ballot. London, 1831–1832.

*The Bath Elector, or the True Conservator of Public Morals. 1832.

Bennet's Glasgow Magazine. 1831–1832.

*Berthold's Political Handkerchief. London, 1831.

*The Birmingham Labour Exchange Gazette. 1833.

*Le Bonnet Rouge: The Republican Magazine. London, 1833.

The British Co-operator; or, Record and Review of Co-operative and Entertaining Knowledge. London, 1830.

*The Cab. London, 1832.

*The Calendar of Crime and General Advertiser. London, 1832.

*The Calendar of Horrors! A Weekly Register of the Terrific, Wonderful,

Bibliography

Instructive, Legendary, Extraordinary, and Fictitious. London, 1835–1836.

Carpenter's Monthly Political Magazine. London, 1831–1832.

*Chambers' Edinburgh Journal. 1832–1853.

*The Christian Corrector. London, 1831–1832.

*Church and State. London, 1836.

*Church Examiner and Ecclesiastical Record. London, 1832.

*Cleave's Picture Gallery of Grant's Comicalities. London, 1836.

*Cleave's Weekly Police Gazette. London, 1834–1836.

Cobbett's Weekly Political Register. London, 1819–1835.

*The Comet; or, Falvey's Liverpool Observer. 1832.

The Constitutional; (and Public Ledger). London, 1836–1837.

*The Cosmopolite. London, 1832–1833.

*The "Destructive" and Poor Man's Conservative. London, 1833–1834.

The Edinburgh Review.

The Examiner. London.

*Figaro in London. 1831–1839.

*The Gauntlet. London, 1833–1834.

The Glasgow Argus. 1833–1837.

*The Halfpenny Magazine. London, 1832.

*The Half-Penny Magazine, or, Cheap Repository of Amusement and Instruction. Edinburgh, 1832–1833.

*The Herald of the Rights of Industry. Manchester, 1834.

*Herald to the Trades' Advocate, and Co-operative Journal. Glasgow, 1830–1831.

*Hetherington's Twopenny Dispatch, and People's Police Register. London, 1834?–1836.

*The Laughing Philosopher. London, 1832.

The Leicester Corporation and Parochial Reformer. 1835–1836.

The Liberator. Glasgow, 1835–1836.

*Life in Edinburgh, or, the Police Intelligencer, and Dramatic Review. Edinburgh, 1833.

*The Literary Test. London, 1832.

The Liverpool Examiner. 1832.

The London Democrat. 1839.

The London Dispatch; (and People's Political and Social Reformer). 1836–1839.

[282]

Bibliography

The London Mercury. 1836–1837.

*The Loyal Reformers' Gazette. Glasgow, 1831–1836.

*The Magazine of Interest. London, 1833.

*The Magazine of Useful Knowledge, and Co-operative Miscellany. London, 1830.

*The Magician: A Weekly Periodical of General Literature. Glasgow, 1832.

*The Man. London, 1833–1834.

The Manchester and Salford Advertiser. 1831–1848.

The Midland Representative, and Birmingham Herald. 1831–1832.

*The Mirror for Magistrates. London, 1836.

*The Monthly Political Register. London, 1836.

The Monthly Repository (of Theology and General Literature). London.

The Morning Chronicle. London.

The Morning Herald. London.

The New Monthly Magazine (and Universal Register). London.

*New Political Dictionary. Glasgow, 1832.

*The New Political Register. . . . London, 1835–1836.

*The New Weekly True Sun. London, 1836.

Official Kalendar for 1831. London.

*Pamphlets for the People. London, 1835–1836.

The Parliamentary Review, and Family Magazine. London, 1833–1834.

*The Parrot: A Weekly Echo, of Literature, Fine Arts, Drawing-Rooms, Theatres, Balls, Concerts, and Fashions. London, 1832.

*The Patriot. London, 1831.

*The Penny Magazine of the Society for the Diffusion of Useful Knowledge. London, 1832–1845.

*The Penny Papers for the People. London, 1830–1831.

*The People's Conservative; and Trade's Union Gazette (Formerly the *"Destructive"* and *Poor Man's Conservative.*) London, 1833–1834.

*The People's Hue and Cry, or Weekly Police Register. London, 1834.

*The People's Police Gazette, and Tradesman's Advertiser. London, 1833–1834.

*People's Weekly Dispatch. London, 1835–1836.

*People's Weekly Police Gazette. London, 1834–1836.

The Political Letter. London, 1831.

*Political Letters and Pamphlets. London, 1830–1831.

The Political Mirror. London, 1837.

The Political Penny Magazine. London, 1836.

The Political Register; Late the London Police Gazette. London, 1834–1835.

The Political Soldier: A Paper for the Army and People. London, 1833–1834.

The Political Union Register. Birmingham, 1832.

The Political Unionist. London, 1832.

The Poor Man's Advocate, and People's Library. Manchester, 1832–1834.

The Poor Man's Guardian. London, 1831–1835.

The Preston Temperance Advocate. 1834–1837.

The Prompter. London, 1830–1831.

Punchinello! or Sharps, Flats, and Naturals! A Family Gazette of Fun, Fashion, Literature, and the Drama. London, 1832.

The Radical. London, 1831–1832.

The Radical. London, 1836.

Radical Reformer. (Formerly the *Radical.*) London, 1831–1832.

The Radical Reformer's Gazette. Glasgow, 1832–1833.

The Reformer. London, 1833–1834.

The Reformers' Pocket Companion. Glasgow, 1832.

The Regenerator, and Advocate for the Unrepresented: A Legal Substitute for a Stamped Paper. Manchester, 1839.

The Regenerator, or Guide to Happiness. London, 1832.

The Republican. London, 1831–1834.

The Scotsman. Edinburgh.

A Scourge for the Littleness of "Great" Men. London, 1834–1835.

The Spectator. London.

Tait's Edinburgh Magazine.

The Times. London.

The Trades Examiner; or, Political and Literary Review. Edinburgh, 1832.

The True Sun. London, 1832–1837.

The United Trades' Co-operative Journal. Manchester, 1830.

A Voice from the Commons. London, 1836.

The Voice of the People. Manchester, 1831.

The Voice of the West Riding. Huddersfield, 1833–1834.

The Weekly Chronicle. London.

The Weekly Herald. London, 1836.

Bibliography

Weekly Times. London, 1835–1836.

The Weekly True Sun. London, 1833–1839.

The Westminster Review. London.

The Working Man's Friend; and Political Magazine. London, 1832–1833.

The Workman's Expositor, and Weekly Review of Literature, Science, and the Arts. Manchester, 1832.

Contemporary Pamphlets and Tracts

Adams, William B. ("Junius Redivivus"). *The Political Unionist's Catechism: A Manual of Political Instruction for the People, with a View to Make Political Knowledge a Legal Claim to the Elective Franchise, Instead of the Absurd Test of "Property."* London: Effiingham Wilson, 1833.

——. *The Rights of Morality; An Essay on the Present State of Society, Moral, Political, and Physical, in England: Addressed to the Productive Classes of the Community*. London: Effingham Wilson, 1832.

——. *What the People Ought to Do, in Choosing Their Representatives at the General Election, after the Passing of the Reform Bill: A Letter Addressed to the Electors of Great Britain*. London: Effingham Wilson, 1832.

An Address to the Readers of Cleave's Weekly Police Gazette. London: John Cleave, 1836.

Association of Working Men to Procure a Cheap and Honest Press. *Address*. London: The Association, 1836.

[Bailey, Samuel]. *Essays on the Formation and Publication of Opinions, and on Other Subjects*. London: R. Hunter, 1821.

——. *Essays on the Pursuit of Truth, on the Progress of Knowledge, and on the Fundamental Principle of All Evidence and Expectation*. London: R. Hunter, 1829.

Beaumont, Augustus H. *Whig Nullities; or, a Review of a Pamphlet Attributed to the Right Hon. John Cam Hobhouse, M.P. for Nottingham, Privy Councillor, etc. Entitled, "Domestic Policy of the Country under the New Parliament."* London: Henry Hetherington, 1837.

Bell, John. *Report of an Address . . . in the Music Hall, Blackett Street, Newcastle-upon-Tyne, on Tuesday Evening, September 6th, 1836, also the Speech of John Fife, Esq., and Mr. Bell's Reply*. Newcastle-upon-Tyne: Joseph Harris, 1836.

Benbow, William. *Grand National Holiday, and Congress of the Productive Classes.* London: William Benbow, 1831.

A Brief Review of the British Labourer's Protector, and Factory Child's Friend. Leeds: Henry Cullingworth (1833).

Brougham, Henry. "Practical Observations upon the Education of the People, Addressed to the Working-Classes and Their Employers," pp. 417–464 in Henry Brougham, *Works,* Vol. VIII (Edinburgh: Adam and Charles Black, 1872–1873).

———. *Taxes on Knowledge: Stamps on Newspapers: Extracts from the Evidence of the Right Honourable Baron Brougham and Vaux, Lord High Chancellor of England, before the Select Committee of the House of Commons, on Libel Law, in June 1834; in Which the Evil to Society from the Stamp Duty on Newspapers, the Impolicy of the Government in Its Continuance, and Its Impediment to the Spread of Useful Information and Knowledge amongst the Mass of the People Are Clearly Shown.* London: J. R. and C. Childs, 1834.

Bulwer, Edward Lytton. *Taxes on Knowledge: Debate in the House of Commons on the 15th June, 1832, on Mr. Edward Lytton Bulwer's Motion . . . with a Comment in the Form of Notes (by Francis Place); and the Article from the "Examiner" Newspaper, of Sunday, 17th June, 1832.* Southwark: W. Barnes, 1832.

Campbell, Alexander. *Trial and Self-Defence of Alexander Campbell, Operative, before the Exchequer Court, Edinburgh, for Printing and Publishing "The Tradesman," Contrary to the Infamous Gagging Act.* Glasgow: W. and W. Miller, 1835.

Carlile, Richard. *An Address to Men of Science: Calling upon Them to Stand Forward, and Vindicate the Truth from the Foul Grasp and Persecution of Superstition; and Obtain for the Island of Great Britain the Noble Appellation of the Focus of Truth. . . .* London: Richard Carlile, 1822.

———. *Cobbett's Spelling-Book.* London: Richard Carlile, 1831?

———. *Coronation Handkerchief.* London: Richard Carlile, 1831?

———. *A Letter to the Society for the Suppression of Vice, on Their Malignant Efforts to Prevent a Free Enquiry after Truth and Reason.* London: Richard Carlile, 1819.

Carpenter, William. *An Address to the Working Classes on the Reform Bill.* London: William Strange, 1831.

——. *Can the Tories Become Reformers?* London: Wakelin, 1834.

——. *The Life and Times of John Milton.* London: Wakelin, 1836.

——. *The People's Book; Comprising Their Chartered Rights and Practical Wrongs.* London: William Strange, 1831.

——. *The Political Alphabet, with Notes and Illustrations: Embellished by Thirty-one Engravings from Designs by George Cruikshank, Esq.* London: William Carpenter, 1831.

——. *A Report of the Trial of Mr. William Carpenter, in the Court of Exchequer, on Saturday, May 14, 1831, for Publishing a Number of Political Letters and Pamphlets, Charged to be Newspapers, Within the Meaning of the Acts of Parliament.* London: William Carpenter, 1831.

Chadwick, Edwin. *On the Taxes on Knowledge: From the Westminster Review, No. XXIX, for July 1, 1831.* London: Robert Heward, 1831.

Crawfurd, John. *The Newspaper Stamp, and the Newspaper Postage; Compared.* London: J. Reid, 1836.

——. *Taxes on Knowledge: A Financial and Historical View of the Taxes Which Impede the Education of the People.* London: Charles Ely, 1836.

D., R. K. *Letter to Lord Viscount Althorp, on the Proposed Reduction in the Newspaper Stamp and Advertisement Duties.* London: Hurst, Chance, 1831.

Detrosier, Rowland. *An Address, Delivered to Members of the New Mecanics' Institution, Manchester, on Friday Evening, March 25, 1831, on the Necessity of an Extension of Moral and Political Instruction among the Working Classes.* London: William Strange, 1831.

——. *"Lecture on the Utility of Political Unions for the Diffusion of Sound Moral and Political Information amongst the People; on the Necessity for That Information and on the Political Influence of Scientific Knowledge." Delivered to the Members of the National Political Union at Saville House, 26 March, 1832.* London: John Brooks, 1832.

Doherty, John. *A Letter to the Members of the National Association for the Protection of Labour.* Manchester: Alexander Wilkinson, 1832.

Edmonds, George. *Appeal to the Labourers of England, an Exposure of Aristocrat Spies, and the Infernal Machinery of the Poor Law Murder Bill: Accompanied by Appalling Proofs of the Alarming Progress of Cruelty, Cannibalism, Gluttony, Ignorance, Prodigality, Lying, Slandering, Atheism, Blasphemy, Sedition, and Sexual Profligacy, in the High-*

Priced Aristocrat Press, and Especially the Six Shilling Quarterly Review. London: S. Wilson, 1835.

——. *The English Revolution . . . Addressed to My Unrepresented Fellow Millions.* London: William Strange, 1831.

Forster, Joseph. *The Rejected Address to the Editor of the Weekly Dispatch of Sunday, October 5, 1834, on Being Sentenced to Three Months' Imprisonment in That Horrible Bastile, the House of Correction, Cold Bath Fields, for Selling Unstamped Newspapers, Called the Man, Police Gazette, Twopenny Dispatch, Pioneer, etc. . . . to Which Is Added, a Few Remarks on the Present Awful and Momentous Crisis.* London: Howlett and Son, [1835].

Fox, W. J. *The Duties of Christians towards Deists: A Sermon Preached . . . on Occasion of the Recent Prosecution of Mr. Carlile for the Republication of Paine's "Age of Reason."* London: George Smallfield, 1819.

——. *Finsbury Lectures: Reports of Lectures Delivered at the Chapel in South Place, Finsbury.* London: Charles Fox, 1835.

——. *Lectures Addressed Chiefly to the Working Classes.* 4 vols. London: Charles Fox, 1845–1849.

——. *On the Parliamentary Pledges to Be Required of Candidates at the Ensuing Elections: An Address to the Electors of Great Britain.* London: Charles Fox, 1832.

Hammersley, Robert. *Hints to the Young Men of Great Britain, on the Progress of Political Opinion.* London: Wakelin, 1836.

Hetherington, Henry. *Cheap Salvation; or, An Antidote to Priestcraft: Being a Succinct, Practical, Essential, and Rational Religion, Deduced from the New Testament, the General Adoption of Which Would Supersede the Necessity for a Hireling Priesthood, and Save This Overtaxed Nation Fifteen Millions per Annum.* London: Henry Hetherington, 1838?

——. *A Full Report of the Trial of Henry Hetherington, on an Indictment for Blasphemy, before Lord Denman and a Special Jury, at the Court of Queen's Bench, Westminster, on Tuesday, December 8, 1840; for Selling Haslam's Letters to the Clergy of All Denominations: With the Whole of the Authorities Cited in the Defence, at Full Length.* London: Henry Hetherington, 1840.

Hickson, William E. *Manifesto of the Chancellor of the Exchequer*

Against the Moral Interests of the Productive Classes. London: T. C. Hansard, 1836.

———. *Mister Spring Rice and His Penny Stamp: From the London and Westminster Review.* London: 1836.

———. *Taxes on Knowledge: Reduction or Abolition of the Newspaper Stamp-Duty?* London: C. Ely, 1836.

Hill, Matthew Davenport. *Speech . . . on Mr. Bulwer's Motion for a Repeal of the Stamp Duty on Newspapers, in the House of Commons, on Thursday, May 22, 1834: Extracted from the Mirror of Parliament.* London: *Mirror of Parliament*, 1834.

Howitt, William. *A Popular History of Priestcraft in All Ages and Nations.* London: Effingham Wilson, 1833.

Hunt, Henry. *An Appeal to the People of England by the Council of the Metropolitan Political Union: Reprinted from a Monitory Letter to Sir Robert Peel.* London: Metropolitan Political Union, 1830.

———. *Lecture on the Conduct of the Whigs, to the Working Classes: Delivered at Laurence Street Chapel, Birmingham, on Wednesday, October 31st, 1832.* London: William Strange, 1832.

———. *The Preston Cock's Reply to the Kensington Dunghill: A Two-Penny Exposure of Cobbett's Fourteen-Pennyworth of Falsehoods . . . Addressed to the Electors of Preston.* 4th ed. London: William Strange, 1831.

Knight, Charles. *The Newspaper Stamp and the Duty on Paper, Viewed in Relation to Their Effects upon the Diffusion of Knowledge.* London: Charles Knight, 1836.

Lamennais, F. *The Book of the People.* Trans. with notes by James H. B. Lorymer. London: Henry Hetherington, 1838.

Lee, R. E. *Victimization, or, Benbowism Unmasked: Addressed to the National Union of the Working Classes.* London: R. E. Lee, 1832.

———. *A Whisper to the Whigs, or, What Is Treason? Answered by Lords Grey, Brougham, and Company: His Majesty's Whig Tinkers of the "Glorious Constitution," and Military Law Makers to the People of Ireland.* London: R. E. Lee, 1833.

Lorymer, James H. B. *A National Convention, the Only Proper Remedy.* London: Henry Hetherington, 1833.

Macconnell, Thomas. *A Lecture on the Signs of the Times: Delivered in the Great Lecture Room of Robert Owen's Institution, Gray's Inn Road, on the Morning of November 18, 1832*. London: Eamonson, 1832.

McCulloch, J. R. *Observations, Illustrative of the Practical Operation and Real Effect of the Duties on Paper, Showing the Expediency of Their Reduction or Repeal*. London: Longman, Rees, Orme, Brown, Green, and Longman, 1836.

Martin, R. Montgomery. *Taxation of the British Empire*. London: Effingham Wilson, 1833.

Mill, James. "Liberty of the Press," *Supplement to the 4th, 5th, and 6th Editions of the Encyclopaedia Britannica*, V, 258–272 (Edinburgh, A. Constable, 1824).

Milton, John. *A Speech on the Liberty of Unlicensed Printing, to the Parliament of England*. London: John Cleave, 1834.

The Moral and Political Evils of the Taxes on Knowledge . . . London: Effingham Wilson, 1830.

The Newspaper Stamp and Advertisement Duties: A Form of a Petition to Parliament, Accurately Setting Forth, as is Presumed, the Merits of Much of the Present Newspaper Press; and Suggesting with Respect to the Above Duties, an Entirely Novel Mode of Proceeding. London: Roake and Varty, 1836.

Newspaper Stamps: Deputation to Lord Viscount Melbourne, to Procure the Total Repeal of the Stamp Duty on Newspapers: From Cleave's Gazette, of the 20th of Feb., 1836. London: C. Ely, 1836.

Northern Political Union. *Objects and Rules*. Newcastle-upon-Tyne: The Union, 1831.

Petrie, George. *The Works of George Petrie: Comprising Equality, and Other Poems: Select Extracts from the Letters of Agrarius: With a Biographical Memoir of the Author*. London: John Cleave, [1841].

Place, Francis. *The Examiner and the Tax on Newspapers*. London: G. Morgan, 1836.

——. *Improvement of the Working People: Drunkenness—Education*. London: Charles Fox, 1834.

——. *A Letter to a Minister of State, Respecting Taxes on Knowledge*. 2d ed. London: Privately distributed, 1831.

——. *On the Law of Libel with Strictures on the Self-Styled "Constitutional Association."* London: John Hunt, 1823.

——. *On Pledges to Be Given by Candidates*. London: National Political Union, 1832.

——. *The Stamp Duty on Newspapers*. London: G. Morgan, 1836.

——. *The Stamp Tax Bill.* London: G. Morgan, 1836.

——. *The Whigs and the Penny Stamp.* London: Henry Hetherington, 1836.

Proceedings of the Third Co-operative Congress: Held in London . . . on the 23rd of April, 1832, and by Adjournment on Each of the Six Following Days, Sunday Excepted. Reported and ed. William Carpenter. London: William Strange, 1832.

Reid, Francis. *Prosecution and Committal to Jail of Mr. Francis Reid, At the Instance of the Glasgow Stamped Newspaper Press, Under a Charge of Selling Unstamped Newspapers.* John Thomson: Glasgow, 1835.

Report of the Public Reception, and the Speeches Delivered at the Dinner to Lord Durham . . . on Wednesday, 29th October 1834. Glasgow: W. R. M'Phun, 1834.

Roebuck, John A. *To the Electors of Bath.* London: W. Barnes, 1832.

Roebuck, John A. *Report of the Council to the First Annual General Meeting of the Members: Held at Saville House, on Thursday, February 2nd, 1832.* London: Effingham Wilson, 1832.

Some Notices of John Crawfurd, Esq., One of the Candidates for Representation of This City. Glasgow: Privately pub., 1832.

Thompson, T. Perronet. *The Article on the Six Acts, Especially Taxes on Literature: Reprinted (by Permission) from the Westminster Review, No. XXIV, for April, 1830.* London: William Strange, 1830.

Wade, Rev. Arthur S. *A Voice from the Church: or, a Sermon (with a Few Notes and Amplifications) on Church Reform, Pledges, Cheap Government—Cheap Justice—Cheap Food—Cheap Knowledge—and on a Cheap and Efficient Medium of Exchange; Also, on the Duties Which the Electors and Elected Will Owe to the Represented People of Great Britain and Ireland, Especially to the Working Classes.* London: James Ridgway, 1832.

Wakley, Thomas. *A Letter to the People of England, on the New Project for Gagging the Press.* London: G. Churchill, 1836.

[Watson, James]. *An Address to the Members of Trade Unions, and the Working Classes Generally: Being an Exposition of the Relative Situation, Condition, and Future Prospects of Working People in England, Scotland, and Ireland: Together With a Suggestion and Outline of a Plan, by Which They May Gradually and Indefinitely Improve Their Condition.* London: James Watson, 1833.

Watson, James. *A Report of the Trial of James Watson, for Having Sold a*

Bibliography

Copy of Palmer's Principles of Nature, at the Shop of Mr. Carlile, 201 Strand: Tried at the Clerkenwell Sessions House . . . on the 24th day of April, 1823 before Mr. Const, as Chairman and a Common Jury. London: Richard Carlile, 1825.

Westmacott, C. M. *The Stamp Duties: Serious Considerations on the Proposed Alteration of the Stamp Duty on Newspapers; Addressed to the Right Honourable Thomas Spring Rice, Chancellor of the Exchequer.* London: *Age,* 1836.

SECONDARY SOURCES

Adams, William E. *Memoirs of a Social Atom.* 2 vols. London: Hutchinson, 1903.

Altick, Richard D. *The English Common Reader: A Social History of the Mass Reading Public, 1800–1900.* Chicago: University of Chicago Press, 1963.

Andrews, Alexander. *The History of British Journalism from the Foundation of the Newspaper Press in England, to the Repeal of the Stamp Act in 1855, with Sketches of Press Celebrities.* 2 vols. London: Richard Bentley, 1859.

Arnould, Sir Joseph. *Life of Thomas, First Lord Denman: Formerly Lord Chief Justice of England.* 2 vols. Boston: Estes and Lauriat, 1874.

Ashton, John, ed. *Chap-Books of the Eighteenth Century.* London: Chatto and Windus, 1882.

Aspinall, Arthur. "The Irish 'Proclamation' Fund, 1800–1846," *English Historical Review,* LVI (1941), 265–280.

——. *Lord Brougham and the Whig Party.* Manchester: Manchester University Press, 1927.

——. *Politics and the Press, c. 1780–1850.* London: Home and Van Thal, 1949.

——. "Statistical Accounts of the London Newspapers in the Eighteenth Century," *English Historical Review,* LXIII (1948), 201–232.

——. "Statistical Accounts of the London Newspapers, 1800–1836," *English Historical Review,* LXV (1950), 222–234.

Bain, Alexander. *James Mill: A Biography.* London: Longmans, Green, 1882.

Barker, A. G. *Henry Hetherington, 1792–1849: A Pioneer in the Free Thought and Working Class Struggles of a Hundred Years Ago for the Freedom of the Press.* London: Pioneer Press, 1938.

Beer, M. *A History of British Socialism.* 2 vols. London: George Allen and Unwin, 1953.

Beer, Samuel H. "The Representation of Interests in British Government: Historical Background," *American Political Science Review,* LI (1957), 613–650.

Black, Eugene C. *The Association: British Extraparliamentary Political Organization, 1769–1793.* Cambridge, Mass.: Harvard University Press, 1963.

Bourne, H. R. Fox. *English Newspapers: Chapters in the History of Journalism.* 2 vols. London: Chatto and Windus, 1887.

Briggs, Asa. *The Age of Improvement, 1783–1867.* London: Longmans, Green, 1959.

——. "The Background of the Parliamentary Reform Movement in Three English Cities (1830–2)," *Cambridge Historical Journal,* X (1952), 293–317.

——. "Chartism Reconsidered," *Historical Studies,* II (1959), 42–59.

——. "The Language of 'Class' in Early Nineteenth-Century England," in *Essays in Labour History,* pp. 43–73, ed. Asa Briggs and John Saville. London: Macmillan, 1960.

——. "Social Structure and Politics in Birmingham and Lyons (1825–1848)," *British Journal of Sociology,* I (1950), 67–76.

——. "Thomas Attwood and the Economic Background of the Birmingham Political Union," *Cambridge Historical Journal,* IX (1948), 190–216.

Brougham, Henry. *Life and Times: Written by Himself.* 3 vols. New York: Harper and Bros., 1871.

——. "On the Diffusion of Knowledge," in National Association for the Promotion of Social Science, *Transactions,* II (1858), 25–42.

——. *Speeches . . . upon Questions Relating to Public Rights, Duties, and Interests: with Historical Introductions, and a Critical Dissertation upon the Eloquence of the Ancients.* 4 vols. Edinburgh: Adam and Charles Black, 1838.

——. *Works.* 11 vols. Edinburgh: Adam and Charles Black, 1872–1873.

Broughton, Lord (John Cam Hobhouse). *Recollections of a Long Life.* Ed. Lady Dorchester. 6 vols. London: John Murray, 1909–1911.

Buckley, Jessie K. *Joseph Parkes of Birmingham and the Part Which He Played in Radical Reform Movements from 1825 to 1845.* London: Methuen, 1926.

Campbell, Theophila C. *The Battle of the Press as Told in the Story of the Life of Richard Carlile*. London: A and H. B. Bonner, 1899.

Carpenter, Niles. "William Benbow and the Origin of the General Strike," *Quarterly Journal of Economics*, XXXV (1920–1921), 491–499.

Chambers, William. *Memoir of William and Robert Chambers*. Edinburgh: W. and R. Chambers, 1884.

——. *Story of a Long and Busy Life*. Edinburgh: W. and R. Chambers, 1882.

Chartist Studies. Ed. Asa Briggs. London: Macmillan, 1960.

Checkland, S. G. "The Birmingham Economists, 1815–50," *Economic History Review*, Ser. 2, I (1948), 1–19.

Clark, G. Kitson. *The Making of Victorian England*. London: Methuen, 1962.

Cockburn, Henry. *Journal . . . Being a Continuation of the Memorials of his Time, 1831–1854*. 2 vols. Edinburgh: Edmonston and Douglas, 1874.

Cole, G. D. H. *Attempts at General Union: A Study in British Trade Union History, 1818–1834*. London: Macmillan, 1953.

——. *A Century of Co-operation*. Manchester: Co-operative Union, 1944.

——. *Chartist Portraits*. London: Macmillan, 1941.

——. *The Life of William Cobbett*. 3d ed. London: Home and Van Thal, 1947.

——. *Richard Carlile, 1790–1843*. London: Victor Gollancz, 1943.

——. *A Short History of the British Working-Class Movement, 1789–1947*. London: George Allen and Unwin, 1948.

—— and A. W. Filson, eds. *British Working Class Movements: Select Documents, 1789–1875*. London: Macmillan, 1965.

Coleman, D. C. *The British Paper Industry, 1495–1860: A Study in Industrial Growth*. Oxford: Clarendon Press, 1958.

Collet, Collet D. *History of the Taxes on Knowledge: Their Origin and Repeal*. 2 vols. London: T. Fisher Unwin, 1899.

Cowan, R. M. W. *The Newspaper in Scotland: A Study of its First Expansion, 1815–1860*. Glasgow: G. Outram, 1946.

Creevey, Thomas. *The Creevey Papers: A Selection from the Correspondence and Diaries of the Late Thomas Creevey, M.P.* Ed. Sir Herbert Maxwell. 2 vols. London: John Murray, 1903.

Croker, John Wilson. *The Correspondence and Diaries of the Late Right*

Bibliography

Honourable John Wilson Croker, LL.D., F.R.S., Secretary to the Admiralty from 1809 to 1830. Ed. Louis Jennings. 3 vols. London: John Murray, 1884.

Davenport-Hill, Rosamond and Florence. *The Recorder of Birmingham: A Memoir of Matthew Davenport Hill; With Selections from His Correspondence.* London: Macmillan, 1878.

Driver, Cecil. *Tory Radical: The Life of Richard Oastler.* New York: Oxford University Press, 1946.

Edgell, Rev. Edgell W. "Moral Statistics of the Parishes of St. James, St. George, and St. Anne, Soho, in the City of Westminster . . . ," *Journal of the Statistical Society of London,* I (1838), 485.

Fawcett, Millicent G. *Life of the Right Honourable Sir William Molesworth, Bart., M.P., F.R.S.* London: Macmillan, 1901.

Felkin, W. "Moral Statistics of a Section of the City of Norwich," *Journal of the Statistical Society of London,* I (1838), 540–541.

Fetter, Frank W. "Economic Articles in the Westminster Review and Their Authors, 1824–51," *Journal of Political Economy,* LXX (1962), 570–596.

Finer, S. E. *The Life and Times of Sir Edwin Chadwick.* London: Methuen, 1952.

Fonblanque, Albany. *England Under Seven Administrations.* 3 vols. London: Richard Bentley, 1837.

——. *The Life and Labours of Albany Fonblanque.* Ed. E. B. de Fonblanque. London: Richard Bentley and Son, 1874.

Francis, John C. *John Francis, Publisher of The Athenaeum: A Literary Chronicle of Half a Century.* 2 vols. London: Richard Bentley and Son, 1888.

Gammage, R. G. *History of the Chartist Movement, 1837–1854.* Newcastle-on-Tyne: Browne and Browne, 1894.

Garnett, Richard. *The Life of W. J. Fox, Public Teacher and Social Reformer: 1786–1864.* London: J. Lane, 1910.

Gash, Norman. *Reaction and Reconstruction in English Politics, 1832–1852.* Oxford: Clarendon Press, 1965.

Glasgow, Eric. "The Establishment of the Northern Star Newspaper," *History,* n.s. XXXIX (1954), 54–67.

Graham, Alan H. "The Lichfield House Compact—1835," *Irish Historical Studies,* XII (1961), 209–225.

Grant, James. *The Newspaper Press: Its Origin, Progress and Present Position.* 2 vols. London: Tinsley Bros., 1871.

Greville, Charles. *The Greville Memoirs: A Journal of the Reigns of King George IV and King William IV.* Ed. Henry Reeve. 2 vols. New York: D. Appleton, 1886.

Grobel, Monica C. "The Society for the Diffusion of Useful Knowledge, 1826–1846." 4 vols. Unpub. M.A. thesis, University of London, 1933.

Grote, Harriet. *The Personal Life of George Grote: Compiled from Family Documents, Private Memoranda, and Original Letters to and from Various Friends.* London: John Murray, 1873.

Guest, James. "A Free Press, and How It Became Free," in W. Hutton, *The History of Birmingham* (6th ed.; Birmingham: James Guest, 1861), pp. 493–507.

Halévy, Elie. *The Triumph of Reform, 1830–1841.* Trans. from the French by E. I. Watkin. London: Ernest Benn, 1950.

Hall, Samuel C. *Retrospect of a Long Life: From 1815 to 1883.* 2 vols. London: Richard Bentley and Son, 1883.

Hamburger, Joseph. *Intellectuals in Politics: John Stuart Mill and the Philosophic Radicals.* New Haven, Conn.: Yale University Press, 1965.

——. *James Mill and the Art of Revolution.* New Haven, Conn.: Yale University Press, 1963.

Harrison, J. F. C. *Learning and Living, 1790–1960: A Study in the History of the English Adult Education Movement.* London: Routledge and Kegan Paul, 1961.

Heywood, Abel, Jr. *English Almanacks during the First Third of the Century.* Manchester: Privately pub., 1904.

Heywood, George B. *Abel Heywood, Abel Heywood and Son, Abel Heywood and Son Ltd., 1832–1932.* Manchester: Abel Heywood and Son, 1932.

Hill, Christopher. "The Norman Yoke," *Democracy and the Labour Movement,* ed. John Saville (London: Lawrence and Wishart, 1954), pp. 11–66.

Holyoake, George Jacob. *The History of Co-operation.* London: T. Fisher Unwin, 1908.

——. *The Life and Character of Henry Hetherington.* London: James Watson, 1849.

——. *The Life and Character of Richard Carlile.* London: J. Watson, 1849.

———. *Sixty Years of an Agitator's Life.* 2 vols. London: T. Fisher Unwin, 1893.

Hovell, Mark. *The Chartist Movement.* 2d ed. Manchester: Manchester University Press, 1959.

Hume, L. J. "Jeremy Bentham and the Nineteenth-Century Revolution in Government," *Historical Journal*, X (1967), 361–75.

Hunt, Frederick Knight. *The Fourth Estate: Contributions towards a History of Newspapers, and of the Liberty of the Press.* 2 vols. London: David Bogue, 1850.

Inglis, Brian. *The Freedom of the Press in Ireland, 1784–1841.* London: Faber and Faber, 1954.

James, Louis. *Fiction for the Working Man, 1830–1850: A Study of the Literature Produced for the Working Classes in Early Victorian Urban England.* London: Oxford University Press, 1963.

Kellet, E. E. "The Press," *Early Victorian England*, ed. G. M. Young, (London: Oxford University Press, 1934), II, 1–97.

Kelly, Thomas. *George Birkbeck: Pioneer of Adult Education.* Liverpool: Liverpool University Press, 1957.

Kennedy, William F. "Lord Brougham, Charles Knight, and the 'Rights of Industry,'" *Economica*, XXIX (1962), 58–71.

Knight, Charles. *The Old Printer and the Modern Press.* London: John Murray, 1854.

———. *Passages of a Working Life during Half a Century: With a Prelude of Early Reminiscences.* 3 vols. London: Bradbury and Evans, 1864–1865.

Le Marchant, Denis. *Memoir of John Charles Viscount Althorp, Third Earl Spencer.* London: Richard Bentley and Son, 1876.

Leader, Robert E. *Life and Letters of John Arthur Roebuck; with Chapters of Autobiography.* London: Edward Arnold, 1897.

Lillibridge, C. D. *Beacon of Freedom: The Impact of American Democracy upon Great Britain, 1830–1870.* New York: A. S. Barnes, 1961.

Linton, W. J. *James Watson: A Memoir.* Hamden, Conn.: Appledore Private Press, 1879.

———. *Memories.* London: Laurence and Bullen, 1895.

Lovett, William. *Life and Struggles of William Lovett, in His Pursuit of Bread, Knowledge, and Freedom: With Some Short Account of the Different Associations He Belonged to and of the Opinions He Entertained.* 2 vols. London: G. Bell and Sons, 1920.

Lytton, Earl of. *The Life of Edward Bulwer, First Lord Lytton.* 2 vols. London: Macmillan, 1913.

Lytton, Baron. *The Life, Letters, and Literary Remains of Edward Bulwer, Lord Lytton.* 2 vols. London: Kegan Paul, Trench, 1883.

Maccoby, S. *English Radicalism, 1832–1852.* London: George Allen and Unwin, 1935.

Marshall, L. S. "The First Parliamentary Election in Manchester," *American Historical Review,* XLVII (1942), 518–538.

Martin, John E. "Statistics of an Agricultural Parish in Bedfordshire," *Journal of the Statistical Society of London,* VI (1843), 255.

Martin, Sir Theodore. *A Life of Lord Lyndhurst.* London: John Murray, 1883.

Mather, F. C. *Chartism.* London: Historical Association, 1965.

The Mayor of Manchester and His Slanderers. Manchester: Tubbs and Brook, 1877.

Melbourne, 2nd Viscount. *Lord Melbourne's Papers.* Ed. Charles Sanders. London: Longmans, Green, 1889.

Mill, John Stuart. *The Earlier Letters of John Stuart Mill, 1812–1848.* Ed. Francis Mineka. 2 vols. London: Routledge and Kegan Paul, 1963.

Mineka, Francis E. *The Dissidence of Dissent: The Monthly Repository, 1806–1838.* Chapel Hill, N.C.: University of North Carolina Press, 1944.

Moore, M. G. "The History of the Agitation against the Stamp Duty on Newspapers, 1830–1855," Unpub. M.A. thesis, University of London, 1935.

Morison, Stanley. *The English Newspaper: Some Account of the Physical Development of Journals Printed in London between 1622 and the Present Day.* Cambridge: Cambridge University Press, 1932.

Morris, David C. "The History of the Labour Movement in England, 1825–1852: The Problem of Leadership and the Articulation of Demands." Unpub. Ph.D. thesis, University of London, 1952.

New, Chester. *The Life of Henry Brougham to 1830.* Oxford: Clarendon, Press, 1961.

——. *Lord Durham: A Biography of John George Lambton, First Earl of Durham.* Oxford: Clarendon Press, 1929.

Oliphant, Margaret. *Annals of a Publishing House: William Blackwood and His Sons: Their Magazine and Friends.* Edinburgh: William Blackwood and Sons, 1897–1898.

Bibliography

Paterson, Alexander. *Yorkshire Journalism: Past and Present.* Barnsley: The Institute of Journalists, 1901.

Patterson, A. Temple. *Radical Leicester: A History of Leicester, 1780–1850.* Leicester: University College, Leicester, 1954.

Patterson, M. W. *Sir Francis Burdett and His Times (1770–1844).* 2 vols. London: Macmillan, 1931.

Peel, Robert. *Sir Robert Peel from His Private Papers.* Ed. C. S. Parker. 3 vols. London: J. Murray, 1891–1899.

Podmore, Frank. *Robert Owen: A Biography.* 2 vols. London: Hutchinson, 1906.

Read, Donald. *Press and People, 1790–1850: Opinion in Three English Cities.* London: Edward Arnold, 1961.

—— and Eric Glasgow. *Feargus O'Connor: Irishman and Chartist.* London: Edward Arnold, 1961.

Rees, R. D. "Glamorgan Newspapers under the Stamp Acts," *Morgannwg: Transactions of the Glamorgan Local History Society,* III (1959), 61–94.

——. "South Wales and Monmouthshire Newspapers under the Stamp Acts," *Welsh History Review,* I (1962), 301–324.

Roebuck, John A. *History of the Whig Ministry of 1830, to the Passing of the Reform Bill.* 2 vols. London: John W. Parker and Son, 1852.

Rose, J. Holland. "The Unstamped Press, 1815–1836," *English Historical Review,* XII (1897), 711–726.

Rowe, D. J. "The London Working Men's Association and the 'People's Charter,'" *Past and Present,* No. 36 (1967), pp. 73–86.

Ruter, A. J. C. "William Benbow as Publisher," *Bulletin of the International Institute for Social History,* IV (1940), 1–14.

——. "William Benbow's 'Grand National Holiday and Congress of the Productive Classes,'" *International Review for Social History,* I (1936), 217–256.

Salmon, Lucy M. *The Newspaper and Authority.* New York: Oxford University Press, 1923.

Schoyen, A. R. *The Chartist Challenge: A Portrait of George Julian Harney.* London: Heinemann, 1958.

Siebert, Frederick S. *Freedom of the Press in England, 1476–1776: The Rise and Decline of Government Control.* Urbana, Ill.: University of Illinois Press, 1965.

Simon, Brian. *Studies in the History of Education, 1780–1870.* London: Laurence and Wishart, 1960.

[299]

Smith, William Allan. *"Shepherd" Smith the Universalist; the Story of a Mind: Being a Life of the Rev. James E. Smith.* London: Samson Low, 1892.

Spriggs, S. S. *The Life and Times of Thomas Wakley: Founder and First Editor of the "Lancet," Member of Parliament for Finsbury, and Coroner for West Middlesex.* London: Longmans, Green, 1897.

Thompson, E. P. *The Making of the English Working Class.* London: Victor Gallancz, 1963.

Thompson, T. Perronet. *Exercises, Political and Others.* 6 vols. London: Effingham Wilson, 1842.

"The Times," *The History of the Times: "The Thunderer" in the Making, 1785–1841.* London: *Times,* 1935.

Timperley, C. H. *An Encyclopaedia of Literary and Typographical Anecdotes.* London: Henry G. Bohn, 1842.

Wadsworth, Alfred P. "Newspaper Circulations, 1800–1914," *Paper Read for Manchester Statistical Society, 9 March 1955.* Manchester: Norwood, Lockbury, 1955.

Wakefield, C. M. *Life of Thomas Attwood.* London: Harrison and Sons, 1885.

Wallas, Graham. *The Life of Francis Place, 1771–1854.* London: George Allen and Unwin, 1925.

Ward, J. T. *The Factory Movement, 1830–1855.* London: Macmillan, 1962.

——. "The Factory Movement in Scotland," *Scottish Historical Review,* XLI (1962), 100–123.

Wearmouth, R. F. *Some Working Class Movements of the Nineteenth Century.* London: Epworth Press, 1948.

Webb, R. K. *The British Working Class Reader, 1790–1848: Literacy and Social Tension.* London: George Allen and Unwin, 1955.

——. "Literacy among the Working Classes in Nineteenth Century Scotland," *Scottish Historical Review,* XXXIII (1954), 100–114.

——. Working Class Readers in Victorian England," *English Historical Review,* LXV (1950), 333–351.

Weld, C. R. "On the Condition of the Working Classes in the Inner Ward of St. George's Parish, Hanover Square," *Journal of the Statistical Society of London,* VI (1843), 17–23.

White, R. J. *Radicalism and Its Results, 1760–1837.* London: Historical Association, 1965.

Bibliography

———. *Waterloo to Peterloo*. London: William Heinemann, 1957.

Wickwar, William H. *The Struggle for the Freedom of the Press, 1819–1832*. London: George Allen and Unwin, 1928.

Wiener, Joel H. *A Descriptive Finding List of Unstamped Periodicals, 1830–1836*. London: Bibliographical Society, 1969.

Williams, Francis. *Dangerous Estate: The Anatomy of Newspapers*. London: Longmans, Green, 1957.

Williams, Gwyn A. *Rowland Detrosier: A Working-Class Infidel, 1800–34*. York: St. Anthony's Press, 1965.

Williams, Raymond. *The Long Revolution*. New York: Columbia University Press, 1961.

Index

Index

Index

Pare, William, 193, 228
Parkes, Joseph, 272 n.
Parkin, Thomas, 215, 217, 233, 249
Patriot, 172
Peel, Sir Robert, 7, 62, 80-81, 97, 196
Penny, Charles, 176-177, 198-199
Penny Cyclopaedia, 14
Penny Magazine, 6 n., 14, 39-40, 124-125, 171-172, 200
Penny Papers for the People, 16, 138, 144, 154-155, 188, 245-246
Penny Story-Teller, 177 n.
People's Conservative, 148 n., 207
People's Hue and Cry, 177, 184
People's Police Gazette, 176-177
People's Weekly Police Gazette, 169, 243
Perry, Erskine, 75-76, 86, 91, 93-94, 101
Perry, Thomas Riley, 206
Petrie, George, 119, 167, 177, 212, 218-219, 226, 242-243, 245
Physician, 179
Pilgrim, George, 182 n., 205
Pioneer, 88, 163, 192-193, 228
Place, Francis, 10, 16, 29, 35, 40 n., 57, 61, 66, 68, 70, 72, 81-84, 135-136, 142 n., 149-150, 180-181, 188 n., 264 n., 274-276; activities on behalf of repeal, 53-56, 253; aids imprisoned vendors, 135, 151 n., 177 n.; and the Association for the Abolition of the Stamp Duty on newspapers, 73-74, 97-114, 249-250, 256; and the *Constitutional*, 27, 273; criticism of unstamped journals, 23 n., 24, 231; *Letter to a Minister of State*, 43-45, 76, 87; on libel, 58-59, 74; and the National Political Union, 91-94; opposes reduction of the newspaper duty in 1836, 266-267; on political economy, 33, 53; on postal reform, 44-46; and the *S.C. on Libel Law*, 75-78; and the Society for the Diffusion of Political and Moral Knowledge, 95-97
Police gazettes, circulation of unstamped, 175-177

Political Anecdotist and Popular Instructor, 141
Political journals, circulation of, 162-171
Political Letter, 5 n., 141
Political Letters and Pamphlets, 5 n., 16, 25, 88, 138, 140-141, 153-154, 166, 170, 185-186, 188, 210-211, 228, 235
Political Penny Magazine, 212 n., 223, 226-227
Political Register, 165
Political Soldier, 133
Poor law, 20-21, 223-224
Poor Man's Advocate, 156-157, 163, 189, 218-219
Poor Man's Guardian, 119, 128 n., 130, 137-139, 144, 146-147, 150, 154, 162-164, 166-171, 173, 184, 187 n., 194, 200-202, 207, 210, 213-214, 217-219, 221, 231, 234-235, 238, 245, 248
Postal reform, 43-48
Prentice, Archibald, 113
Prest, Thomas, 174
Preston, unstamped periodicals, 191-192
Prompter, 132, 158-159, 166-168, 182, 194, 234
Prosecutions of vendors and publishers, 195-209, 233, 251-253, 263-264
Pseudonyms, use of, 157-158, 165, 167
Public Ledger, 96-97, 262 n., 264 n.
Punch in London, 177-178, 232
Punchinello, 177-179, 202 n., 232

Radical (1831-1832), 144, 161 n., 168, 216
Radical (1836), 267
Radical associations, 90, 121, 143, 147 n., 248-249, 254-257; *see also* British Association for Promoting Co-operative Knowledge; London Working Men's Association; Metropolitan Political Union; National Political Union; National Union of the Working Classes
Radical Reformer, 170 n.

[308]

Index